I had my first case of acute gastroenteritis. It didn't last that long, but I was in a lot of pain for half a day. Since it was caused by neither bacteria nor a virus, I guess it was caused by stress? Or maybe my excessive daily drinking and eating? I will now only eat food that is gentle on my stomach and intestines. I've stopped snacking and only eat three square meals a day as part of a well-balanced diet. I also make sure to take the time to carefully chew and swallow until my stomach is three-quarters full. Thanks to that, my body has been feeling great! But I still can't escape the stress of weekly serialization…
(My current weight…68 kg!!)

—Mitsutoshi Shimabukuro, 2014

Mitsutoshi Shimabukuro made his debut in **Weekly Shonen Jump** in 1996. He is best known for **Seikimatsu Leader Den Takeshi!**, for which he won the 46th Shogakukan Manga Award for children's manga in 2001. His current series, **Toriko**, began serialization in Japan in 2008.

TORIKO VOL. 32
SHONEN JUMP Manga Edition

STORY AND ART BY **MITSUTOSHI SHIMABUKURO**

Translation/Christine Dashiell
Weekly Shonen Jump Lettering/Erika Terriquez
Graphic Novel Touch-Up Art & Lettering/Elena Diaz
Design/Matt Hinrichs
Weekly Shonen Jump Editor/Hope Donovan
Graphic Novel Editor/Marlene First

Printed in the U.S.A.

Published by VIZ Media, LLC
P.O. Box 77010
San Francisco, CA 94107

10 9 8 7 6 5 4 3 2 1
First printing, February 2016

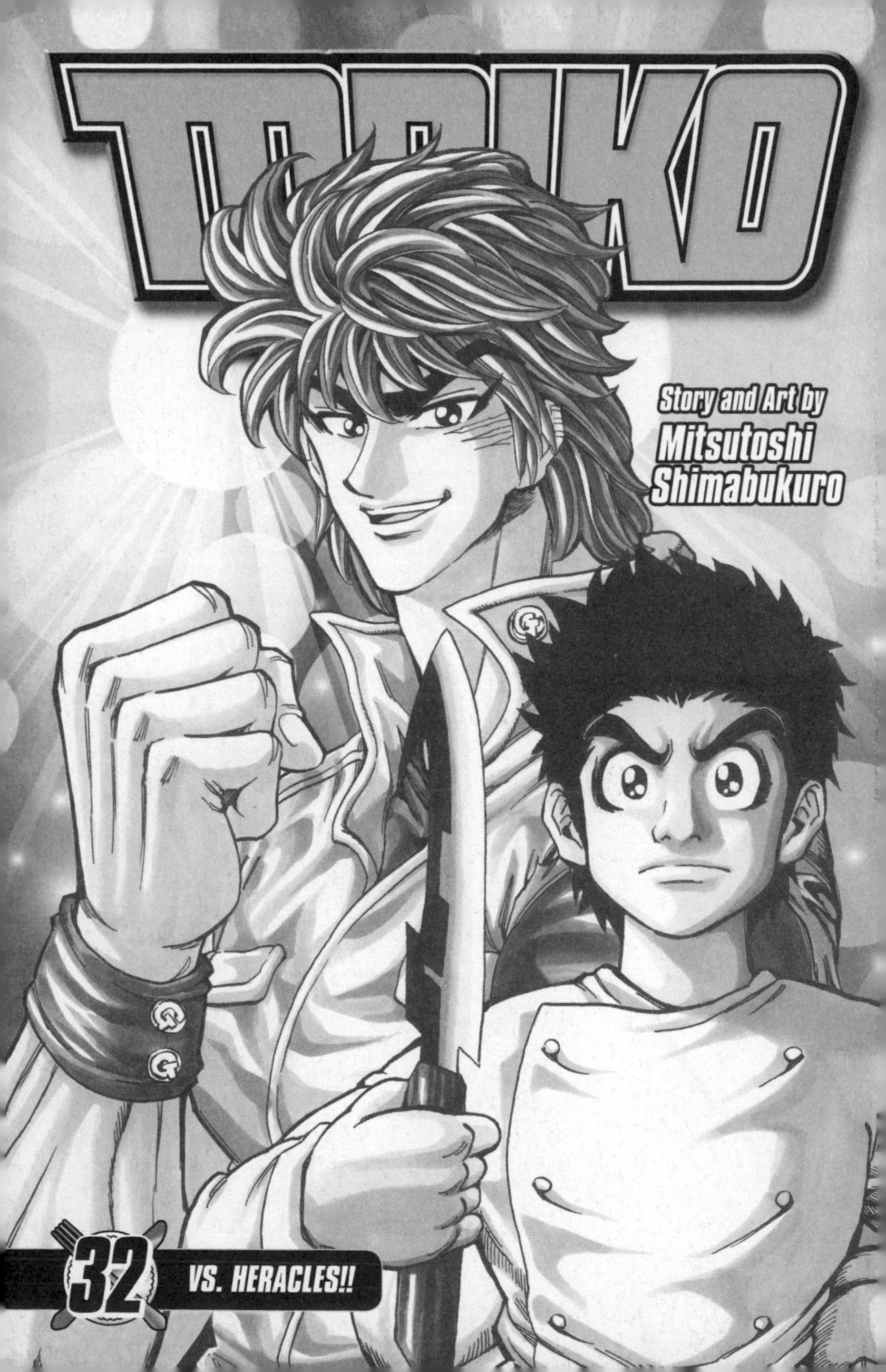
TORIKO
Story and Art by
Mitsutoshi
Shimabukuro
32
VS. HERACLES!!

TORIKO

THE ULTIMATE GOURMET HUNTER WHO'S ON A NEVER-ENDING QUEST TO FIND AND SCARF UP THE RAREST FOODS ON EARTH! HE FIGHTS WITH A KNIFE (HIS FIST), A FORK (HIS FIST), AND SPIKED PUNCH (ALSO HIS FISTS).

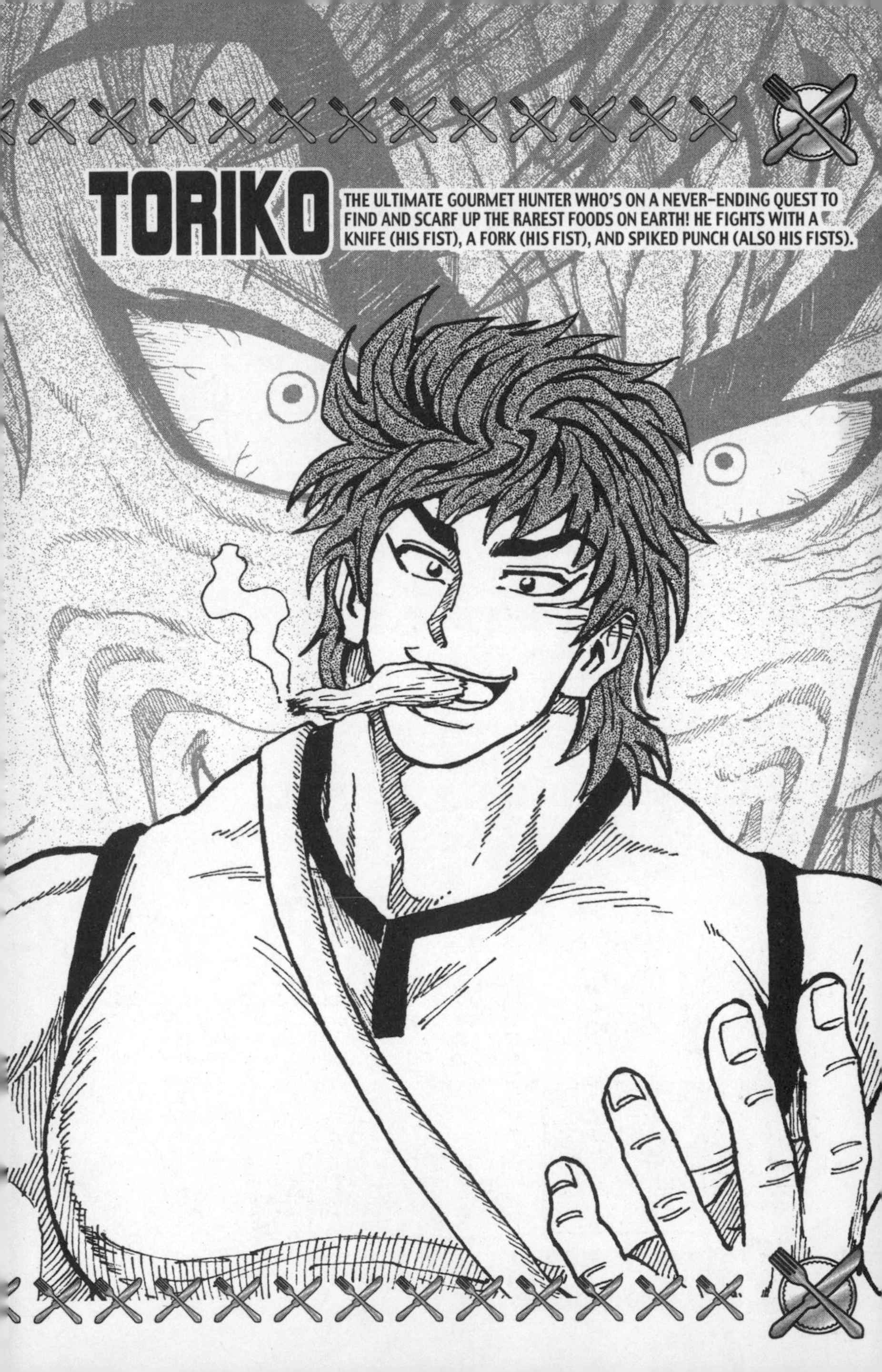

WHAT'S FOR DINNER

THE AGE OF GOURMET IS DECLARED OVER. IN ORDER TO GET KOMATSU BACK FROM GOURMET CORP., TORIKO VENTURES INTO THE GOURMET WORLD ON HIS OWN. EIGHTEEN MONTHS LATER, THE PAIR RETURNS HOME ALONG WITH A MASSIVE AMOUNT OF PROVISIONS TO FEED THE HUMAN WORLD. UPON THEIR RETURN, THE TWO ARE COMMISSIONED BY THE NEW IGO PRESIDENT, MANSOM, TO SEARCH FOR THE REMAINDER OF ICHIRYU'S FULL-COURSE MEAL. JOINING FORCES WITH THE OTHER FOUR KINGS, COCO, SUNNY AND ZEBRA, THEY SUCCEED IN RETRIEVING THE MIRACLE INGREDIENT THAT WILL SAVE HUMANITY FROM STARVATION: THE BILLION BIRD.

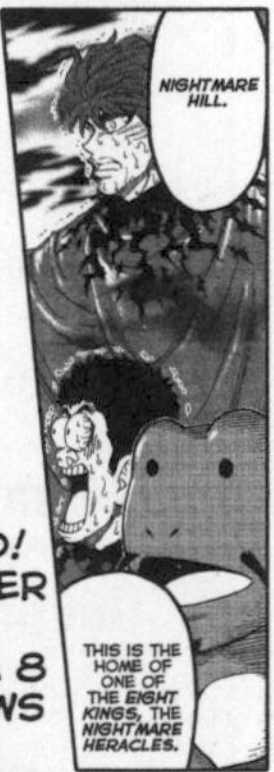
NIGHTMARE HILL.
THIS IS THE HOME OF ONE OF THE EIGHT KINGS, THE NIGHTMARE HERACLES.

IN ORDER TO REVIVE THE AGE OF GOURMET, THE FIVE OF THEM TAKE AN ENORMOUS ORDER! THEY MUST TRAVEL TO THE GOURMET WORLD AND FIND ACACIA'S FULL-COURSE MEAL. ARMED WITH THE INFORMATION AND THE OCTOMELON CAMPER MONSTER GIVEN TO THEM BY ICHIRYU'S MYSTERIOUS FRIEND CHICHI, THE FIVE MEN SET THEIR SIGHTS ON THE GOURMET WORLD!

GUIDED BY A MESSENGER FROM HEX FOOD WORLD, MAPPY, TORIKO AND CO. ARRIVE AT AREA 8 AND MEET THE MAYOR, WHO KNOWS ABOUT ACACIA'S SALAD, AIR. AIR WILL THEN LEAD THEM TO ACACIA'S SOUP, PAIR. AFTER BEING TAUGHT HOW TO PREPARE AIR, THE MEN SET THEIR SIGHTS ON SLOW RAIN HILL.

AT LONG LAST, TORIKO AND KOMATSU REACH THE NIGHTMARE HERACLES, RULER OF THE CONTINENT. HER OVERPOWERING AURA SENDS THEM BOTH SHIVERING! BUT THEN, MAPPY MAKES AN ANNOUNCEMENT: HE WILL SACRIFICE HIMSELF TO HERACLES SO THEY CAN CAPTURE AIR.

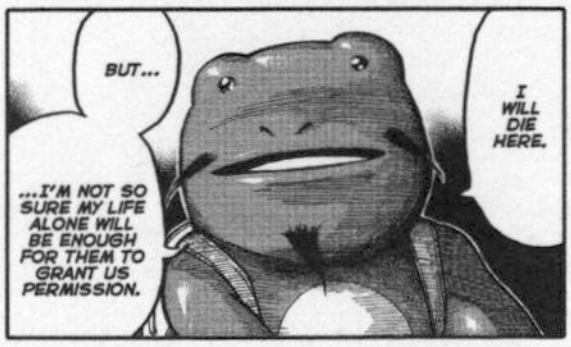
I WILL DIE HERE.
BUT...
...I'M NOT SO SURE MY LIFE ALONE WILL BE ENOUGH FOR THEM TO GRANT US PERMISSION.

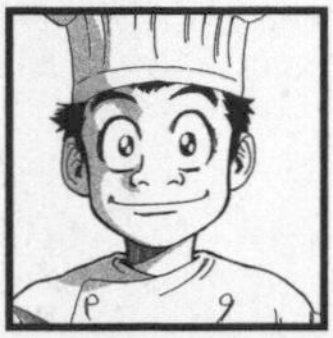

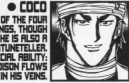

● KOMATSU

TALENTED IGO HOTEL CHEF AND TORIKO'S #1 FAN.

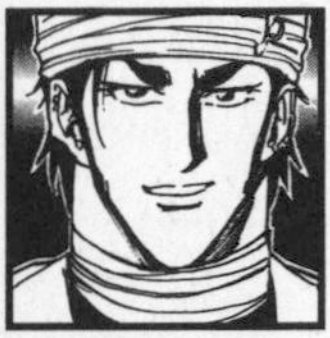

● COCO

ONE OF THE FOUR KINGS, THOUGH HE IS ALSO A FORTUNETELLER. SPECIAL ABILITY: POISON FLOWS IN HIS VEINS.

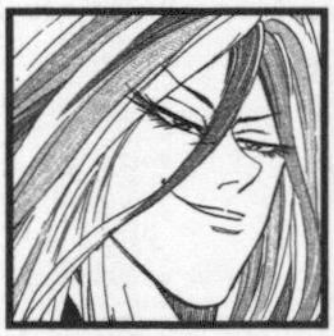

● SUNNY

ONE OF THE FOUR KINGS. SENSORS IN HIS LONG HAIR ENABLE HIM TO "TASTE" THE WORLD. OBSESSED WITH ALL THAT IS BEAUTIFUL.

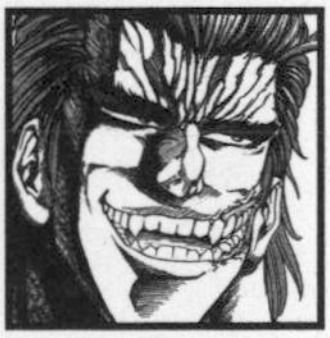

● ZEBRA

ONE OF THE FOUR KINGS. A DANGEROUS INDIVIDUAL WITH SUPERHUMAN HEARING AND VOCAL POWERS.

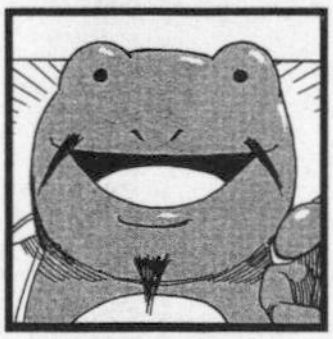

● MAPPY

A GUIDE FROM HEX FOOD WORLD. HE'S A TRAVEL FROG AND SPEAKS CROAKESE.

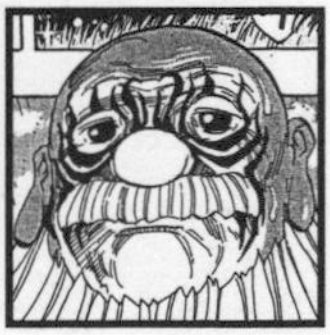

● DARUMA

THE MAYOR OF HEX FOOD WORLD. HE'S THE ONLY PERSON WHO KNOWS HOW TO PROPERLY PREPARE AIR.

Contents

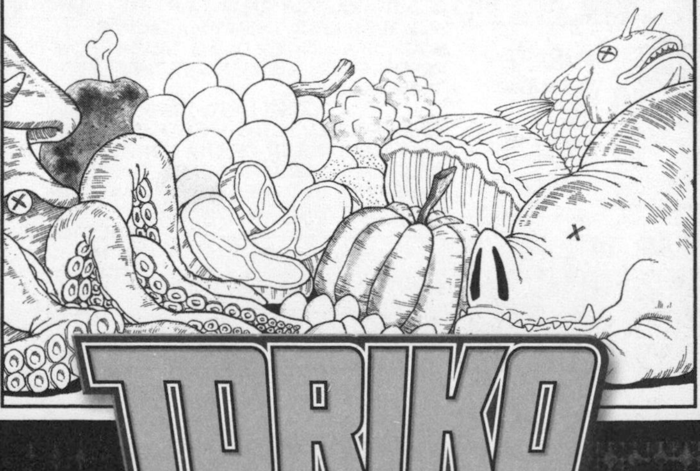

TORIKO

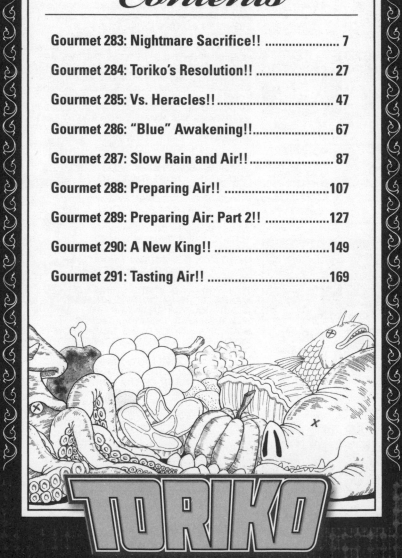

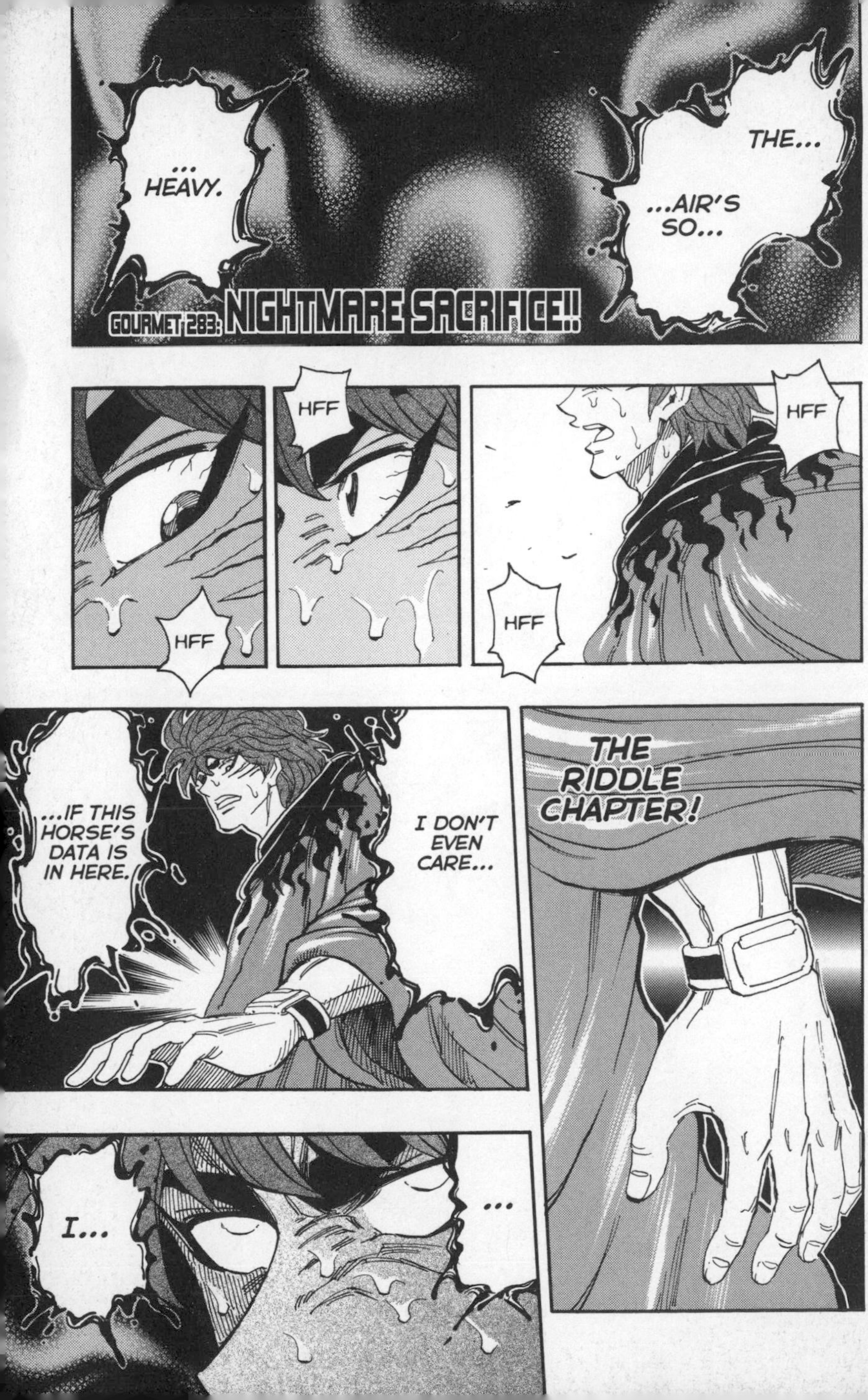
THE...
...AIR'S SO...
...HEAVY.
GOURMET 283: NIGHTMARE SACRIFICE!!
HFF
HFF
HFF
HFF
THE RIDDLE CHAPTER!
I DON'T EVEN CARE...
...IF THIS HORSE'S DATA IS IN HERE.
...
I...

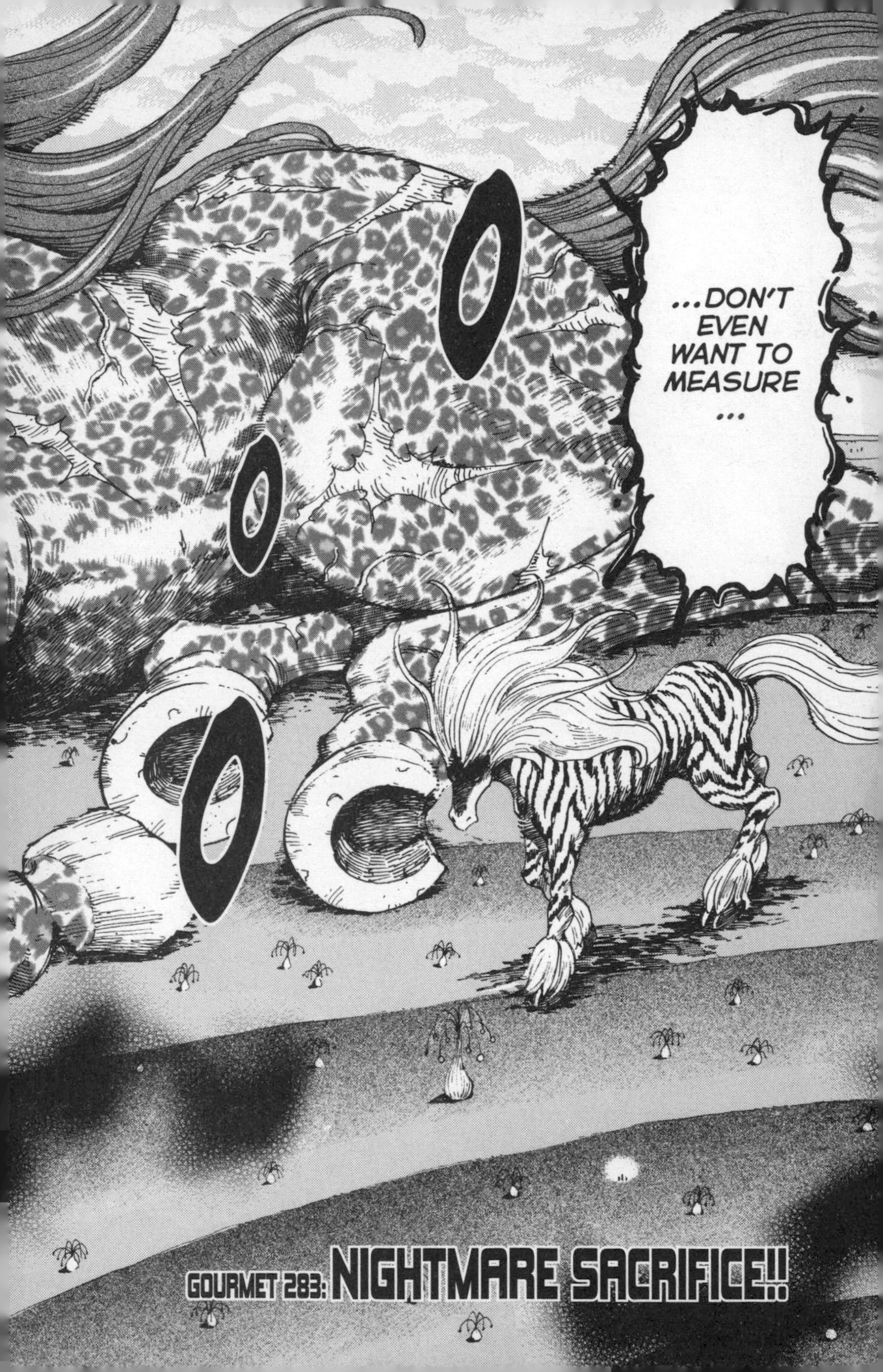
...DON'T EVEN WANT TO MEASURE ...
GOURMET 283: NIGHTMARE SACRIFICE!!

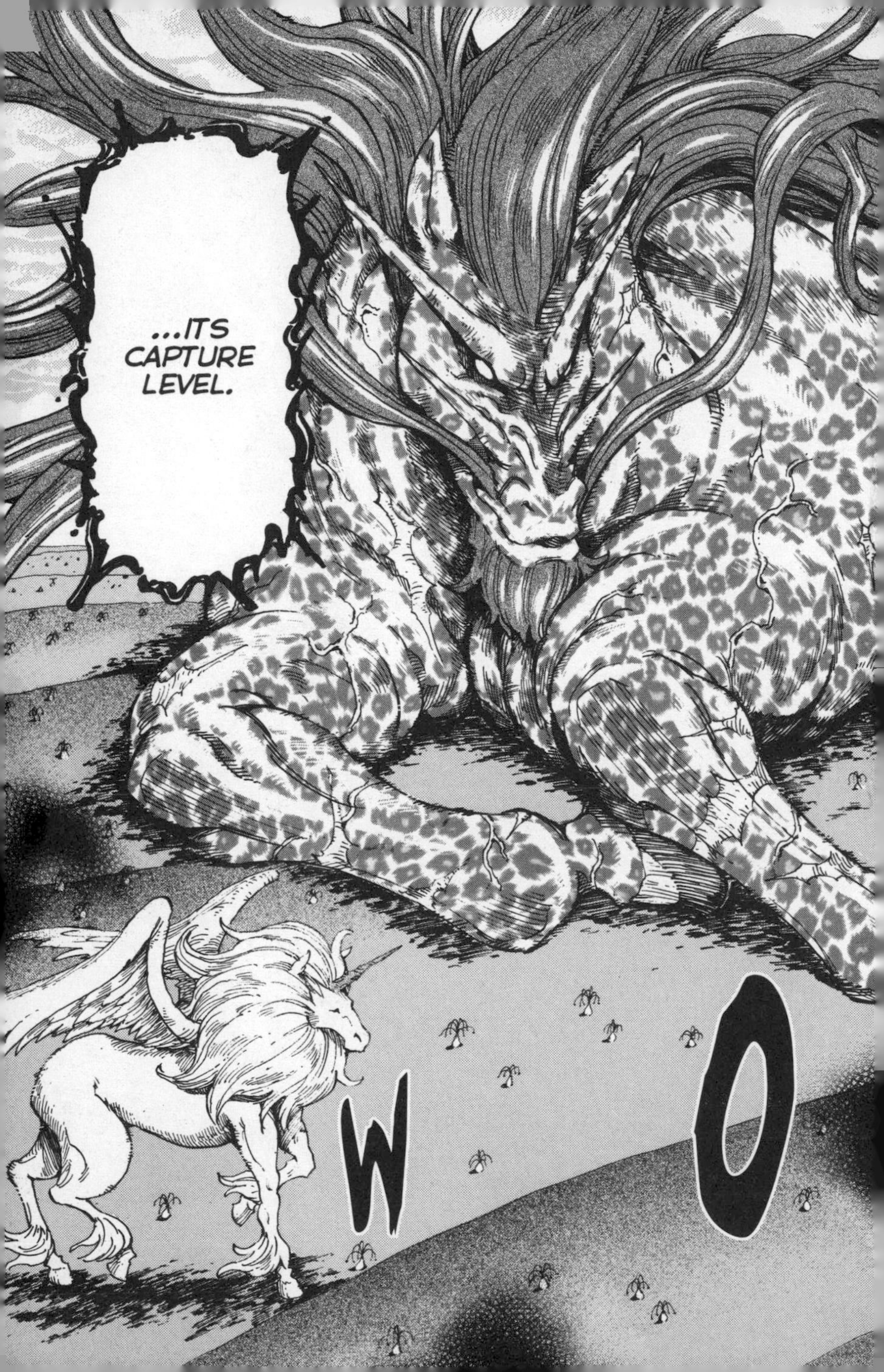
...ITS CAPTURE LEVEL.
W
O

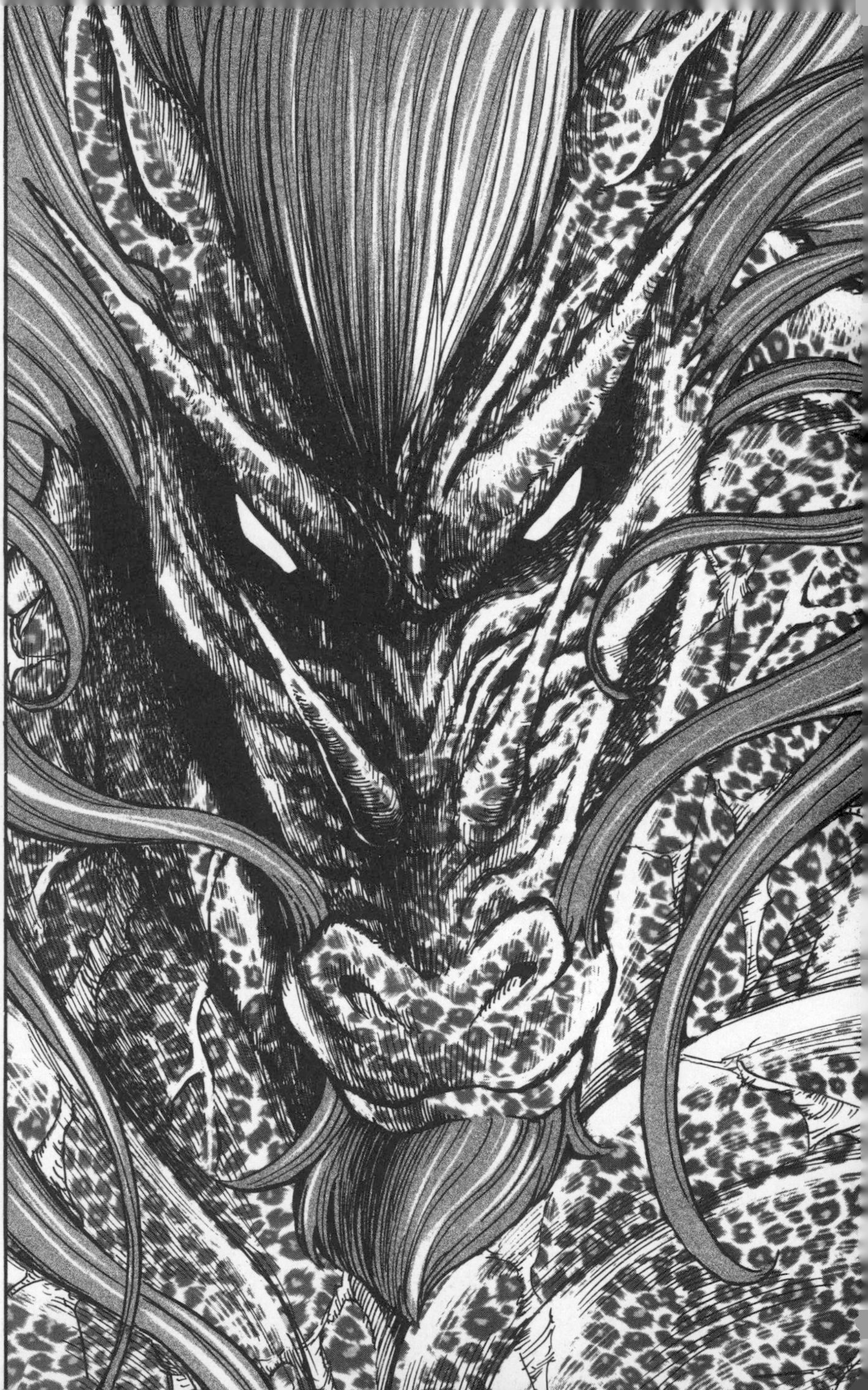

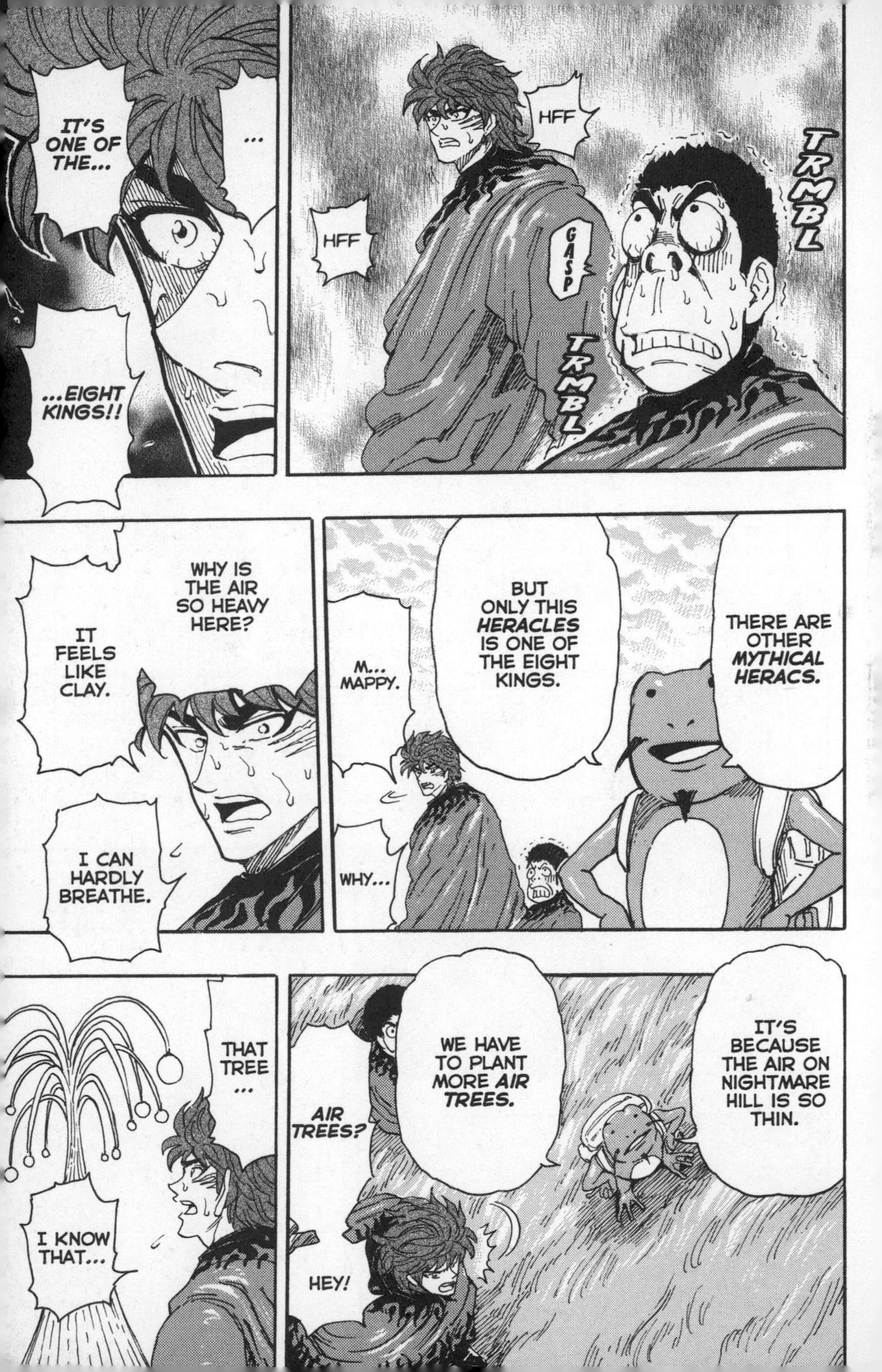
HFF
HFF
GASP
TRMBL
TRMBL
...
IT'S ONE OF THE...
...EIGHT KINGS!!
THERE ARE OTHER *MYTHICAL HERACS.*
BUT ONLY THIS *HERACLES* IS ONE OF THE EIGHT KINGS.
M... MAPPY.
WHY...
WHY IS THE AIR SO HEAVY HERE?
IT FEELS LIKE CLAY.
I CAN HARDLY BREATHE.
IT'S BECAUSE THE AIR ON NIGHTMARE HILL IS SO THIN.
WE HAVE TO PLANT MORE *AIR TREES.*
AIR TREES?
HEY!
THAT TREE ...
I KNOW THAT...

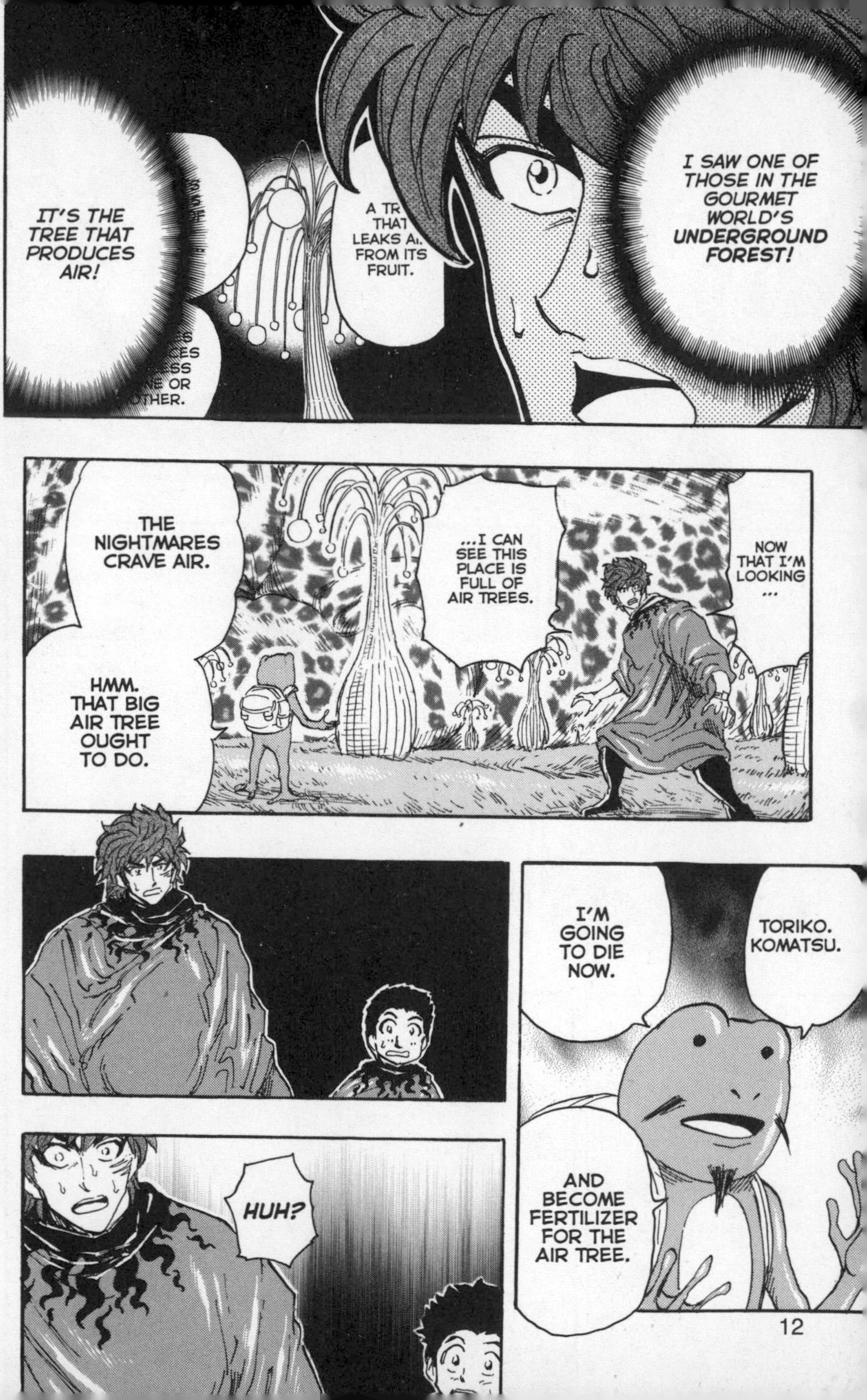

I SAW ONE OF THOSE IN THE GOURMET WORLD'S **UNDERGROUND FOREST!**
A TR THAT LEAKS A FROM ITS FRUIT.
IT'S THE TREE THAT PRODUCES AIR!
NOW THAT I'M LOOKING ...
...I CAN SEE THIS PLACE IS FULL OF AIR TREES.
THE NIGHTMARES CRAVE AIR.
HMM. THAT BIG AIR TREE OUGHT TO DO.
TORIKO. KOMATSU.
I'M GOING TO DIE NOW.
AND BECOME FERTILIZER FOR THE AIR TREE.
HUH?

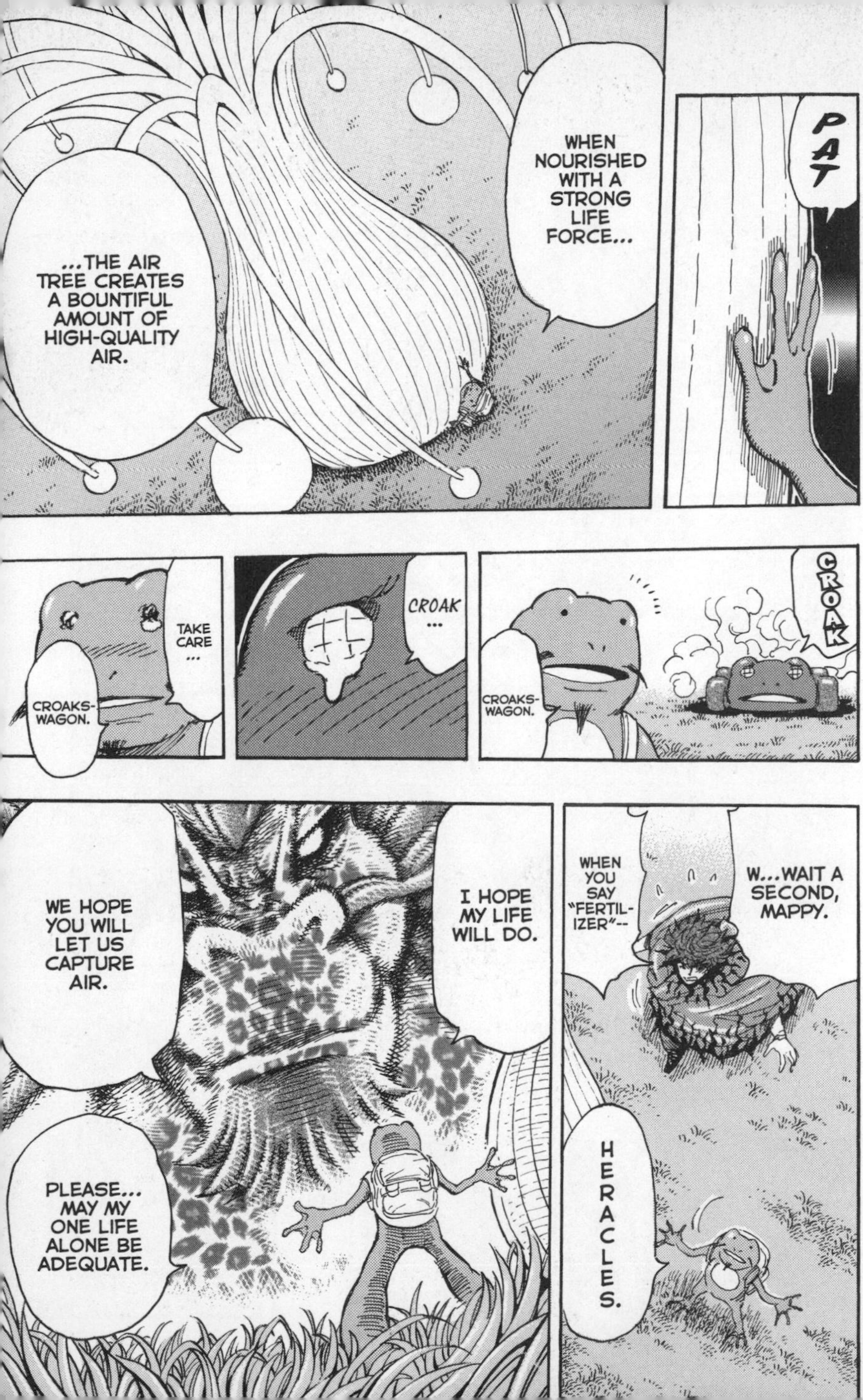
PAT
WHEN NOURISHED WITH A STRONG LIFE FORCE...
...THE AIR TREE CREATES A BOUNTIFUL AMOUNT OF HIGH-QUALITY AIR.
CROAK
CROAKSWAGON.
CROAK...
TAKE CARE...
CROAKSWAGON.
W...WAIT A SECOND, MAPPY.
WHEN YOU SAY "FERTILIZER"--
HERACLES.
I HOPE MY LIFE WILL DO.
WE HOPE YOU WILL LET US CAPTURE AIR.
PLEASE... MAY MY ONE LIFE ALONE BE ADEQUATE.

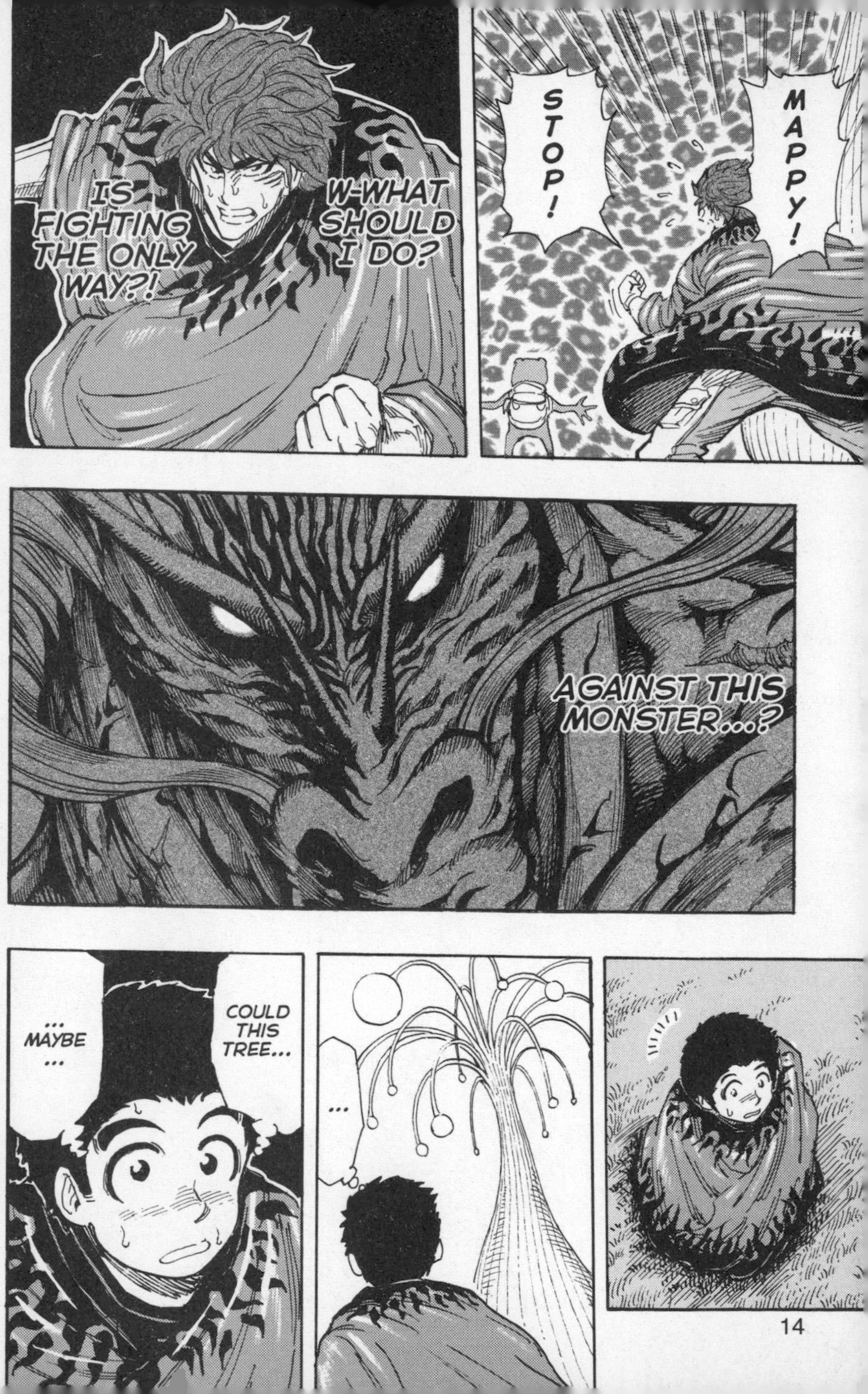
MAPPY!
STOP!
W-WHAT SHOULD I DO?
IS FIGHTING THE ONLY WAY?!
AGAINST THIS MONSTER...?
...
COULD THIS TREE...
...MAYBE...

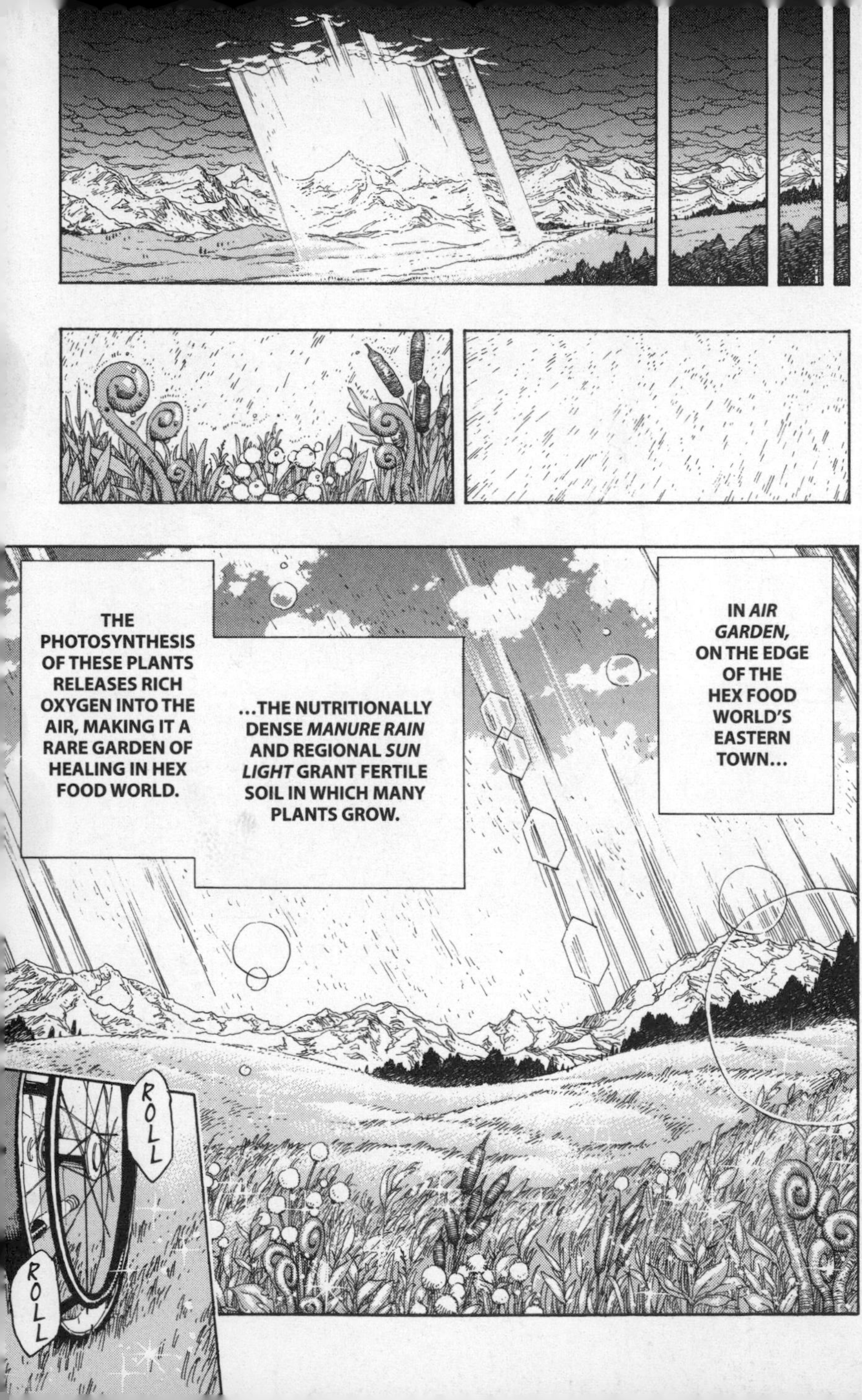
IN *AIR GARDEN,* ON THE EDGE OF THE HEX FOOD WORLD'S EASTERN TOWN…
…THE NUTRITIONALLY DENSE *MANURE RAIN* AND REGIONAL *SUN LIGHT* GRANT FERTILE SOIL IN WHICH MANY PLANTS GROW.
THE PHOTOSYNTHESIS OF THESE PLANTS RELEASES RICH OXYGEN INTO THE AIR, MAKING IT A RARE GARDEN OF HEALING IN HEX FOOD WORLD.
ROLL
ROLL

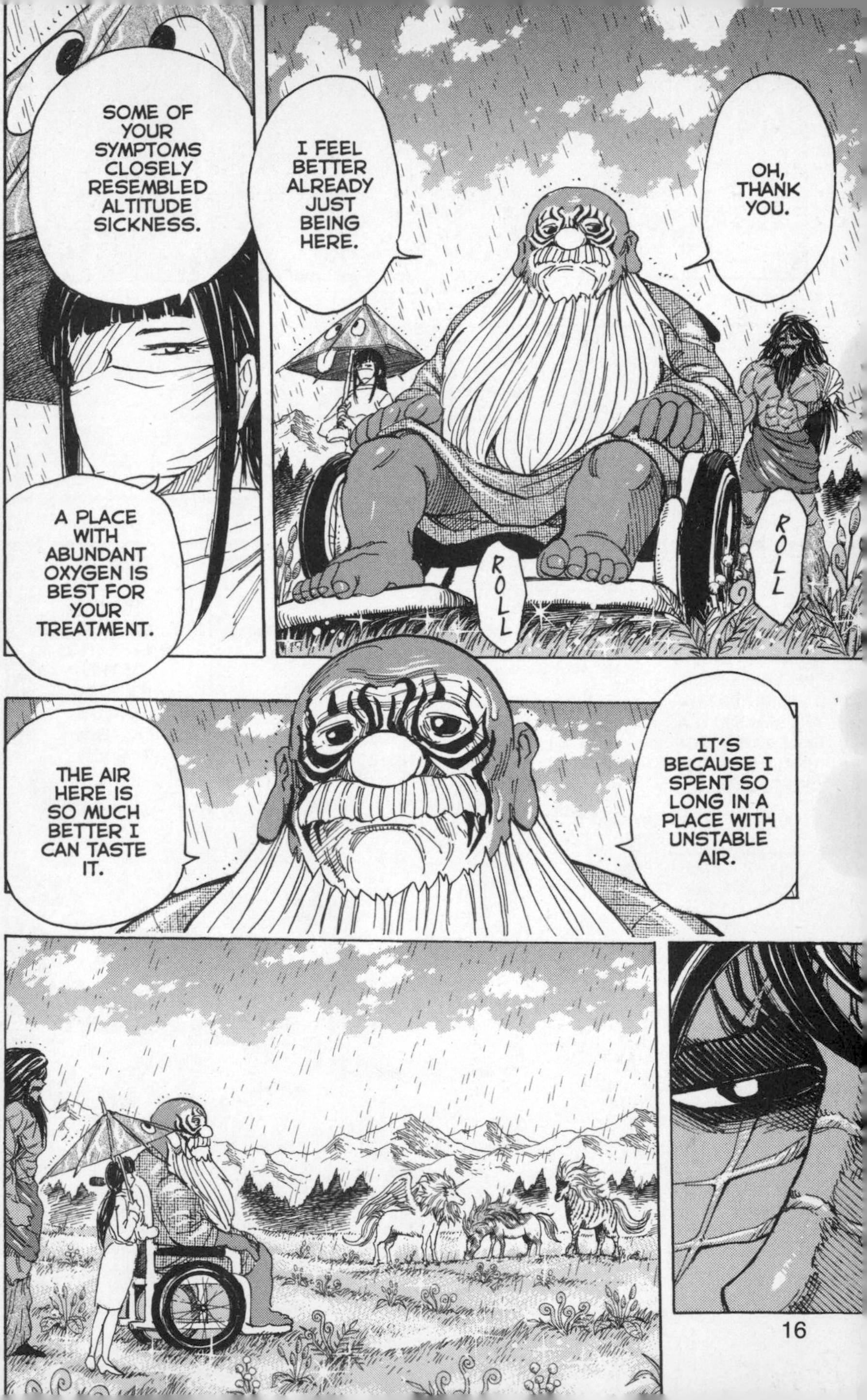
OH, THANK YOU.
I FEEL BETTER ALREADY JUST BEING HERE.
ROLL
ROLL
SOME OF YOUR SYMPTOMS CLOSELY RESEMBLED ALTITUDE SICKNESS.
A PLACE WITH ABUNDANT OXYGEN IS BEST FOR YOUR TREATMENT.
IT'S BECAUSE I SPENT SO LONG IN A PLACE WITH UNSTABLE AIR.
THE AIR HERE IS SO MUCH BETTER I CAN TASTE IT.

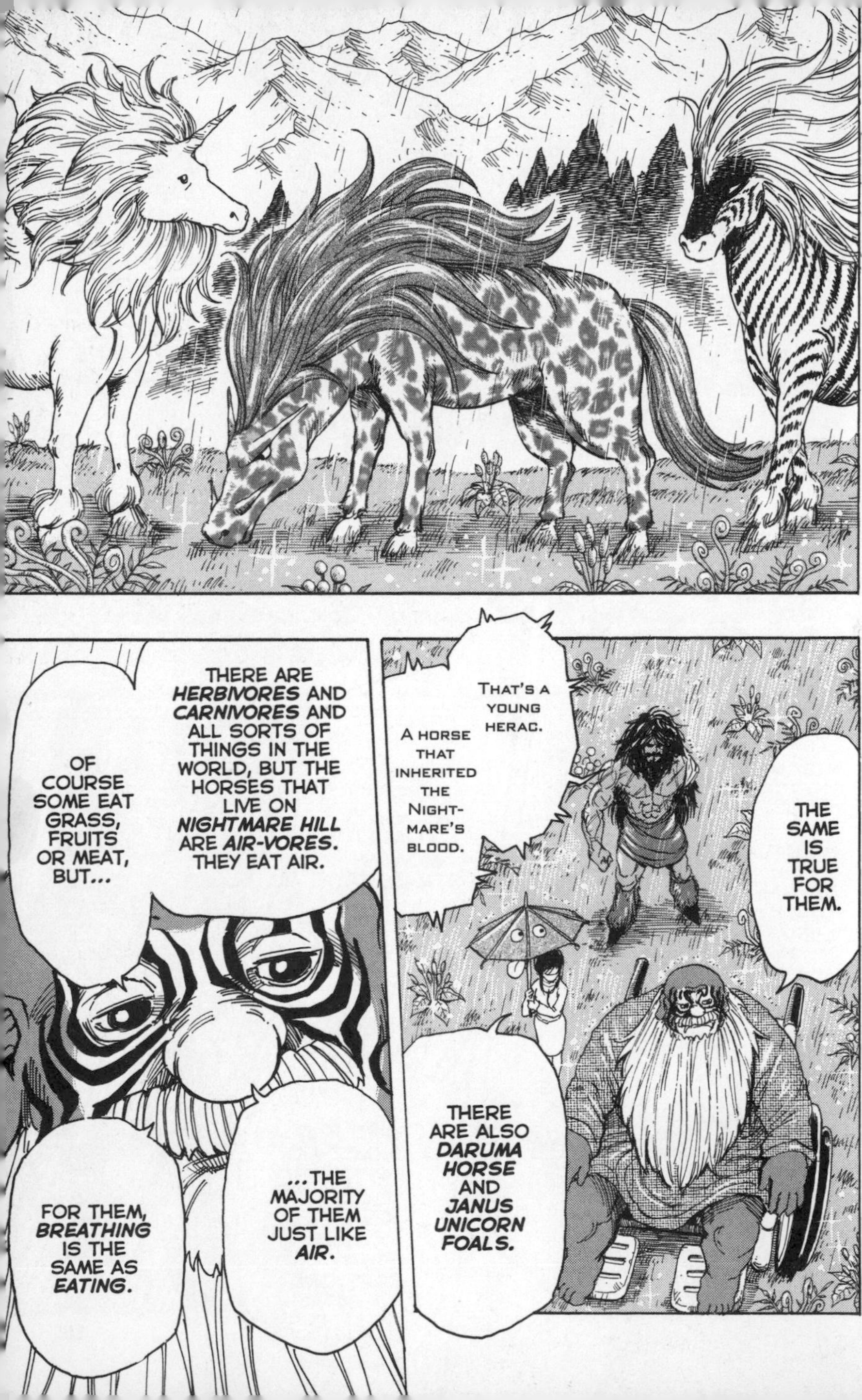

That's a young herac.
A horse that inherited the Nightmare's blood.
There are also *Daruma horse* and *Janus unicorn foals.*
The same is true for them.
There are *herbivores* and *carnivores* and all sorts of things in the world, but the horses that live on *Nightmare Hill* are *air-vores*. They eat air.
Of course some eat grass, fruits or meat, but...
...the majority of them just like *air*.
For them, *breathing* is the same as *eating*.

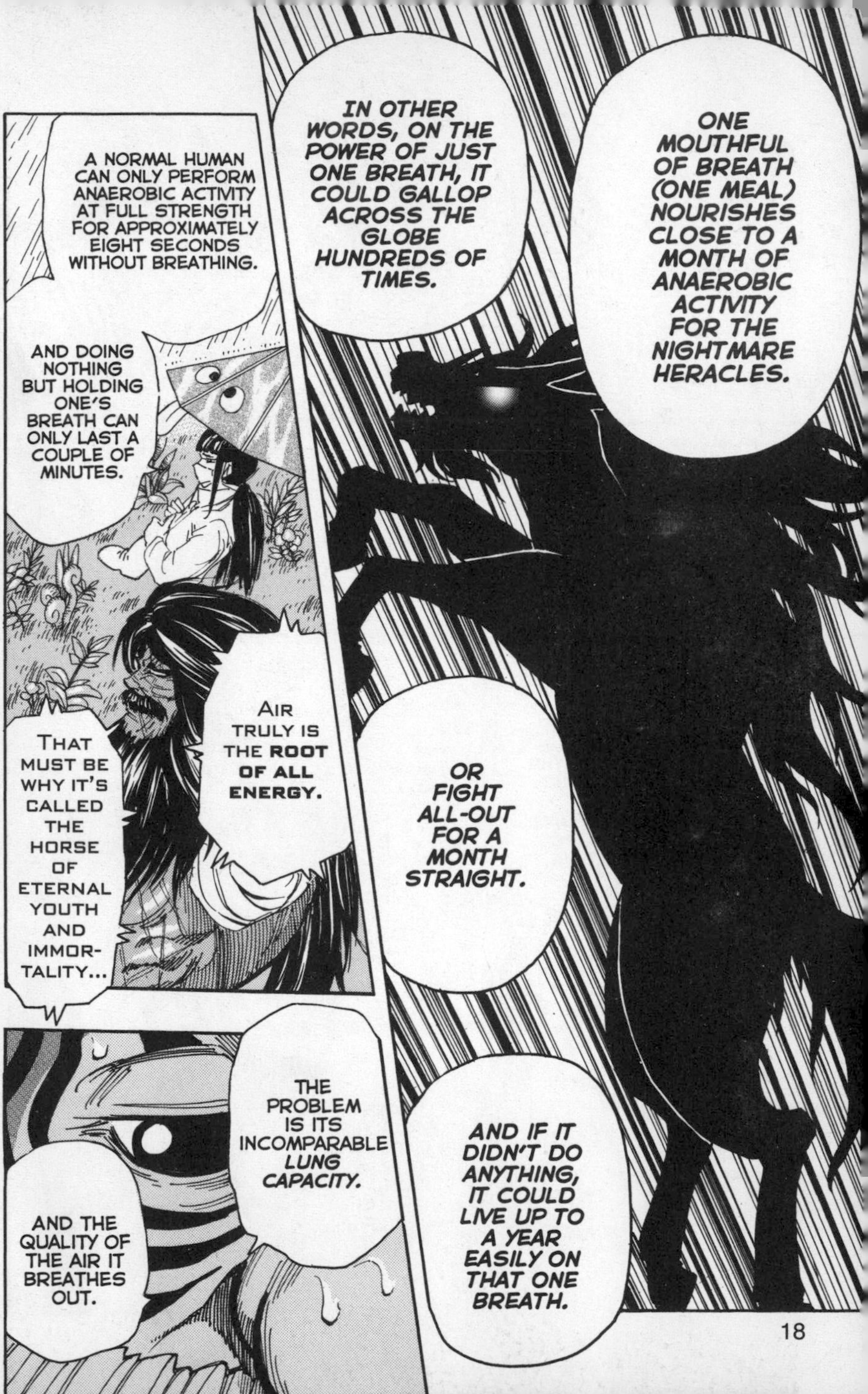
ONE MOUTHFUL OF BREATH (ONE MEAL) NOURISHES CLOSE TO A MONTH OF ANAEROBIC ACTIVITY FOR THE NIGHTMARE HERACLES.
IN OTHER WORDS, ON THE POWER OF JUST ONE BREATH, IT COULD GALLOP ACROSS THE GLOBE HUNDREDS OF TIMES.
OR FIGHT ALL-OUT FOR A MONTH STRAIGHT.
AND IF IT DIDN'T DO ANYTHING, IT COULD LIVE UP TO A YEAR EASILY ON THAT ONE BREATH.
A NORMAL HUMAN CAN ONLY PERFORM ANAEROBIC ACTIVITY AT FULL STRENGTH FOR APPROXIMATELY EIGHT SECONDS WITHOUT BREATHING.
AND DOING NOTHING BUT HOLDING ONE'S BREATH CAN ONLY LAST A COUPLE OF MINUTES.
AIR TRULY IS THE ROOT OF ALL ENERGY.
THAT MUST BE WHY IT'S CALLED THE HORSE OF ETERNAL YOUTH AND IMMORTALITY...
THE PROBLEM IS ITS INCOMPARABLE LUNG CAPACITY.
AND THE QUALITY OF THE AIR IT BREATHES OUT.

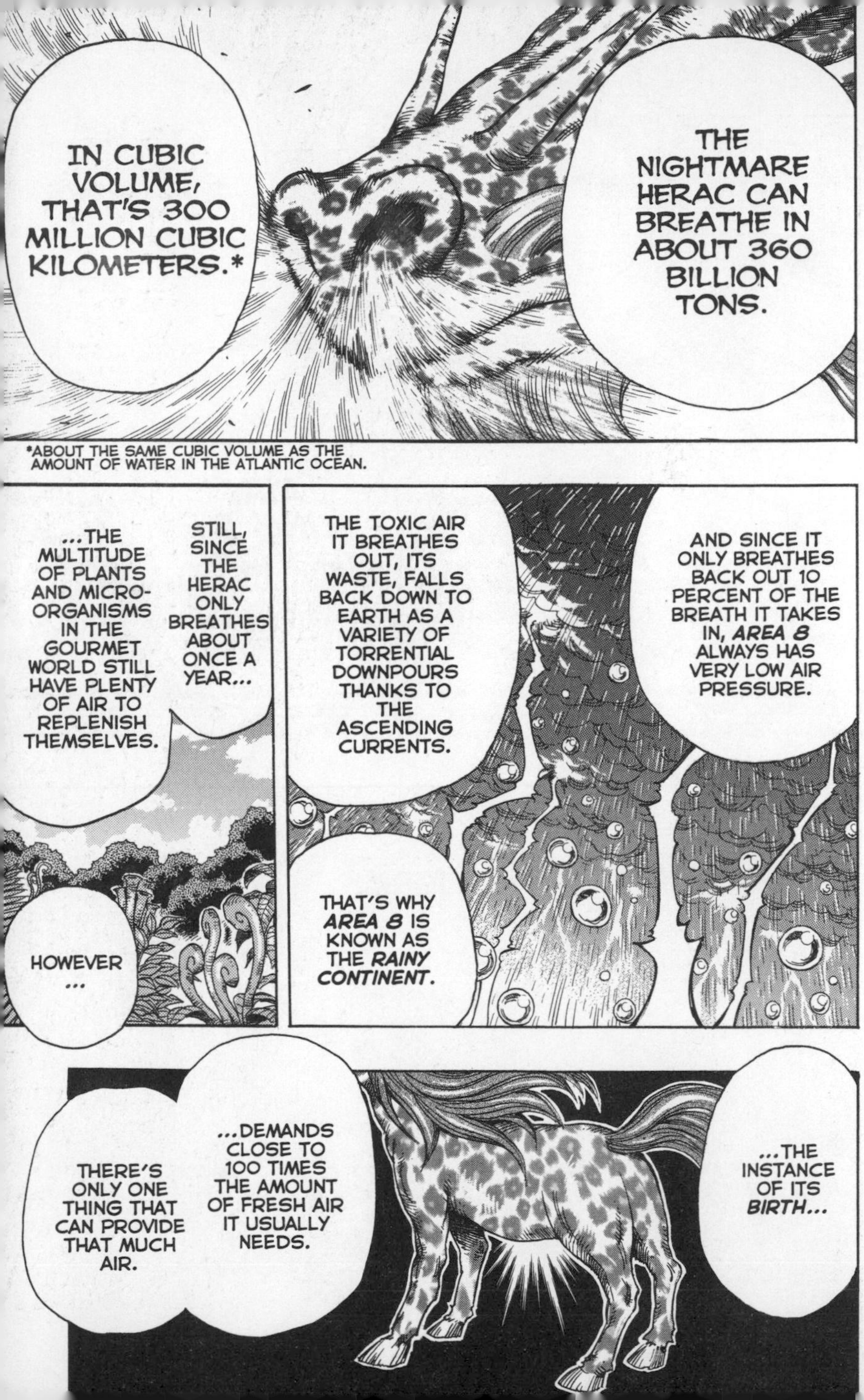
THE NIGHTMARE HERAC CAN BREATHE IN ABOUT 360 BILLION TONS.
IN CUBIC VOLUME, THAT'S 300 MILLION CUBIC KILOMETERS.*
*ABOUT THE SAME CUBIC VOLUME AS THE AMOUNT OF WATER IN THE ATLANTIC OCEAN.
AND SINCE IT ONLY BREATHES BACK OUT 10 PERCENT OF THE BREATH IT TAKES IN, *AREA 8* ALWAYS HAS VERY LOW AIR PRESSURE.
THE TOXIC AIR IT BREATHES OUT, ITS WASTE, FALLS BACK DOWN TO EARTH AS A VARIETY OF TORRENTIAL DOWNPOURS THANKS TO THE ASCENDING CURRENTS.
THAT'S WHY *AREA 8* IS KNOWN AS THE *RAINY CONTINENT*.
STILL, SINCE THE HERAC ONLY BREATHES ABOUT ONCE A YEAR...
...THE MULTITUDE OF PLANTS AND MICRO-ORGANISMS IN THE GOURMET WORLD STILL HAVE PLENTY OF AIR TO REPLENISH THEMSELVES.
HOWEVER ...
...THE INSTANCE OF ITS *BIRTH*...
...DEMANDS CLOSE TO 100 TIMES THE AMOUNT OF FRESH AIR IT USUALLY NEEDS.
THERE'S ONLY ONE THING THAT CAN PROVIDE THAT MUCH AIR.

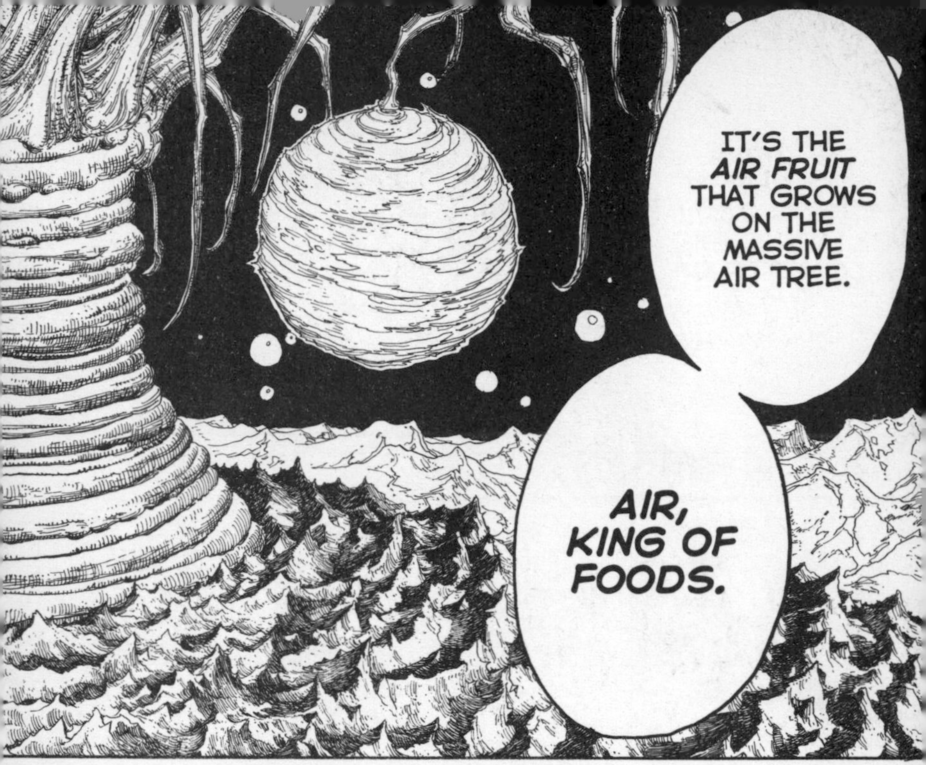
IT'S THE *AIR FRUIT* THAT GROWS ON THE MASSIVE AIR TREE.
AIR, KING OF FOODS.
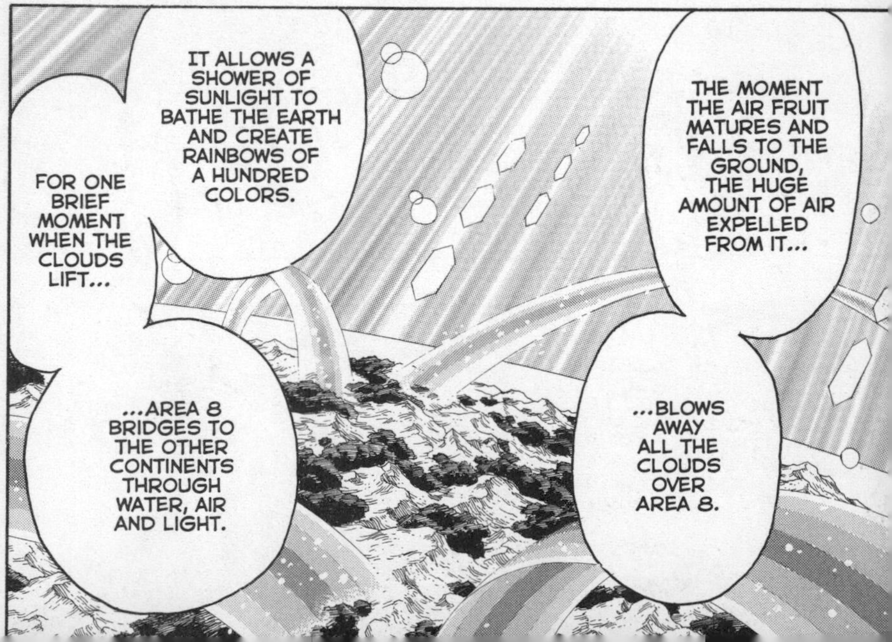
THE MOMENT THE AIR FRUIT MATURES AND FALLS TO THE GROUND, THE HUGE AMOUNT OF AIR EXPELLED FROM IT...
...BLOWS AWAY ALL THE CLOUDS OVER AREA 8.
IT ALLOWS A SHOWER OF SUNLIGHT TO BATHE THE EARTH AND CREATE RAINBOWS OF A HUNDRED COLORS.
FOR ONE BRIEF MOMENT WHEN THE CLOUDS LIFT...
...AREA 8 BRIDGES TO THE OTHER CONTINENTS THROUGH WATER, AIR AND LIGHT.

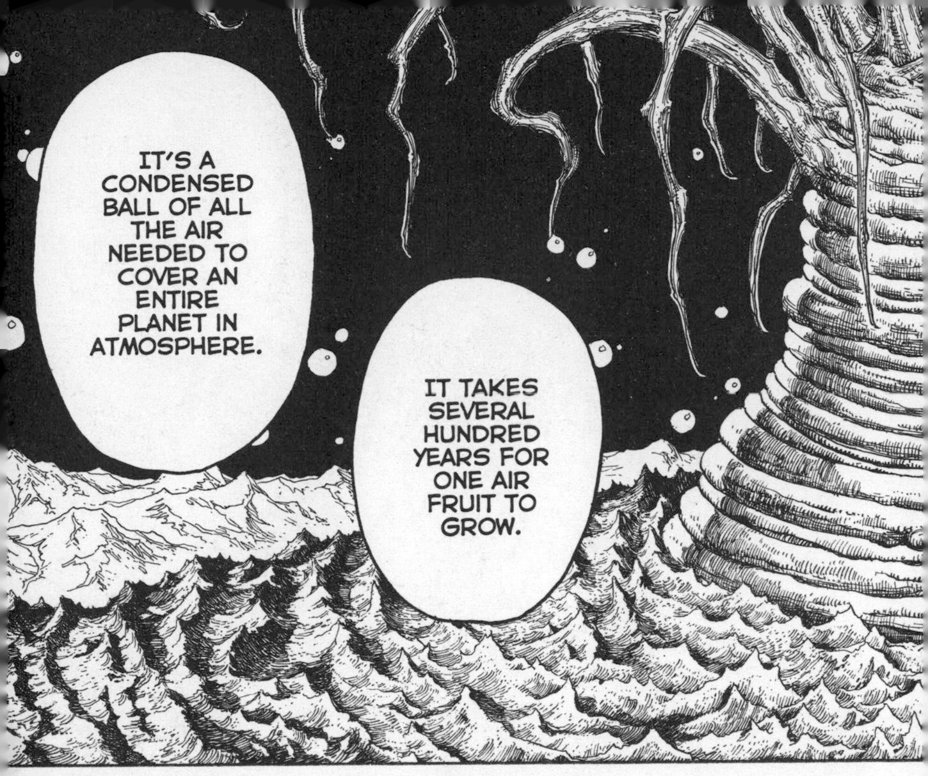
IT'S A CONDENSED BALL OF ALL THE AIR NEEDED TO COVER AN ENTIRE PLANET IN ATMOSPHERE.
IT TAKES SEVERAL HUNDRED YEARS FOR ONE AIR FRUIT TO GROW.

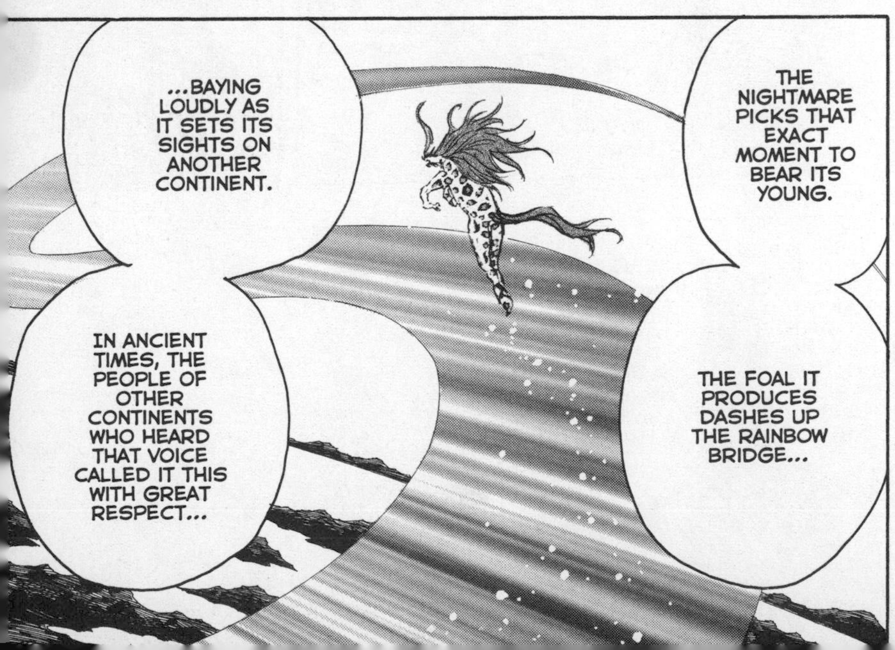
THE NIGHTMARE PICKS THAT EXACT MOMENT TO BEAR ITS YOUNG.
THE FOAL IT PRODUCES DASHES UP THE RAINBOW BRIDGE...
...BAYING LOUDLY AS IT SETS ITS SIGHTS ON ANOTHER CONTINENT.
IN ANCIENT TIMES, THE PEOPLE OF OTHER CONTINENTS WHO HEARD THAT VOICE CALLED IT THIS WITH GREAT RESPECT...

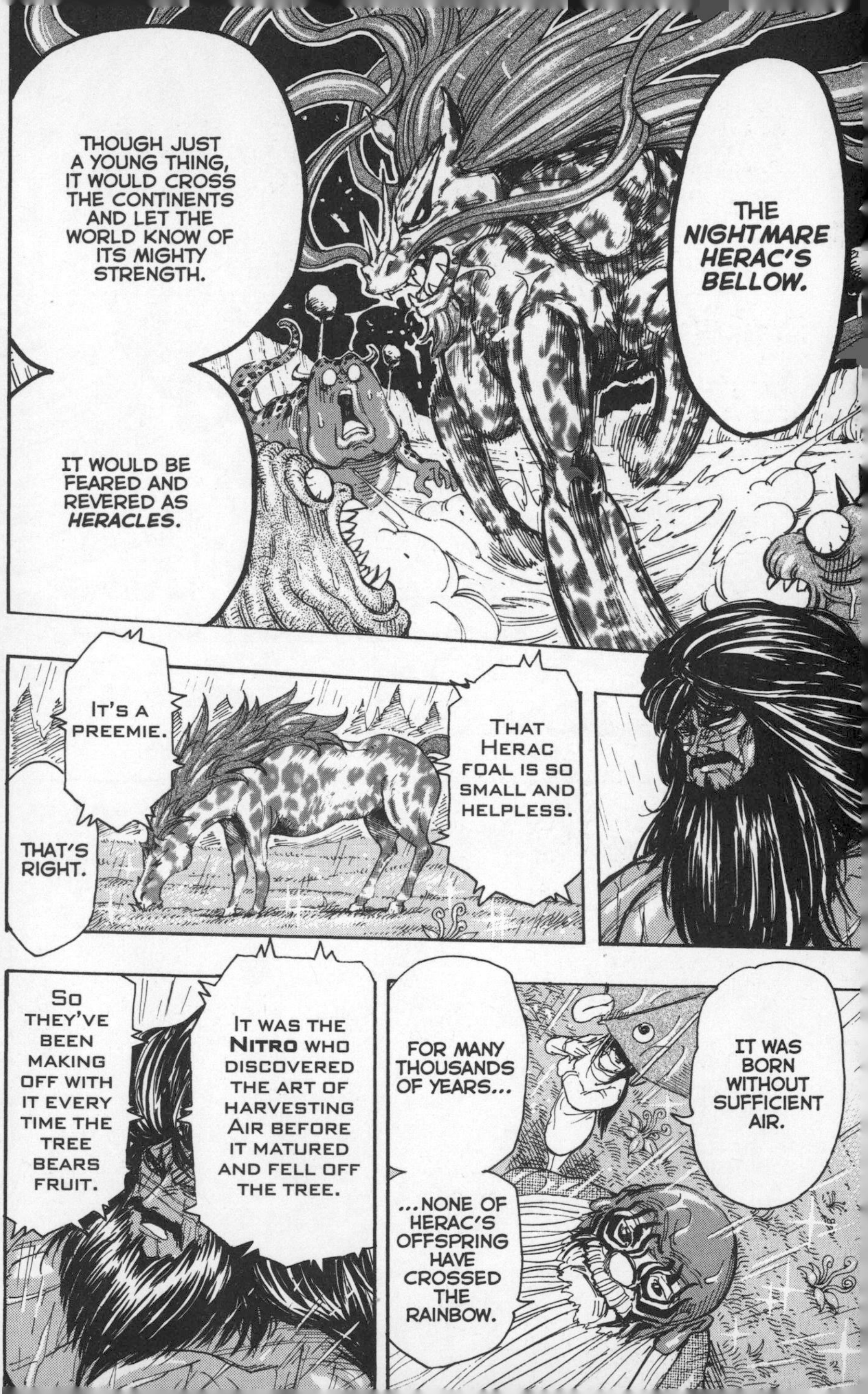
THE NIGHTMARE HERAC'S BELLOW.
THOUGH JUST A YOUNG THING, IT WOULD CROSS THE CONTINENTS AND LET THE WORLD KNOW OF ITS MIGHTY STRENGTH.
IT WOULD BE FEARED AND REVERED AS HERACLES.
THAT HERAC FOAL IS SO SMALL AND HELPLESS.
IT'S A PREEMIE.
THAT'S RIGHT.
IT WAS BORN WITHOUT SUFFICIENT AIR.
FOR MANY THOUSANDS OF YEARS...
...NONE OF HERAC'S OFFSPRING HAVE CROSSED THE RAINBOW.
IT WAS THE NITRO WHO DISCOVERED THE ART OF HARVESTING AIR BEFORE IT MATURED AND FELL OFF THE TREE.
SO THEY'VE BEEN MAKING OFF WITH IT EVERY TIME THE TREE BEARS FRUIT.

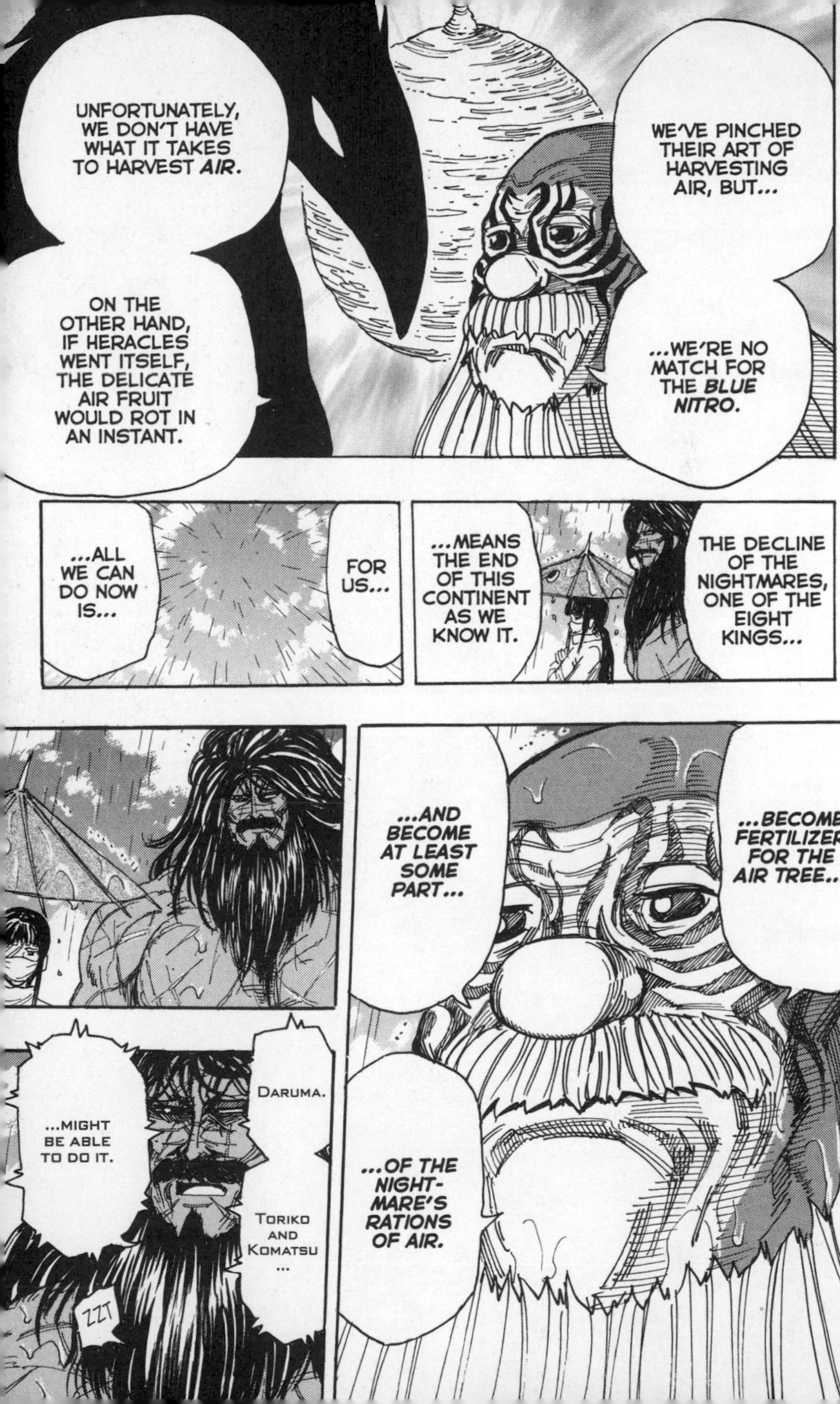
WE'VE PINCHED THEIR ART OF HARVESTING AIR, BUT...
...WE'RE NO MATCH FOR THE *BLUE NITRO*.
UNFORTUNATELY, WE DON'T HAVE WHAT IT TAKES TO HARVEST *AIR*.
ON THE OTHER HAND, IF HERACLES WENT ITSELF, THE DELICATE AIR FRUIT WOULD ROT IN AN INSTANT.
THE DECLINE OF THE NIGHTMARES, ONE OF THE EIGHT KINGS...
...MEANS THE END OF THIS CONTINENT AS WE KNOW IT.
FOR US...
...ALL WE CAN DO NOW IS...
...BECOME FERTILIZER FOR THE AIR TREE...
...AND BECOME AT LEAST SOME PART...
...OF THE NIGHT-MARE'S RATIONS OF AIR.
DARUMA.
TORIKO AND KOMATSU ...
...MIGHT BE ABLE TO DO IT.
ZZT

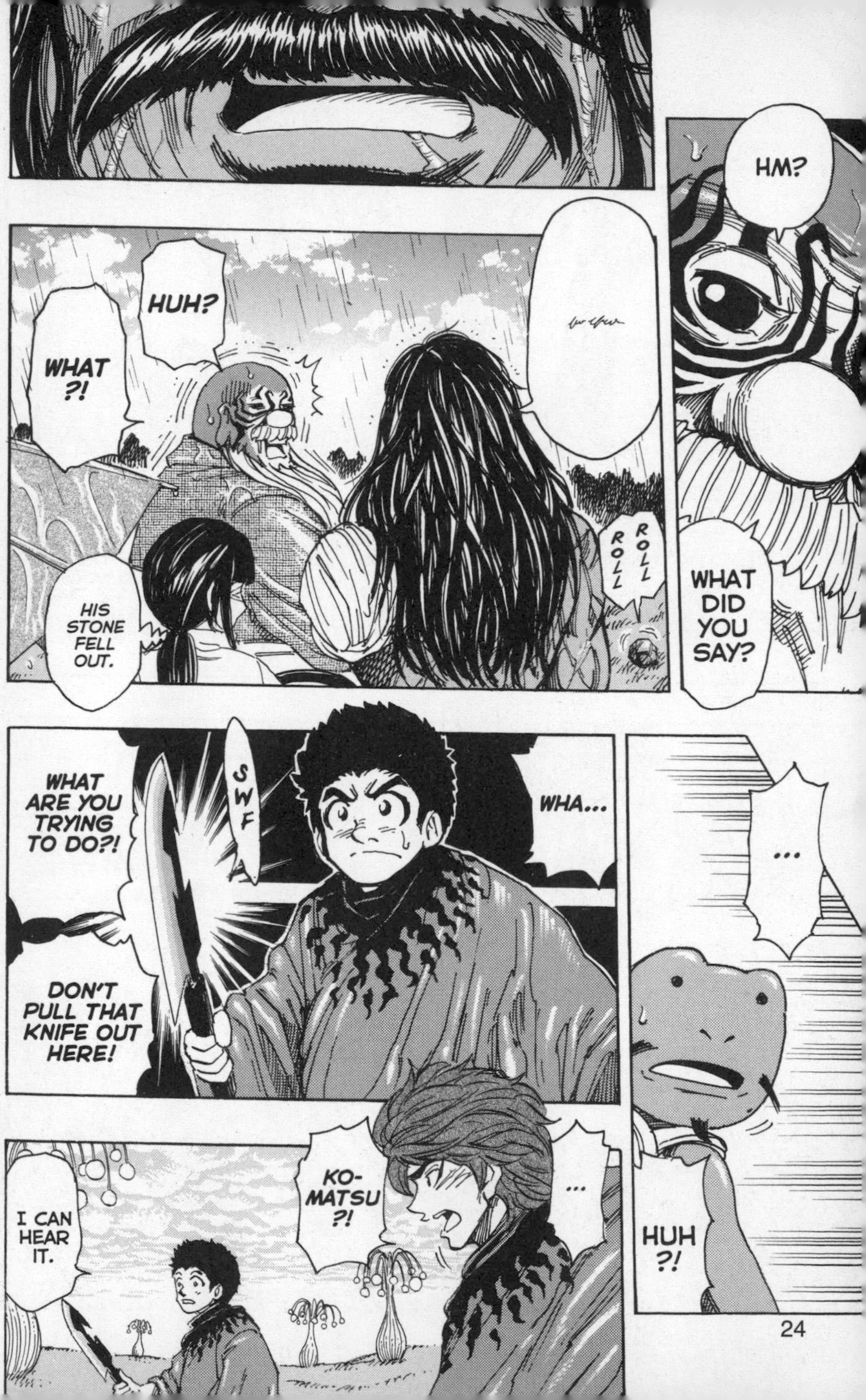
HM?
WHAT DID YOU SAY?
HUH?
WHAT?!
ROLL ROLL
HIS STONE FELL OUT.
...
HUH?!
WHA...
SWF
WHAT ARE YOU TRYING TO DO?!
DON'T PULL THAT KNIFE OUT HERE!
...
KO-MATSU?!
I CAN HEAR IT.

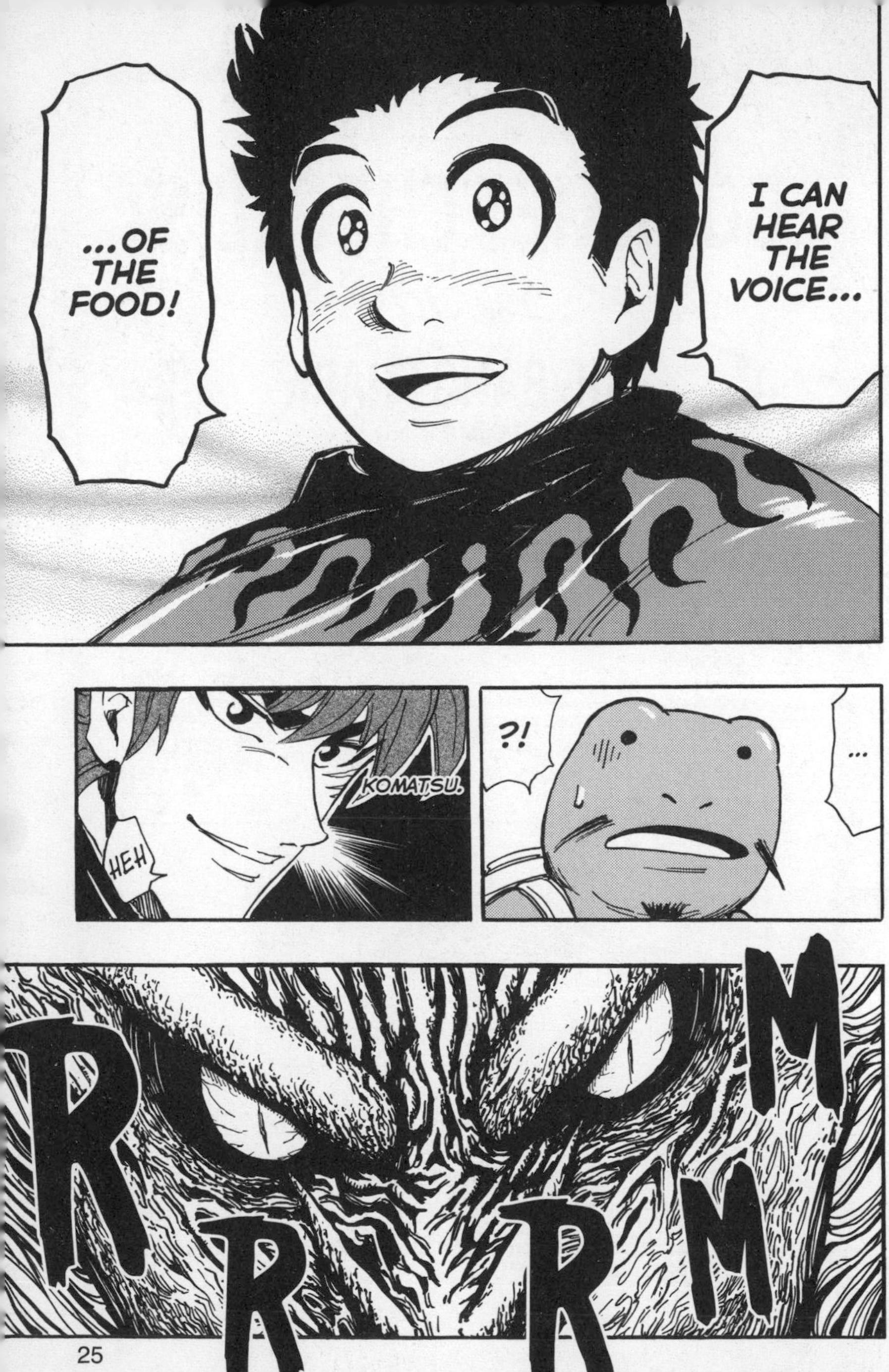
I CAN HEAR THE VOICE...
...OF THE FOOD!
...
?!
KOMATSU.
HEH
RRRMMM

TORIKO

GOURMET CHECKLIST

Vol. 309

BIG BANG SHARK
(MAMMAL FISH)

CAPTURE LEVEL: UNKNOWN
HABITAT: GOURMET WORLD
SIZE: 120 M
HEIGHT: ---
WEIGHT: 700 TONS
PRICE: UNKNOWN

SCALE

THIS CREATURE LIVES IN THE GOURMET WORLD. ITS ENTIRE BODY IS BLACK SO ITS PITCH-BLACK DEEP-SEA ENVIRONMENT MAKES IT DIFFICULT TO FIND. BUT NOT TO WORRY, IT CAN ALSO FLY THANKS TO THE WINGS ON EITHER SIDE OF ITS BODY AND ITS DORSAL FIN. ITS GIANT MOUTH CAN CATCH ANYTHING THAT CROSES ITS PATH. IT HAS AN INSANELY HIGH CAPTURE LEVEL, BUT THOSE WHO ARE STRONG ENOUGH CAN TAME THEM...NAMELY, GOURMET CORP.

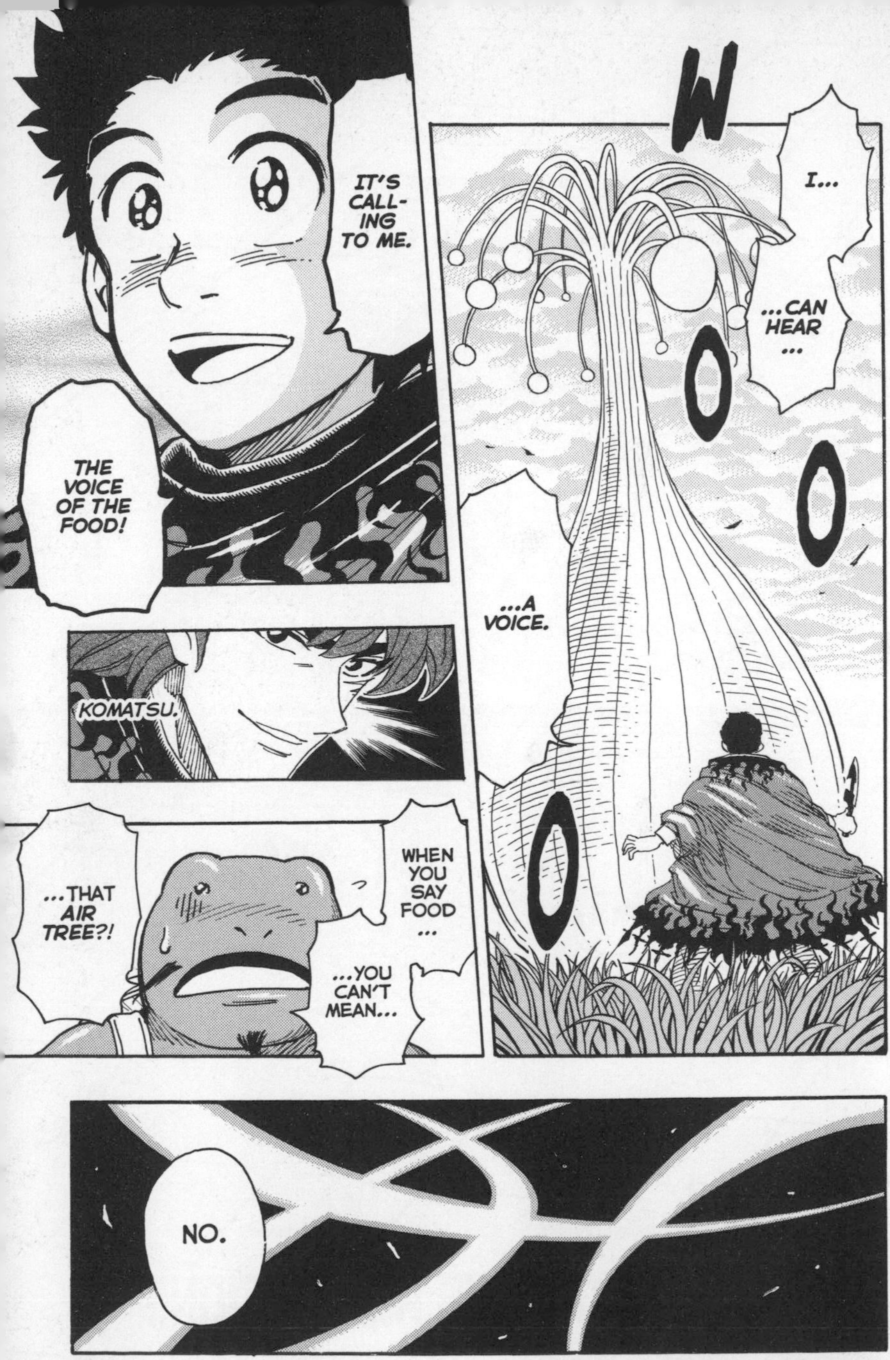
W
I...
...CAN HEAR...
OOO
...A VOICE.
IT'S CALLING TO ME.
THE VOICE OF THE FOOD!
KOMATSU.
WHEN YOU SAY FOOD...
...YOU CAN'T MEAN...
...THAT AIR TREE?!
NO.

GOURMET 284: TORIKO'S RESOLUTION!!

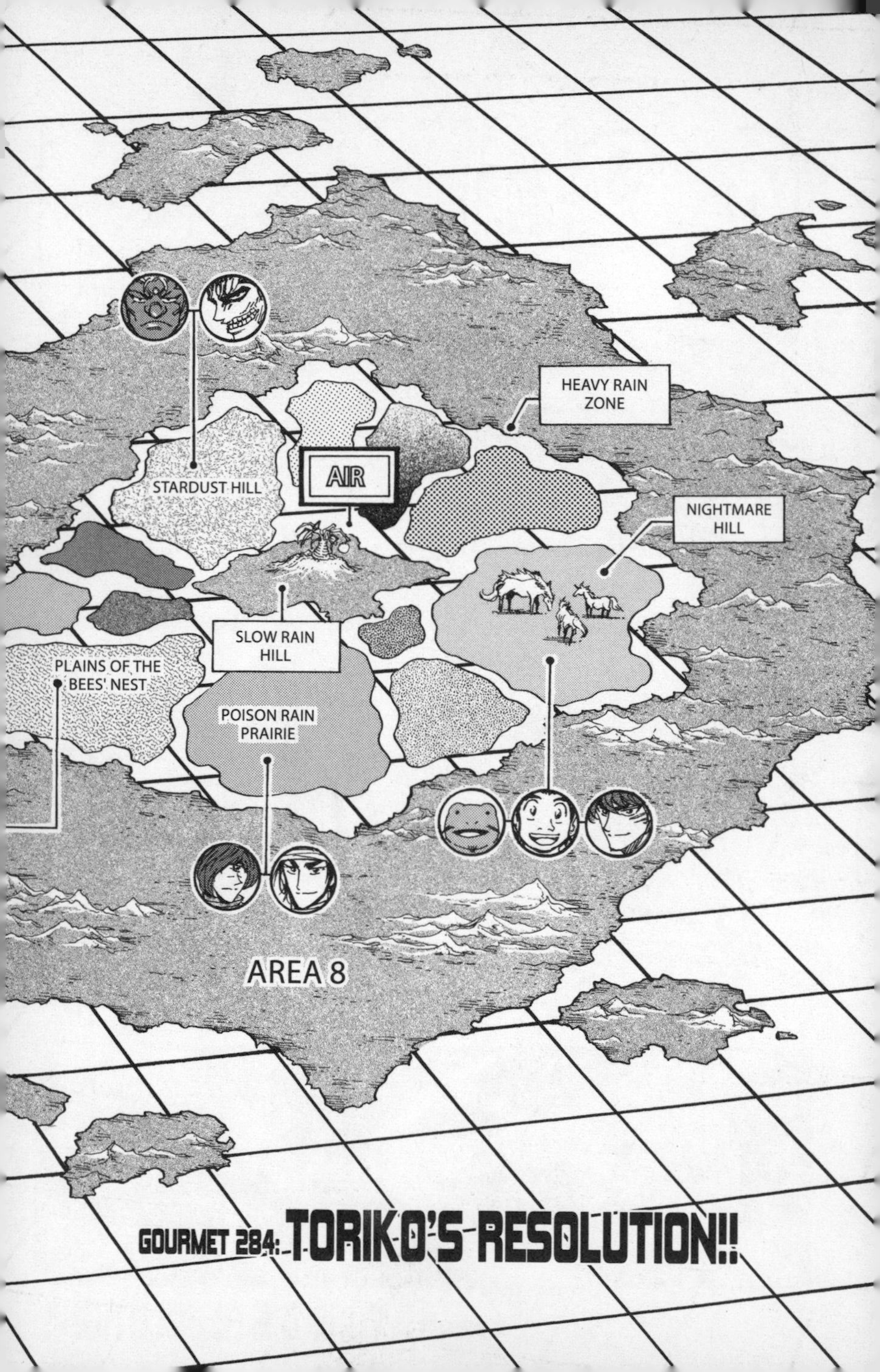
HEAVY RAIN ZONE
AIR
STARDUST HILL
NIGHTMARE HILL
SLOW RAIN HILL
PLAINS OF THE BEES' NEST
POISON RAIN PRAIRIE
AREA 8

GOURMET 284: TORIKO'S RESOLUTION!!

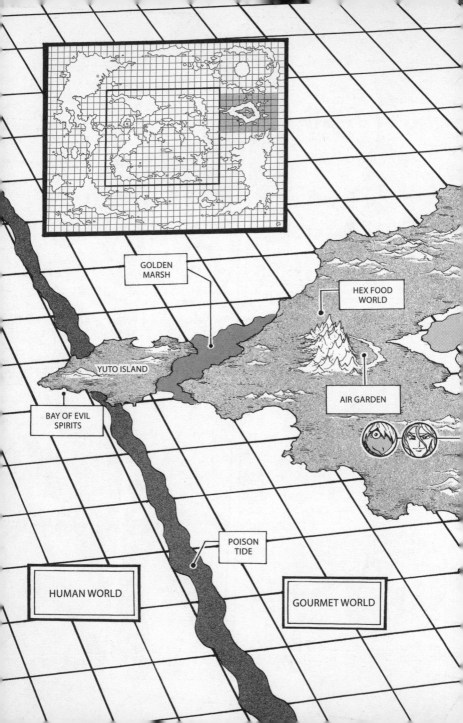

GOLDEN MARSH

HEX FOOD WORLD

YUTO ISLAND

AIR GARDEN

BAY OF EVIL SPIRITS

POISON TIDE

HUMAN WORLD

GOURMET WORLD

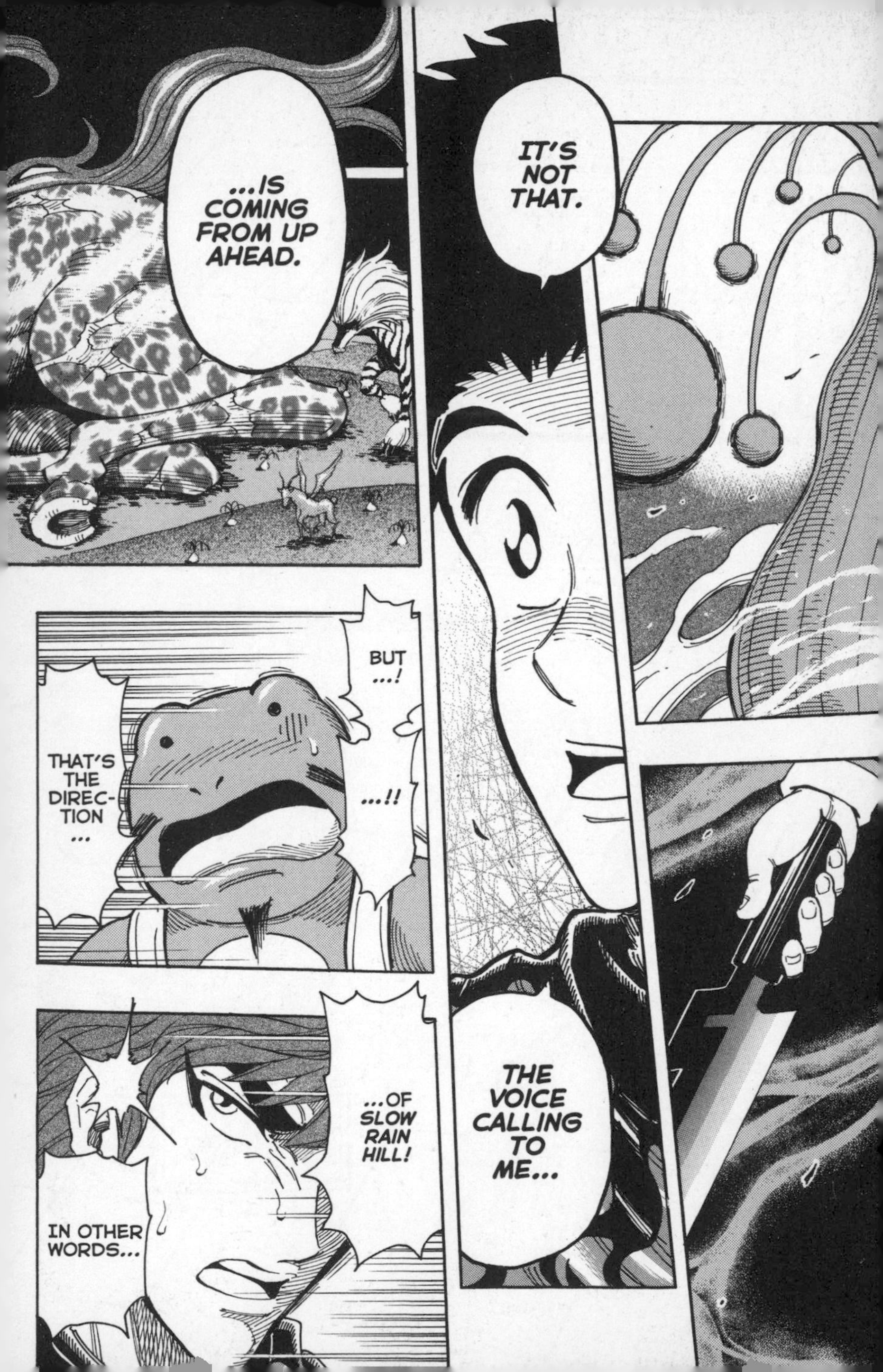
IT'S NOT THAT.
THE VOICE CALLING TO ME...
...IS COMING FROM UP AHEAD.
BUT...!
...!!
THAT'S THE DIRECTION...
...OF SLOW RAIN HILL!
IN OTHER WORDS...

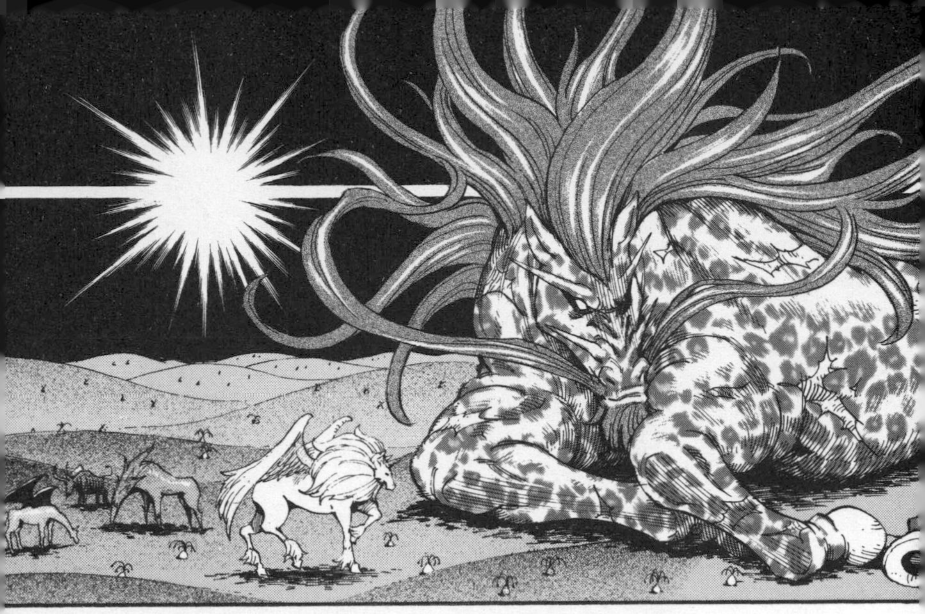

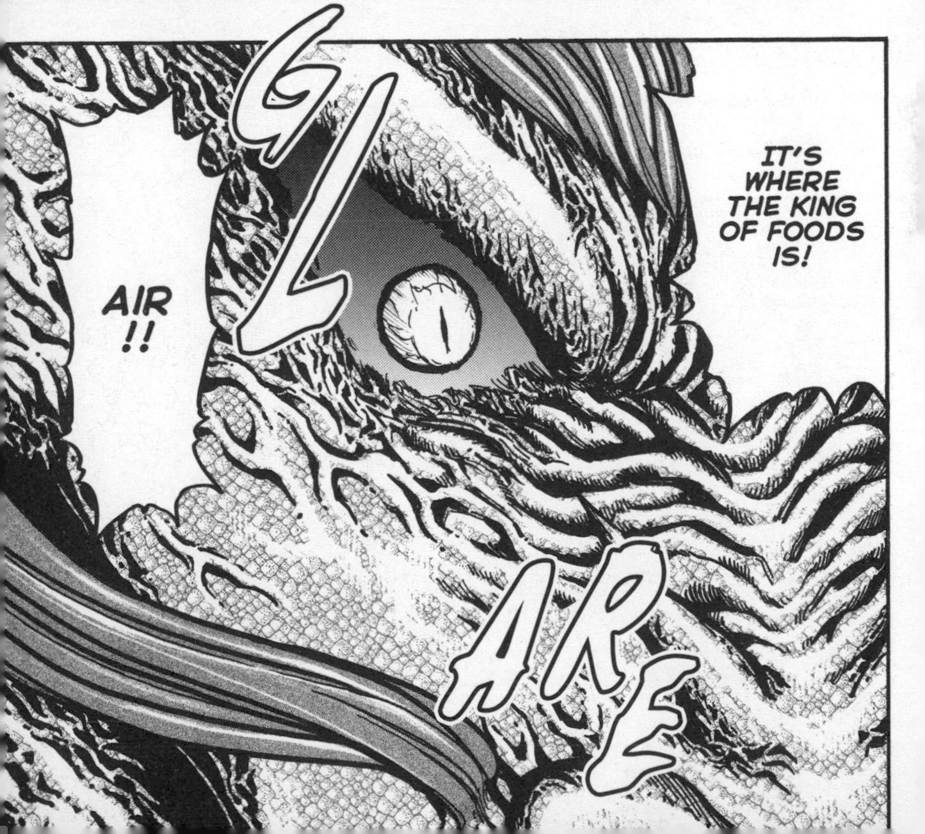
IT'S WHERE THE KING OF FOODS IS!
AIR !!
GLARE

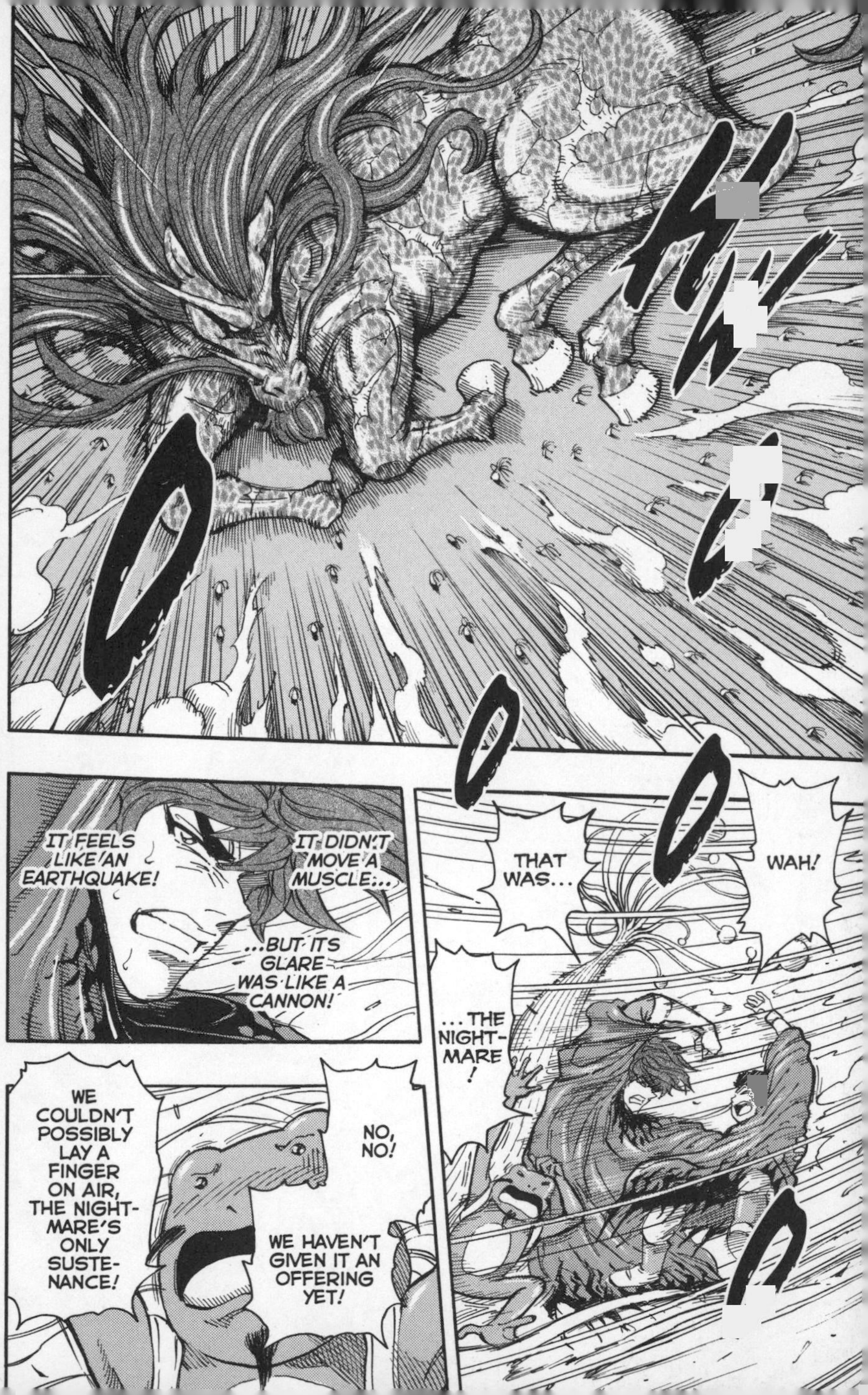
WAH!
THAT WAS...
...THE NIGHT-MARE!
IT DIDN'T MOVE A MUSCLE...
...BUT ITS GLARE WAS LIKE A CANNON!
IT FEELS LIKE AN EARTHQUAKE!
NO, NO!
WE HAVEN'T GIVEN IT AN OFFERING YET!
WE COULDN'T POSSIBLY LAY A FINGER ON AIR, THE NIGHT-MARE'S ONLY SUSTE-NANCE!

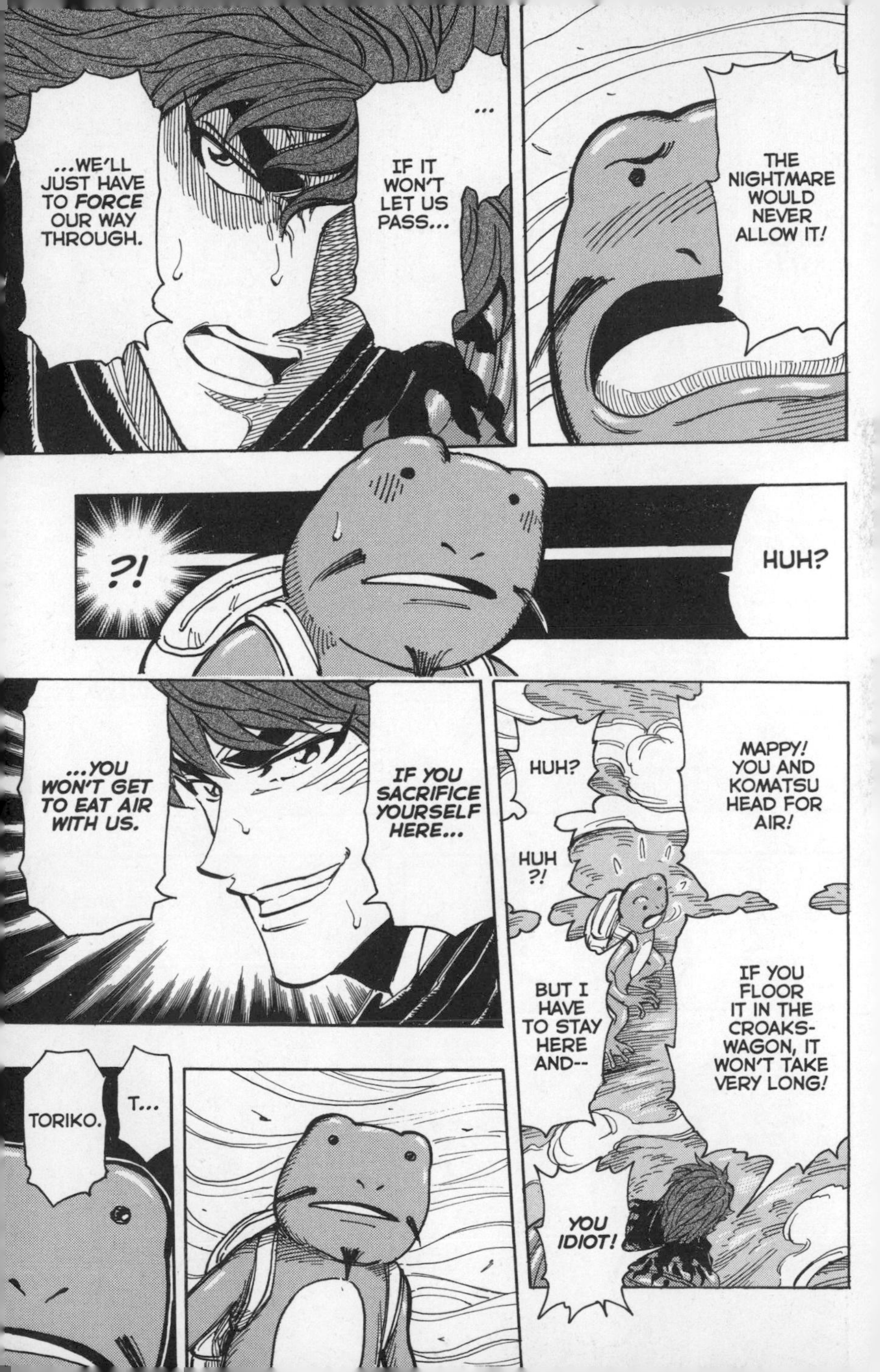
THE NIGHTMARE WOULD NEVER ALLOW IT!
...
IF IT WON'T LET US PASS...
...WE'LL JUST HAVE TO *FORCE* OUR WAY THROUGH.
HUH?
?!
MAPPY! YOU AND KOMATSU HEAD FOR AIR!
HUH?
HUH ?!
IF YOU FLOOR IT IN THE CROAKS-WAGON, IT WON'T TAKE VERY LONG!
BUT I HAVE TO STAY HERE AND--
YOU IDIOT!
IF YOU SACRIFICE YOURSELF HERE...
...YOU WON'T GET TO EAT AIR WITH US.
T...
TORIKO.

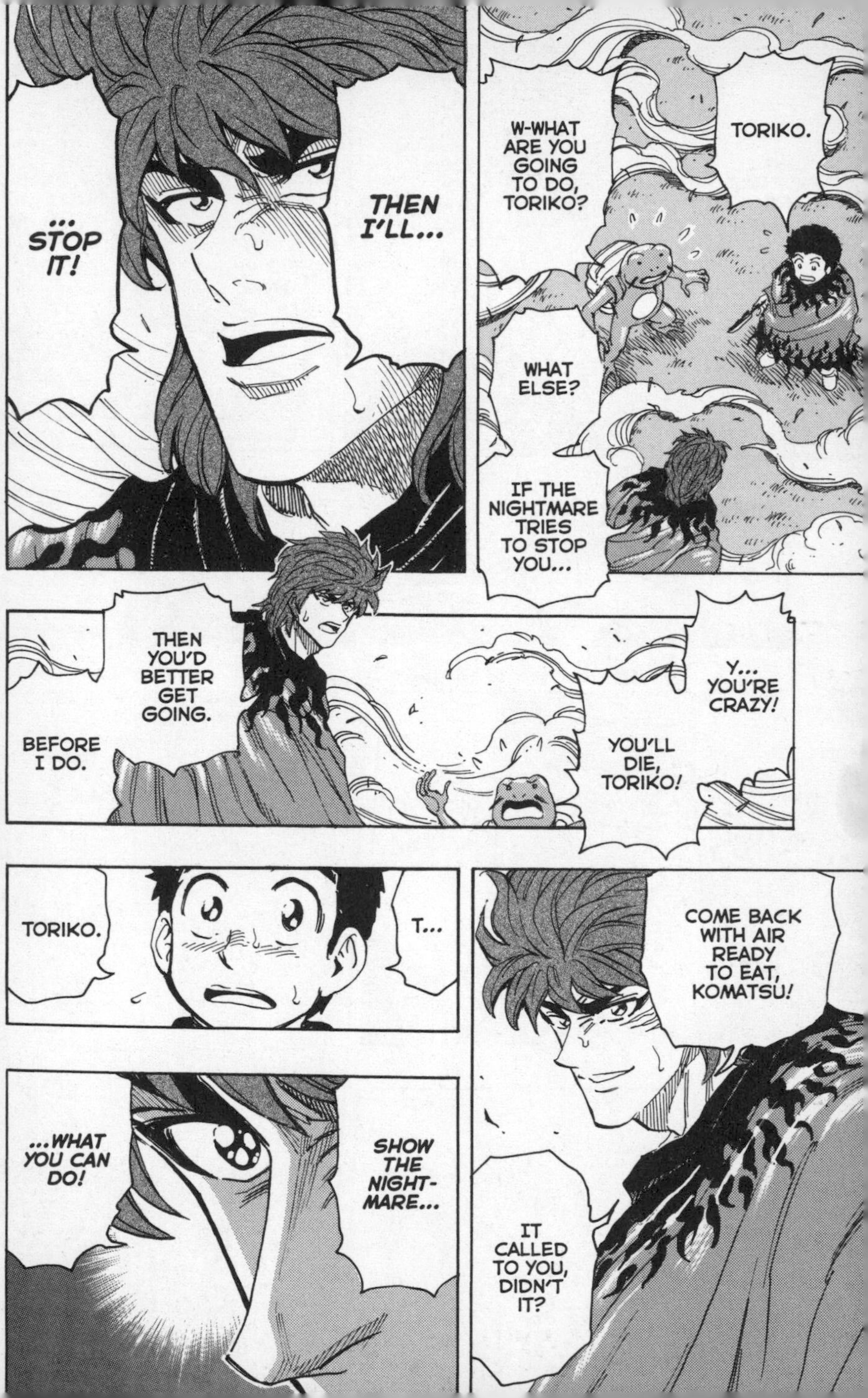
TORIKO.
W-WHAT ARE YOU GOING TO DO, TORIKO?
WHAT ELSE?
IF THE NIGHTMARE TRIES TO STOP YOU...
THEN I'LL...
...STOP IT!
Y... YOU'RE CRAZY!
YOU'LL DIE, TORIKO!
THEN YOU'D BETTER GET GOING.
BEFORE I DO.
COME BACK WITH AIR READY TO EAT, KOMATSU!
IT CALLED TO YOU, DIDN'T IT?
T...
TORIKO.
SHOW THE NIGHTMARE...
...WHAT YOU CAN DO!

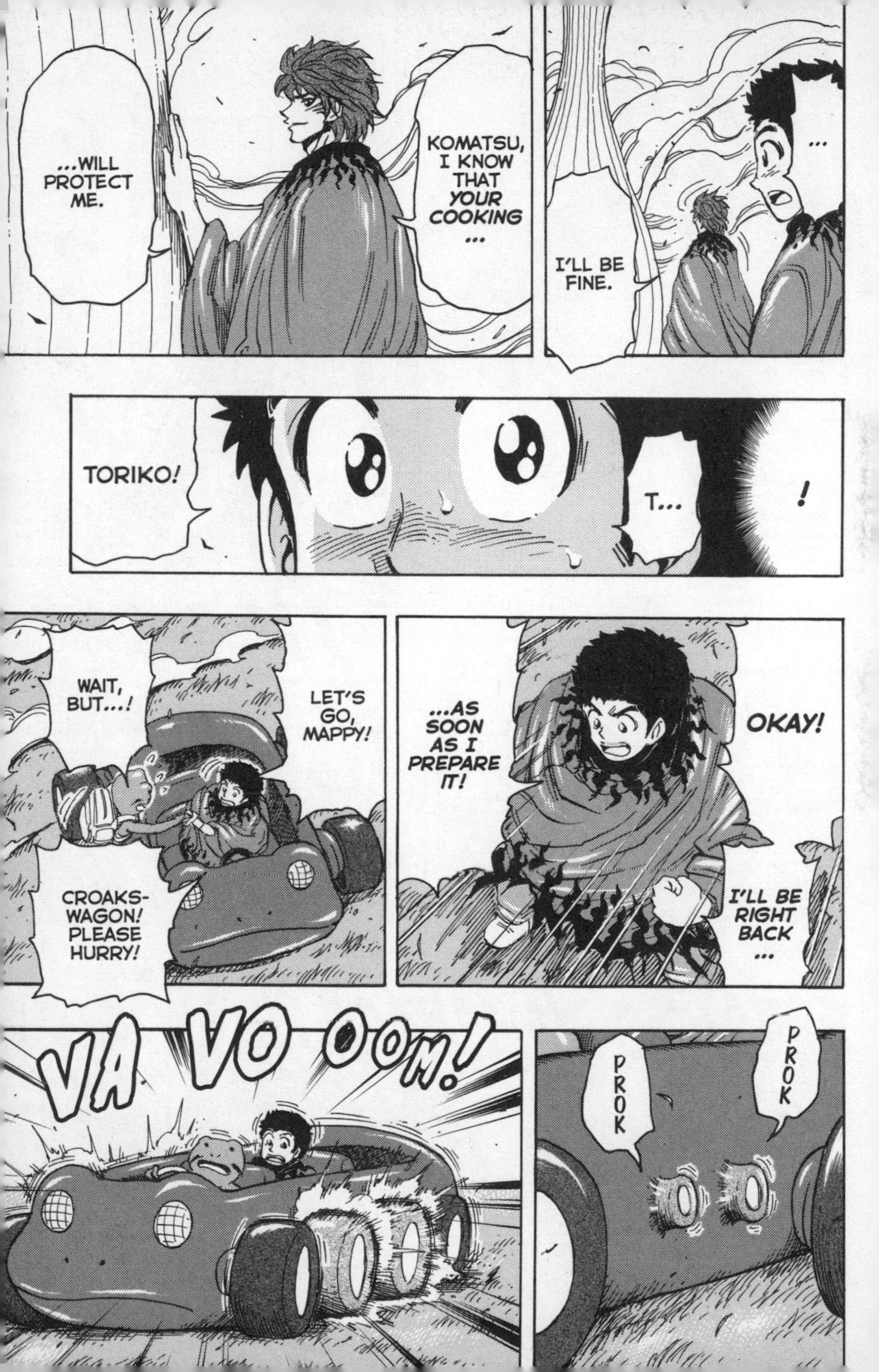
...
I'LL BE FINE.
KOMATSU, I KNOW THAT *YOUR COOKING* ...
...WILL PROTECT ME.
!
T...
TORIKO!
OKAY!
I'LL BE RIGHT BACK ...
...AS SOON AS I PREPARE IT!
LET'S GO, MAPPY!
WAIT, BUT...!
CROAKS-WAGON! PLEASE HURRY!
PROK
PROK
VA VO OOM!

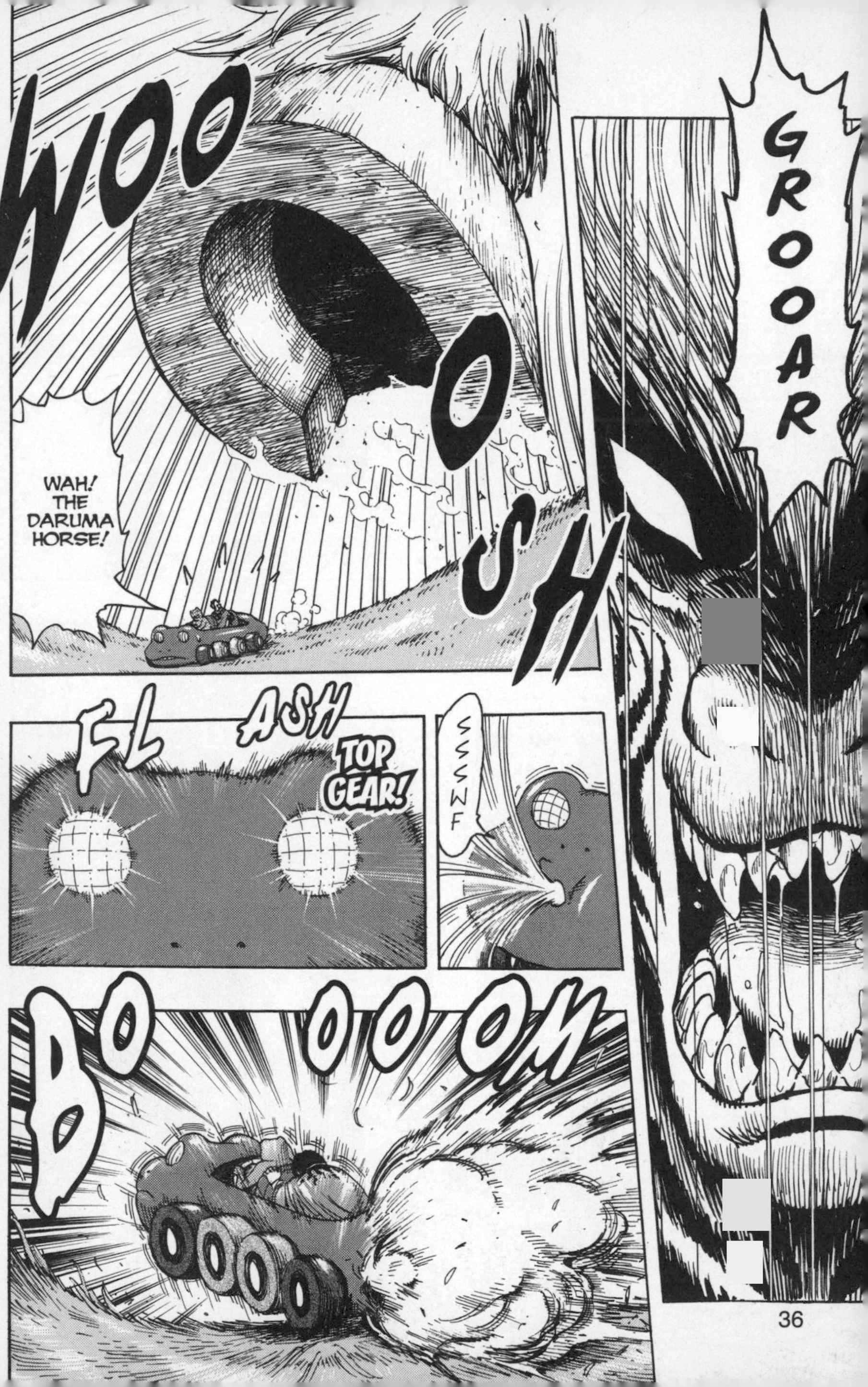
GROOOAR
WOOOSH
WAH! THE DARUMA HORSE!
SSSWF
FLASH
TOP GEAR!
BOOOOM

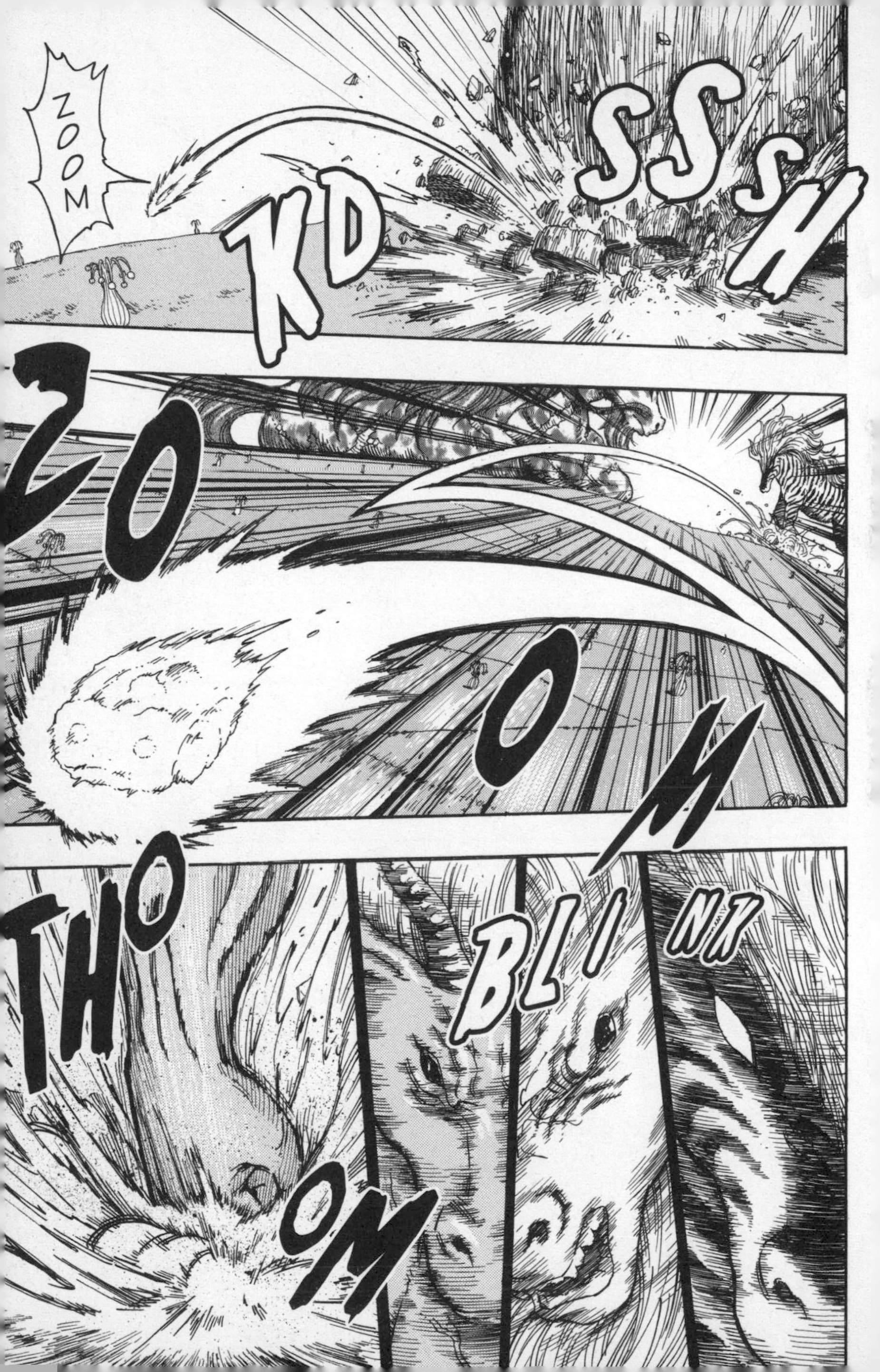
KDSSSH
ZOOM
ZOOOM
THOOM
BLINK

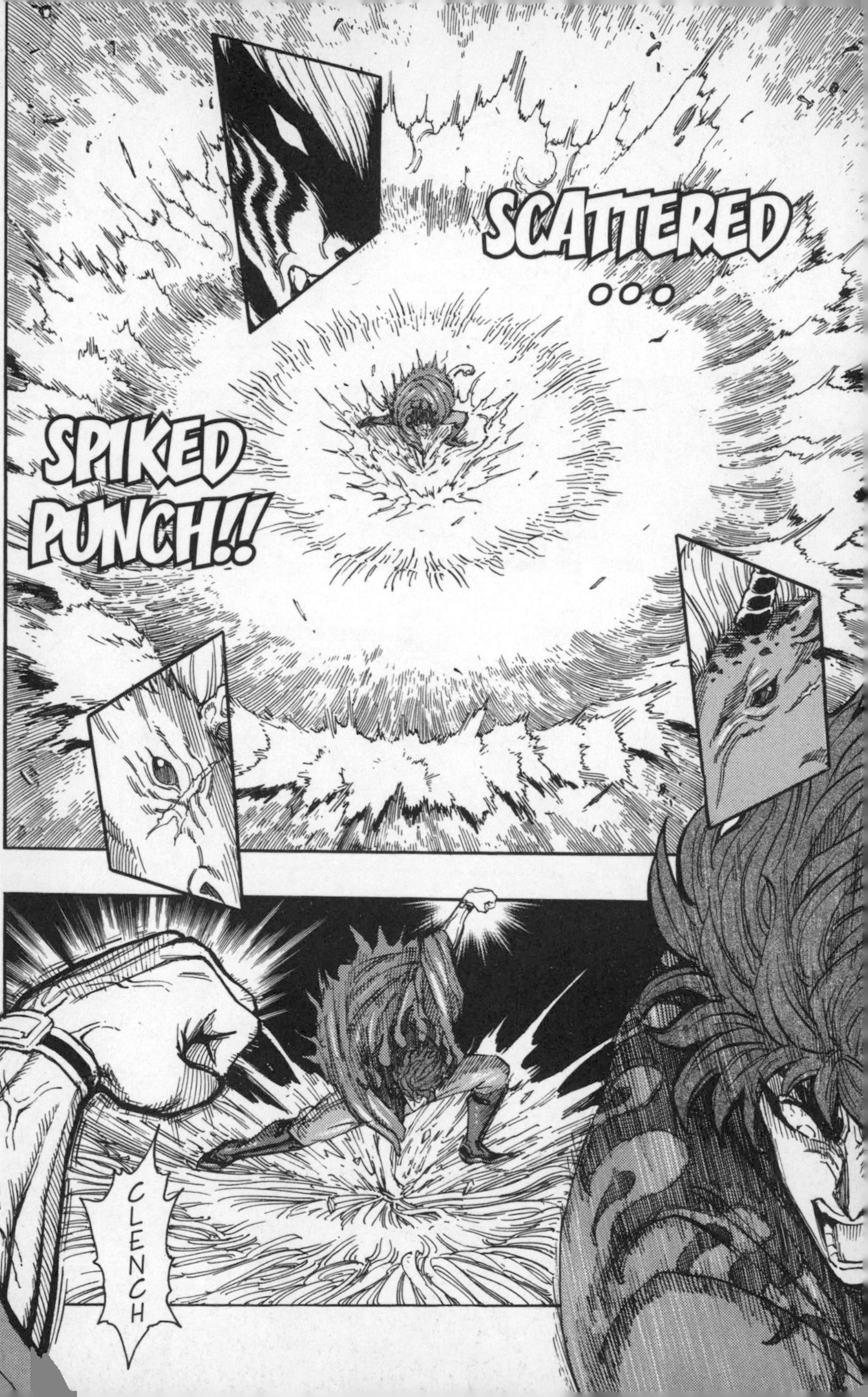
SCATTERED ...
SPIKED PUNCH!!
CLENCH

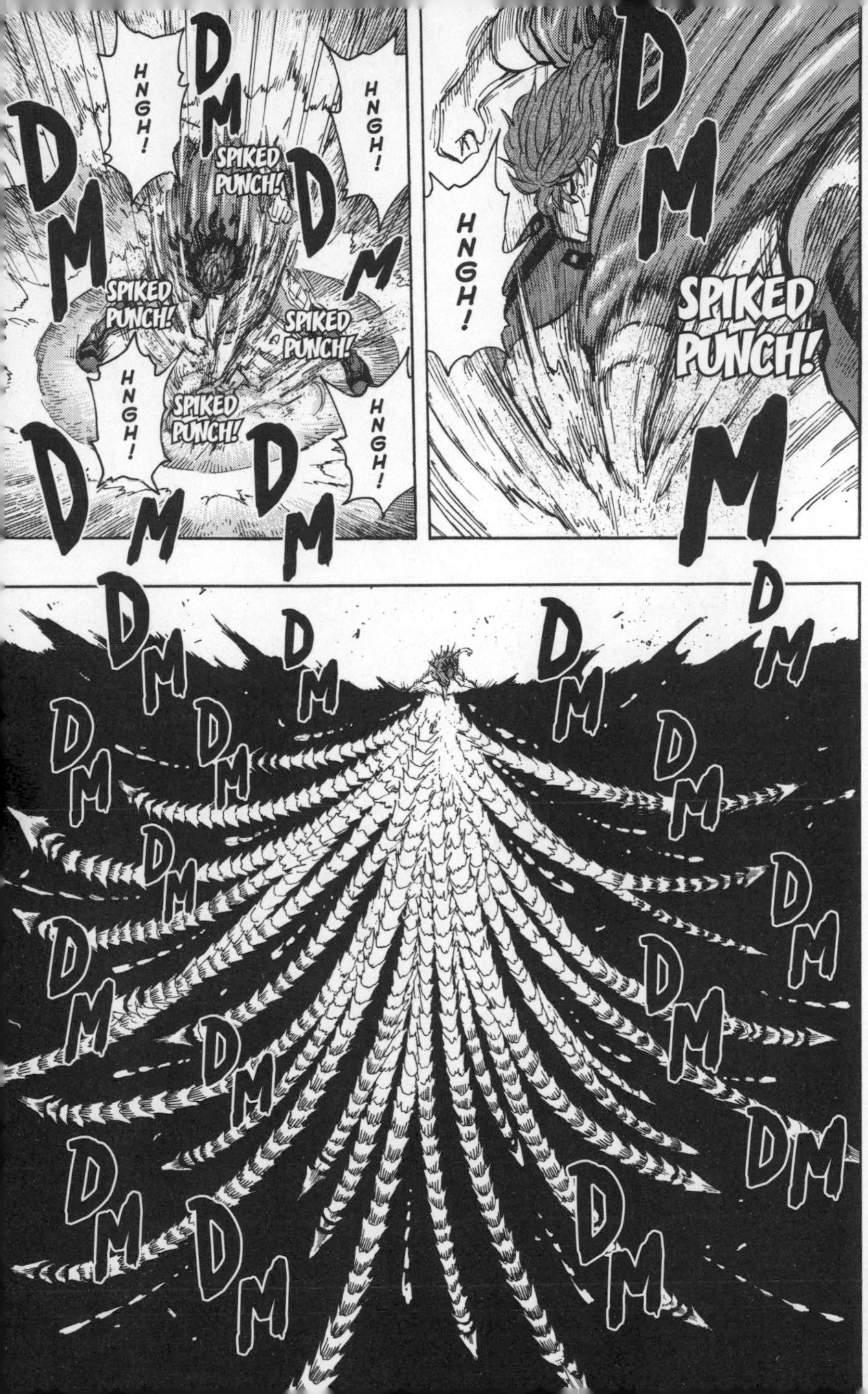
HNGH!
DM
SPIKED PUNCH!
HNGH!
DM
SPIKED PUNCH!
HNGH!
DM
SPIKED PUNCH!
DM
SPIKED PUNCH!
HNGH!
SPIKED PUNCH!
HNGH!
DM
DM
DM
DM
DM
DM
DM
DM
DM
DM
DM
DM
DM
DM
DM
DM
DM
DM
DM
DM

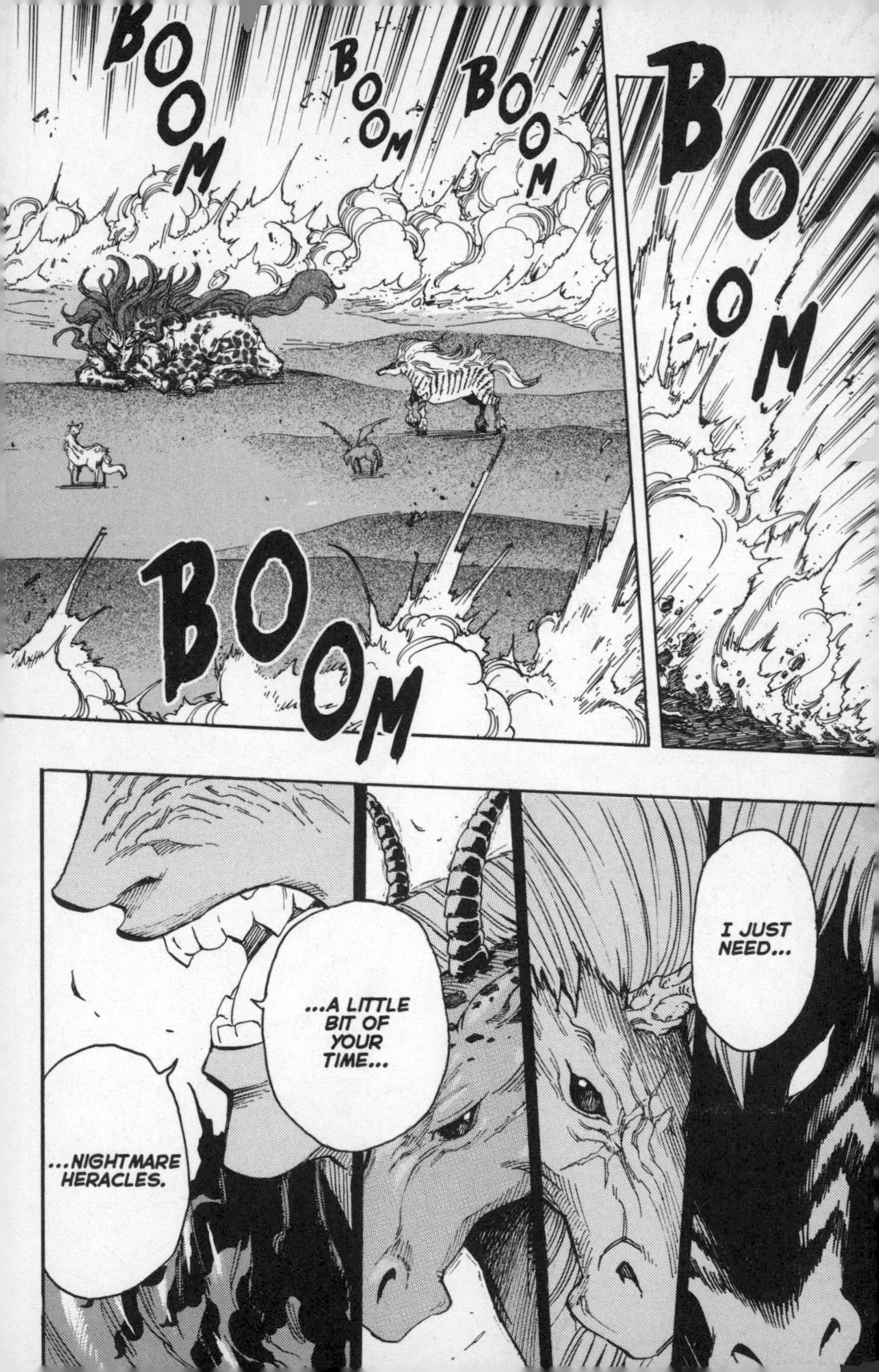
BOOM
BOOM
BOOM
BOOM
BOOM
I JUST NEED...
...A LITTLE BIT OF YOUR TIME...
...NIGHTMARE HERACLES.

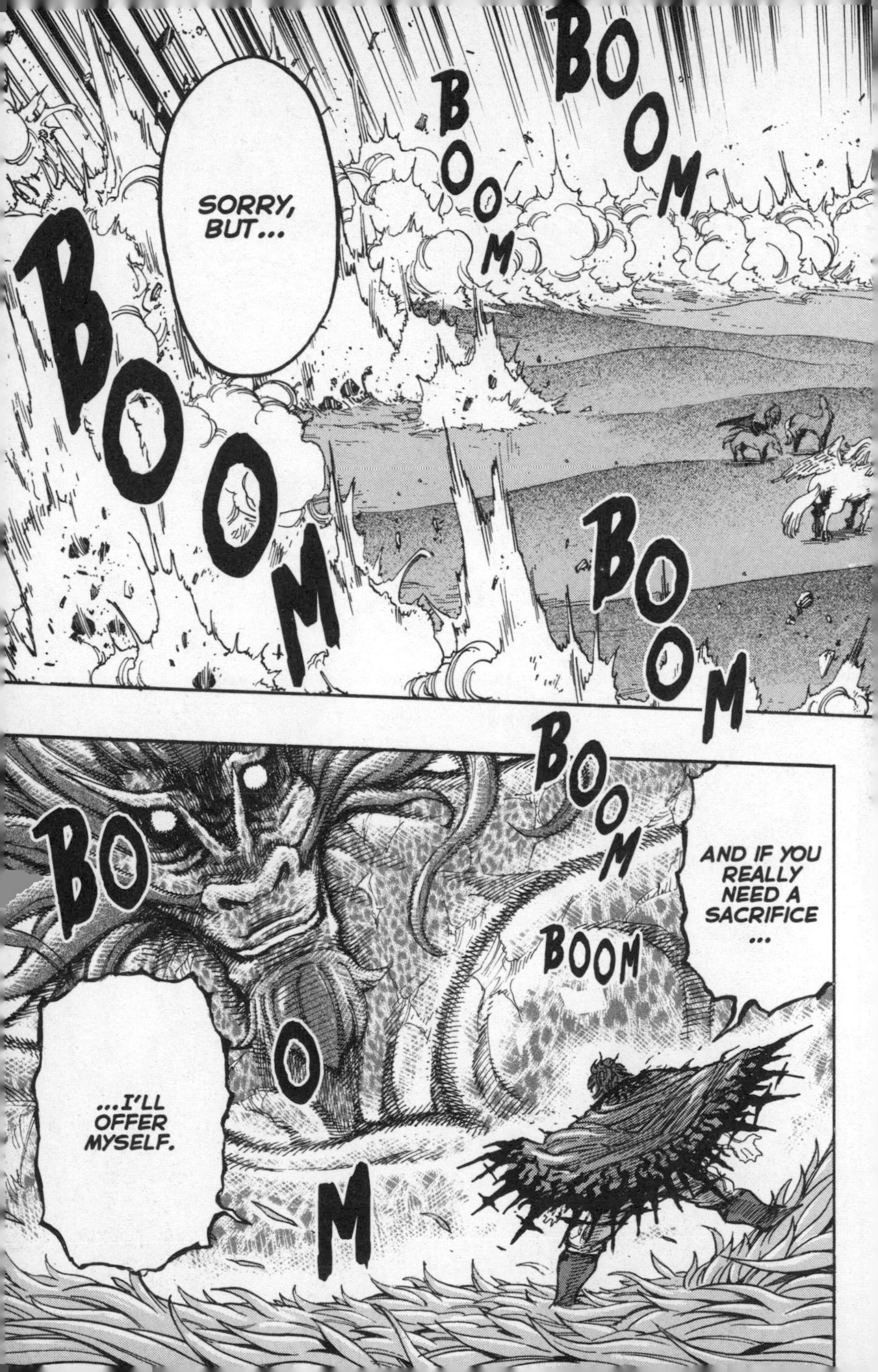
BOOM
BOOM
SORRY, BUT...
BOOM
BOOM
BOOM
AND IF YOU REALLY NEED A SACRIFICE...
BOOM
BOOOM
...I'LL OFFER MYSELF.

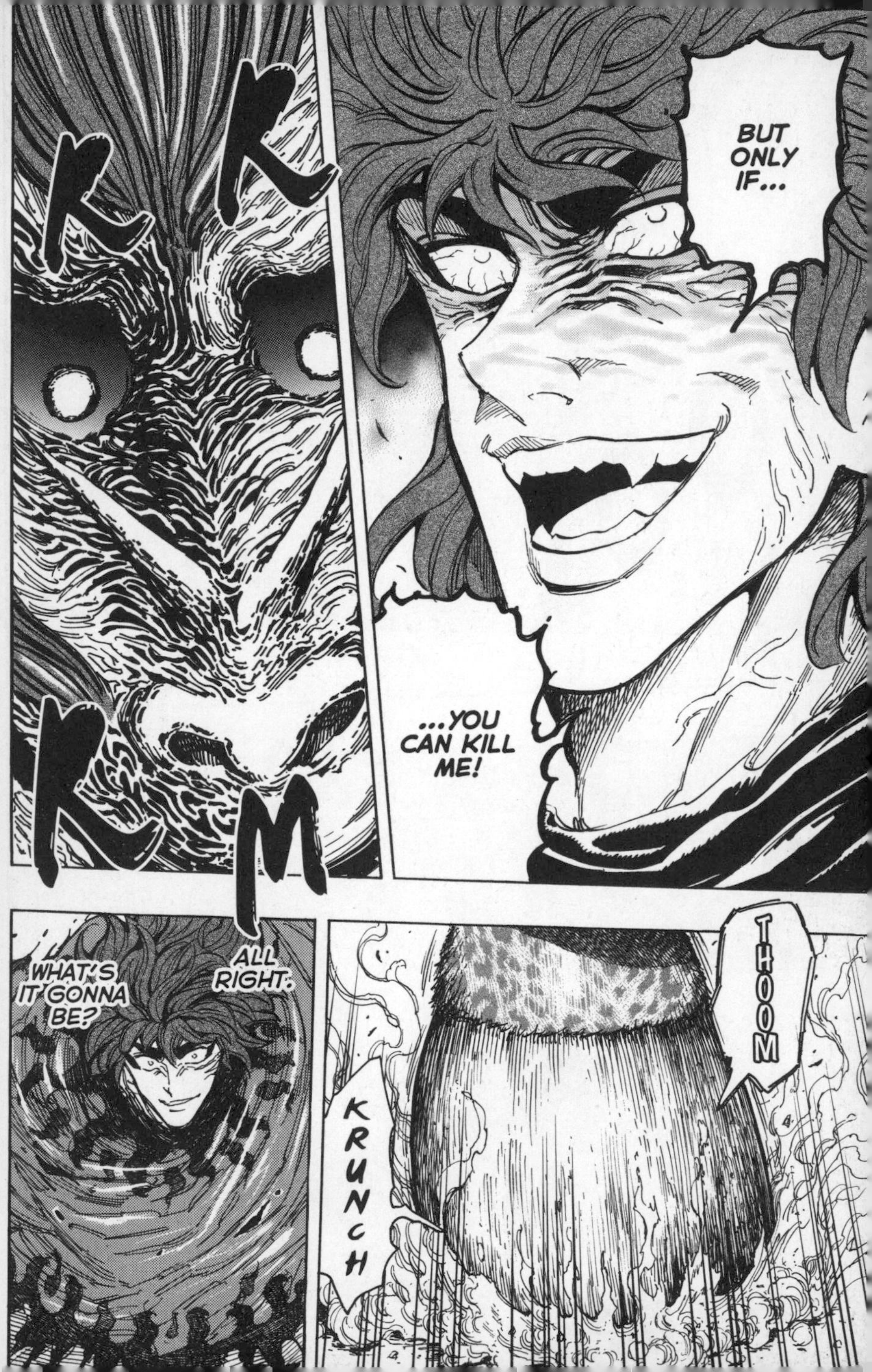
BUT ONLY IF...
...YOU CAN KILL ME!
KK
KM
THOOOM
KRUNCH
ALL RIGHT.
WHAT'S IT GONNA BE?

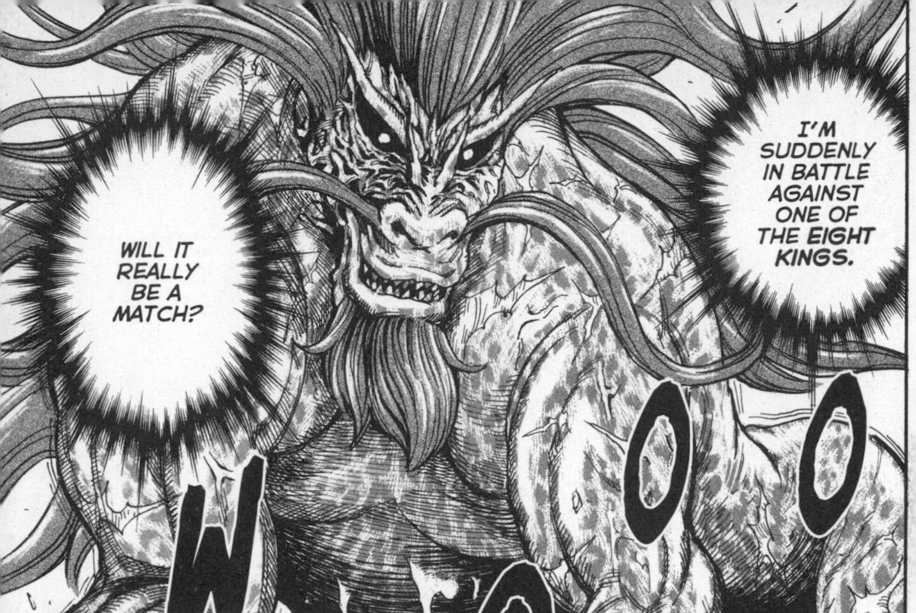
I'M SUDDENLY IN BATTLE AGAINST ONE OF THE EIGHT KINGS.
WILL IT REALLY BE A MATCH?
WOOO
TEN MINUTES... NO, MAKE THAT FIVE MINUTES!
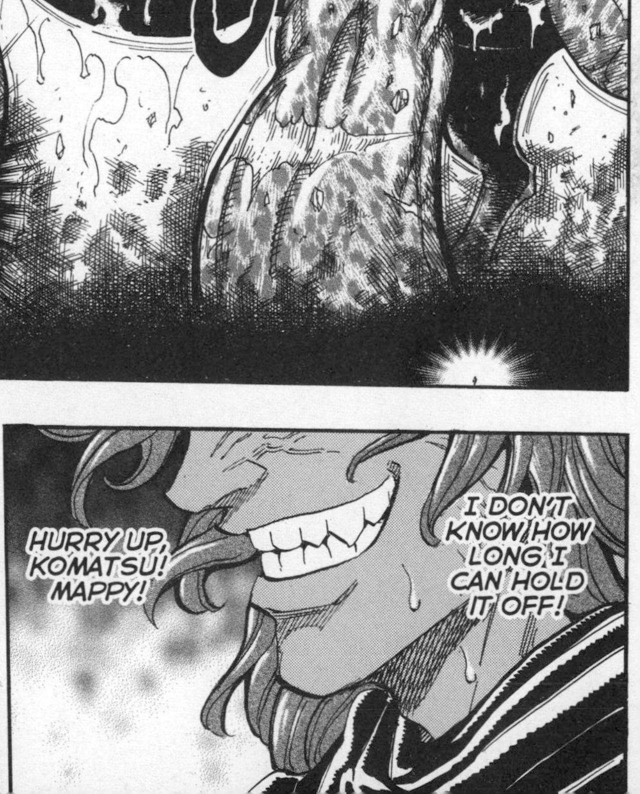
I DON'T KNOW HOW LONG I CAN HOLD IT OFF!
HURRY UP, KOMATSU! MAPPY!
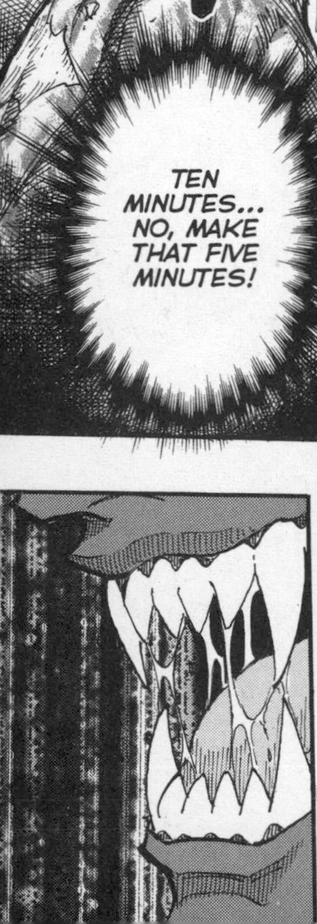

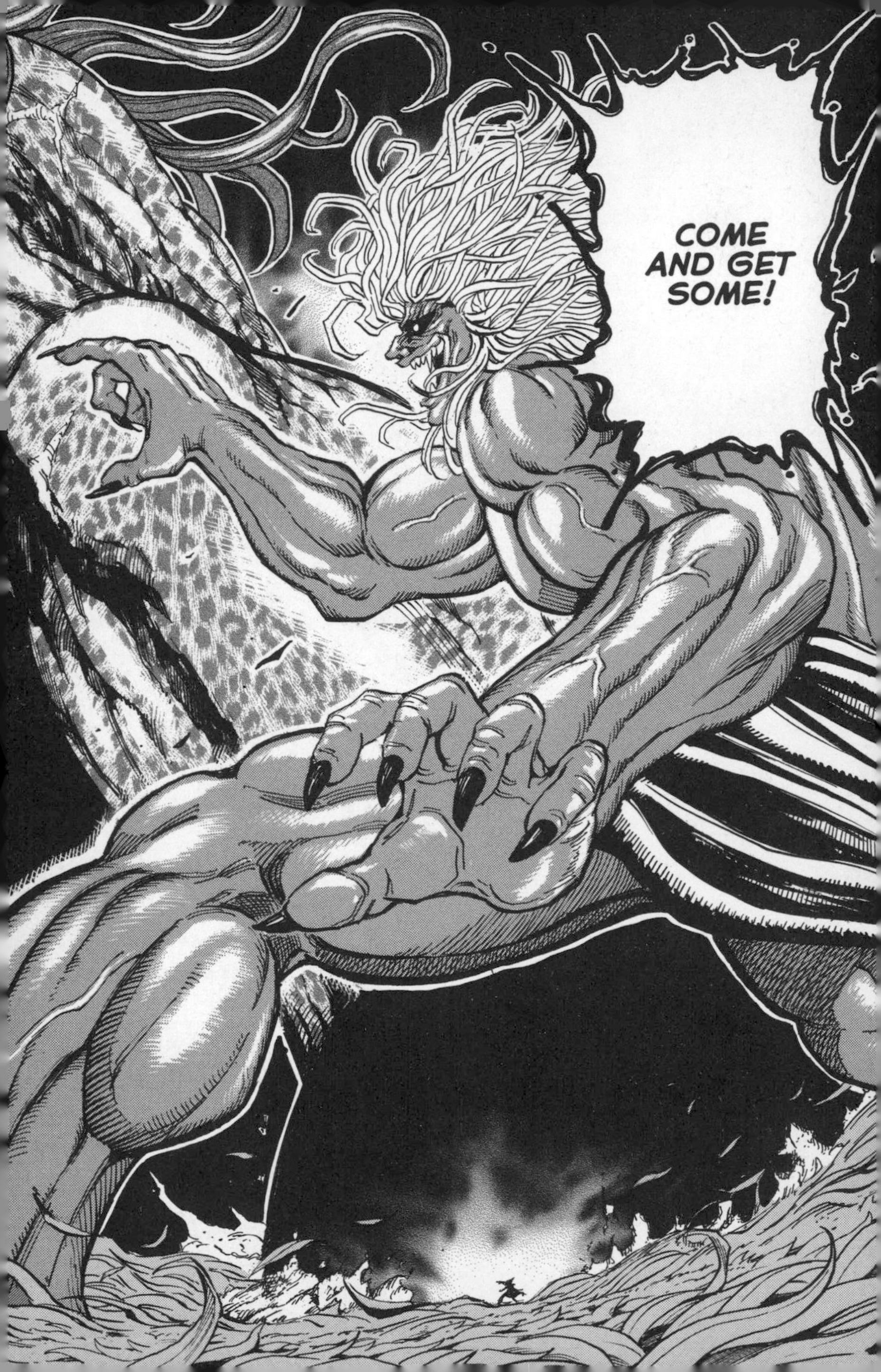
COME AND GET SOME!

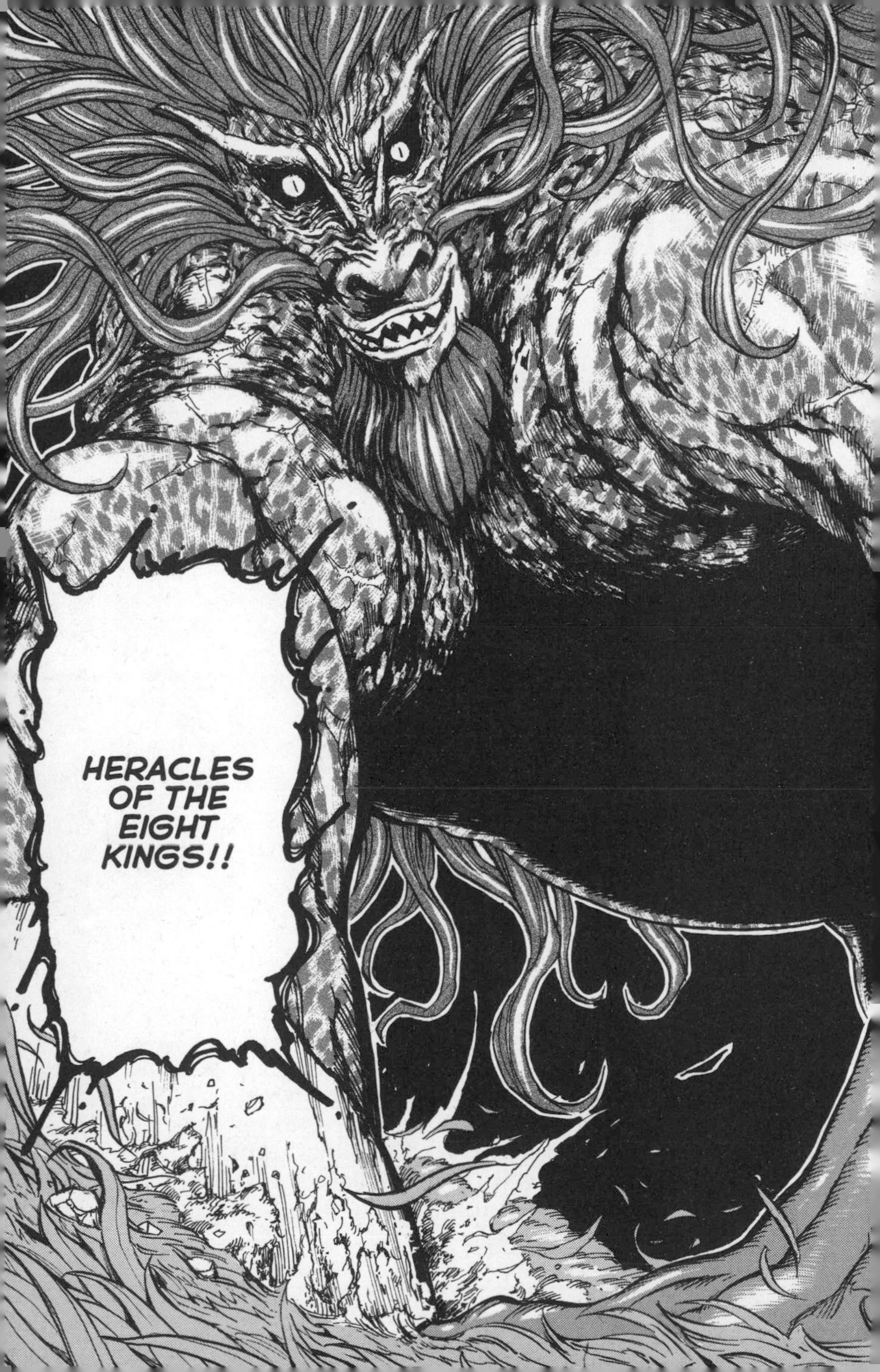
HERACLES OF THE EIGHT KINGS!!

GOURMET CHECKLIST

Vol. 310

⧼ FOUR-BEASTS: FANG KING ⧽
(MAMMAL KING)

CAPTURE LEVEL: 127
HABITAT: GOURMET WORLD
SIZE: 300 M
HEIGHT: 170 M
WEIGHT: 1 MILLION TONS
PRICE: UNKNOWN

SCALE

AN EXTREMITY OF THE MONSTROUS FOUR-BEASTS WHO EMERGES FROM THE GOURMET WORLD EVERY SEVERAL YEARS. IT CHOOSES THE TIME WHEN HUMANITY IS AT ITS PEAK AND THEN FEASTS ON THE WORLD. ITS TOUGH MUSCLE MAKES IT SUPER POWERFUL AND ITS GIANT FANGS ARE THE PERFECT WEAPONS FOR CAPTURING PREY. IT'S A BRUTAL CREATURE WITH A CAPTURE LEVEL OF OVER 100, WHICH COULD SPELL DESTRUCTION FOR THE HUMAN WORLD.

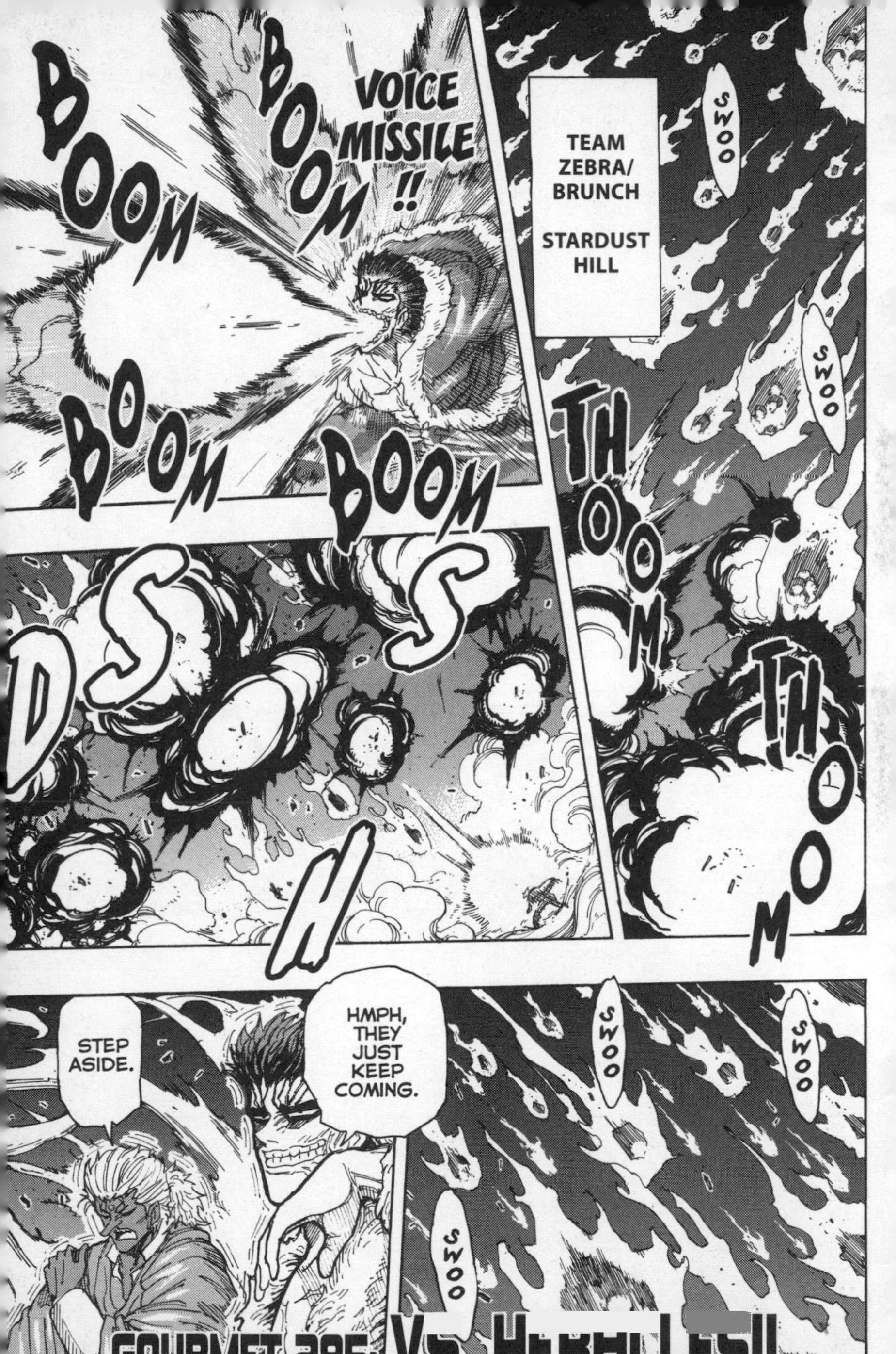
TEAM ZEBRA/ BRUNCH
STARDUST HILL
SWOO
SWOO
THOOM
THOOM
VOICE MISSILE!!
BOOM
BOOM
BOOM
BOOM
DSSH
SWOO
SWOO
SWOO
SWOO
HMPH, THEY JUST KEEP COMING.
STEP ASIDE.

GOURMET 285: VS. HERACLES!!

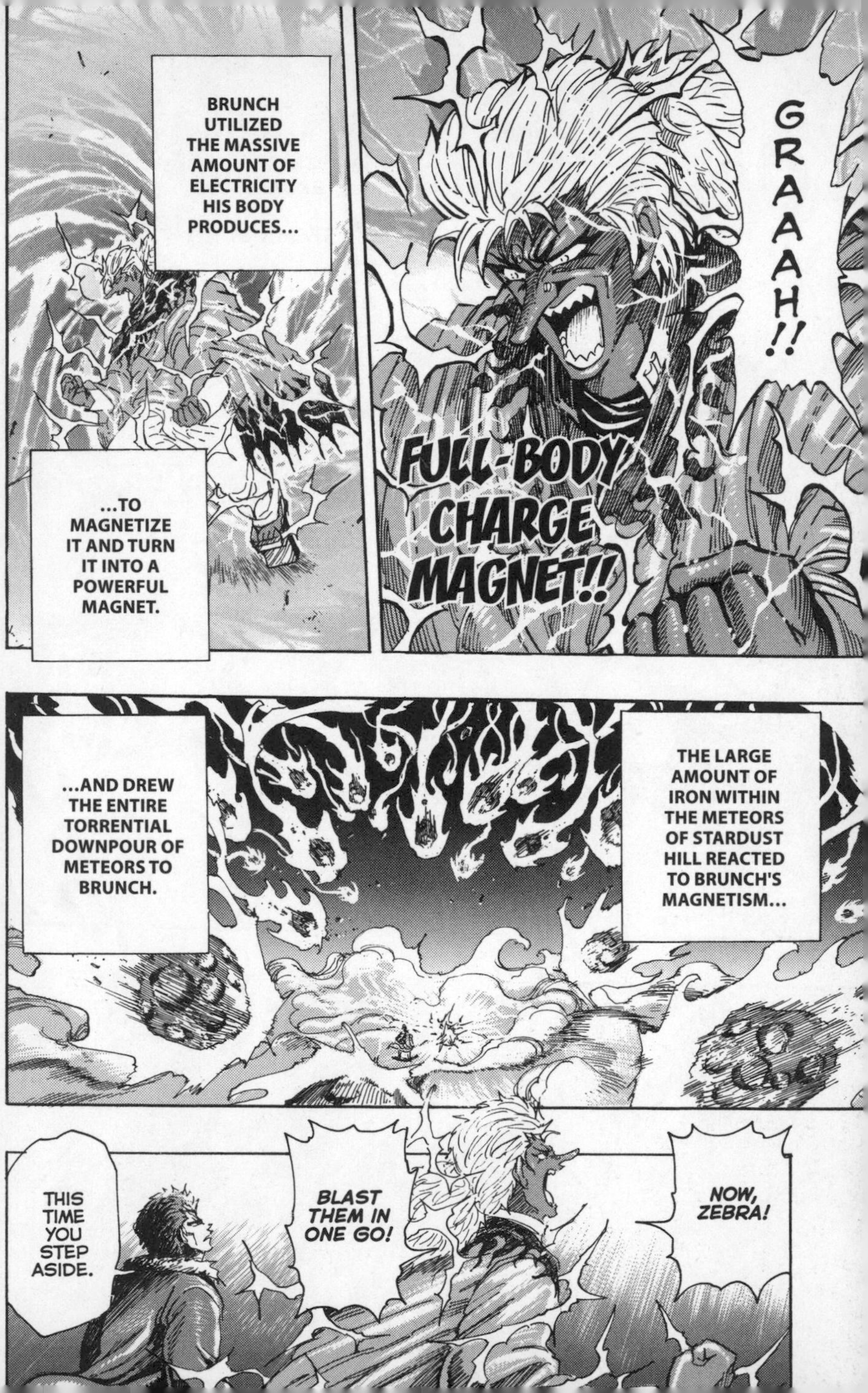
GRAAAH!!
FULL-BODY CHARGE MAGNET!!
BRUNCH UTILIZED THE MASSIVE AMOUNT OF ELECTRICITY HIS BODY PRODUCES...
...TO MAGNETIZE IT AND TURN IT INTO A POWERFUL MAGNET.
THE LARGE AMOUNT OF IRON WITHIN THE METEORS OF STARDUST HILL REACTED TO BRUNCH'S MAGNETISM...
...AND DREW THE ENTIRE TORRENTIAL DOWNPOUR OF METEORS TO BRUNCH.
NOW, ZEBRA!
BLAST THEM IN ONE GO!
THIS TIME YOU STEP ASIDE.

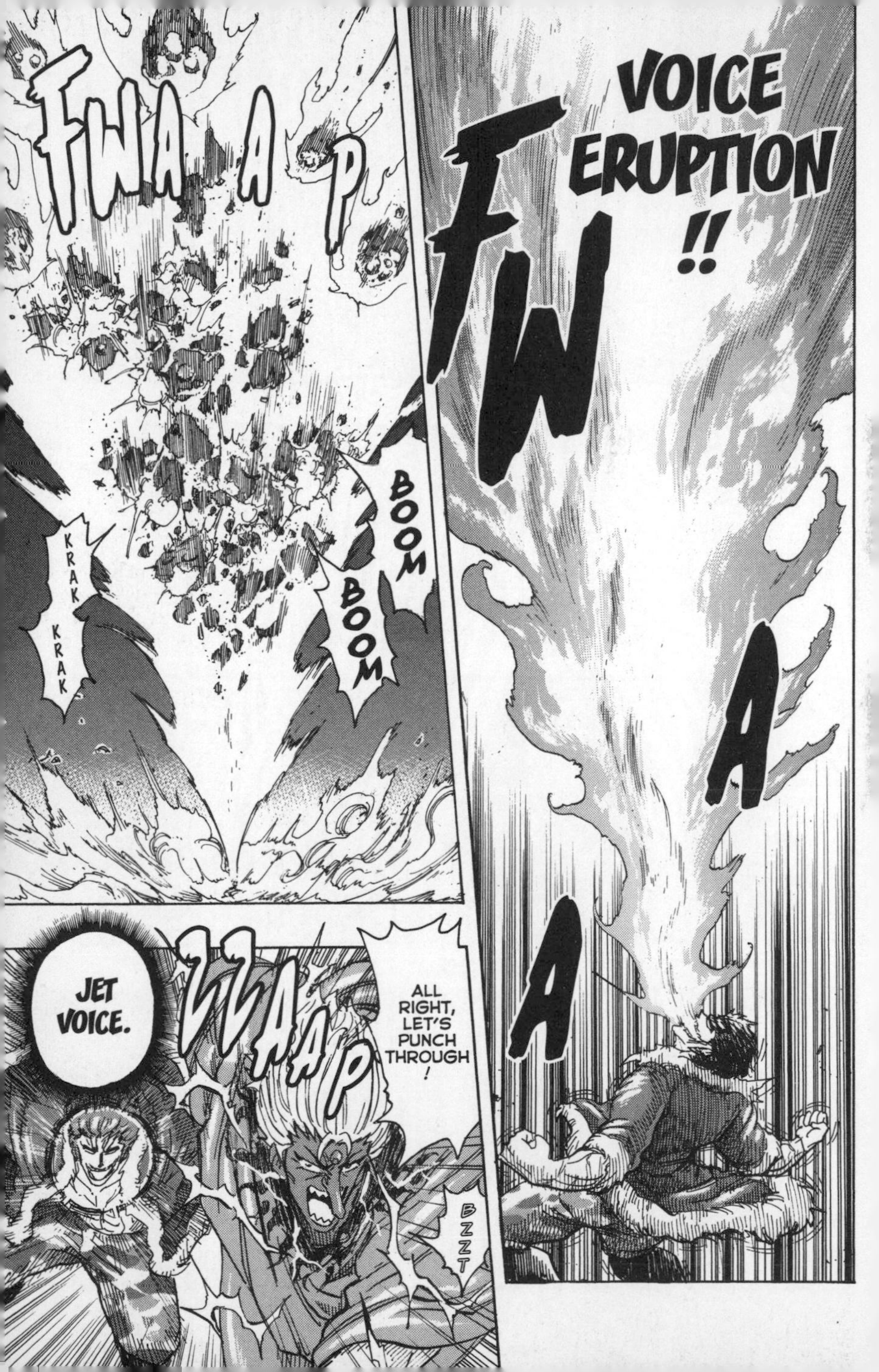
VOICE ERUPTION!!
FWAAA
FWAAAP
BOOM
BOOM
KRAK KRAK
ALL RIGHT, LET'S PUNCH THROUGH!
ZZAAP
JET VOICE.
BZZT

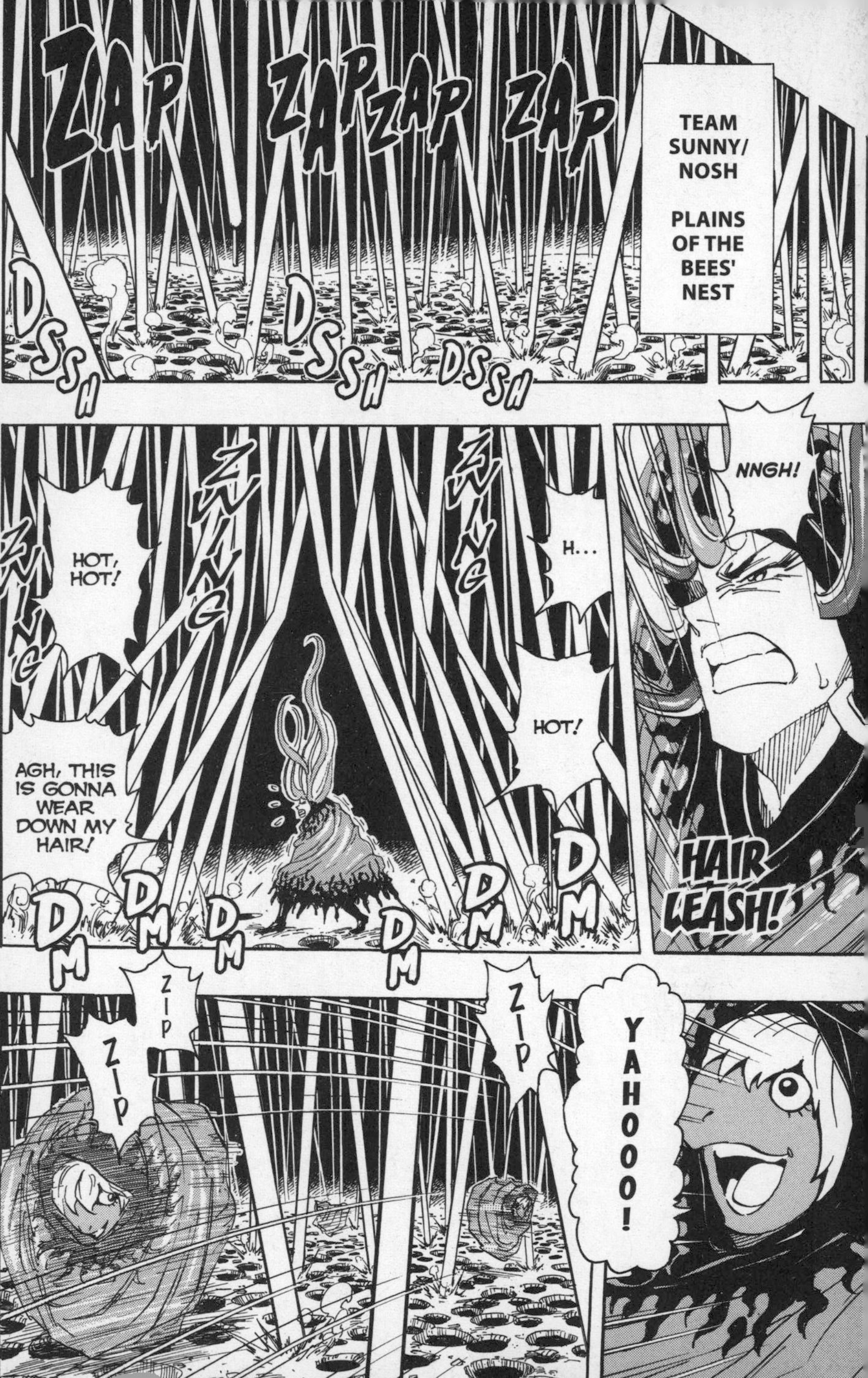
TEAM SUNNY/ NOSH
PLAINS OF THE BEES' NEST
ZAP ZAP ZAP ZAP
DSSH DSSH DSSH
NNGH!
HAIR LEASH!
H...
HOT!
ZWING ZWING ZWING
HOT, HOT!
AGH, THIS IS GONNA WEAR DOWN MY HAIR!
DM DM DM DM DM DM
YAHOOOO!
ZIP
ZIP ZIP

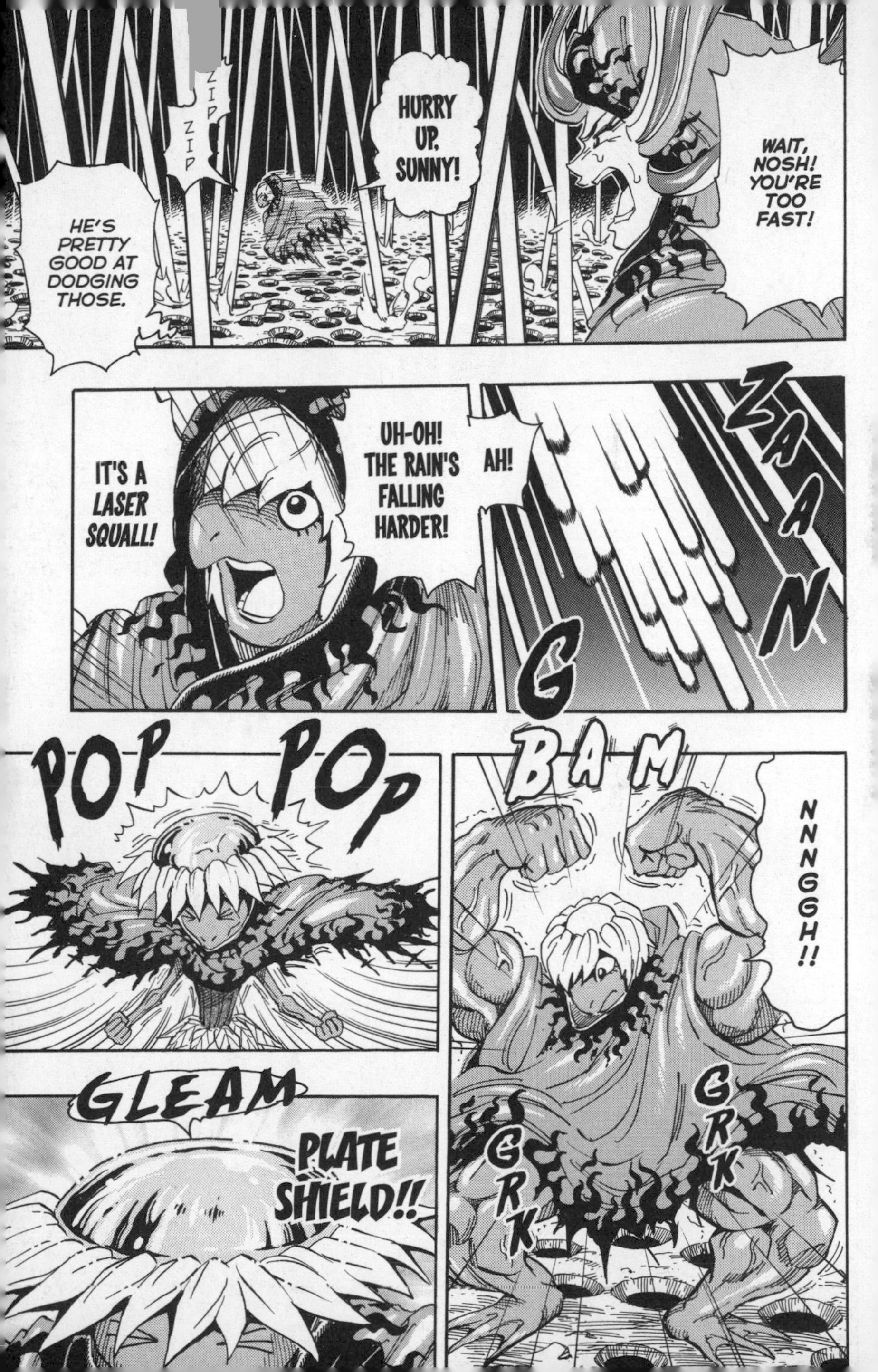
WAIT, NOSH! YOU'RE TOO FAST!
HURRY UP, SUNNY!
ZIP ZIP
HE'S PRETTY GOOD AT DODGING THOSE.
ZAAAN
AH!
UH-OH! THE RAIN'S FALLING HARDER!
IT'S A LASER SQUALL!
G BAM
NNNGGH!!
GRK GRK
POP POP
GLEAM
PLATE SHIELD!!

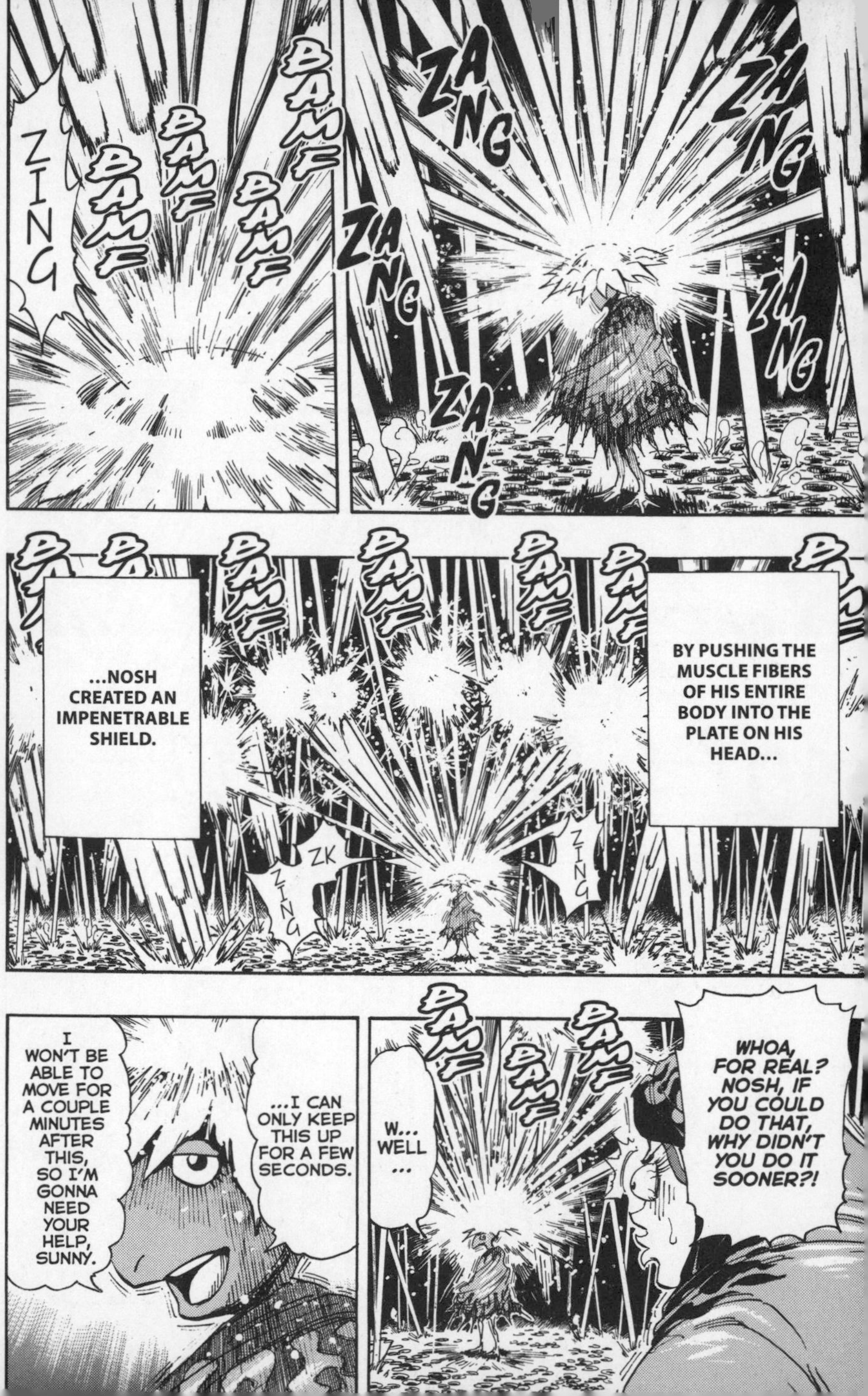
ZANG
ZANG
ZANG
ZANG
ZANG
BAMF
BAMF
BAMF
BAMF
ZING
BAMF
BY PUSHING THE MUSCLE FIBERS OF HIS ENTIRE BODY INTO THE PLATE ON HIS HEAD...
...NOSH CREATED AN IMPENETRABLE SHIELD.
ZING
ZK
ZING
WHOA, FOR REAL? NOSH, IF YOU COULD DO THAT, WHY DIDN'T YOU DO IT SOONER?!
BAMF
BAMF
BAMF
W... WELL...
...I CAN ONLY KEEP THIS UP FOR A FEW SECONDS.
I WON'T BE ABLE TO MOVE FOR A COUPLE MINUTES AFTER THIS, SO I'M GONNA NEED YOUR HELP, SUNNY.

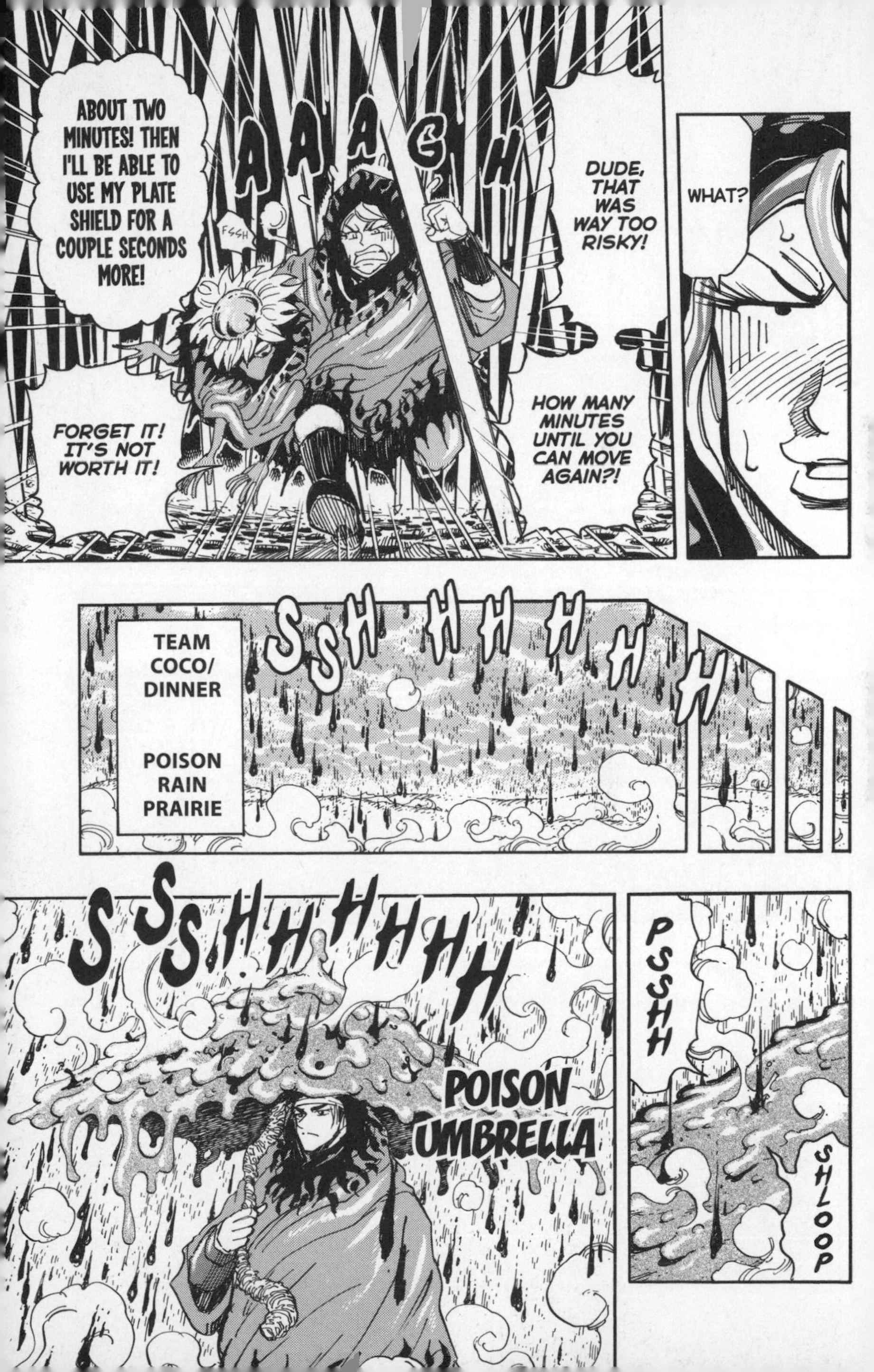
WHAT?
DUDE, THAT WAS WAY TOO RISKY!
AAAGH
HOW MANY MINUTES UNTIL YOU CAN MOVE AGAIN?!
ABOUT TWO MINUTES! THEN I'LL BE ABLE TO USE MY PLATE SHIELD FOR A COUPLE SECONDS MORE!
FSSH
FORGET IT! IT'S NOT WORTH IT!
SSHHHHHHH
TEAM COCO/ DINNER
POISON RAIN PRAIRIE
PSSHH
SHLOOP
SSSHHHHHH
POISON UMBRELLA

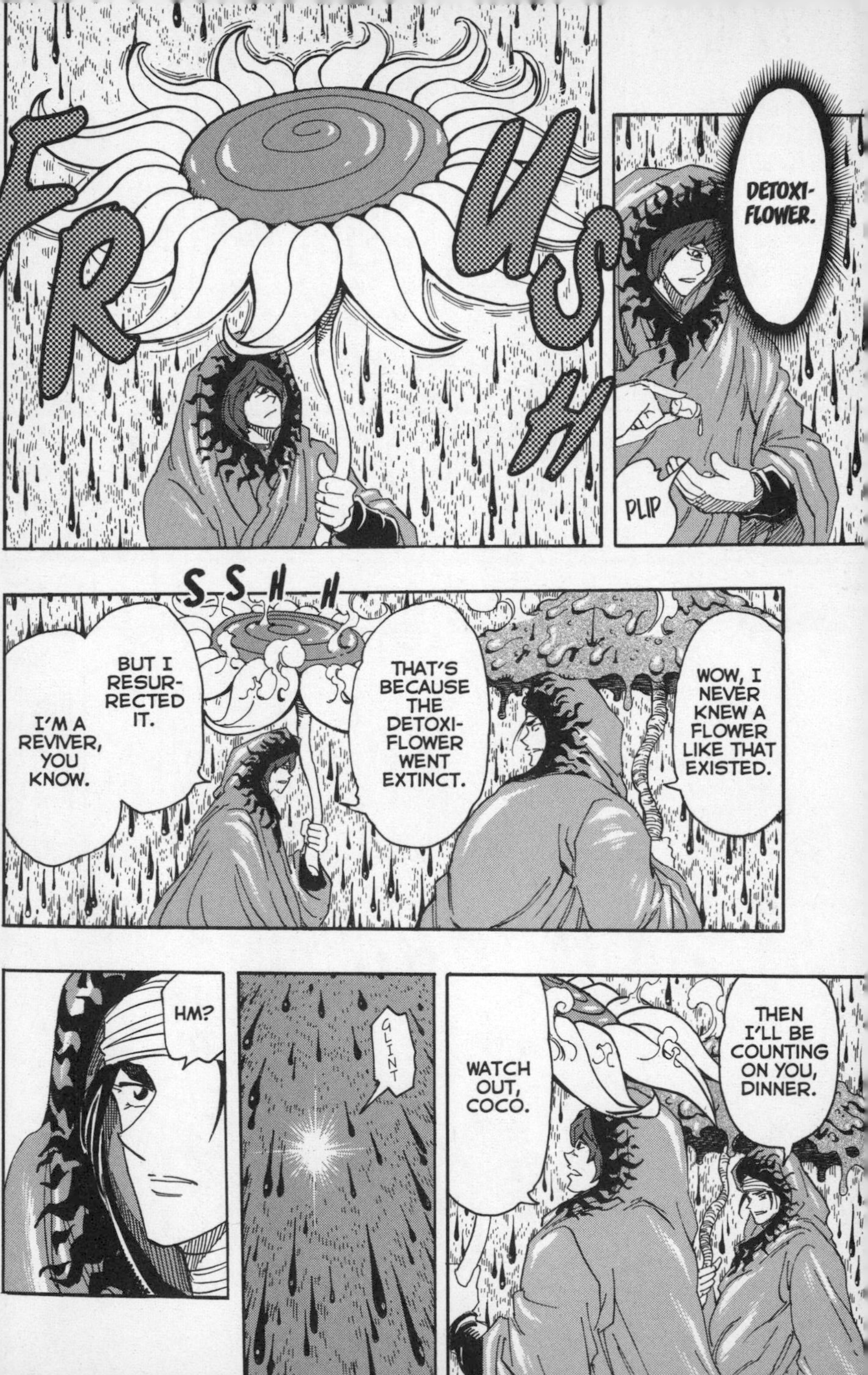
DETOXI-FLOWER.
PLIP
FRUSH
SSHH
WOW, I NEVER KNEW A FLOWER LIKE THAT EXISTED.
THAT'S BECAUSE THE DETOXI-FLOWER WENT EXTINCT.
BUT I RESURRECTED IT.
I'M A REVIVER, YOU KNOW.
THEN I'LL BE COUNTING ON YOU, DINNER.
WATCH OUT, COCO.
GLINT
HM?

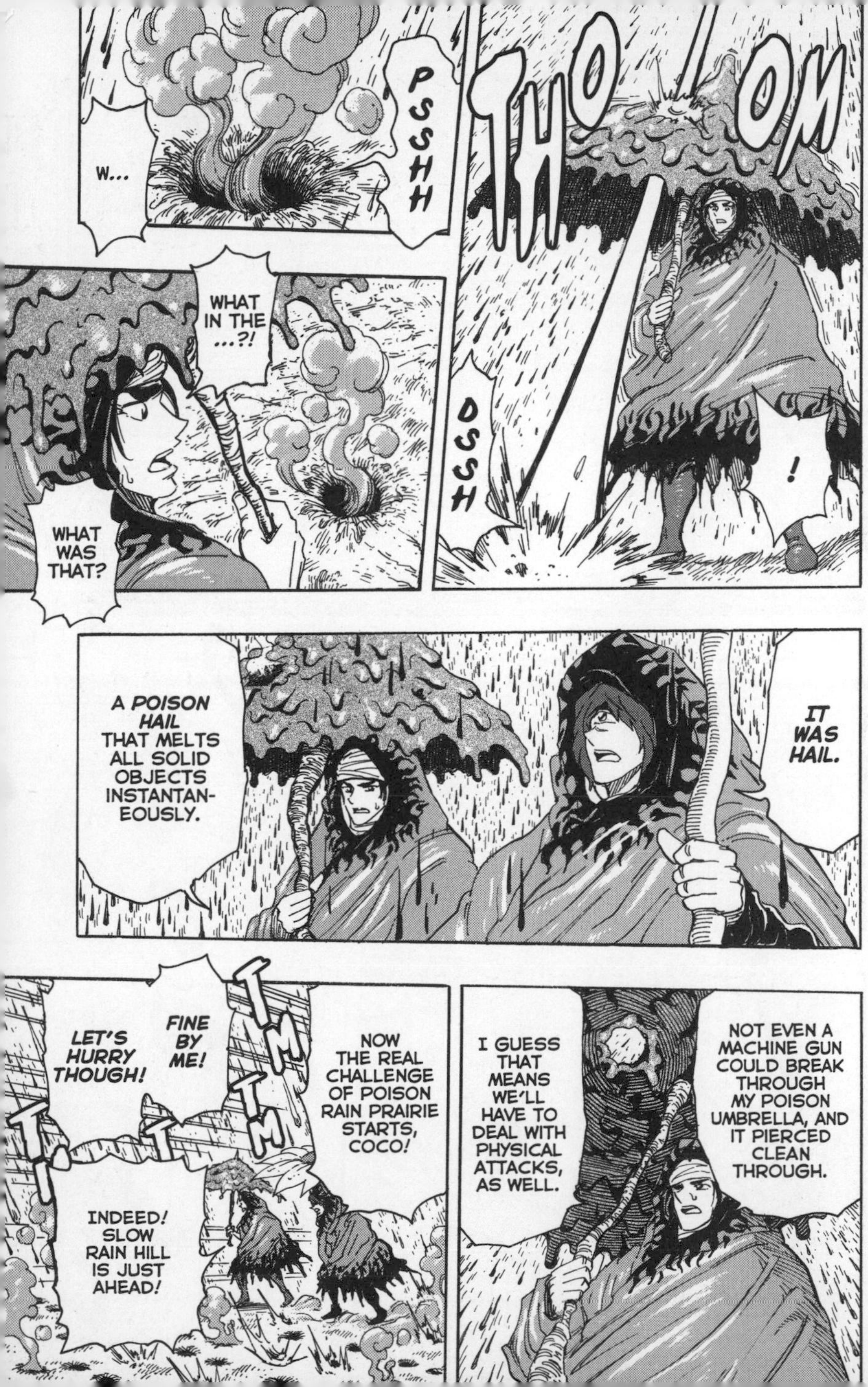
THOOM
DSSH
!
PSSHH
W...
WHAT IN THE ...?!
WHAT WAS THAT?
IT WAS HAIL.
A POISON HAIL THAT MELTS ALL SOLID OBJECTS INSTANTANEOUSLY.
NOT EVEN A MACHINE GUN COULD BREAK THROUGH MY POISON UMBRELLA, AND IT PIERCED CLEAN THROUGH.
I GUESS THAT MEANS WE'LL HAVE TO DEAL WITH PHYSICAL ATTACKS, AS WELL.
NOW THE REAL CHALLENGE OF POISON RAIN PRAIRIE STARTS, COCO!
TMTM
FINE BY ME!
LET'S HURRY THOUGH!
INDEED! SLOW RAIN HILL IS JUST AHEAD!
T T

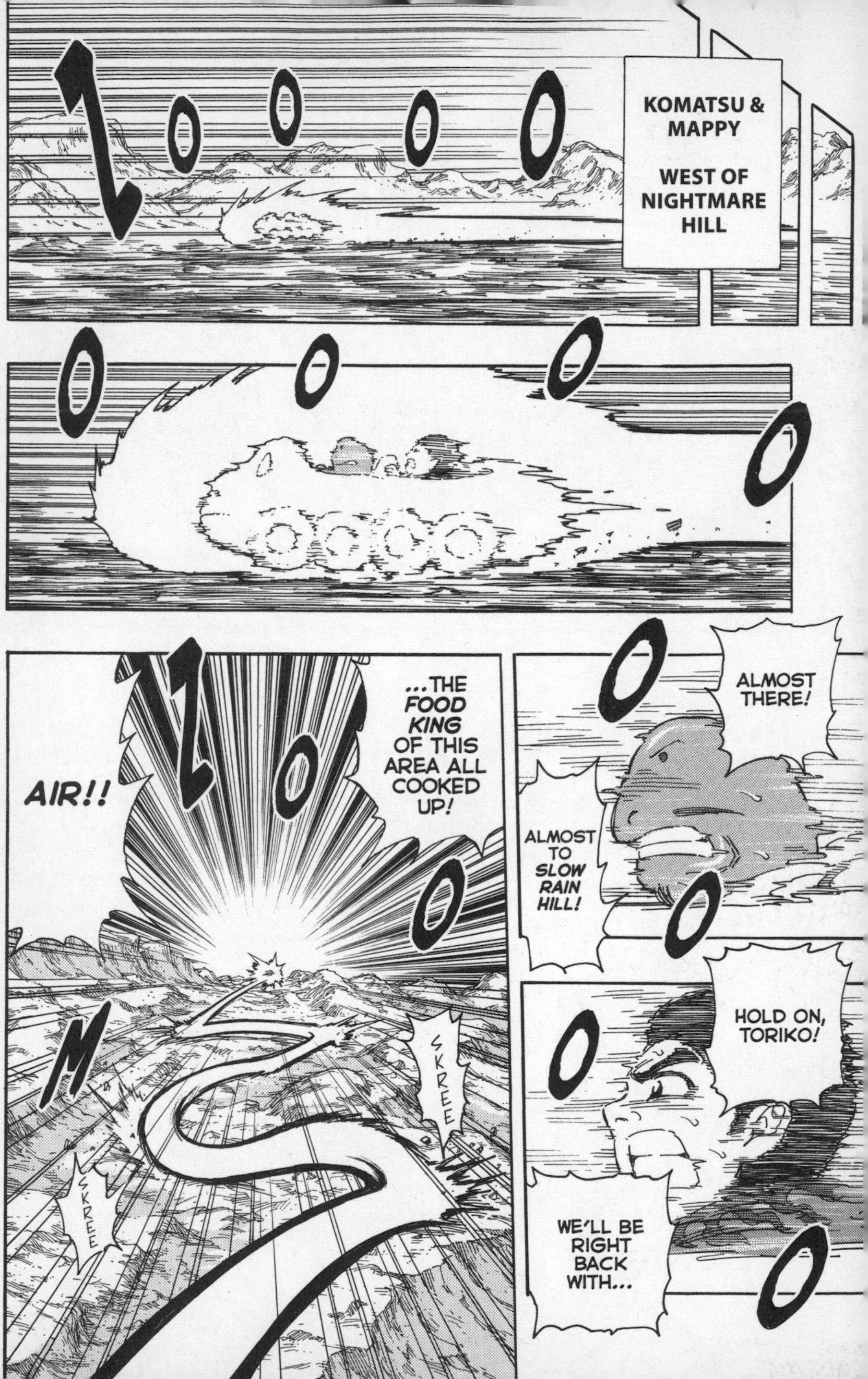
KOMATSU & MAPPY
WEST OF NIGHTMARE HILL
ALMOST THERE!
ALMOST TO SLOW RAIN HILL!
HOLD ON, TORIKO!
WE'LL BE RIGHT BACK WITH...
...THE FOOD KING OF THIS AREA ALL COOKED UP!
AIR!!
SKREE
SKREE

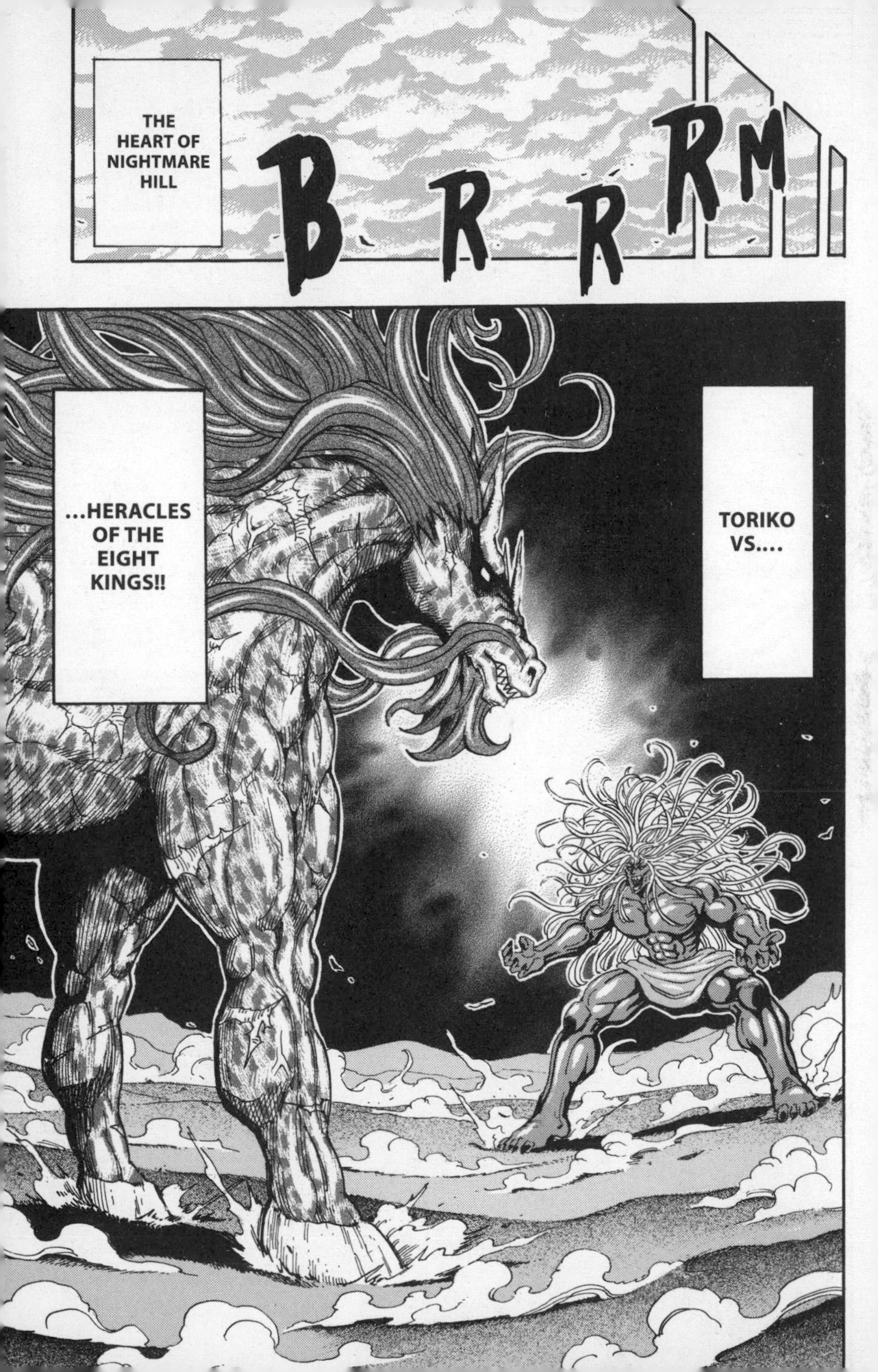
THE HEART OF NIGHTMARE HILL
BRRRM
TORIKO VS....
...HERACLES OF THE EIGHT KINGS!!

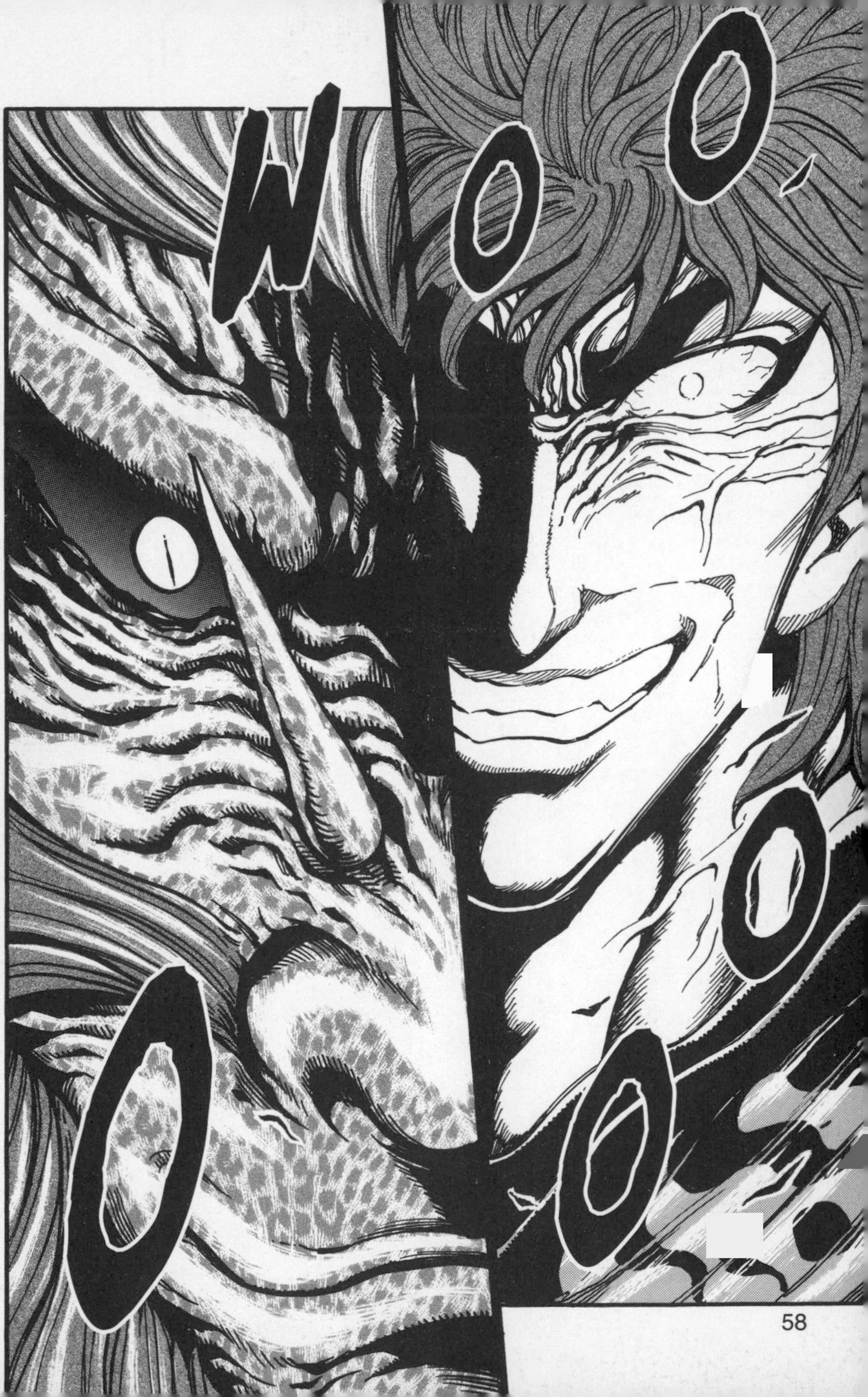
WOOO.
OOOOO

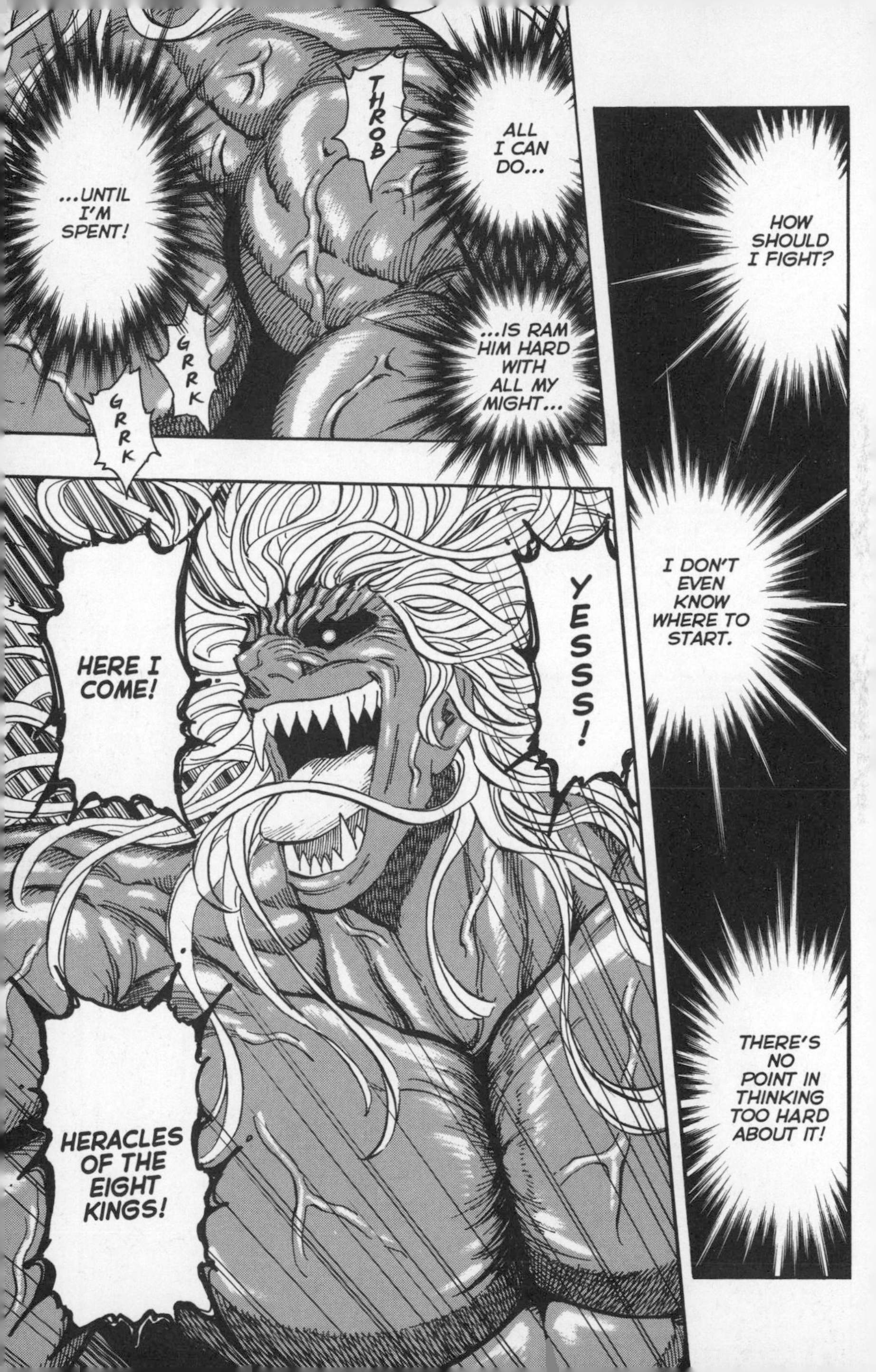
HOW SHOULD I FIGHT?
I DON'T EVEN KNOW WHERE TO START.
THERE'S NO POINT IN THINKING TOO HARD ABOUT IT!
ALL I CAN DO...
THROB
...IS RAM HIM HARD WITH ALL MY MIGHT...
...UNTIL I'M SPENT!
GRRK
GRRK
YESSS!
HERE I COME!
HERACLES OF THE EIGHT KINGS!

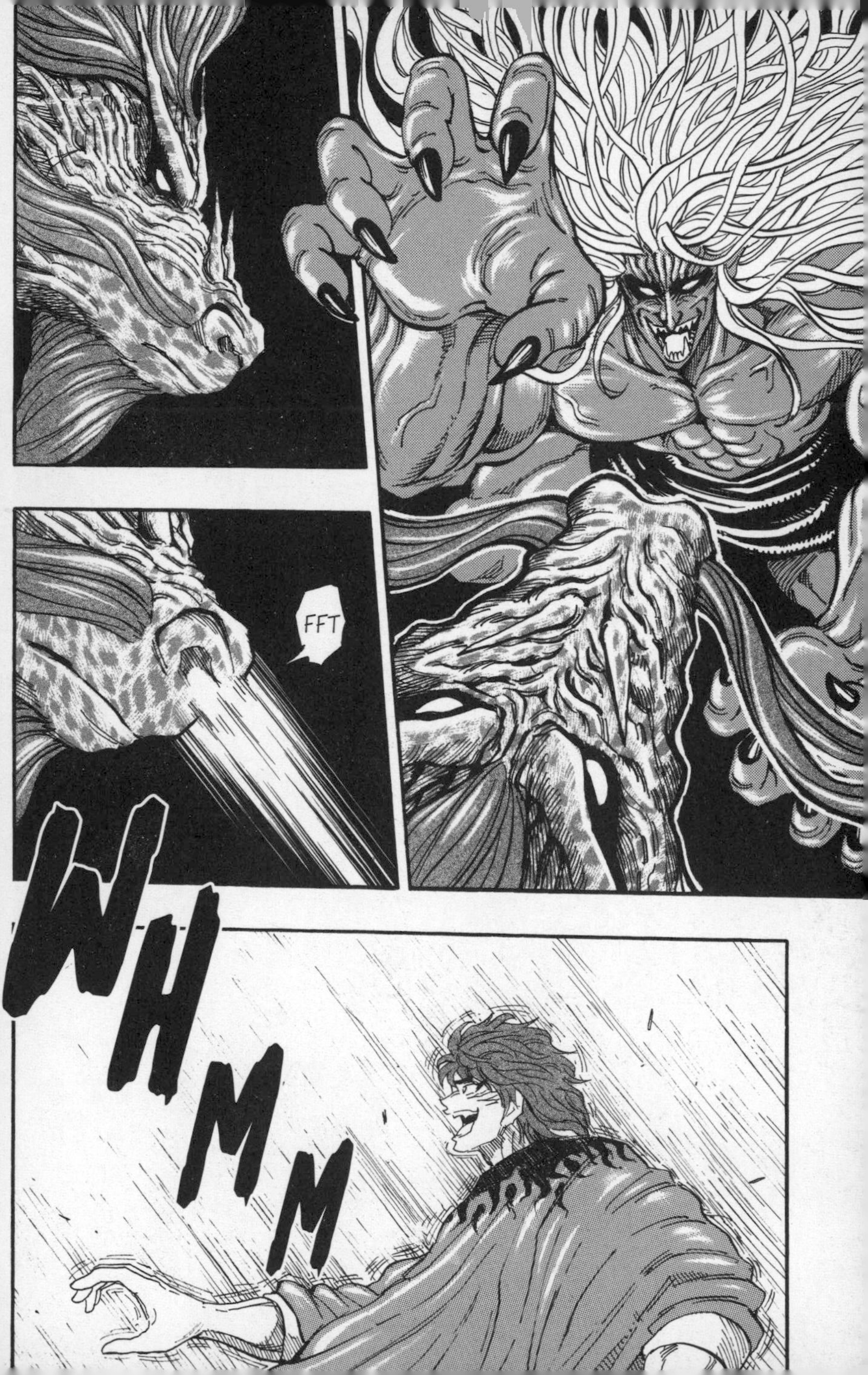
FFT
WHMMM

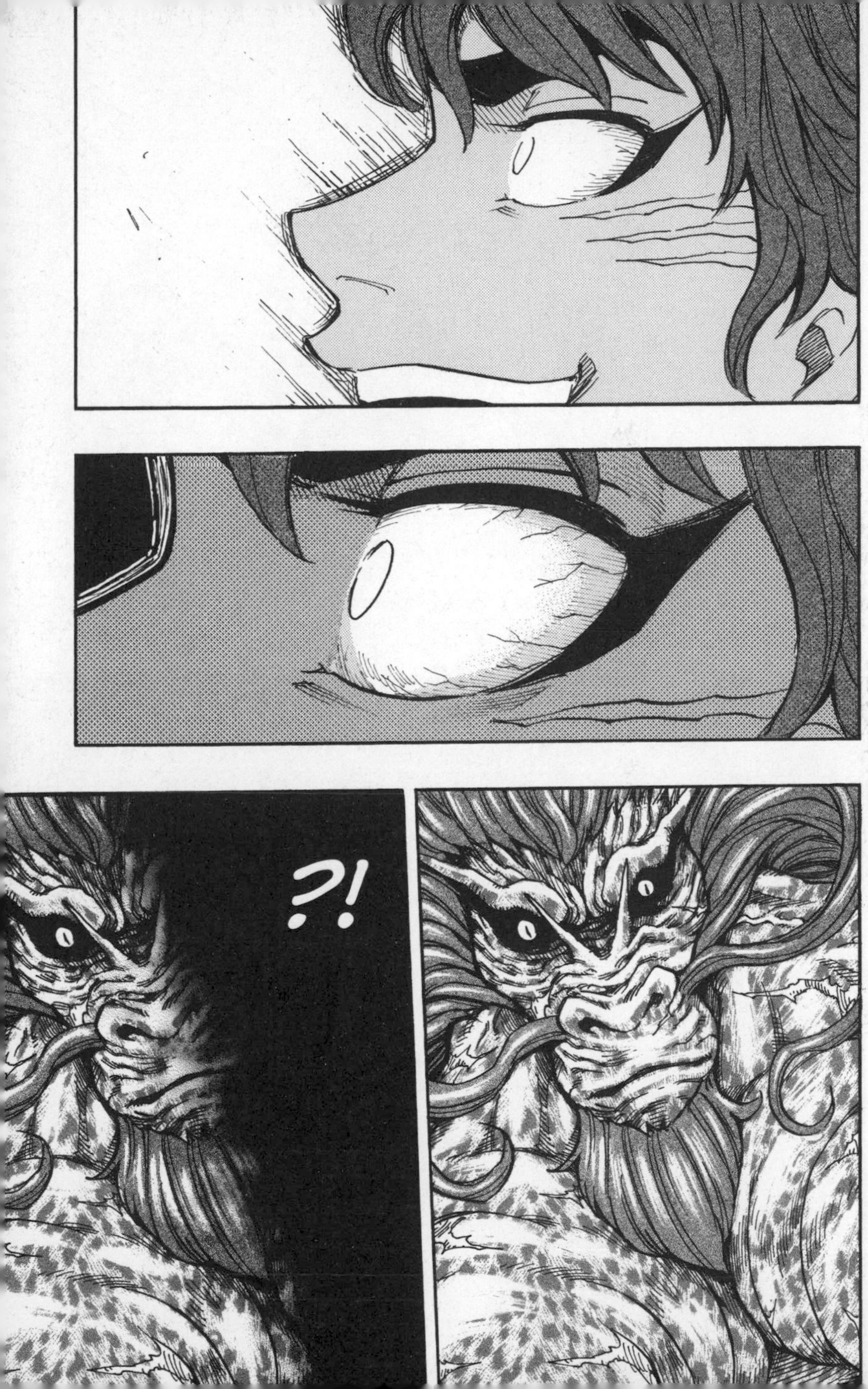
?!

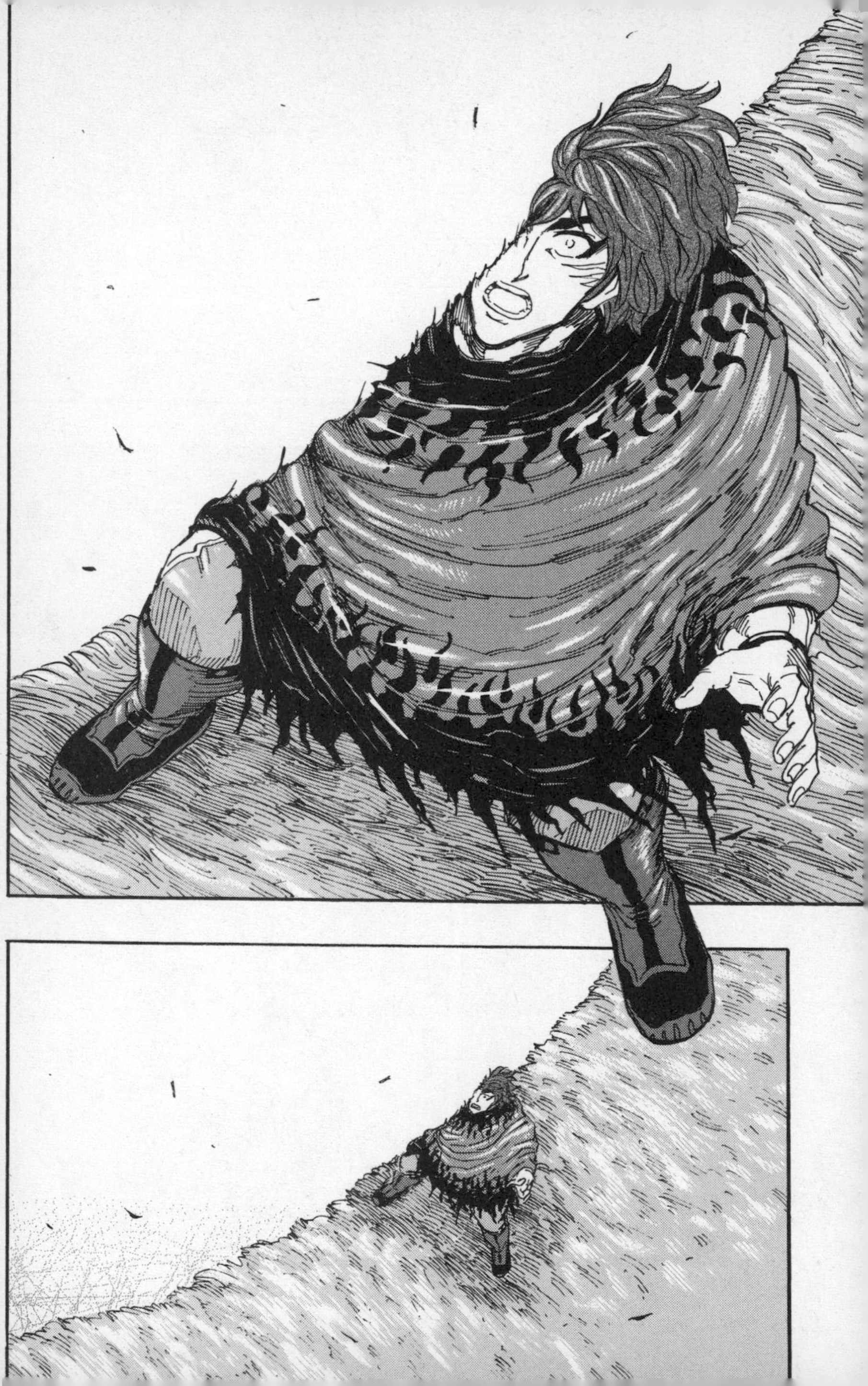

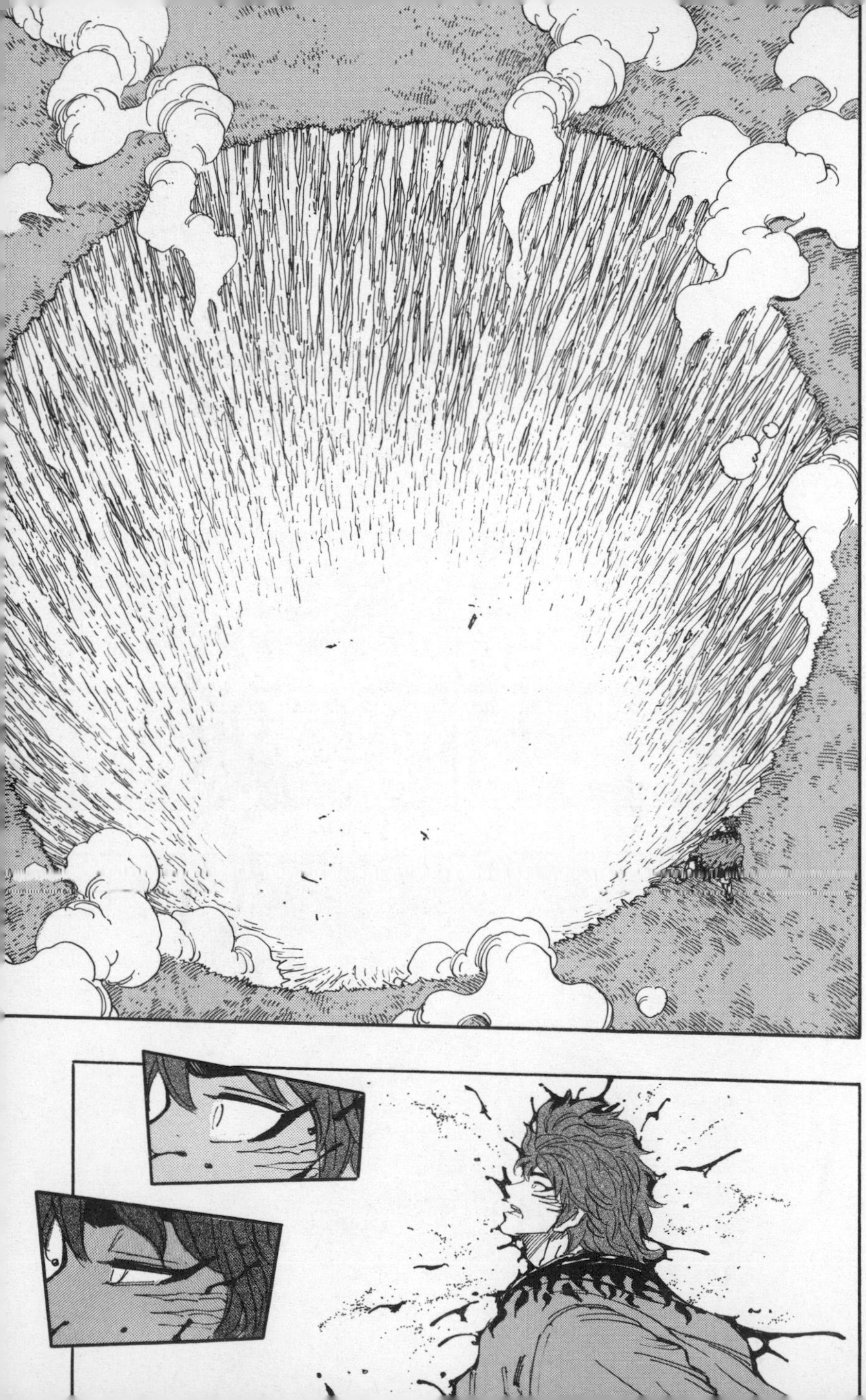

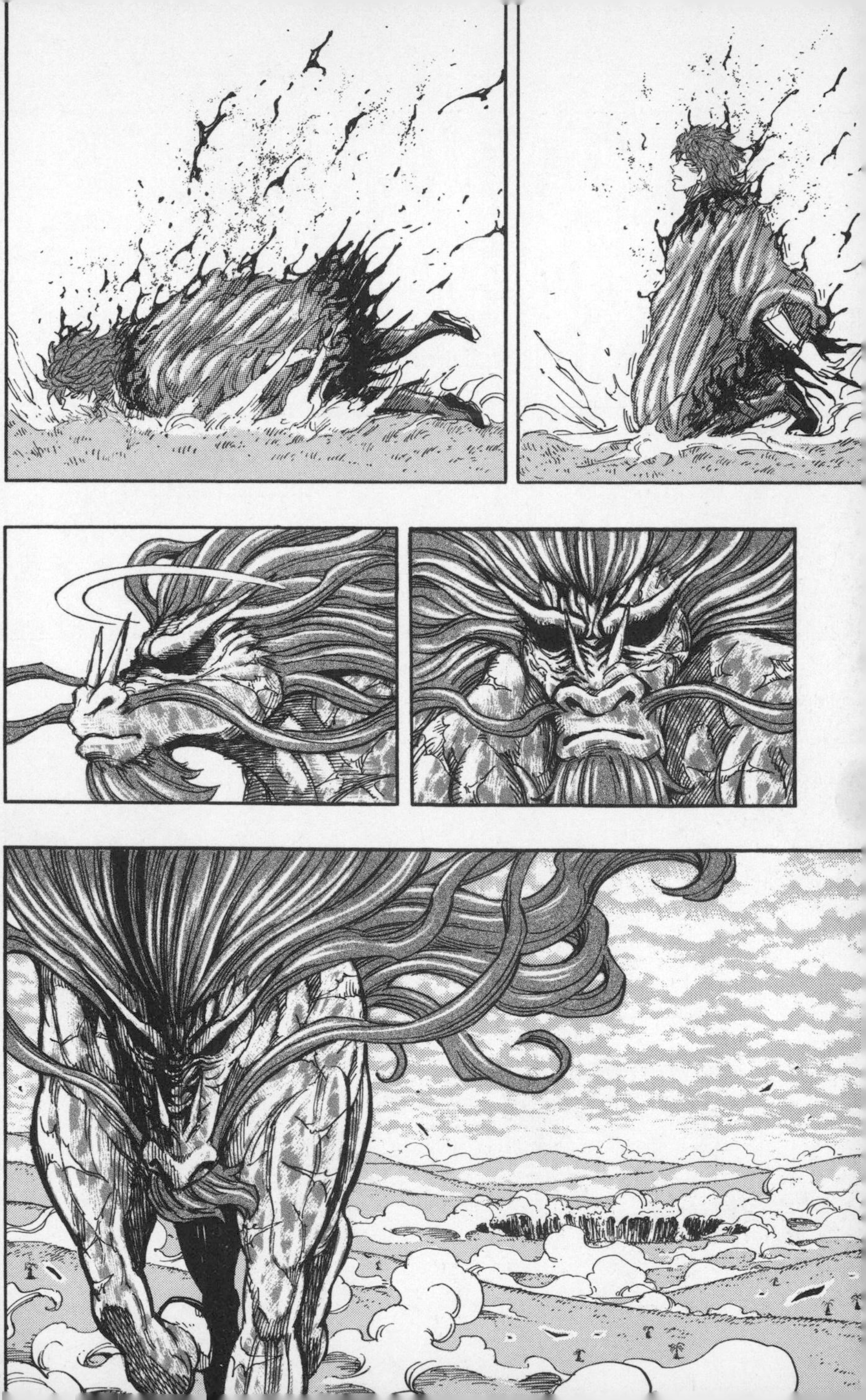

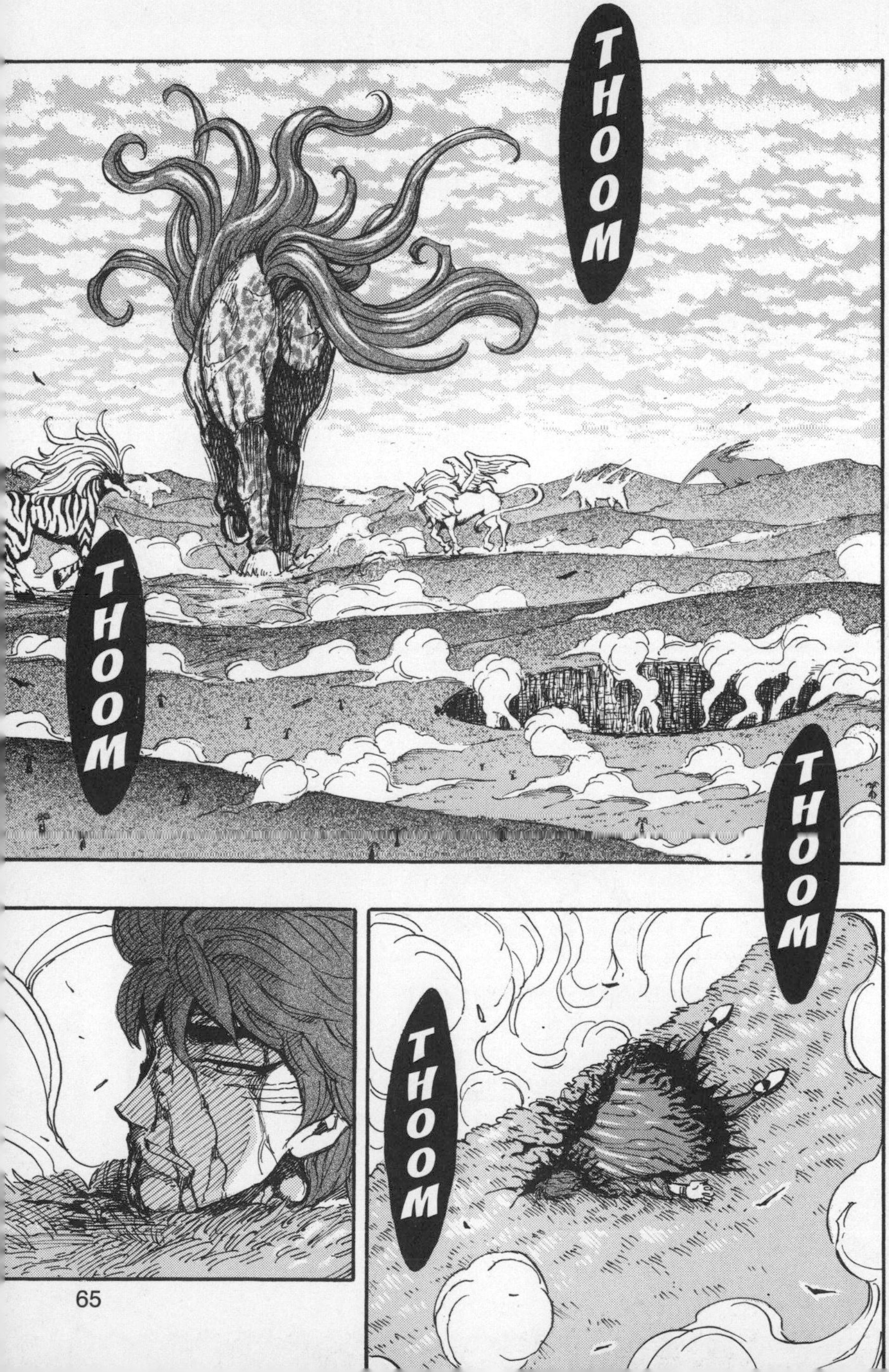
THOOM
THOOM
THOOM
THOOM

TORIKO

GOURMET CHECKLIST

Vol. 311

❧ FOUR-BEASTS: INVITE DEATH ☙
(MOLLUSK MAMMAL)

CAPTURE LEVEL: 140
HABITAT: GOURMET WORLD
SIZE: 260 M
HEIGHT: 180 M
WEIGHT: 2.7 MILLION TONS
PRICE: UNKNOWN

SCALE

AN EXTREMITY OF THE MONSTROUS FOUR-BEASTS WHO EMERGES FROM THE
GOURMET WORLD EVERY SEVERAL YEARS. IT CHOOSES THE TIME WHEN HUMANITY
IS AT ITS PEAK AND THEN FEASTS ON THE WORLD. IT IS A HUNTER OF THE NIGHT,
BRINGING ITS POISON THORN-COVERED LEGS DOWN ON ITS PREY AND THEN
SMOTHERING IT WITH ITS TENTACLES. ITS POISON IS STRONG ENOUGH TO ERODE AN
ENTIRE CONTINENT! OF COURSE, COCO'S POISON IS MUCH STRONGER, BUT THIS GUY'S
POISON PACKS QUITE A PUNCH.

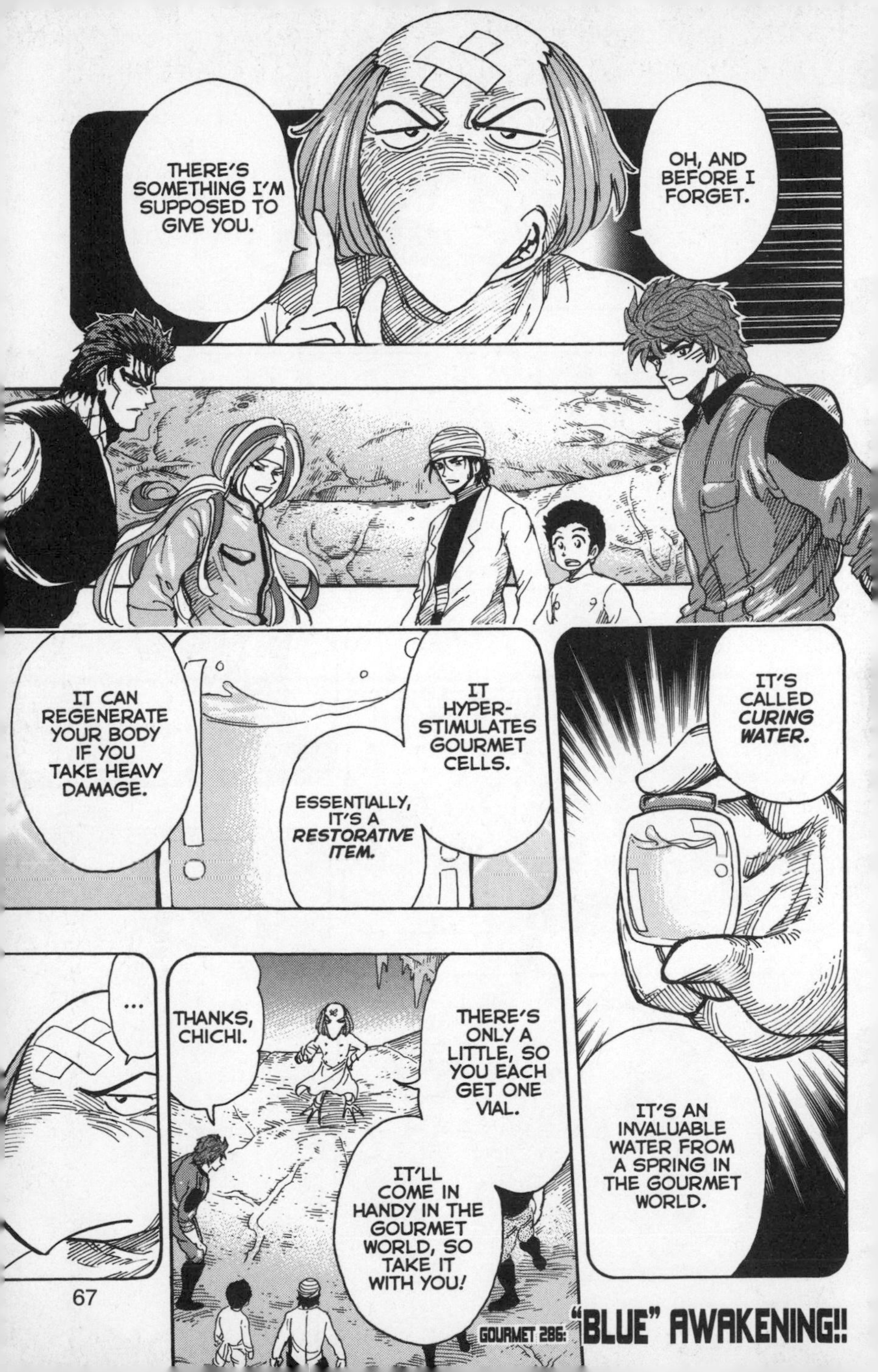
OH, AND BEFORE I FORGET.
THERE'S SOMETHING I'M SUPPOSED TO GIVE YOU.
IT'S CALLED *CURING WATER.*
IT'S AN INVALUABLE WATER FROM A SPRING IN THE GOURMET WORLD.
IT HYPER-STIMULATES GOURMET CELLS.
ESSENTIALLY, IT'S A *RESTORATIVE ITEM.*
IT CAN REGENERATE YOUR BODY IF YOU TAKE HEAVY DAMAGE.
THERE'S ONLY A LITTLE, SO YOU EACH GET ONE VIAL.
IT'LL COME IN HANDY IN THE GOURMET WORLD, SO TAKE IT WITH YOU!
THANKS, CHICHI.
...

GOURMET 286: "BLUE" AWAKENING!!

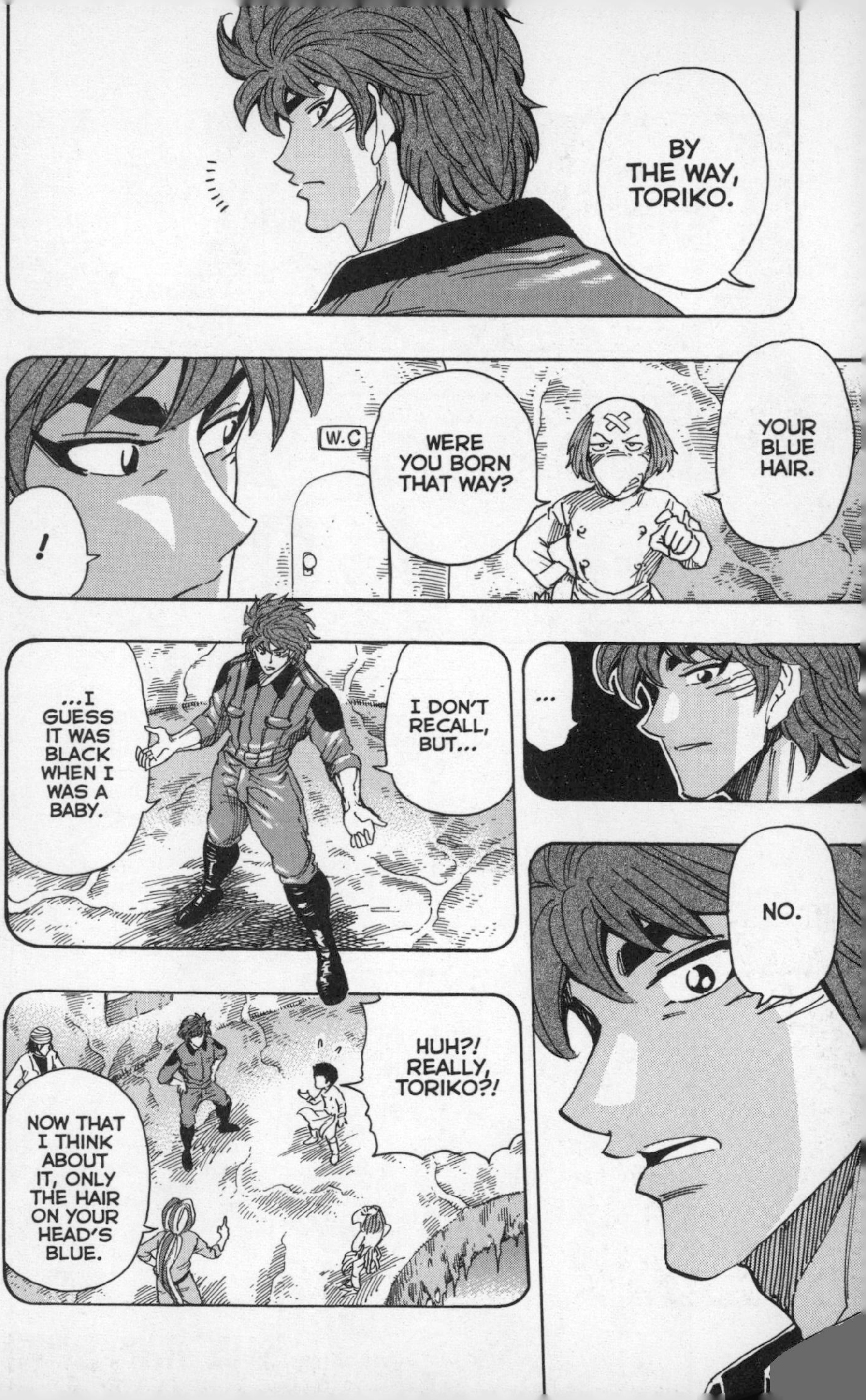
BY THE WAY, TORIKO.
YOUR BLUE HAIR.
WERE YOU BORN THAT WAY?
!
W.C
...
I DON'T RECALL, BUT...
...I GUESS IT WAS BLACK WHEN I WAS A BABY.
NO.
HUH?! REALLY, TORIKO?!
NOW THAT I THINK ABOUT IT, ONLY THE HAIR ON YOUR HEAD'S BLUE.

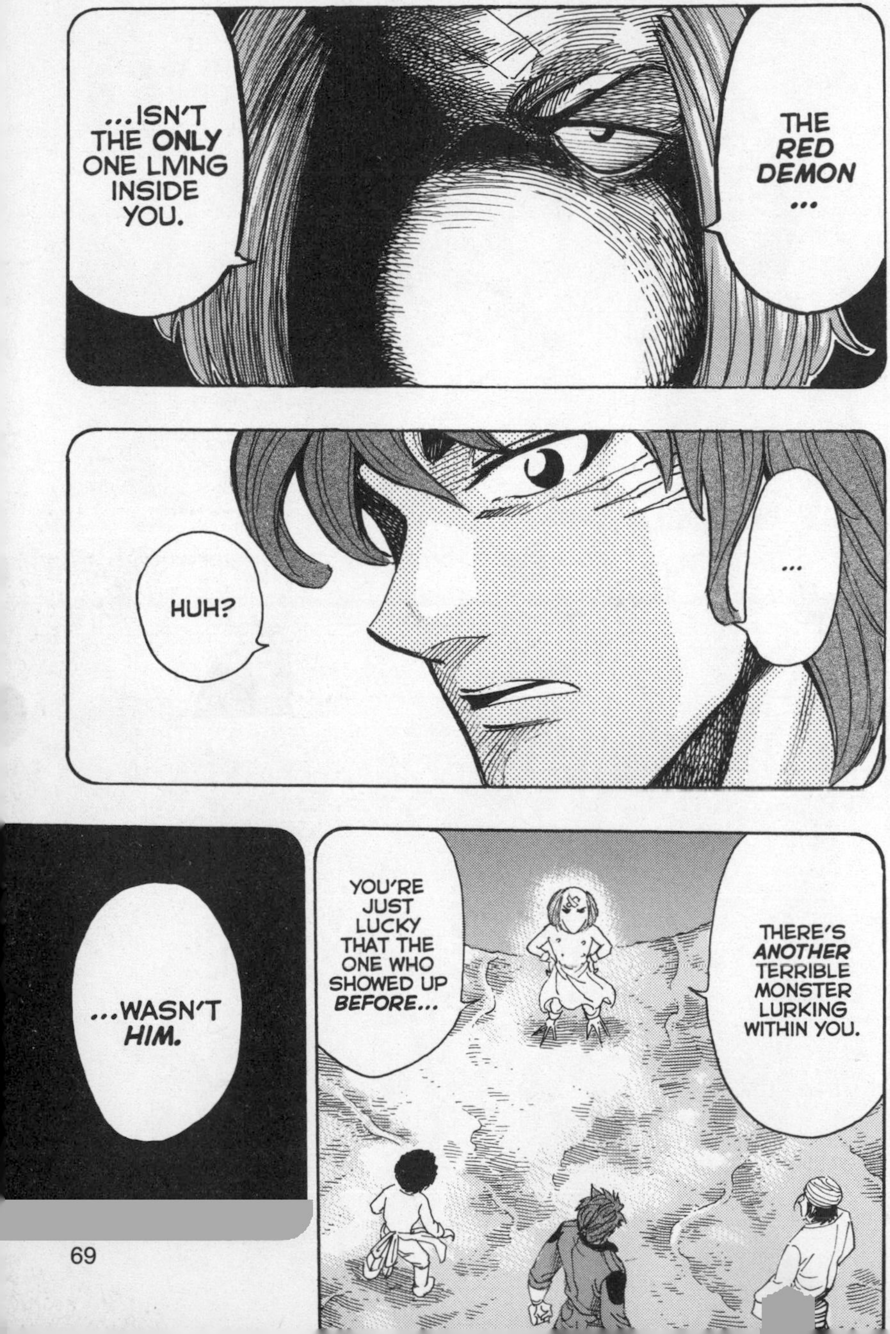
THE *RED DEMON* ...
...ISN'T THE **ONLY** ONE LIVING INSIDE YOU.
...
HUH?
THERE'S *ANOTHER* TERRIBLE MONSTER LURKING WITHIN YOU.
YOU'RE JUST LUCKY THAT THE ONE WHO SHOWED UP *BEFORE*...
...WASN'T *HIM.*

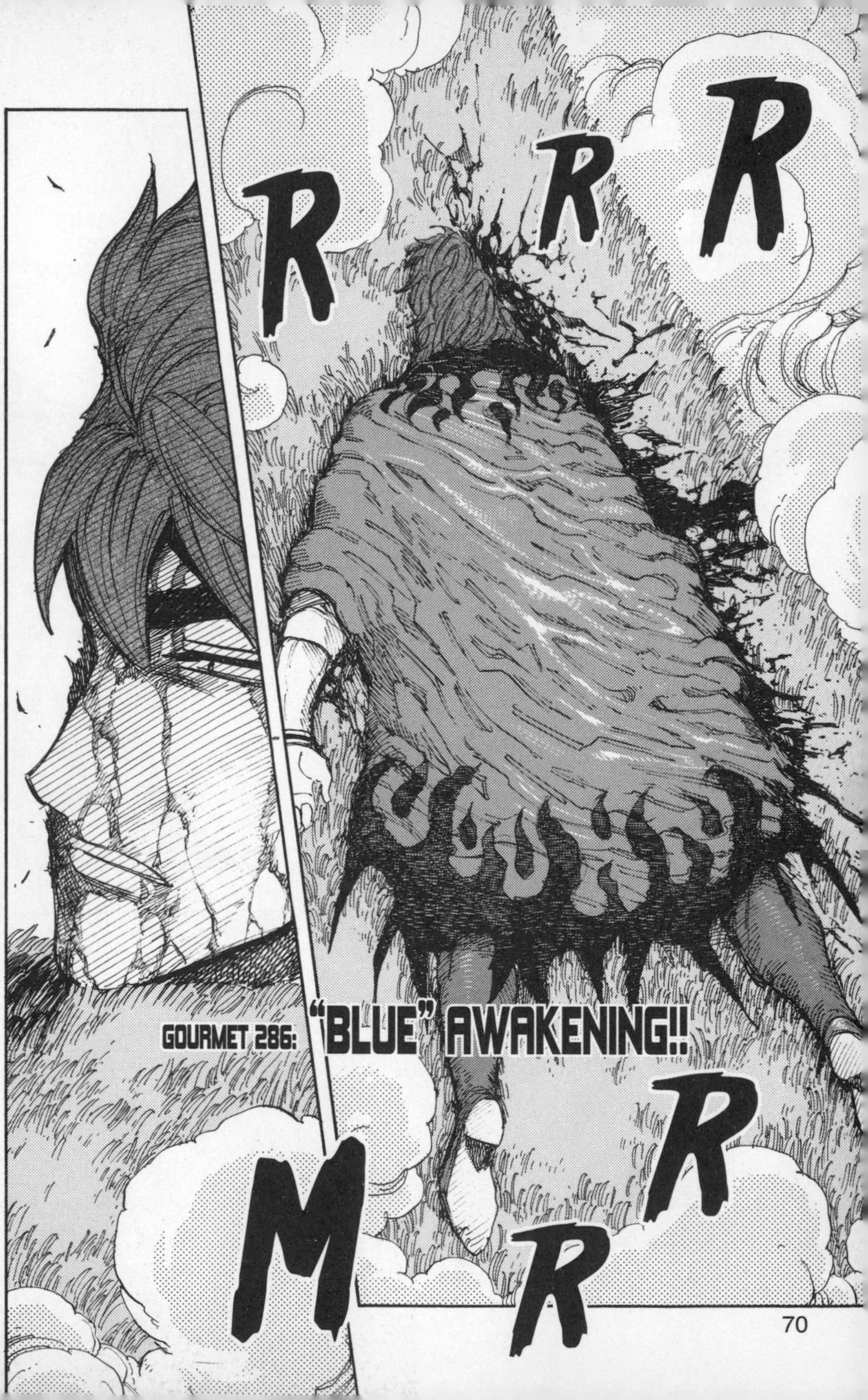
RRRR
GOURMET 286: "BLUE" AWAKENING!!
MRRR

ROLL
ROLL
PERK
THROB
THROB
BLOOP
BLOOP
BLOOPOP

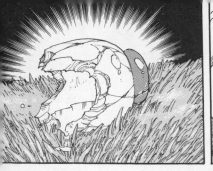

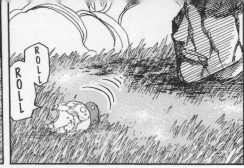

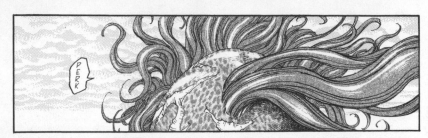

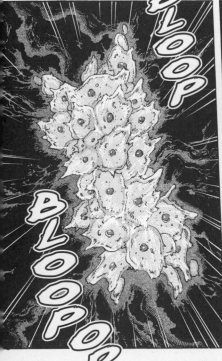

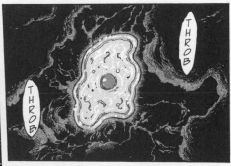

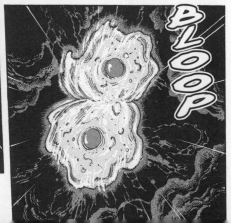

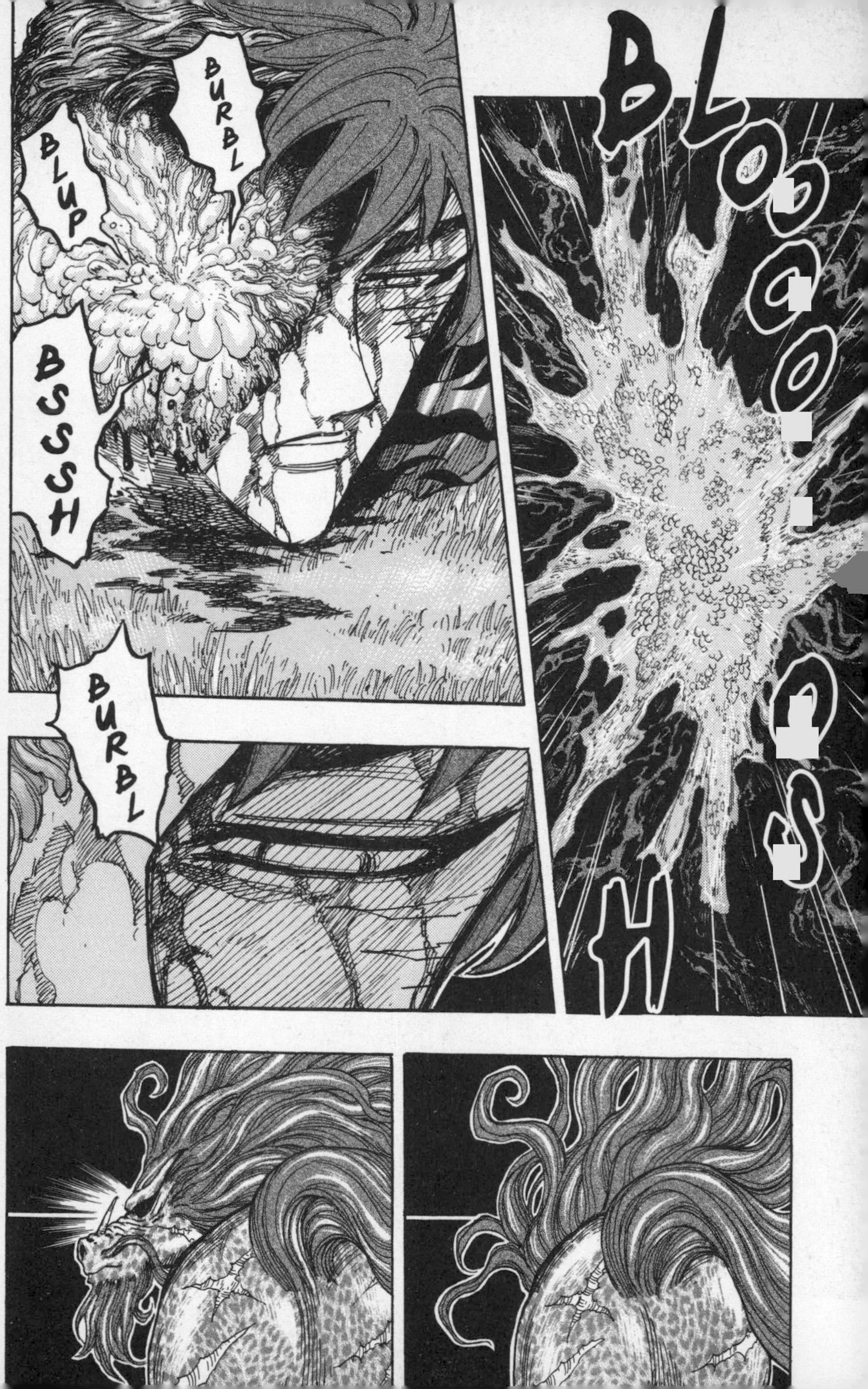
BLOOOOOSH
BURBL
BLUP
BSSSH
BURBL

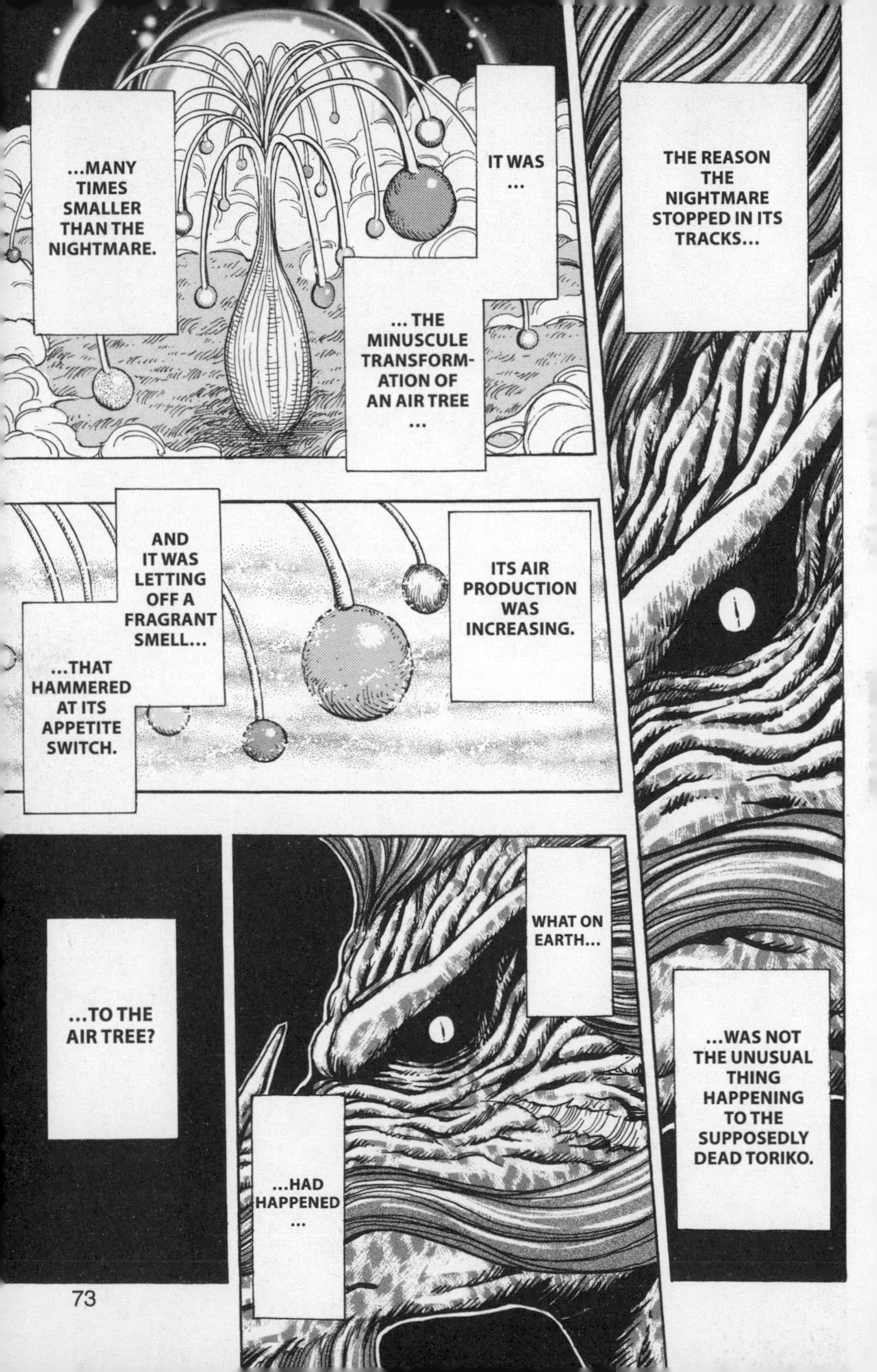
THE REASON THE NIGHTMARE STOPPED IN ITS TRACKS...
...WAS NOT THE UNUSUAL THING HAPPENING TO THE SUPPOSEDLY DEAD TORIKO.
IT WAS ...
... THE MINUSCULE TRANSFORMATION OF AN AIR TREE ...
...MANY TIMES SMALLER THAN THE NIGHTMARE.
ITS AIR PRODUCTION WAS INCREASING.
AND IT WAS LETTING OFF A FRAGRANT SMELL...
...THAT HAMMERED AT ITS APPETITE SWITCH.
WHAT ON EARTH...
...HAD HAPPENED ...
...TO THE AIR TREE?

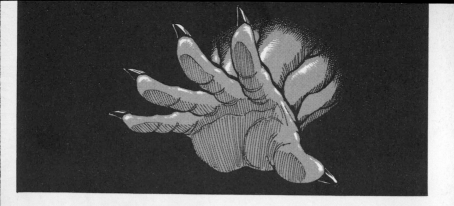

KREEK

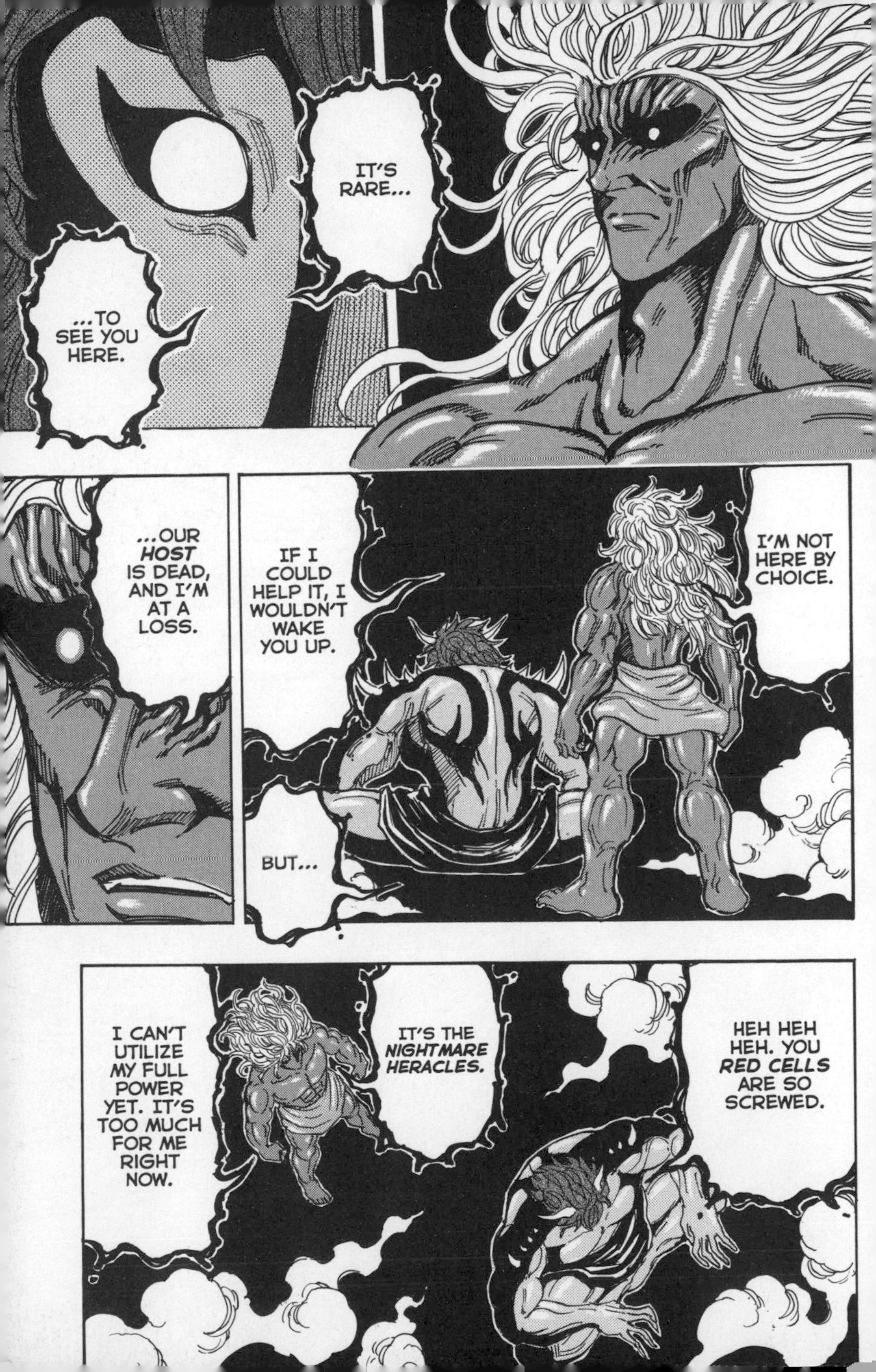
IT'S RARE...
...TO SEE YOU HERE.
I'M NOT HERE BY CHOICE.
IF I COULD HELP IT, I WOULDN'T WAKE YOU UP.
BUT...
...OUR *HOST* IS DEAD, AND I'M AT A LOSS.
HEH HEH HEH. YOU *RED CELLS* ARE SO SCREWED.
IT'S THE *NIGHTMARE* HERACLES.
I CAN'T UTILIZE MY FULL POWER YET. IT'S TOO MUCH FOR ME RIGHT NOW.

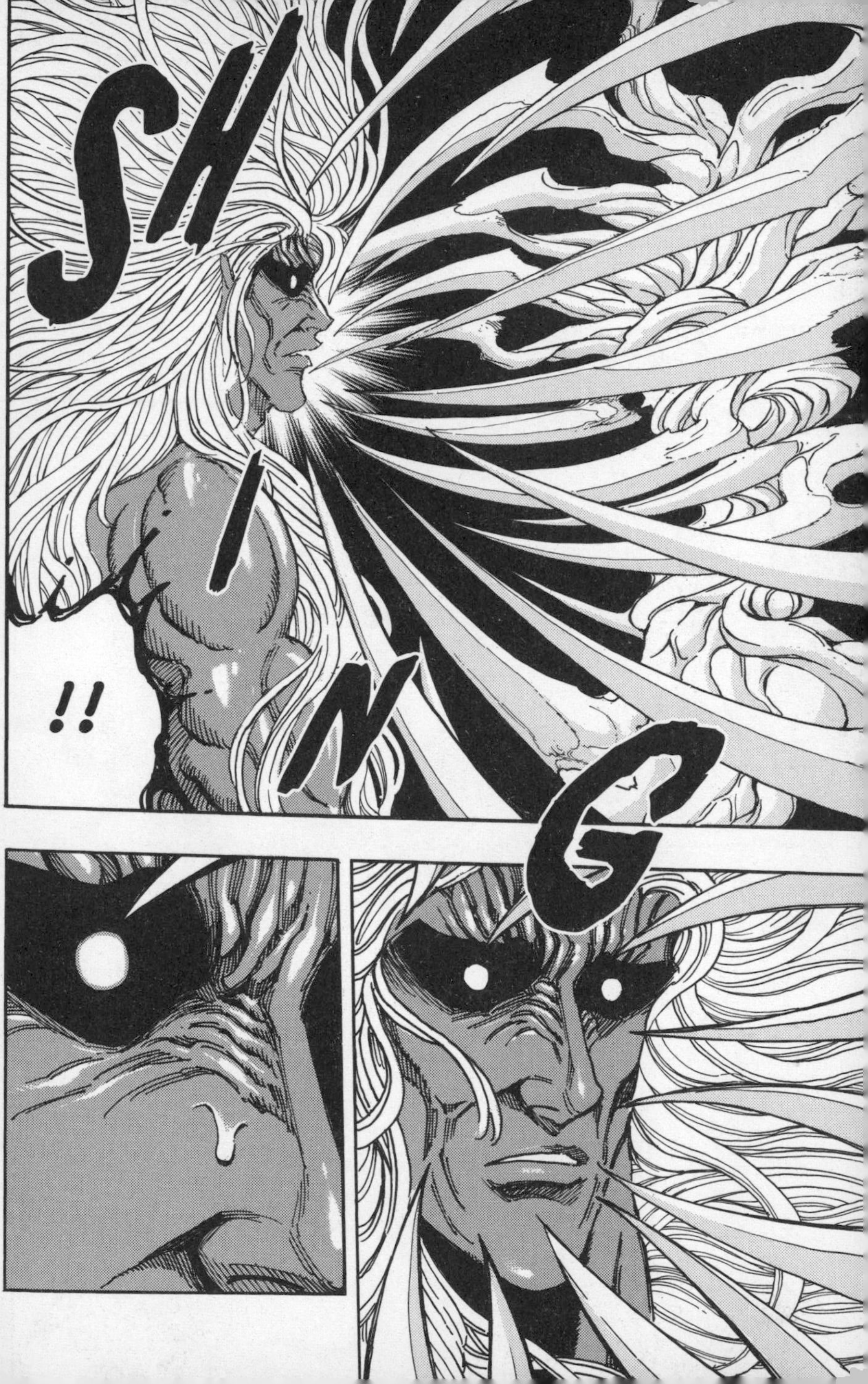
SHING
!!

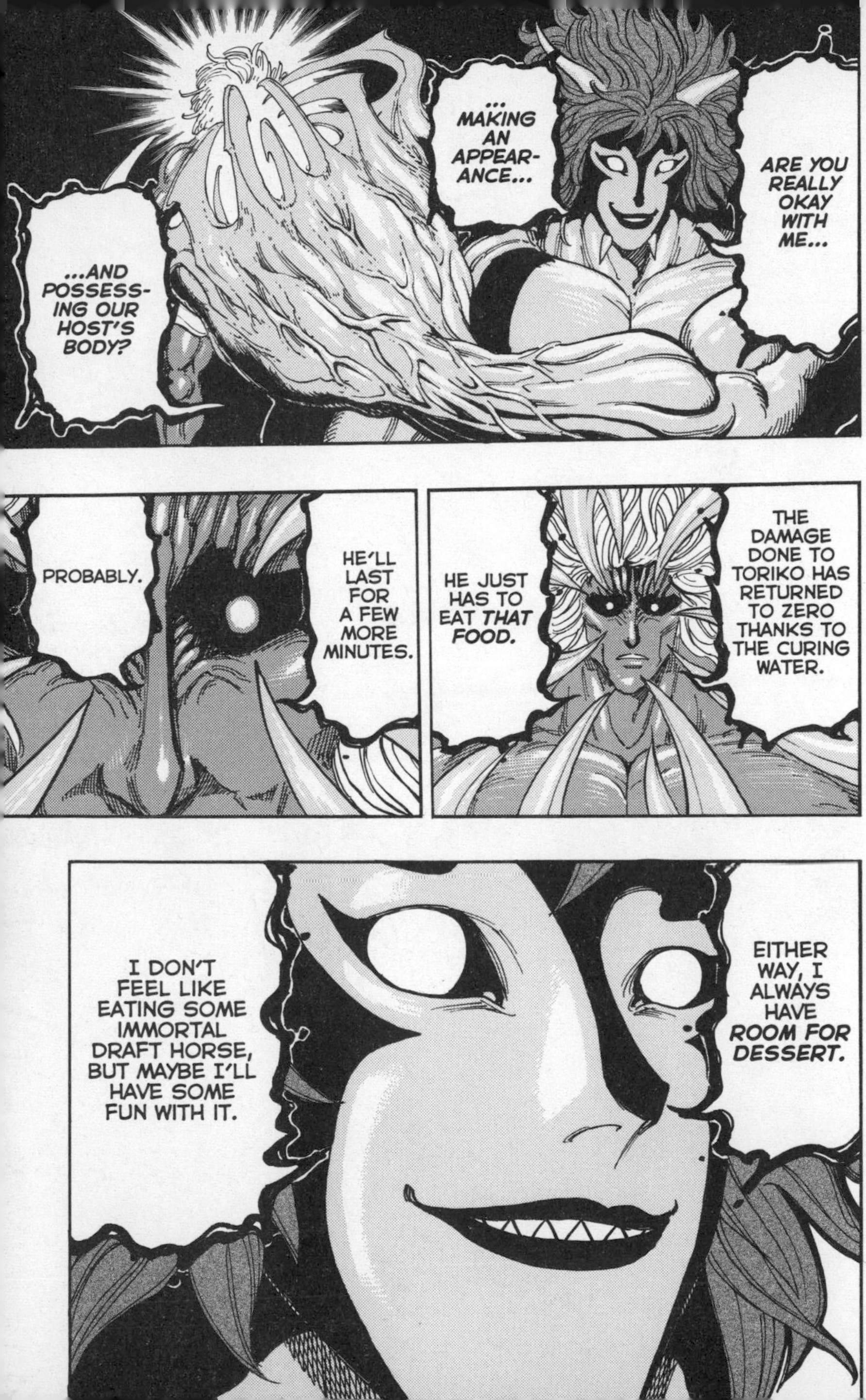
ARE YOU REALLY OKAY WITH ME...
...MAKING AN APPEAR-ANCE...
...AND POSSESS-ING OUR HOST'S BODY?
THE DAMAGE DONE TO TORIKO HAS RETURNED TO ZERO THANKS TO THE CURING WATER.
HE JUST HAS TO EAT *THAT FOOD.*
HE'LL LAST FOR A FEW MORE MINUTES.
PROBABLY.
EITHER WAY, I ALWAYS HAVE *ROOM FOR DESSERT.*
I DON'T FEEL LIKE EATING SOME IMMORTAL DRAFT HORSE, BUT MAYBE I'LL HAVE SOME FUN WITH IT.

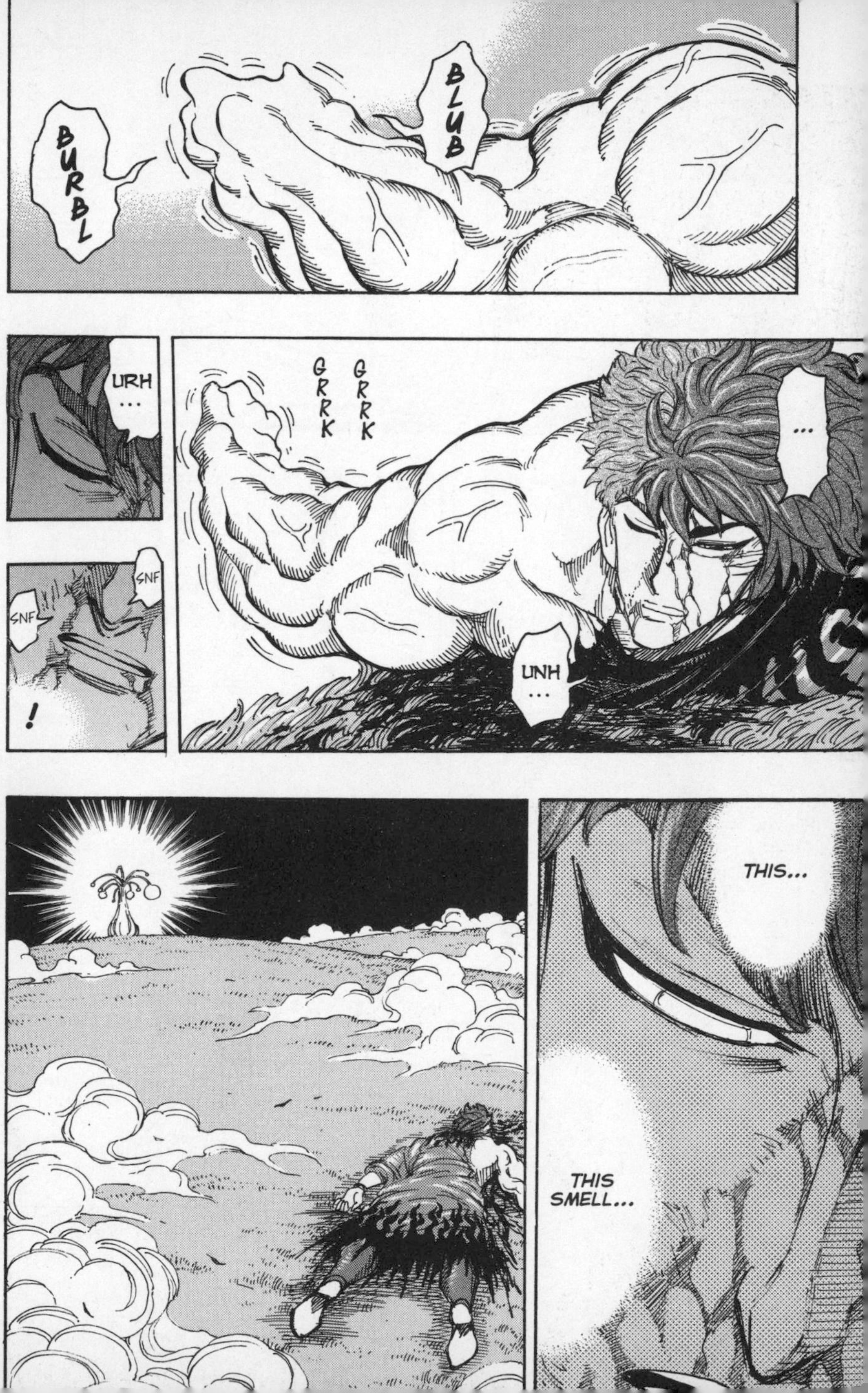
BLUB
BURBL
...
GRRK
GRRK
UNH...
URH...
SNF
SNF
!
THIS...
THIS SMELL...

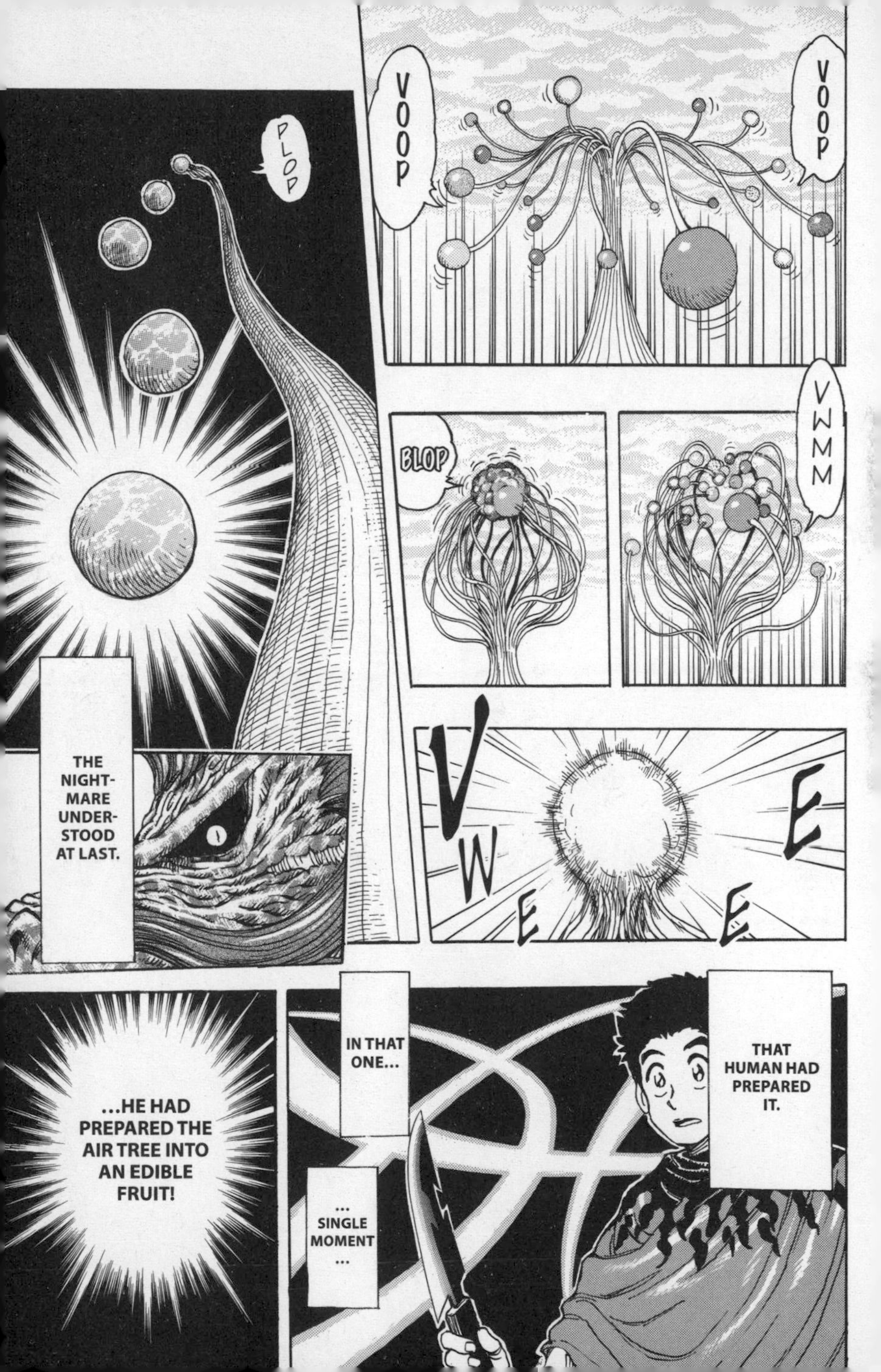

VOOP
VOOP
VWMM
BLOP
VWEEE
PLOP
THE NIGHT-MARE UNDER-STOOD AT LAST.
THAT HUMAN HAD PREPARED IT.
IN THAT ONE...
...SINGLE MOMENT...
...HE HAD PREPARED THE AIR TREE INTO AN EDIBLE FRUIT!

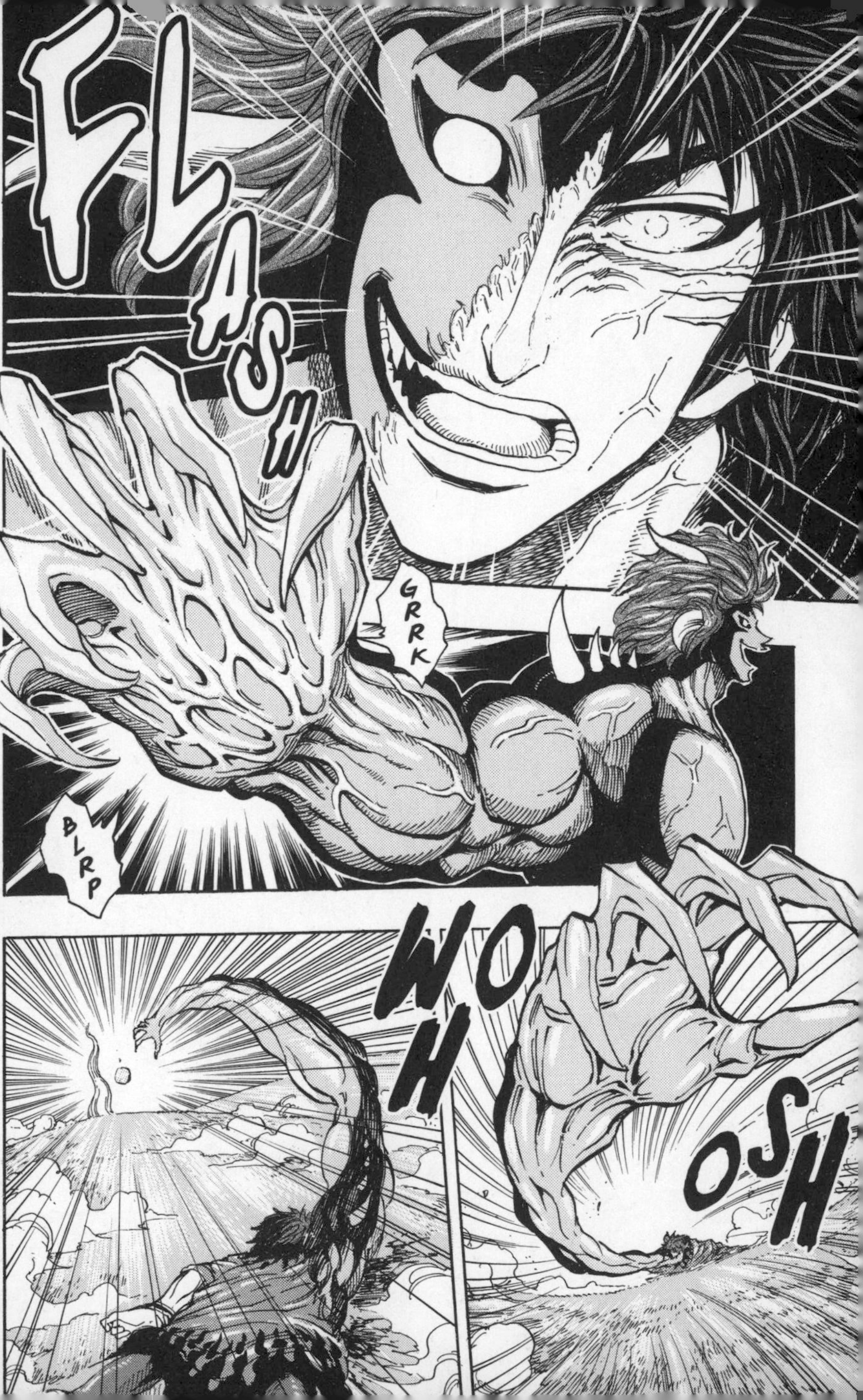
FLASH
GRRK
BLRP
WHOOSH

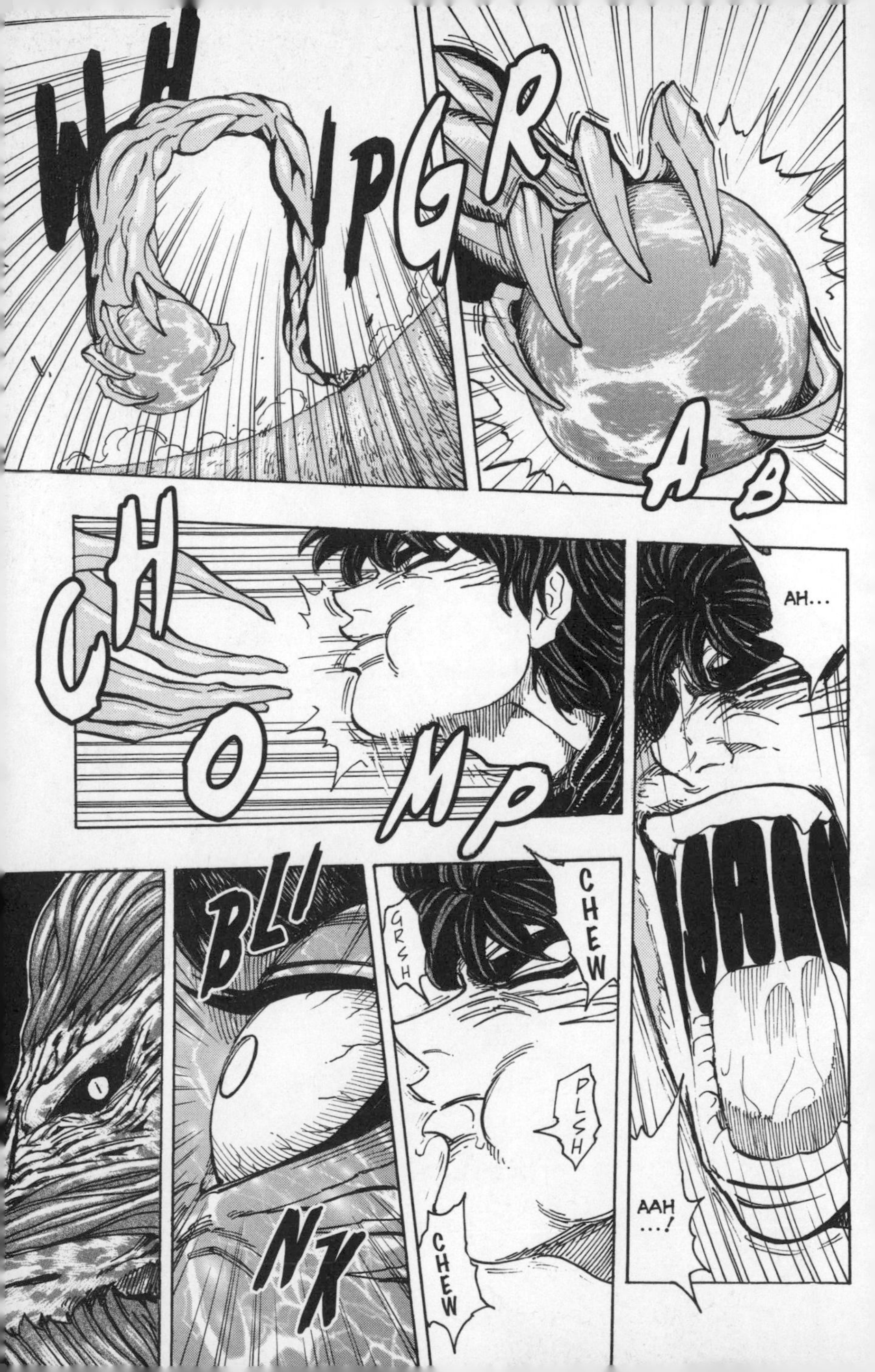
GRAB
WHIP
AH...
CHOMP
AAH...!
CHEW
GRSH
PLSH
CHEW
BLUNK

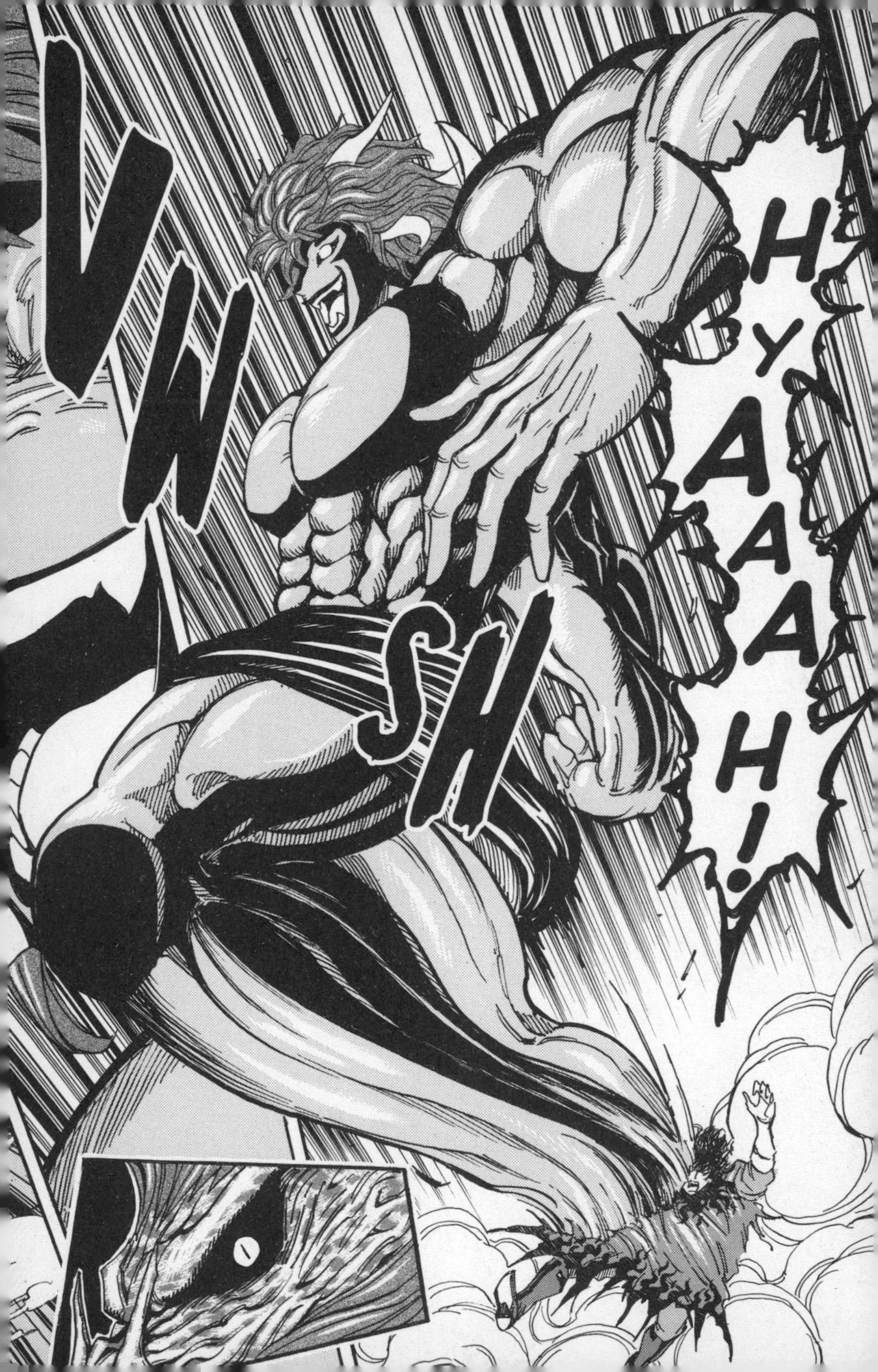
HYAAAH!
VWSH

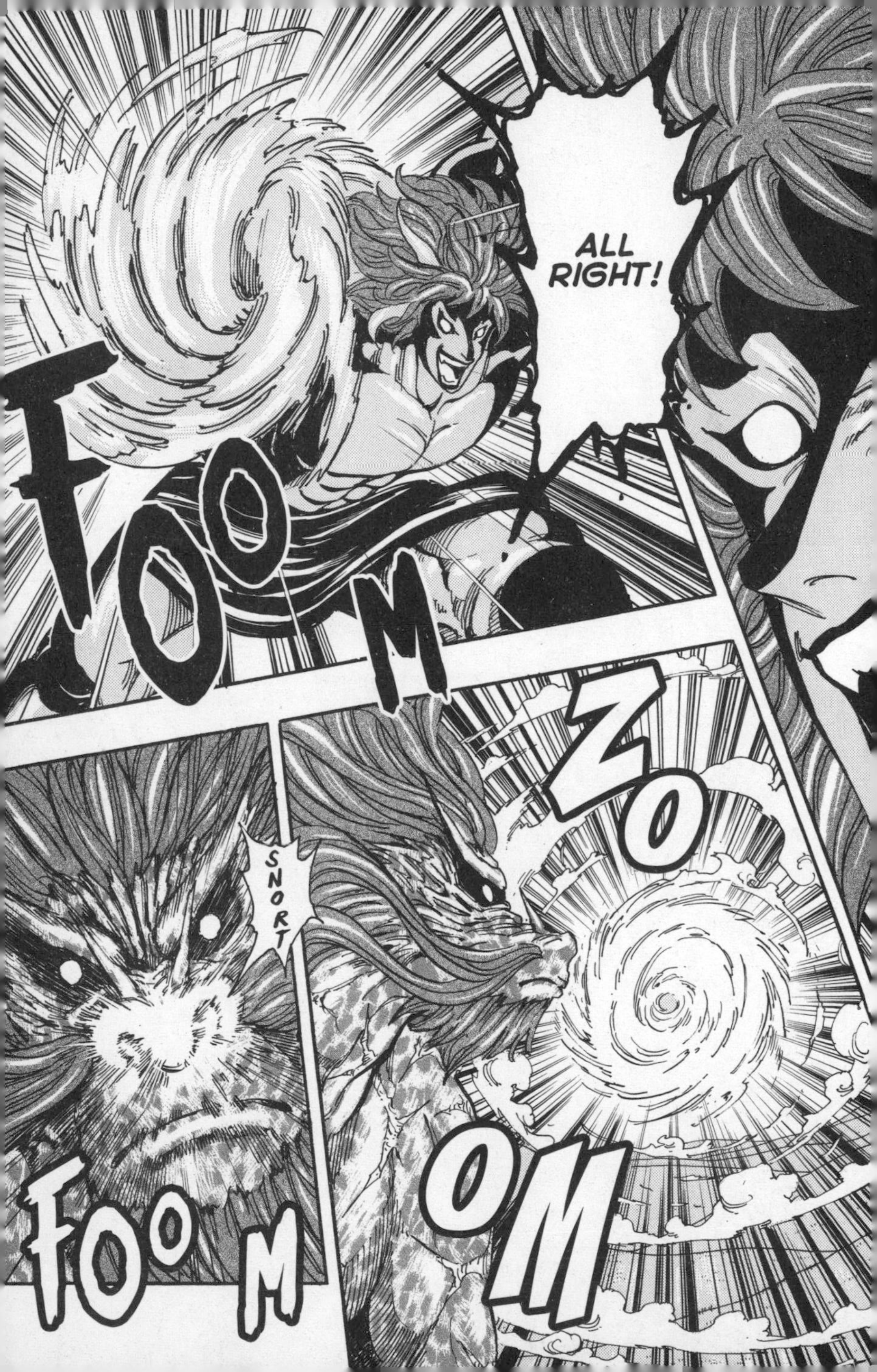
ALL RIGHT!
FOOOM
ZOOOM
SNORT
FOOOM

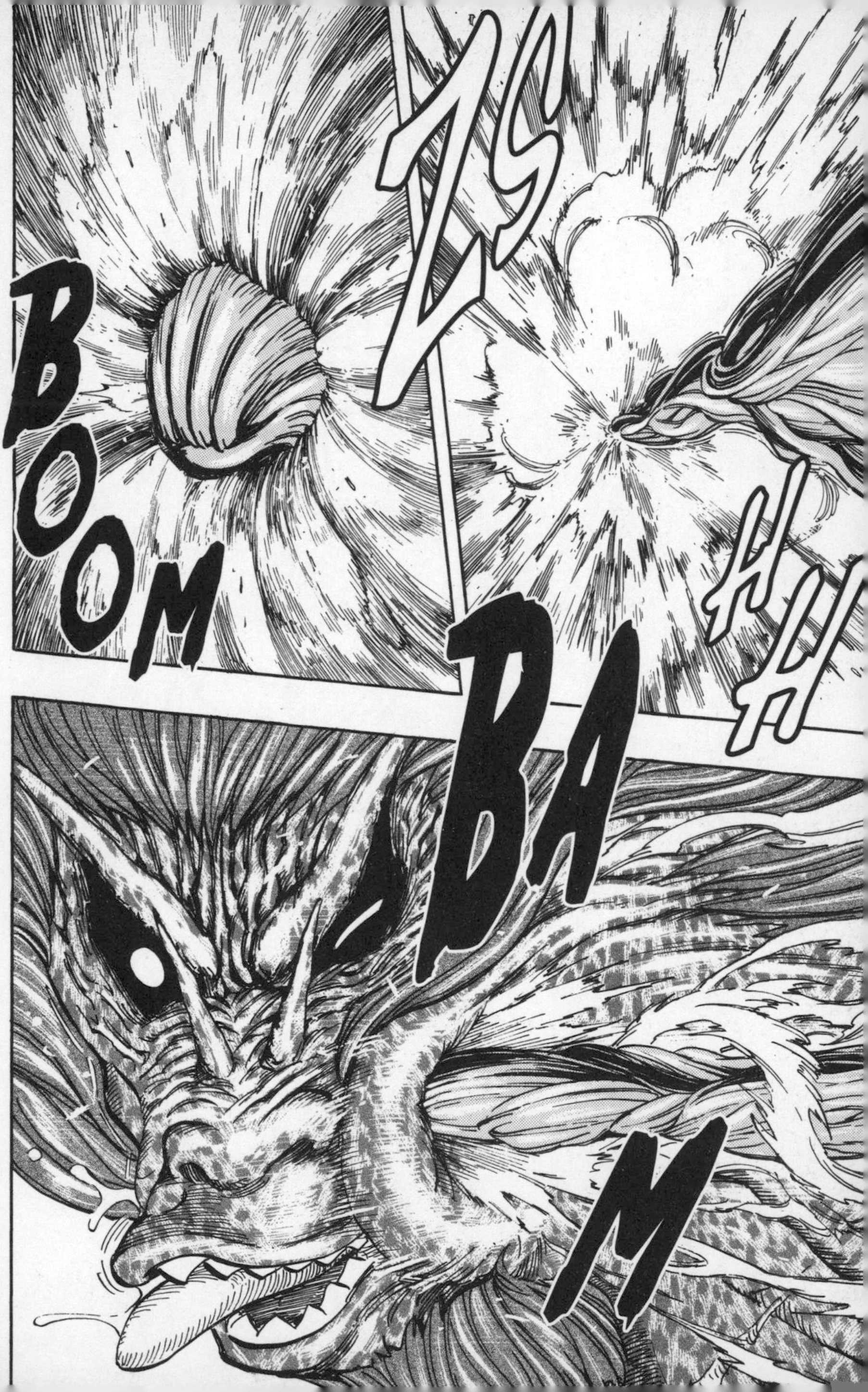
ZSHHH
BOOM
BAM

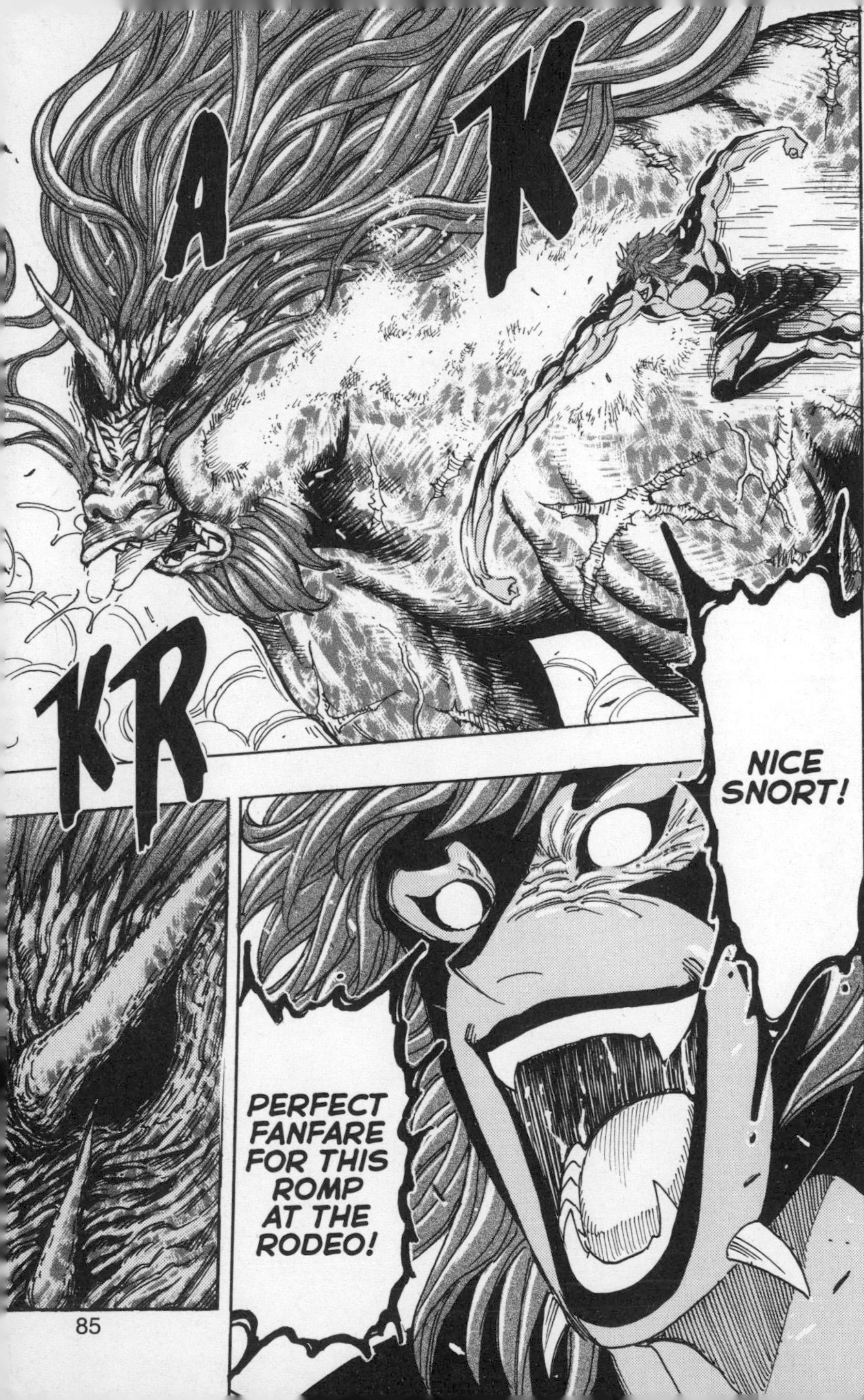
KRAK
NICE SNORT!
PERFECT FANFARE FOR THIS ROMP AT THE RODEO!

TORIKO

GOURMET CHECKLIST

Vol. 312

FOUR-BEASTS: KING OCTOPUS KONG
(MOLLUSK MAMMAL FISH)

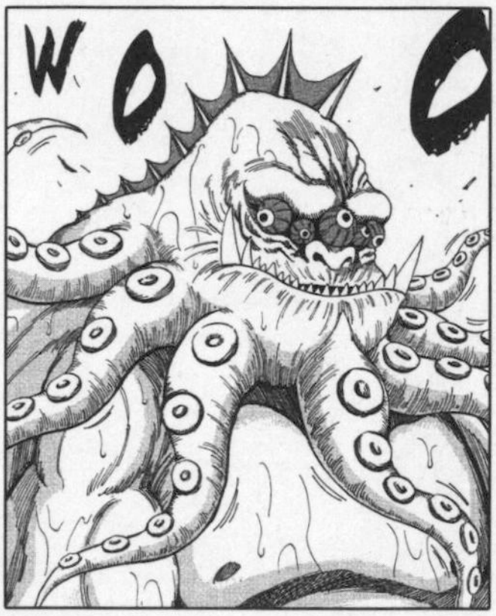
WOO

CAPTURE LEVEL: 132

HABITAT: GOURMET WORLD

SIZE: ---

HEIGHT: 220 M

WEIGHT: 3 MILLION TONS

PRICE: UNKNOWN

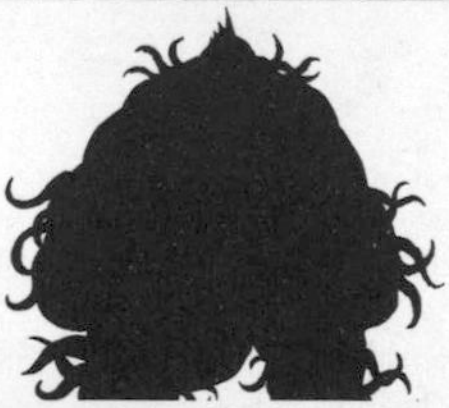

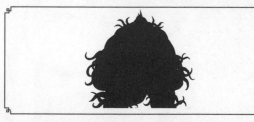

SCALE

AN EXTREMITY OF THE MONSTROUS FOUR-BEASTS WHO EMERGES FROM THE GOURMET WORLD EVERY SEVERAL YEARS. IT CHOOSES THE TIME WHEN HUMANITY IS AT ITS PEAK AND THEN FEASTS ON THE WORLD. THIS HYBRID BEAST BOASTS THE BRAWNY ARMS OF A GORILLA AND THE TENTACLES OF AN OCTOPUS. ITS MOLLUSK SHELL IS THE PERFECT SHIELD, MAKING IT A DIFFICULT ADVERSARY TO DESTROY. OF COURSE, SUNNY'S SUPER HAIR SHOT DID IT IN, BUT IT IS STILL A DANGEROUS CREATURE.

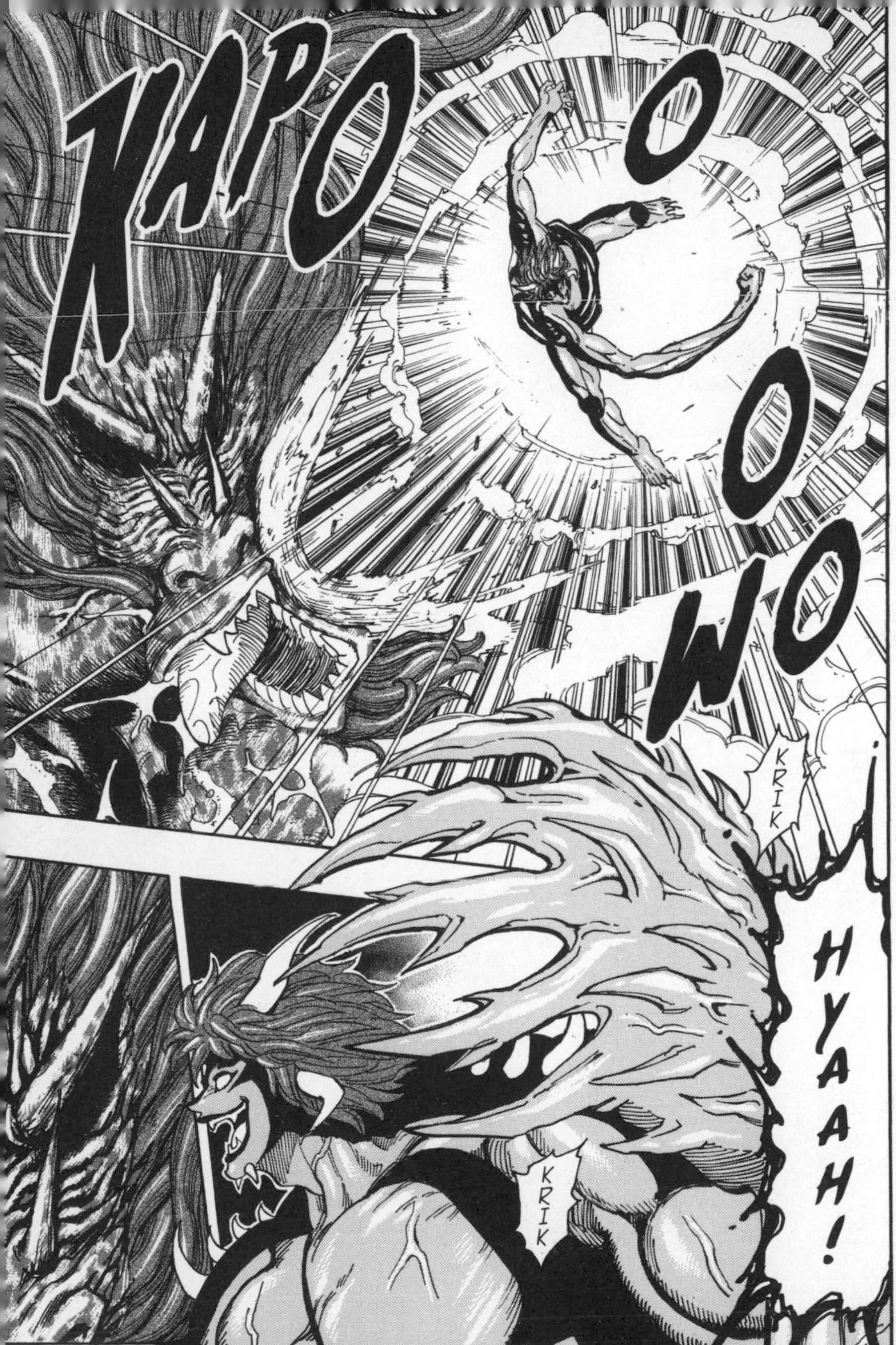
KAPOOOWO
KRIK
HYAAAH!
KRIK

GOURMET 287: SLOW RAIN AND AIR!!

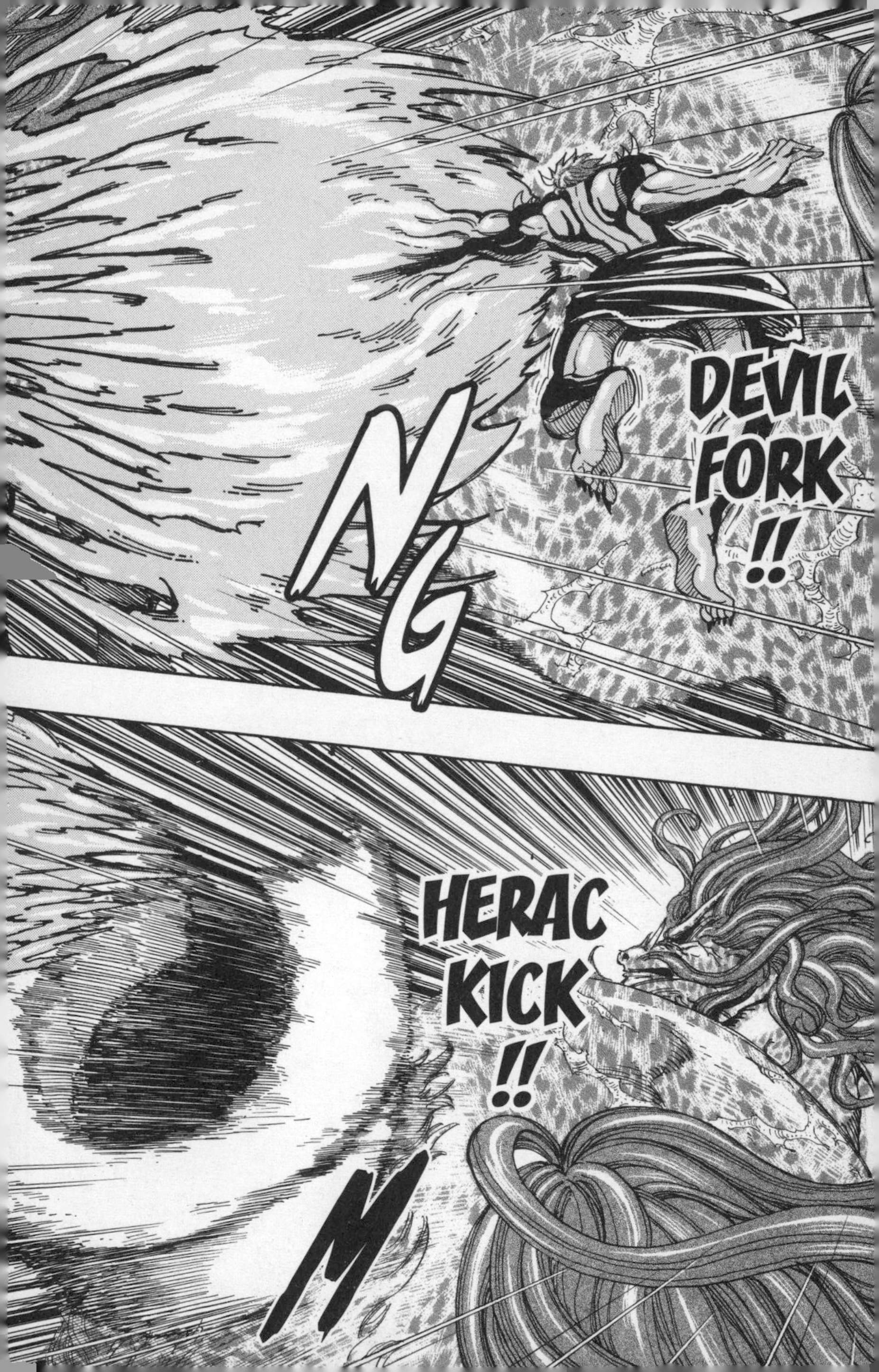
DEVIL FORK!!
NG
HERAC KICK!!
M

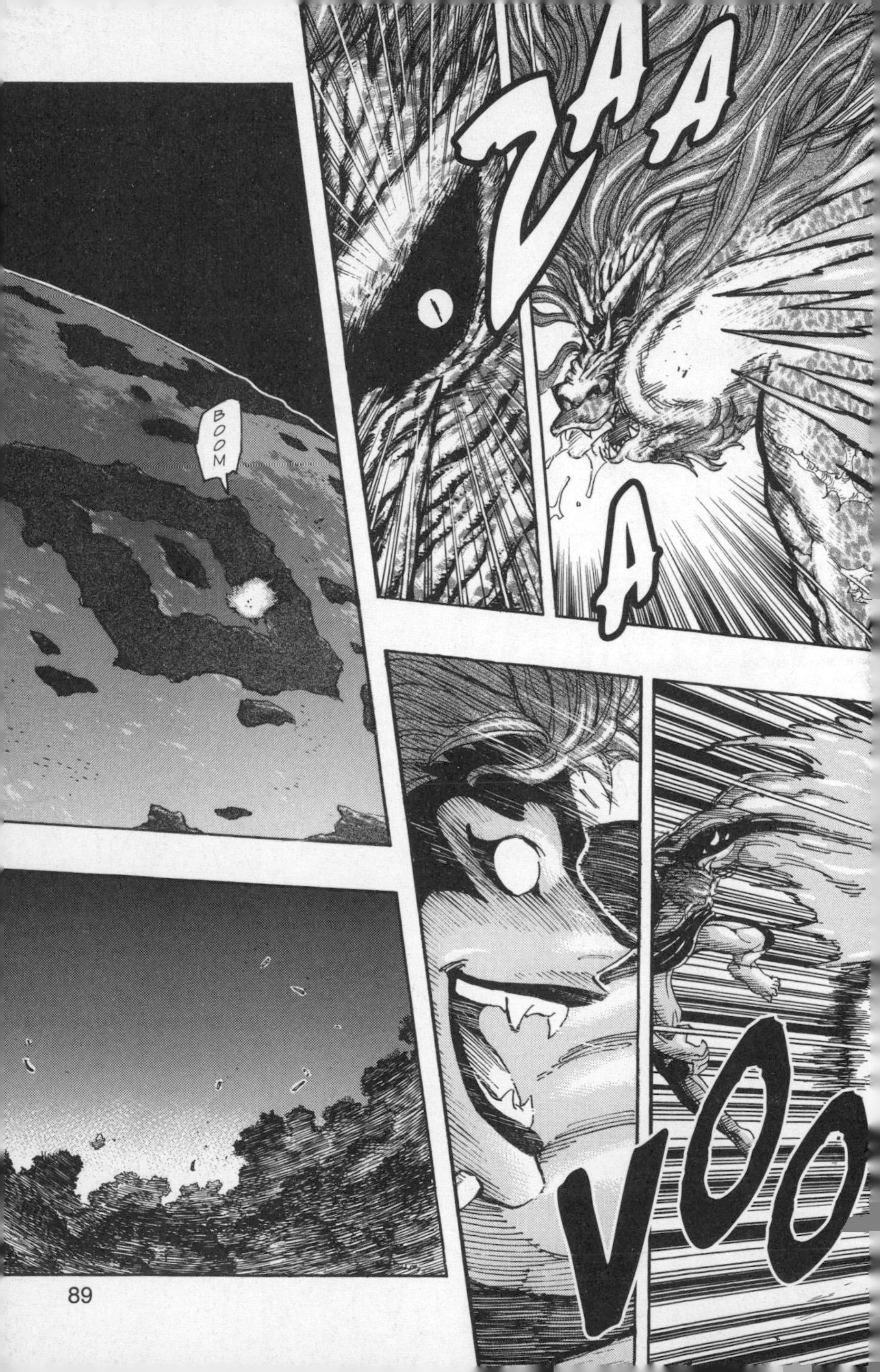
ZAAA
BOOM
VOOO

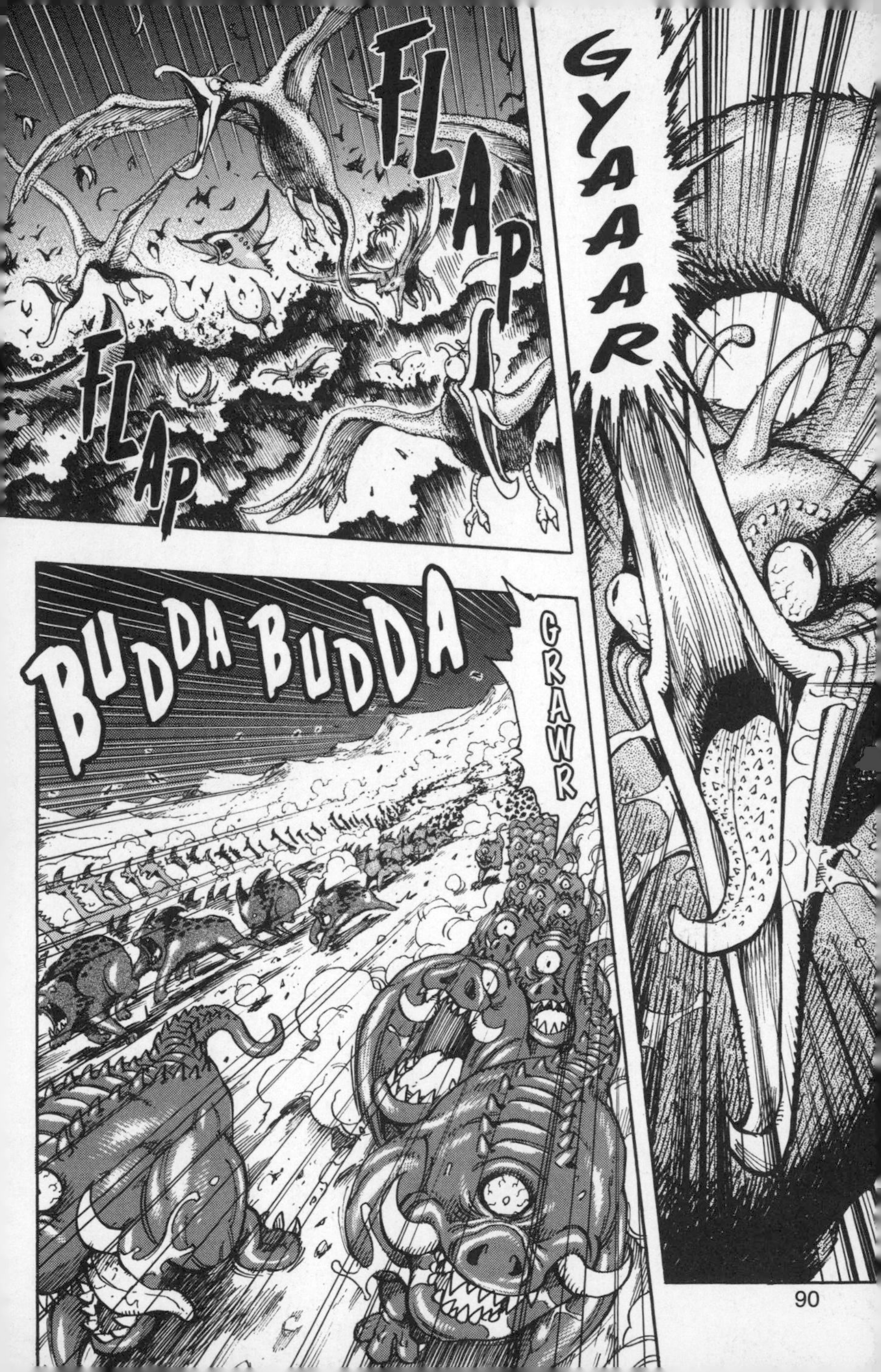
GYAAAR
FLAP
FLAP
GRAWR
BUDDA BUDDA

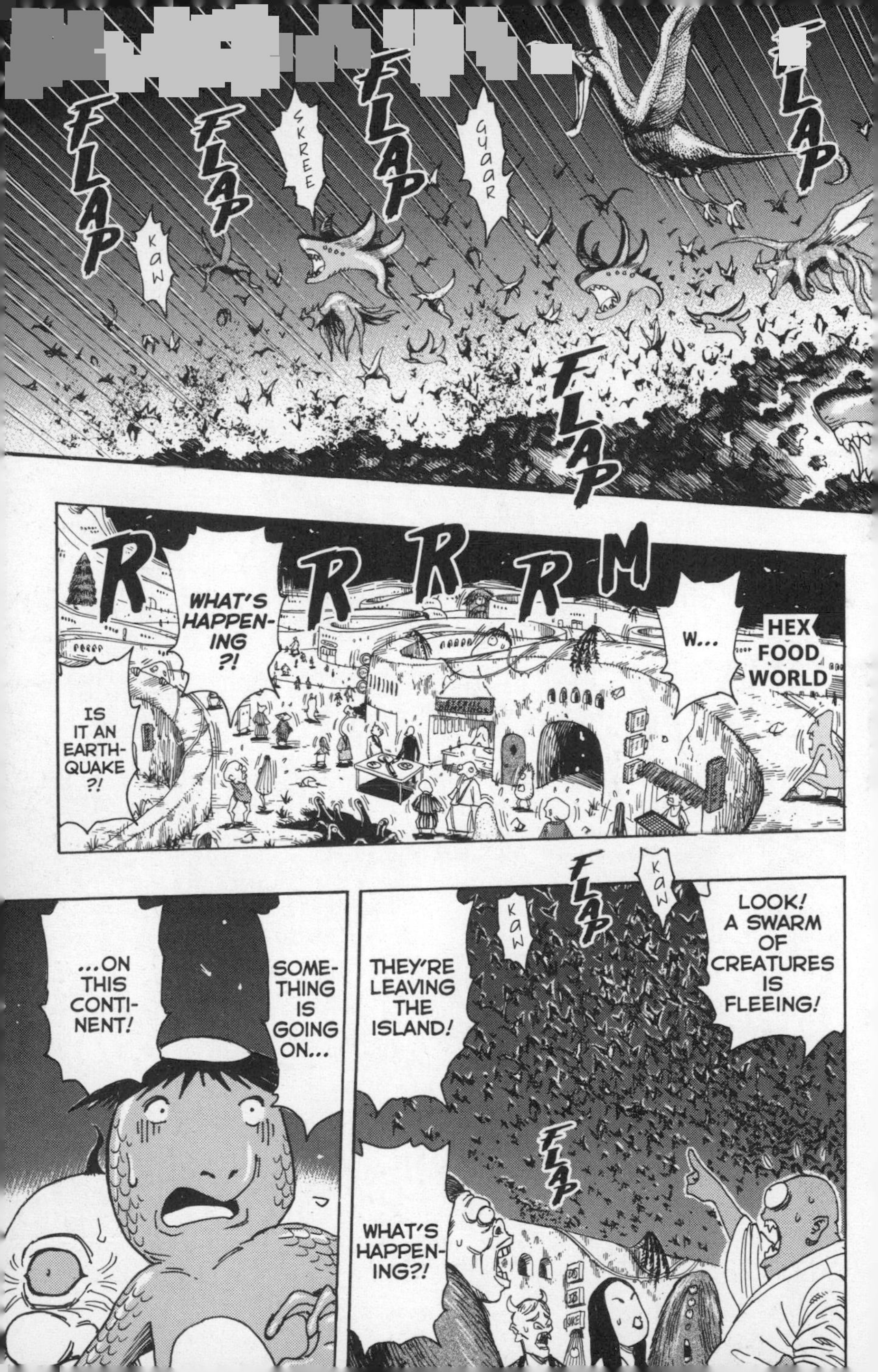
FLAP
GUAAR
FLAP
SKREE
FLAP
FLAP
KAW
FLAP
FLAP
RRRRM
HEX FOOD WORLD
W...
WHAT'S HAPPEN-ING?!
IS IT AN EARTH-QUAKE?!
LOOK! A SWARM OF CREATURES IS FLEEING!
KAW
FLAP
KAW
THEY'RE LEAVING THE ISLAND!
FLAP
WHAT'S HAPPEN-ING?!
SOME-THING IS GOING ON...
...ON THIS CONTI-NENT!

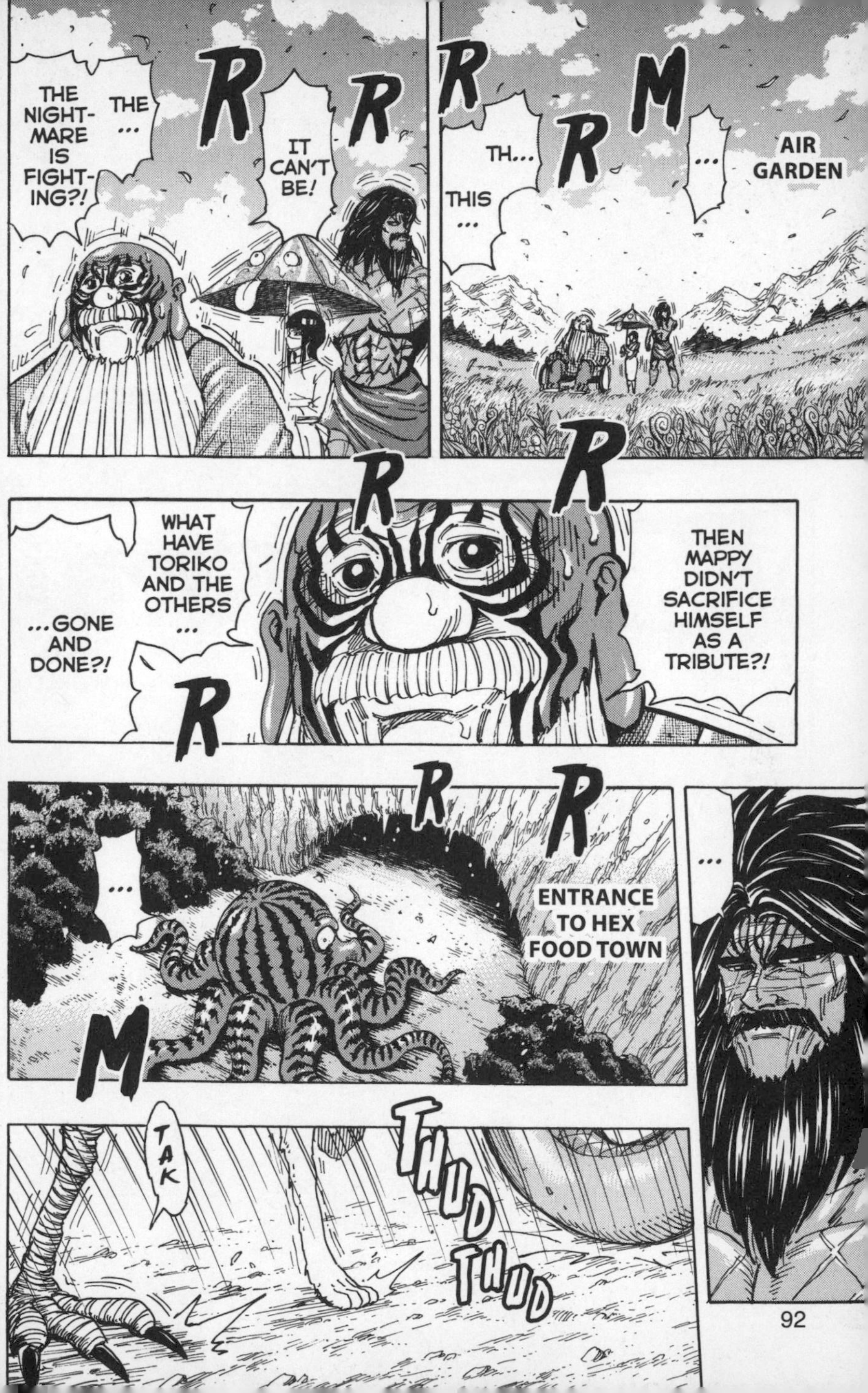
AIR GARDEN
...
TH...
THIS ...
RRRRRRM
IT CAN'T BE!
THE ...
THE NIGHTMARE IS FIGHTING?!
THEN MAPPY DIDN'T SACRIFICE HIMSELF AS A TRIBUTE?!
WHAT HAVE TORIKO AND THE OTHERS ...
...GONE AND DONE?!
RRR
...
RRM
ENTRANCE TO HEX FOOD TOWN
...
THUD THUD
TAK

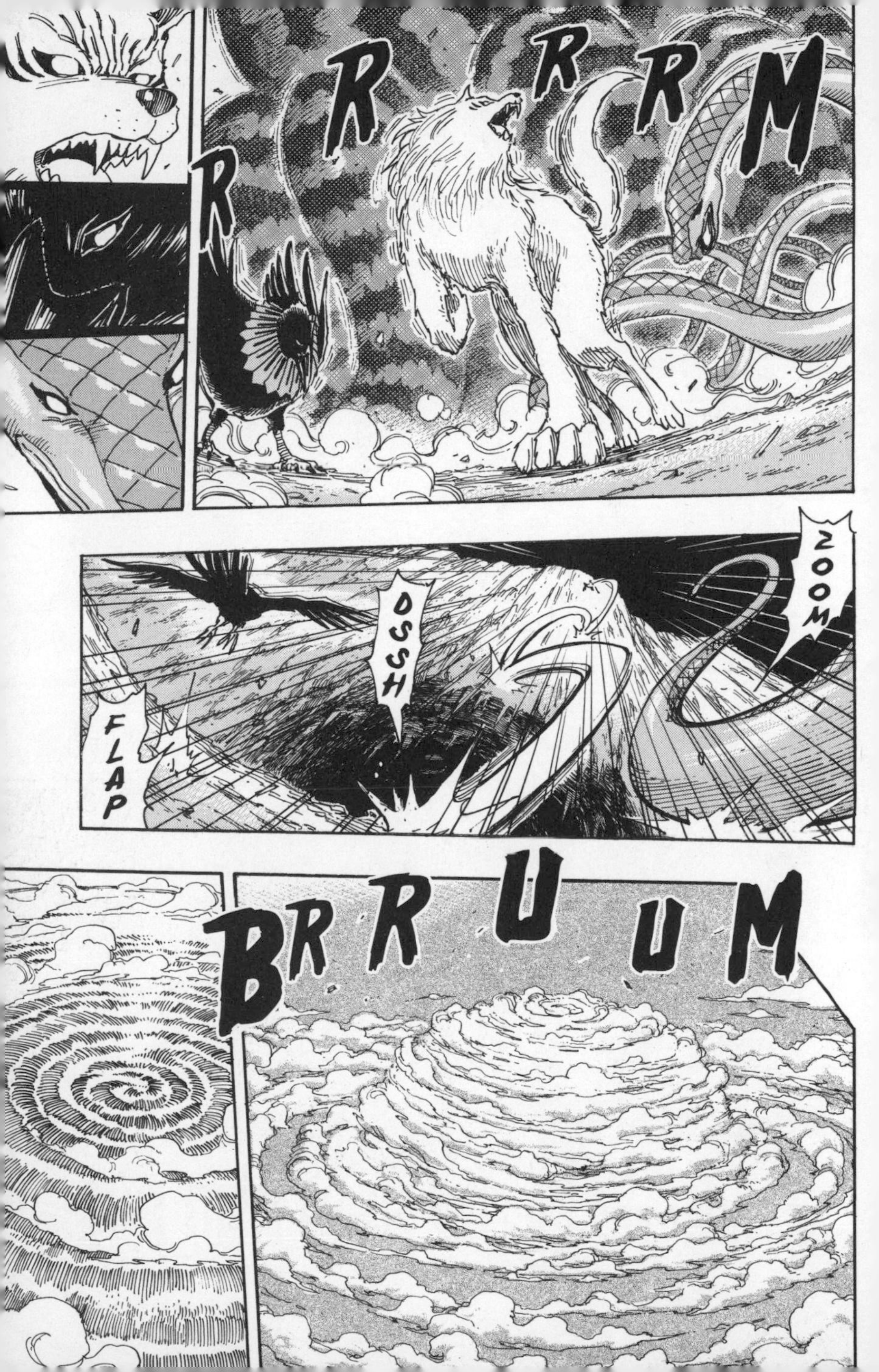
RRRRM
ZOOM
DSSH
FLAP
BRRUUM

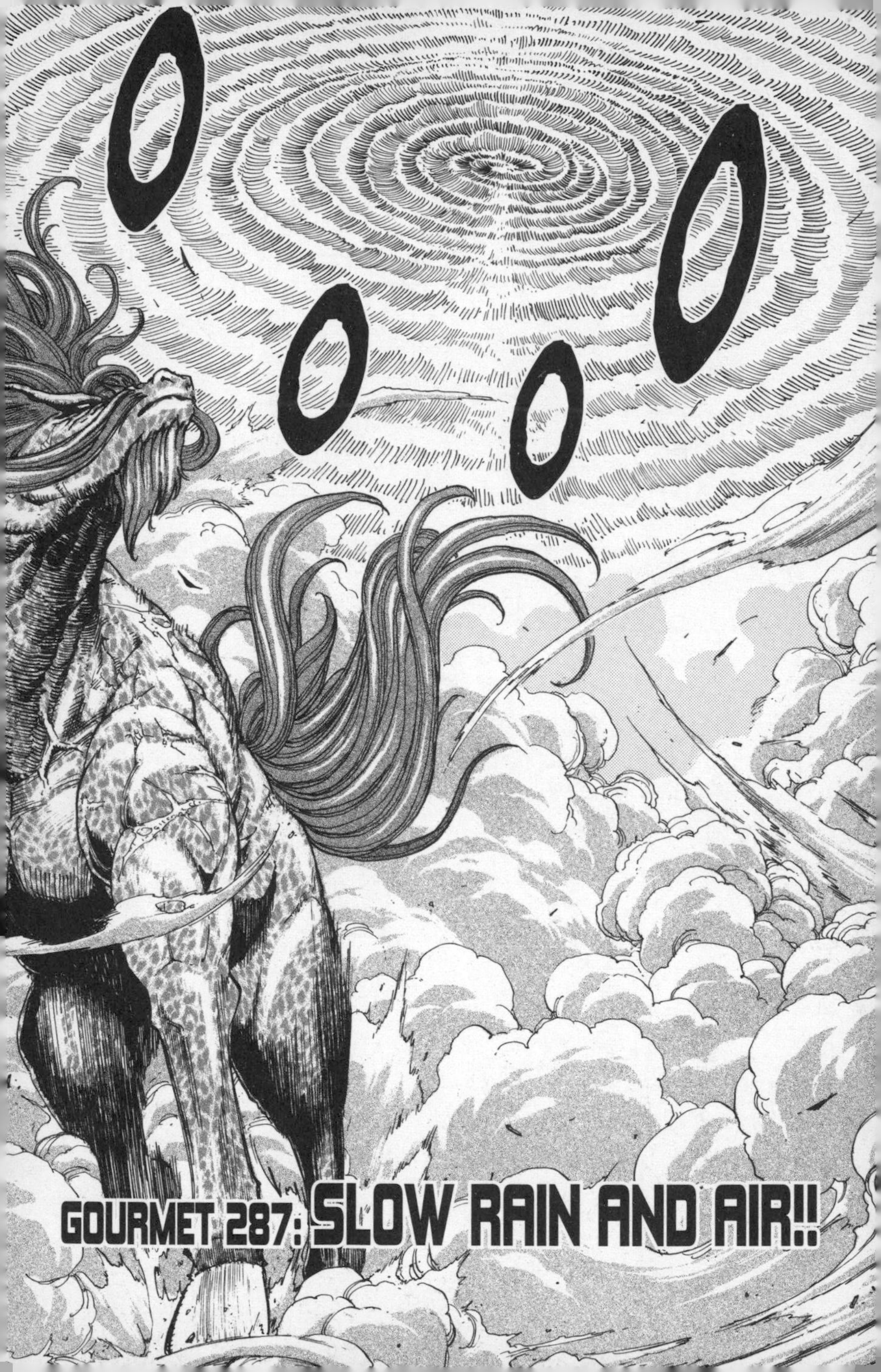
GOURMET 287: SLOW RAIN AND AIR!!

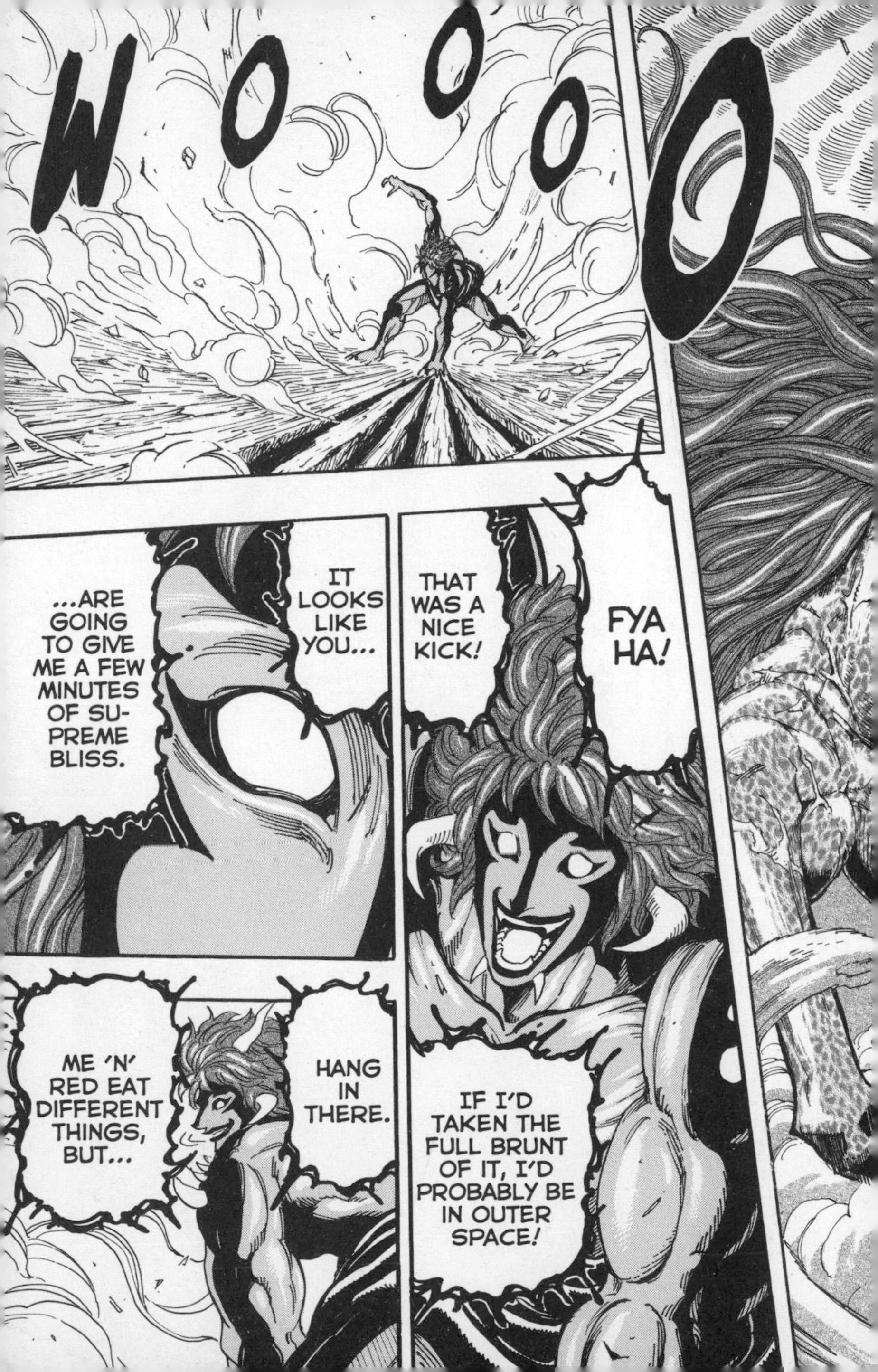
WOOOOO
FYA HA!
THAT WAS A NICE KICK!
IT LOOKS LIKE YOU...
...ARE GOING TO GIVE ME A FEW MINUTES OF SU-PREME BLISS.
IF I'D TAKEN THE FULL BRUNT OF IT, I'D PROBABLY BE IN OUTER SPACE!
HANG IN THERE.
ME 'N' RED EAT DIFFERENT THINGS, BUT...

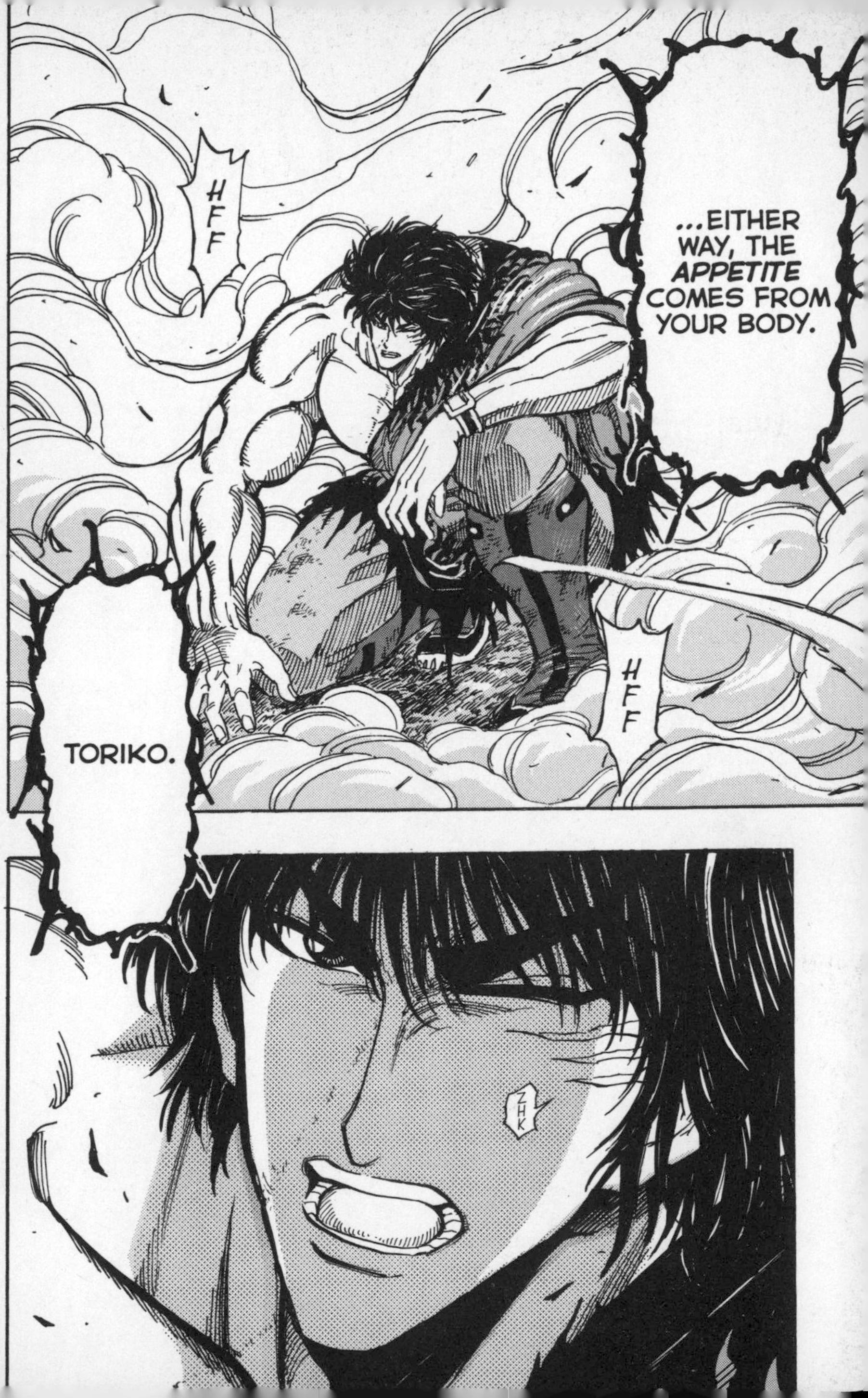
...EITHER WAY, THE *APPETITE* COMES FROM YOUR BODY.
HFF
HFF
TORIKO.
ZHK

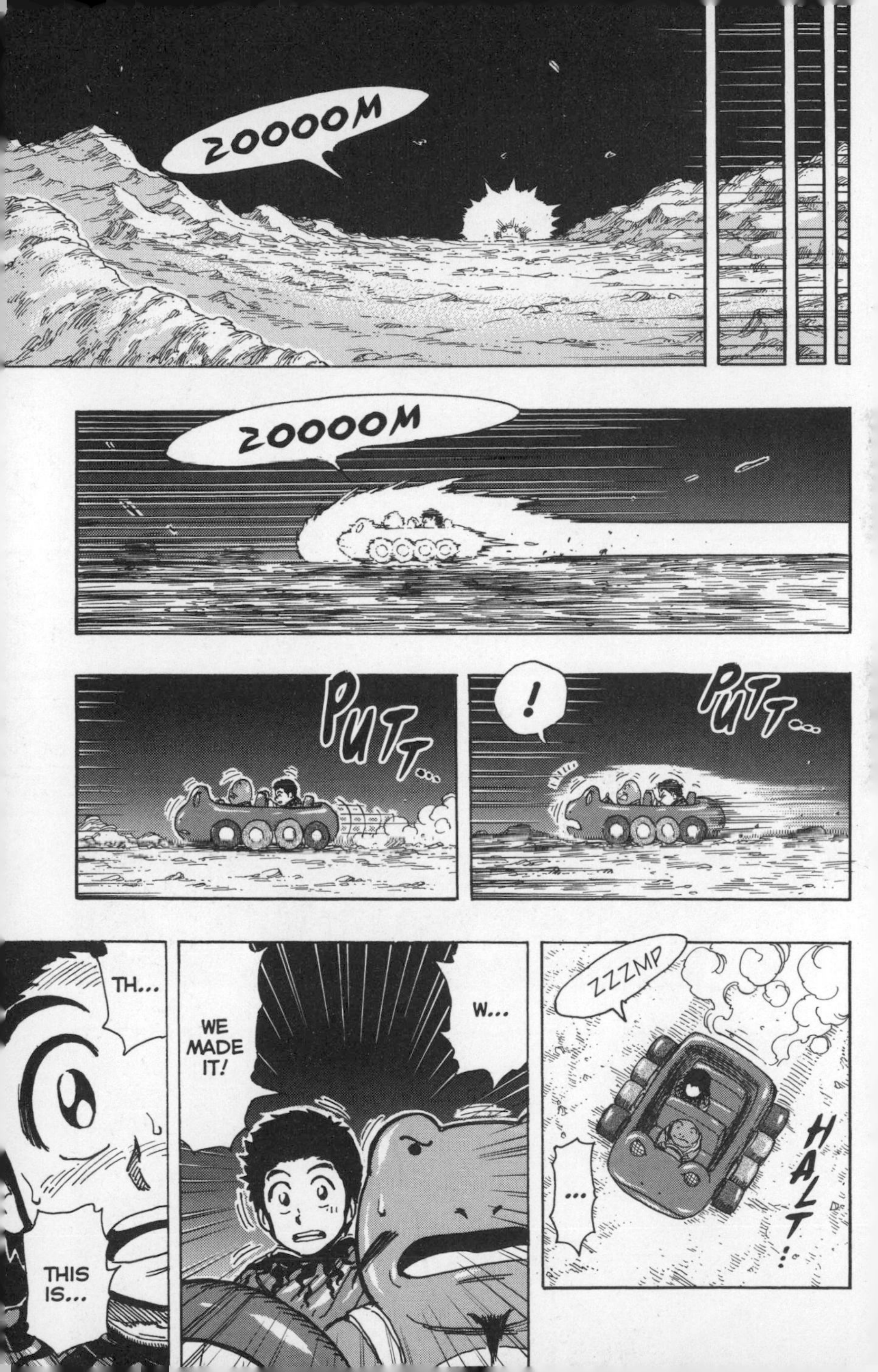
ZOOOOM
ZOOOOM
!
PUTT...
PUTT...
ZZZMP
HALT!!
...
W...
WE MADE IT!
TH...
THIS IS...

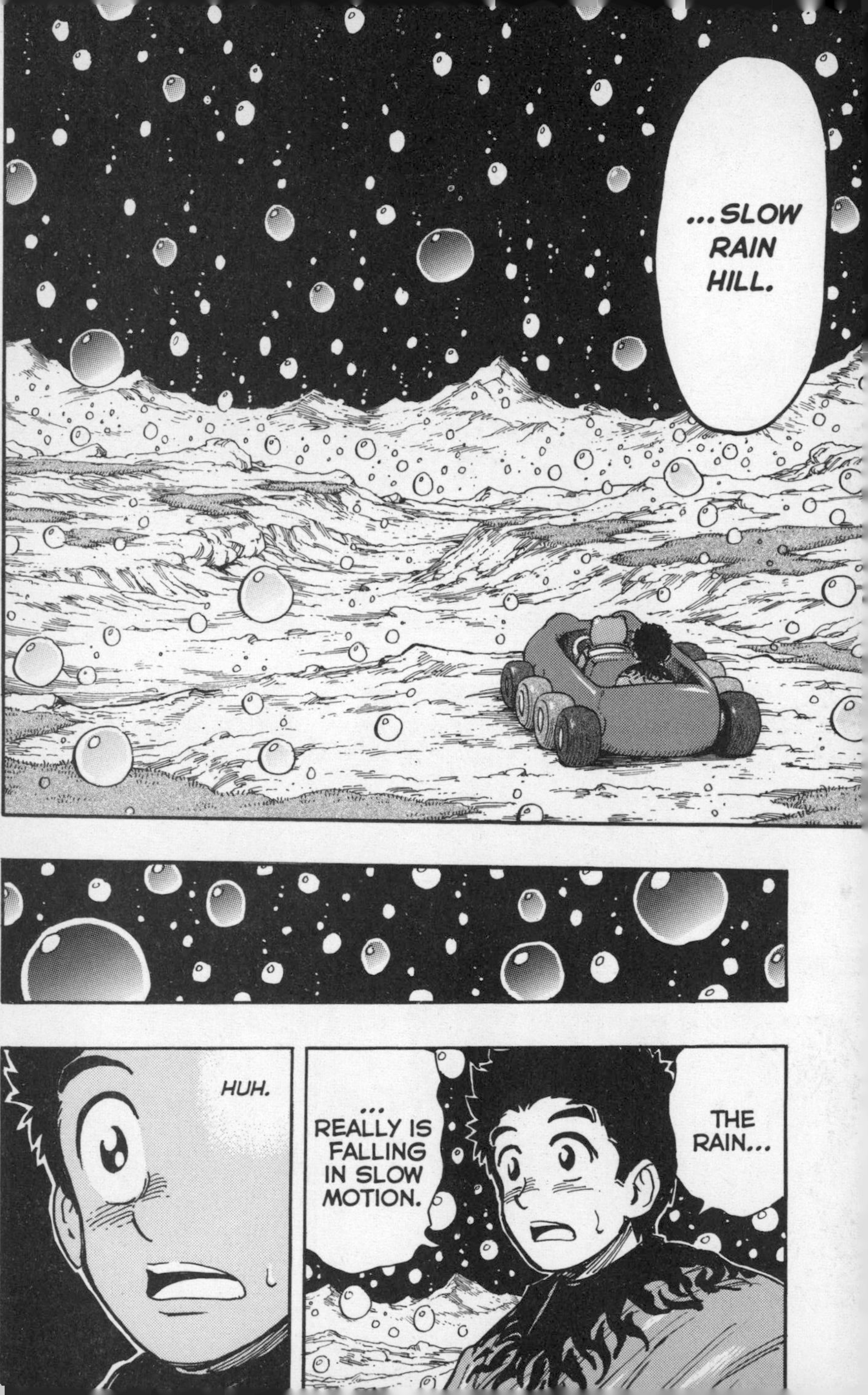
...SLOW RAIN HILL.
THE RAIN...
... REALLY IS FALLING IN SLOW MOTION.
HUH.

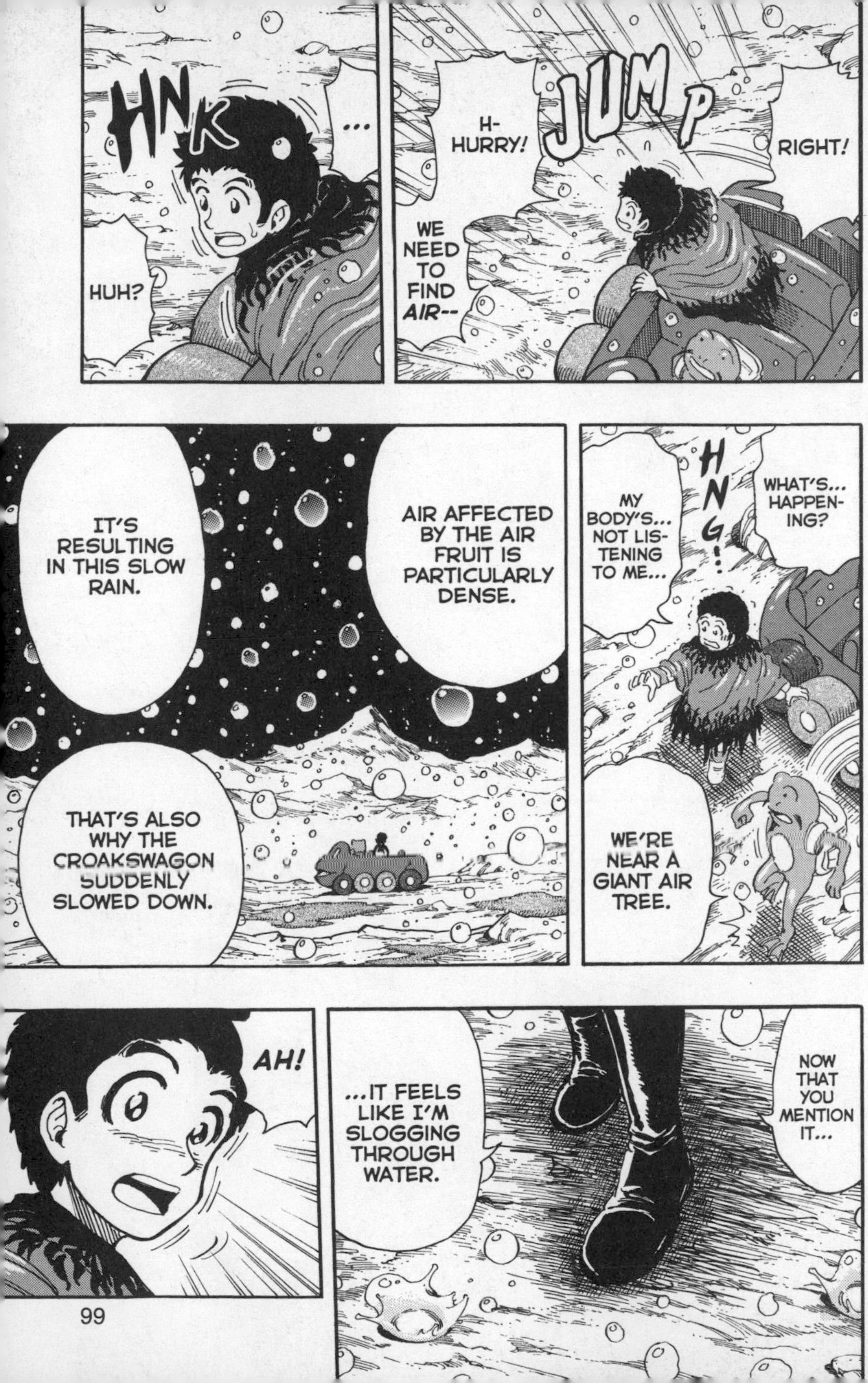
RIGHT!
JUMP
H- HURRY!
WE NEED TO FIND *AIR*--
...
HNK
HUH?
WHAT'S... HAPPENING?
HNG!
MY BODY'S... NOT LISTENING TO ME...
WE'RE NEAR A GIANT AIR TREE.
AIR AFFECTED BY THE AIR FRUIT IS PARTICULARLY DENSE.
IT'S RESULTING IN THIS SLOW RAIN.
THAT'S ALSO WHY THE CROAKSWAGON SUDDENLY SLOWED DOWN.
NOW THAT YOU MENTION IT...
...IT FEELS LIKE I'M SLOGGING THROUGH WATER.
AH!

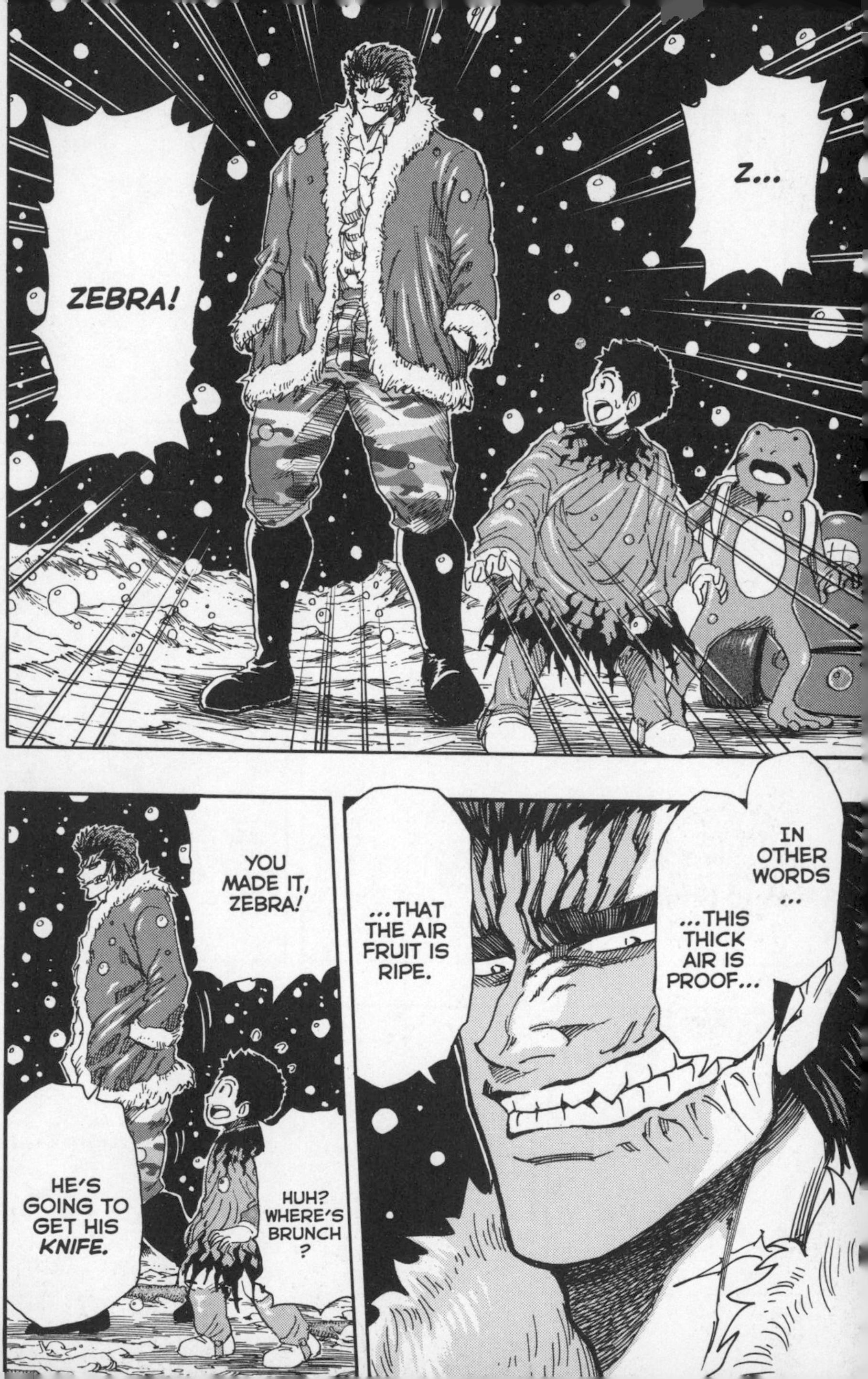
Z...
ZEBRA!
IN OTHER WORDS...
...THIS THICK AIR IS PROOF...
...THAT THE AIR FRUIT IS RIPE.
YOU MADE IT, ZEBRA!
HUH? WHERE'S BRUNCH?
HE'S GOING TO GET HIS KNIFE.

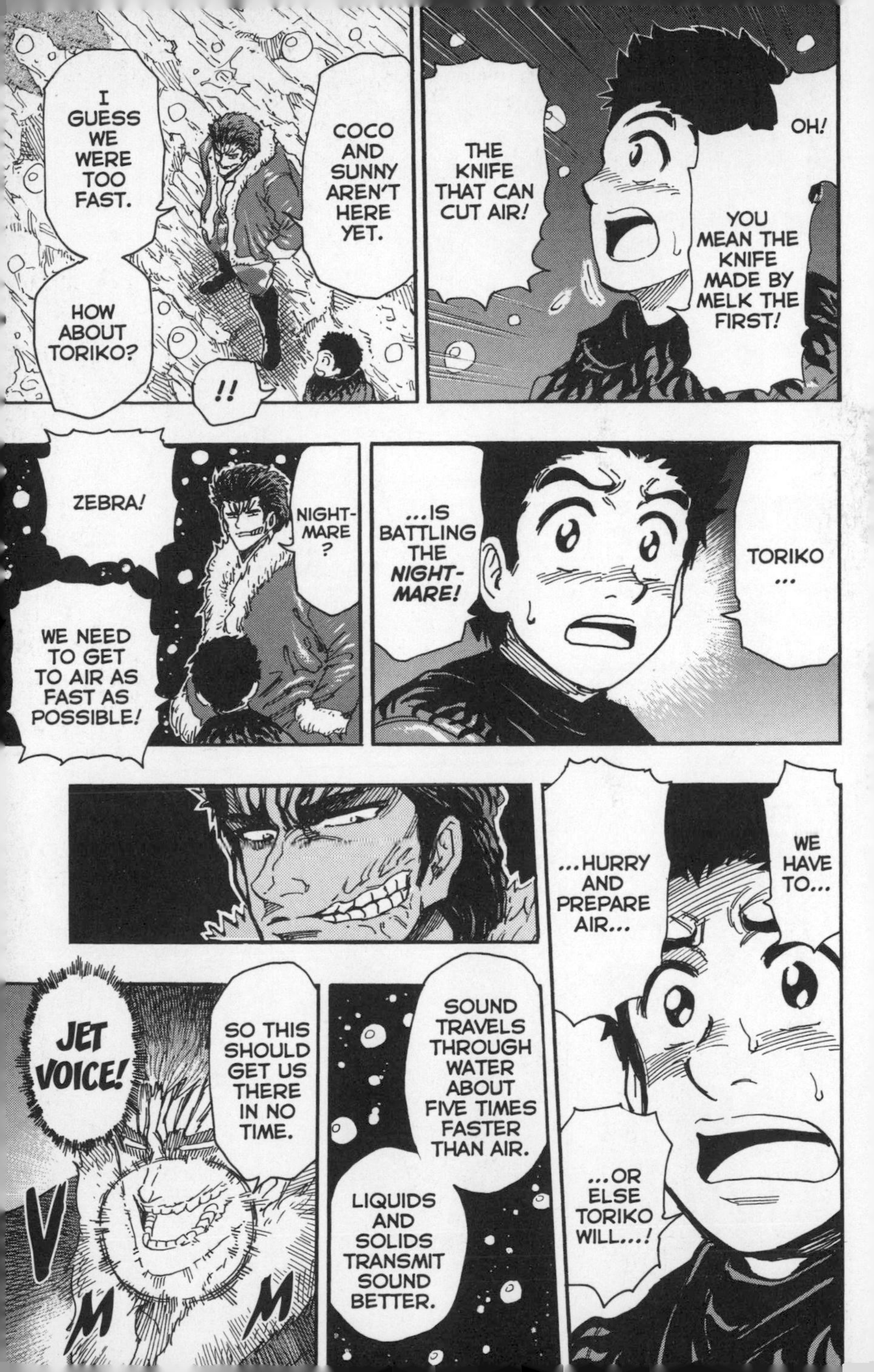
OH!
YOU MEAN THE KNIFE MADE BY MELK THE FIRST!
THE KNIFE THAT CAN CUT AIR!
COCO AND SUNNY AREN'T HERE YET.
I GUESS WE WERE TOO FAST.
HOW ABOUT TORIKO?
!!
TORIKO ...
...IS BATTLING THE NIGHTMARE!
NIGHTMARE?
ZEBRA!
WE NEED TO GET TO AIR AS FAST AS POSSIBLE!
WE HAVE TO...
...HURRY AND PREPARE AIR...
...OR ELSE TORIKO WILL...!
SOUND TRAVELS THROUGH WATER ABOUT FIVE TIMES FASTER THAN AIR.
LIQUIDS AND SOLIDS TRANSMIT SOUND BETTER.
SO THIS SHOULD GET US THERE IN NO TIME.
JET VOICE!
VMM

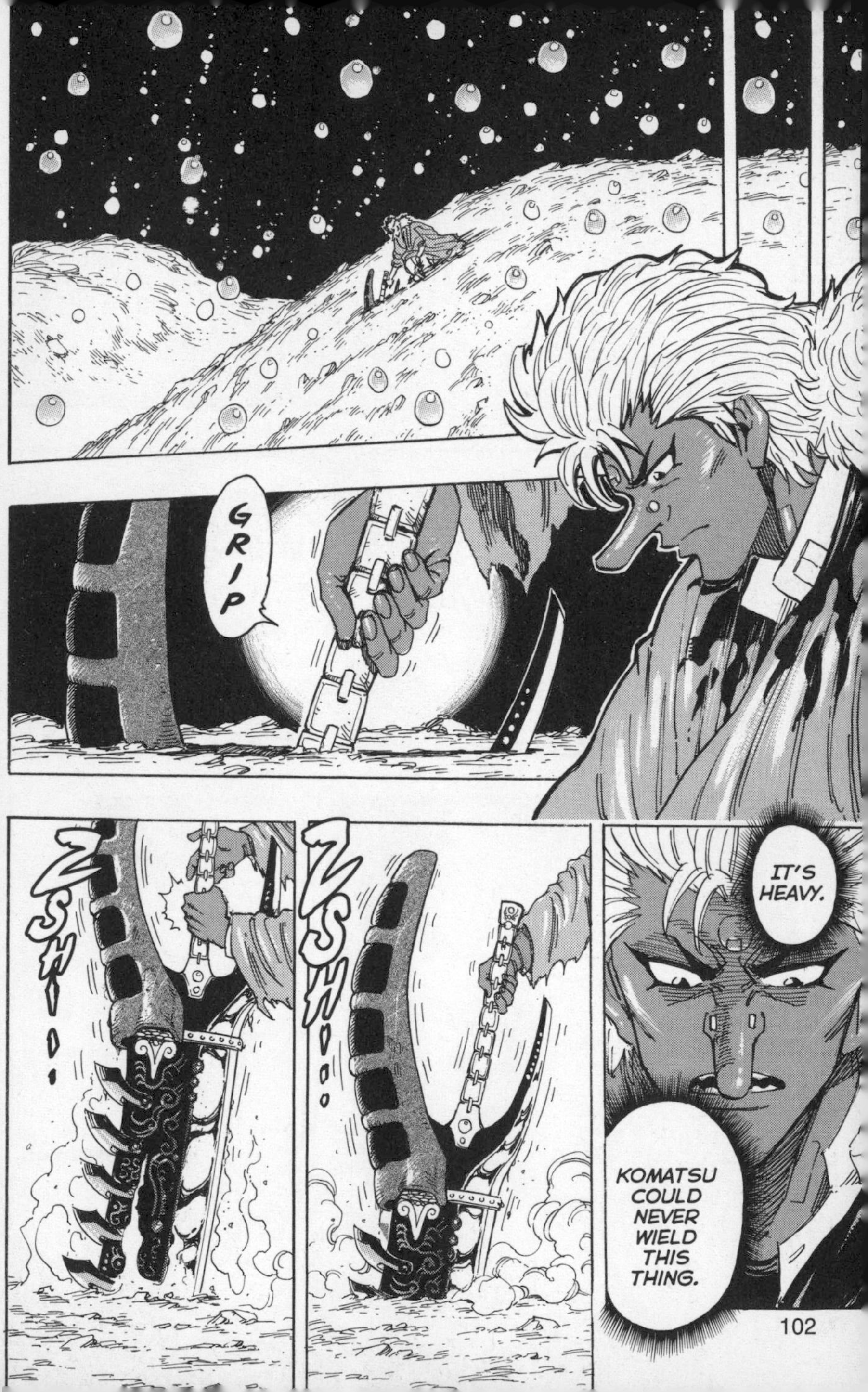
GRIP
IT'S HEAVY.
KOMATSU COULD NEVER WIELD THIS THING.
ZSHOOO
ZSH!!

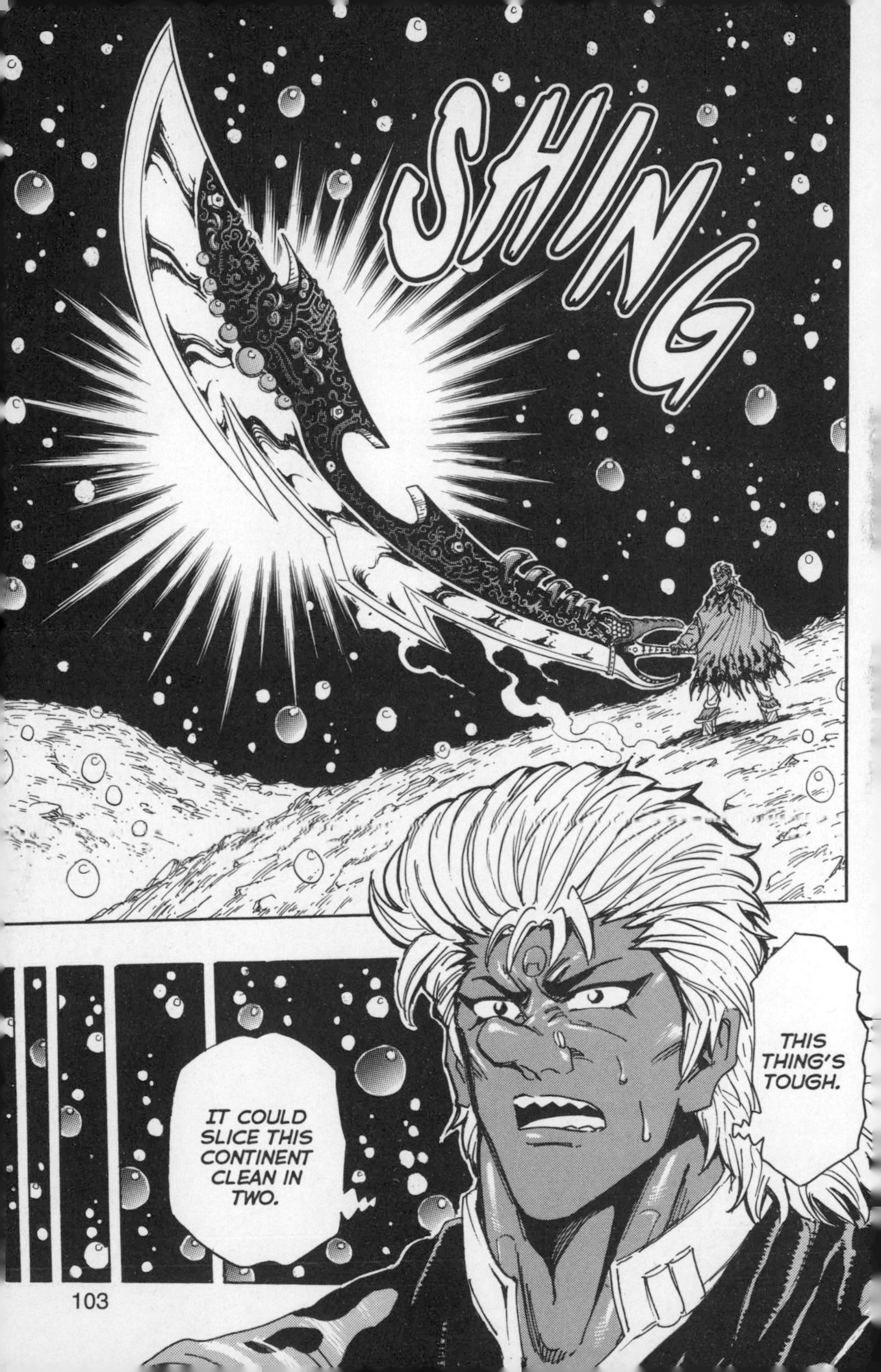
SHING
THIS THING'S TOUGH.
IT COULD SLICE THIS CONTINENT CLEAN IN TWO.

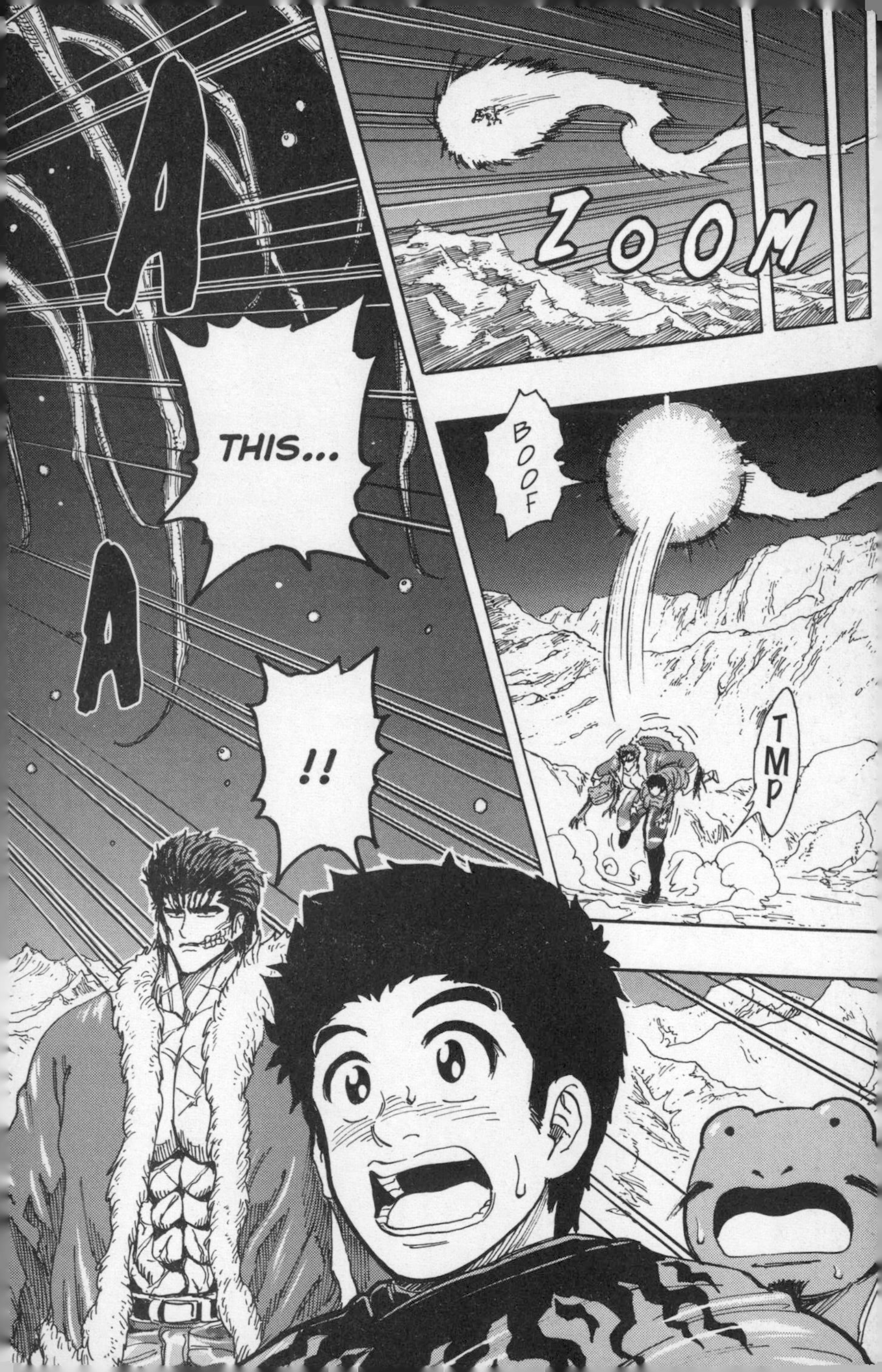
ZOOM
BOOF
TMP
A
A
THIS...
!!

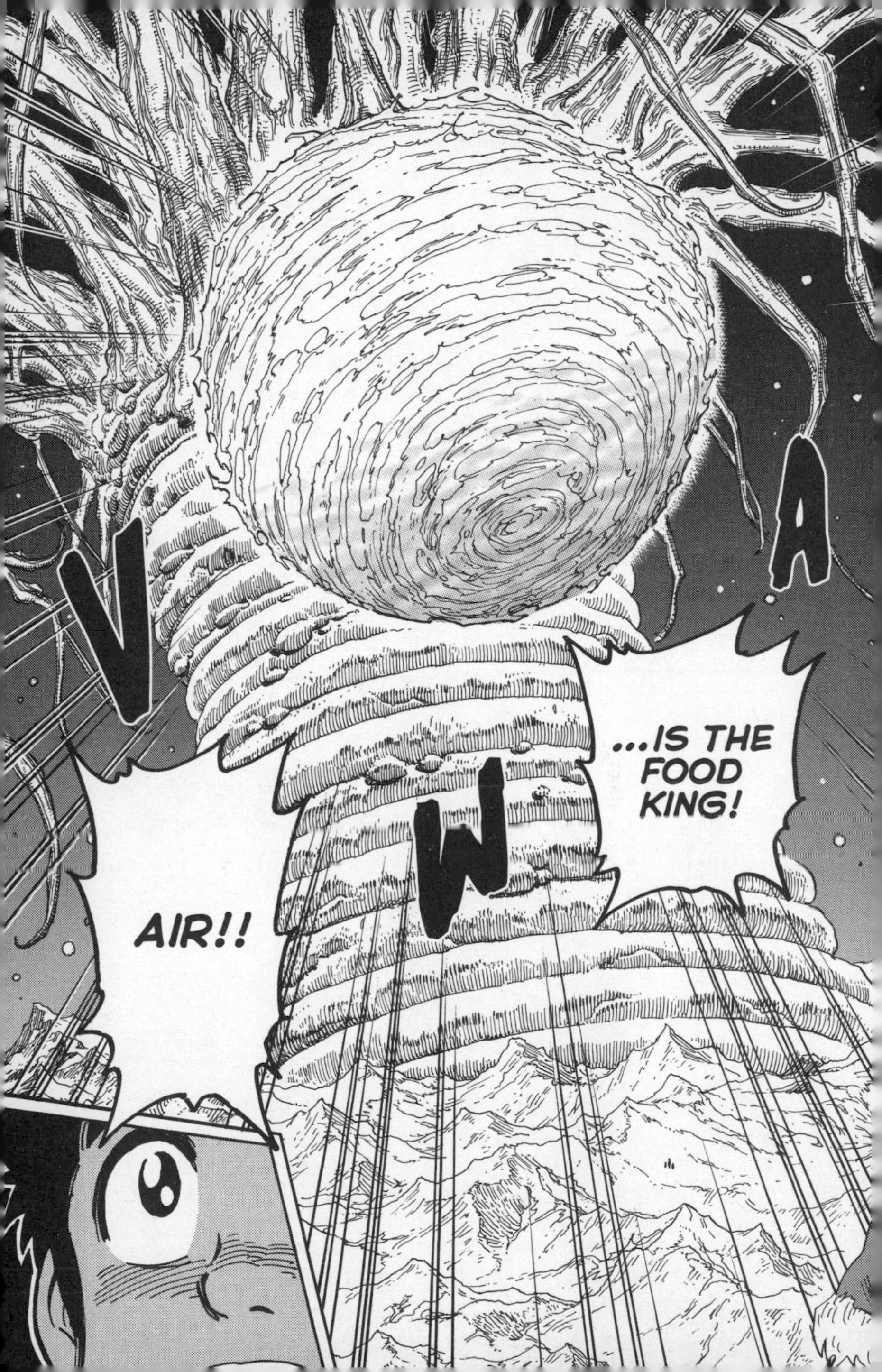
A
...IS THE FOOD KING!
W
V
AIR!!

TORIKO

GOURMET CHECKLIST

Vol. 313

❖ FOUR-BEASTS: MOUNT TURTLE ❖
(VOLCANO CRUSTACEAN BEAST)

CAPTURE LEVEL: 150
HABITAT: GOURMET WORLD
SIZE: 1,200 M
HEIGHT: 1,500 M
WEIGHT: 500,800,000 TONS
PRICE: UNKNOWN

SCALE

AN EXTREMITY OF THE MONSTROUS FOUR-BEASTS WHO EMERGES FROM THE
GOURMET WORLD EVERY SEVERAL YEARS. IT CHOOSES THE TIME WHEN HUMANITY IS
AT ITS PEAK AND THEN FEASTS ON THE WORLD. THIS THING IS MONSTROUS! THE SHELL
ON ITS BACK IS AN ACTIVE VOLCANO SPEWING MAGMA. IT'S LITERALLY THE MOST
DANGEROUS TORTOISE EVER! ITS SHELL IS SUPER HARD, SO EVEN IF THE MAGMA
DOESN'T GET YOU FIRST, BREAKING ITS DEFENSES IS NEAR IMPOSSIBLE. ZEBRA'S
BEAT PUNCH DESTROYED THIS MONSTER, BUT IT'S POSSIBLY THE STRONGEST OF THE
FOUR-BEASTS.

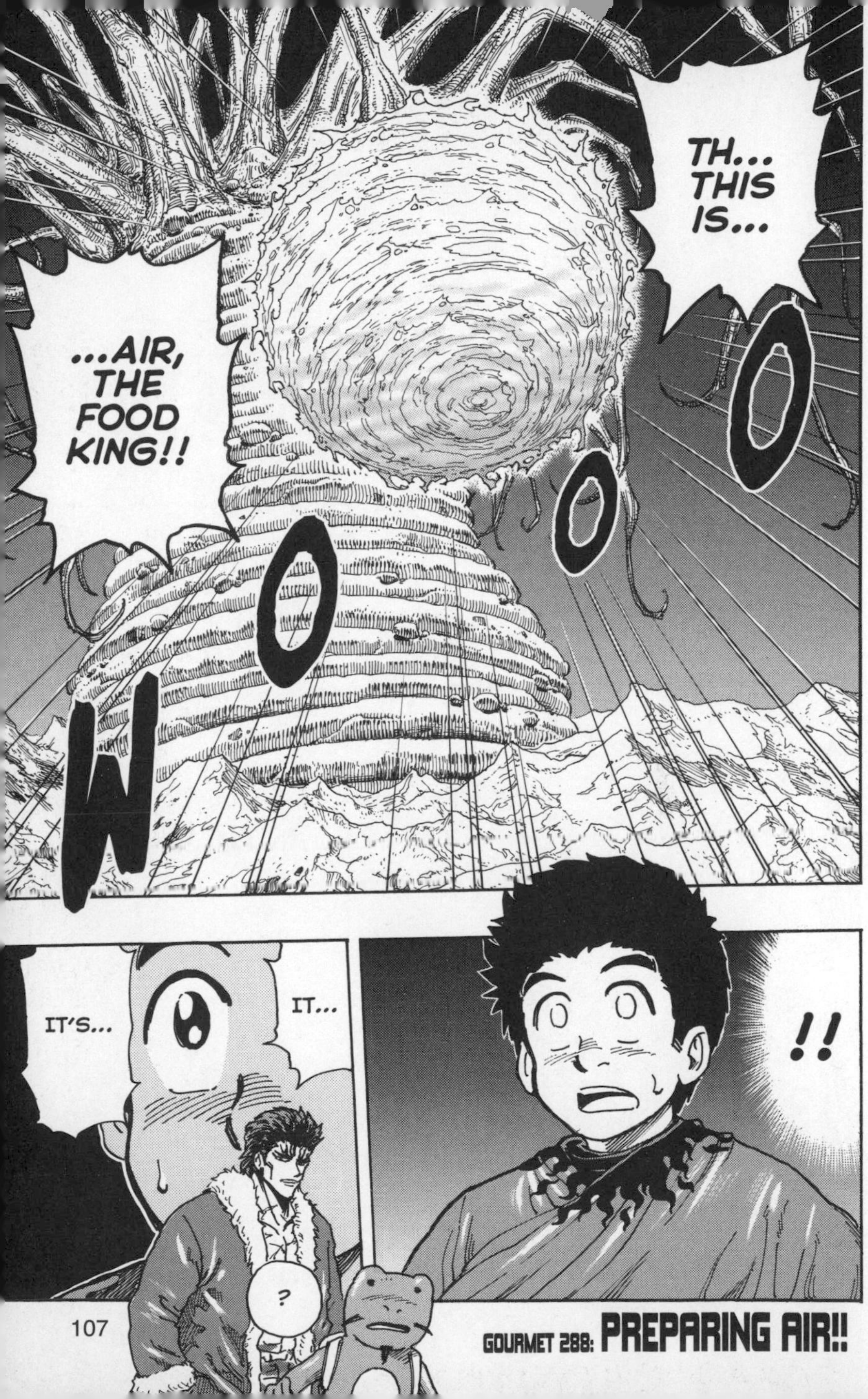
TH... THIS IS...
...AIR, THE FOOD KING!!
WOOO
!!
IT...
IT'S...
?

GOURMET 288: PREPARING AIR!!

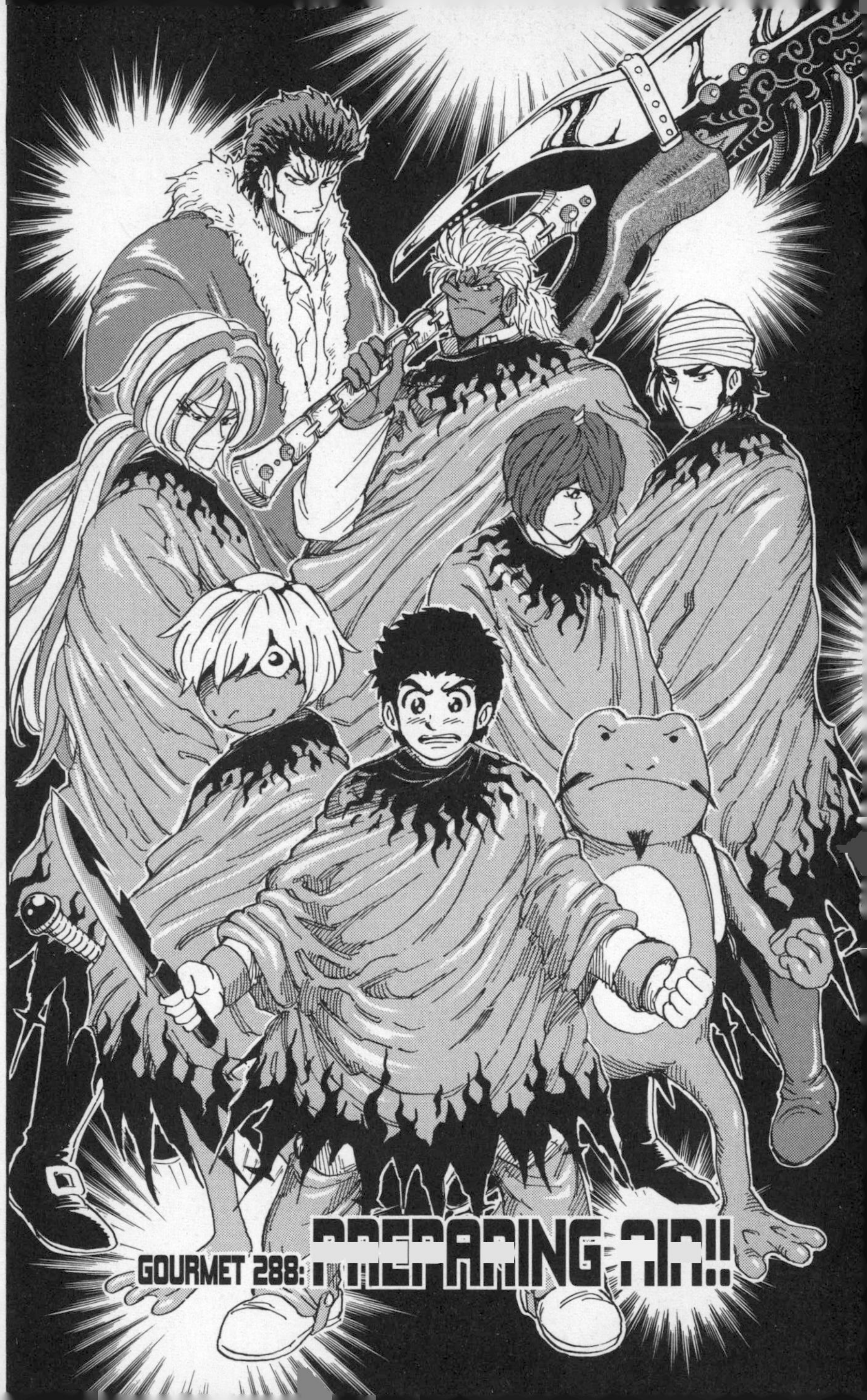
GOURMET 288: PREPARING AIR!!

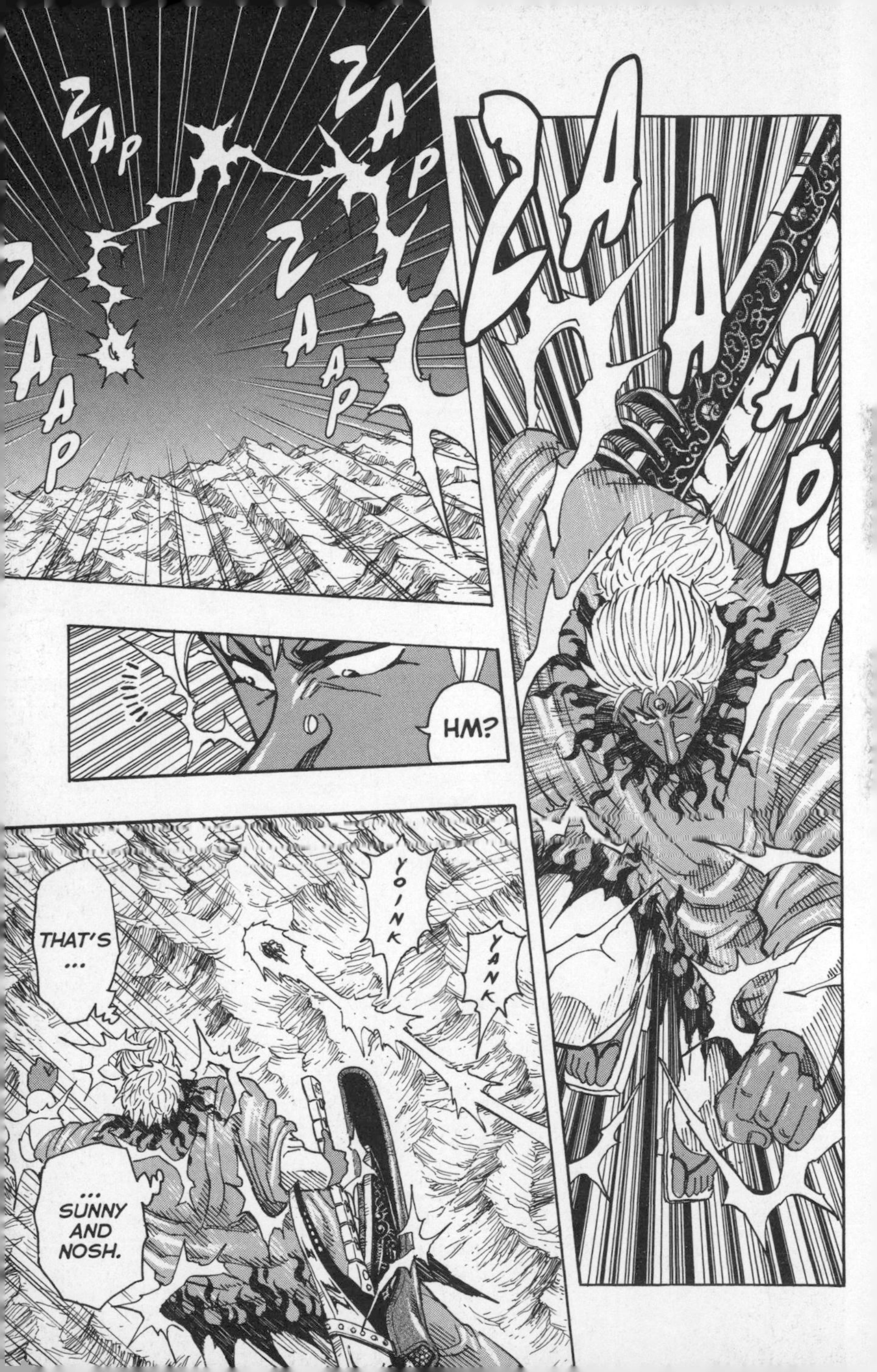
ZAAAP
ZAP
ZAP
ZAAP
ZAAP
HM?
YOINK
YANK
THAT'S ...
... SUNNY AND NOSH.

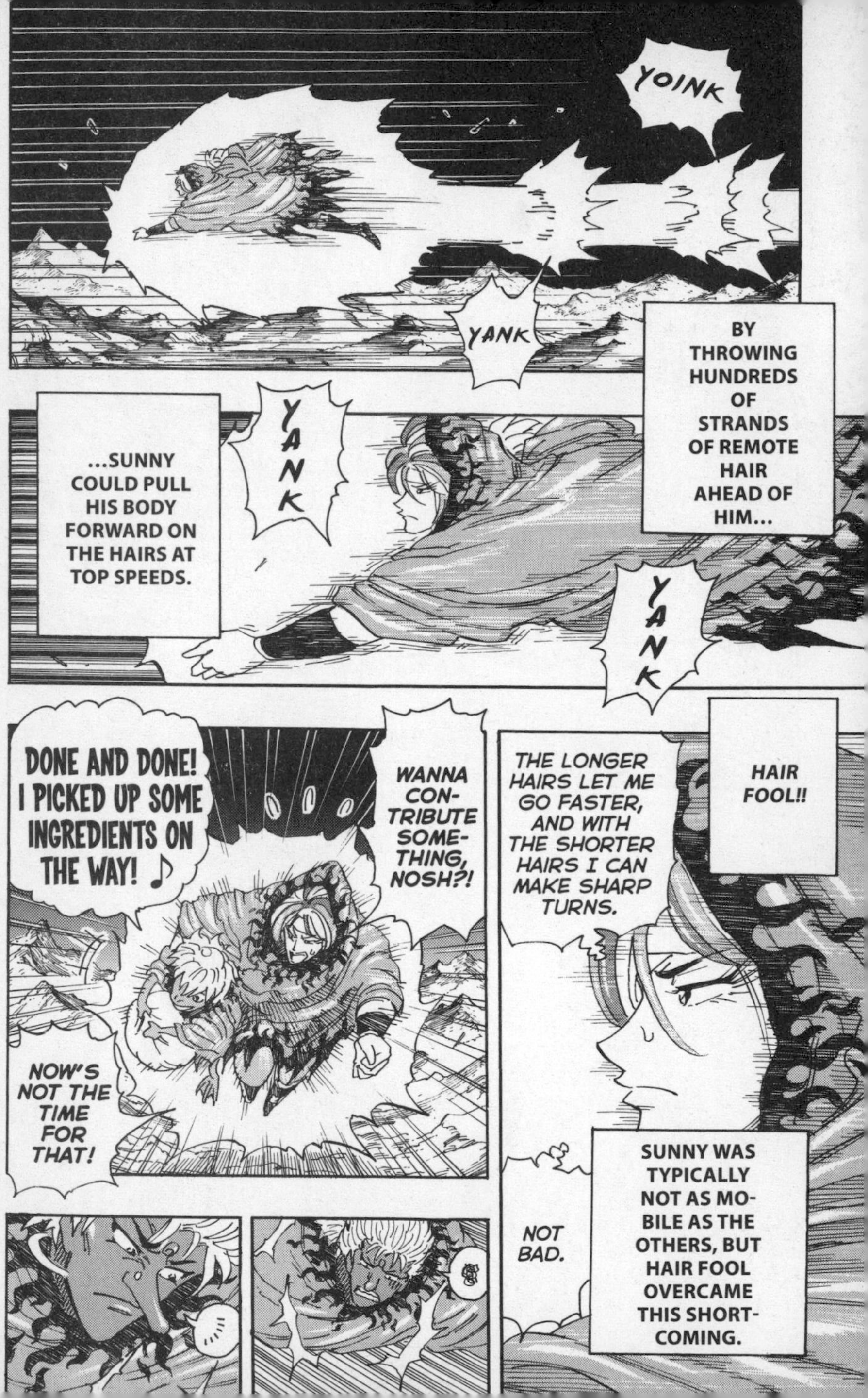
YOINK
YANK
BY THROWING HUNDREDS OF STRANDS OF REMOTE HAIR AHEAD OF HIM...
YANK
...SUNNY COULD PULL HIS BODY FORWARD ON THE HAIRS AT TOP SPEEDS.
YANK
HAIR FOOL!!
THE LONGER HAIRS LET ME GO FASTER, AND WITH THE SHORTER HAIRS I CAN MAKE SHARP TURNS.
NOT BAD.
SUNNY WAS TYPICALLY NOT AS MOBILE AS THE OTHERS, BUT HAIR FOOL OVERCAME THIS SHORTCOMING.
WANNA CONTRIBUTE SOMETHING, NOSH?!
DONE AND DONE! I PICKED UP SOME INGREDIENTS ON THE WAY! ♪
NOW'S NOT THE TIME FOR THAT!

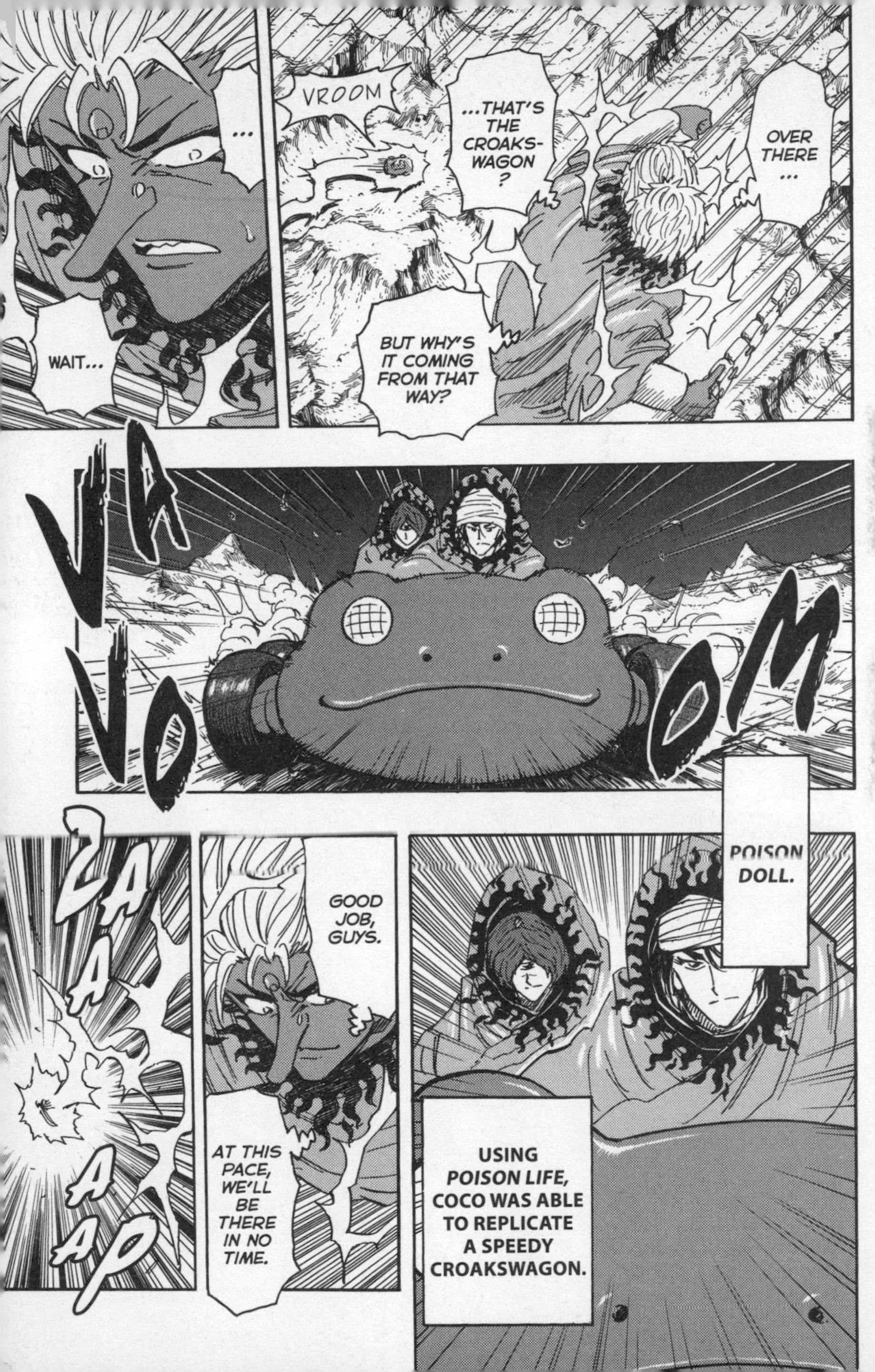
OVER THERE...
...THAT'S THE CROAKS-WAGON?
VROOM
BUT WHY'S IT COMING FROM THAT WAY?
...
WAIT...
VAVOOM
POISON DOLL.
USING POISON LIFE, COCO WAS ABLE TO REPLICATE A SPEEDY CROAKSWAGON.
GOOD JOB, GUYS.
AT THIS PACE, WE'LL BE THERE IN NO TIME.
ZAAAAP

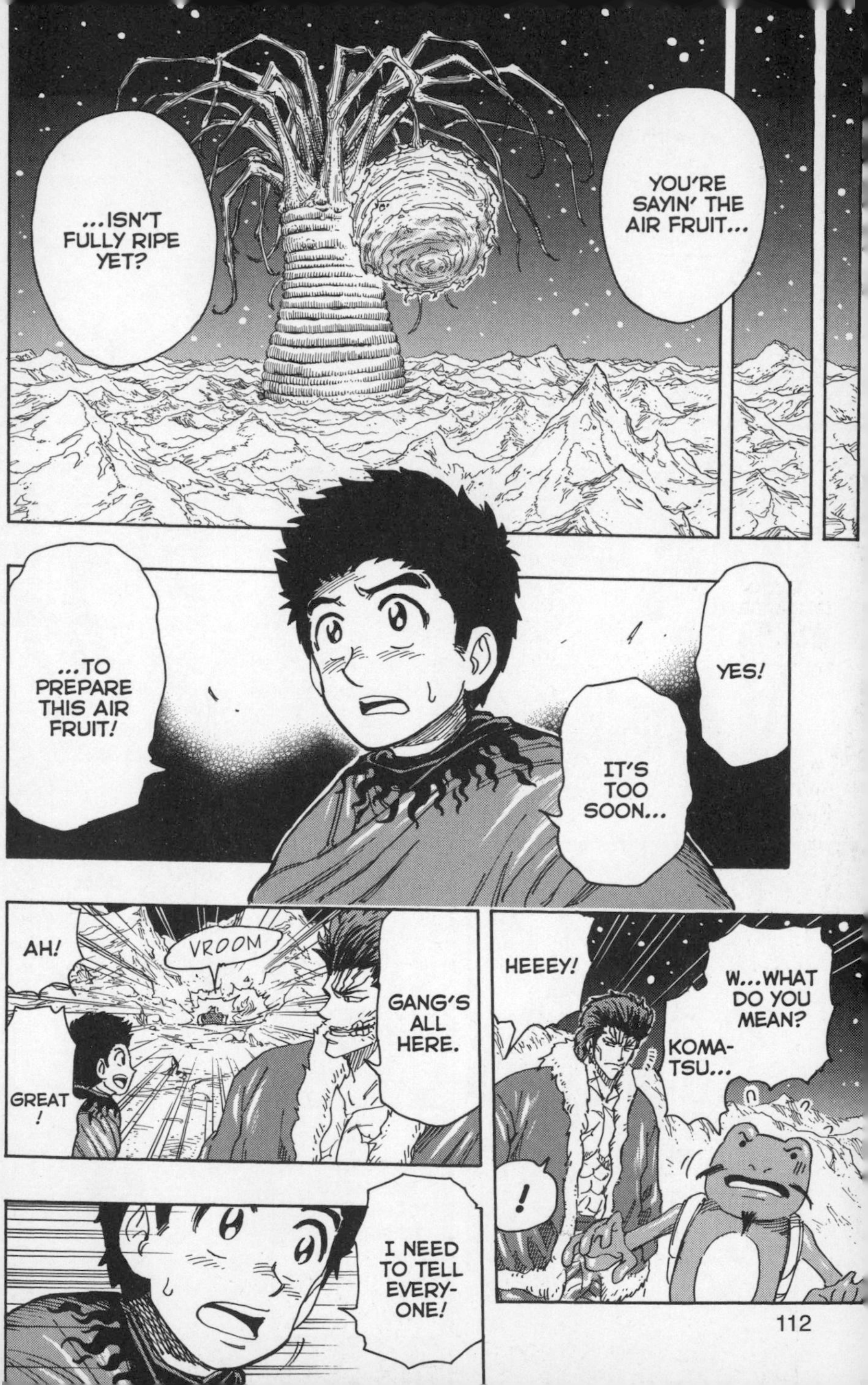
YOU'RE SAYIN' THE AIR FRUIT...
...ISN'T FULLY RIPE YET?
YES!
IT'S TOO SOON...
...TO PREPARE THIS AIR FRUIT!
W...WHAT DO YOU MEAN?
HEEEY!
KOMA-TSU...
!
GANG'S ALL HERE.
VROOM
AH!
GREAT!
I NEED TO TELL EVERY-ONE!

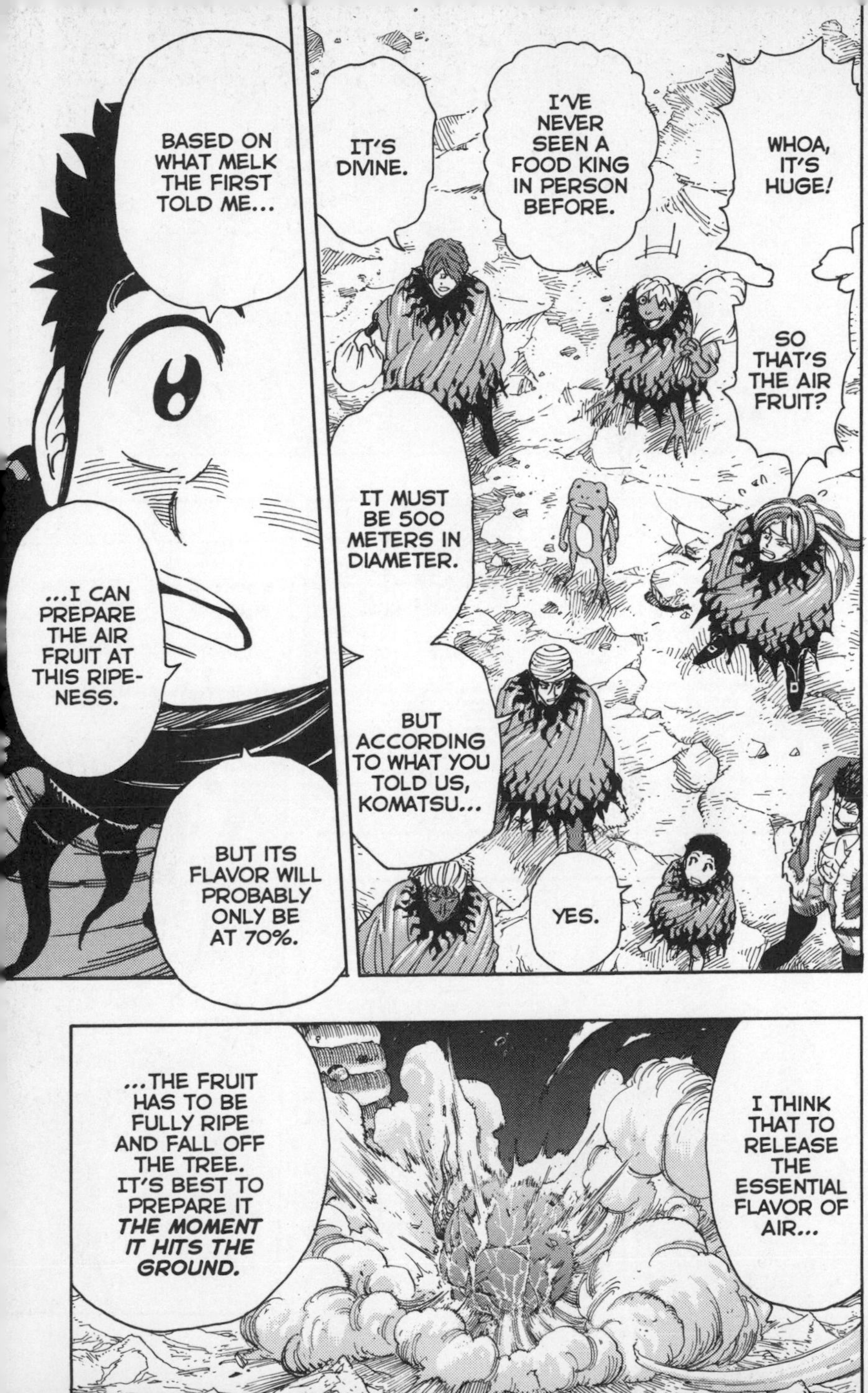
WHOA, IT'S HUGE!
SO THAT'S THE AIR FRUIT?
I'VE NEVER SEEN A FOOD KING IN PERSON BEFORE.
IT'S DIVINE.
IT MUST BE 500 METERS IN DIAMETER.
BUT ACCORDING TO WHAT YOU TOLD US, KOMATSU...
YES.
BASED ON WHAT MELK THE FIRST TOLD ME...
...I CAN PREPARE THE AIR FRUIT AT THIS RIPENESS.
BUT ITS FLAVOR WILL PROBABLY ONLY BE AT 70%.
I THINK THAT TO RELEASE THE ESSENTIAL FLAVOR OF AIR...
...THE FRUIT HAS TO BE FULLY RIPE AND FALL OFF THE TREE. IT'S BEST TO PREPARE IT *THE MOMENT IT HITS THE GROUND.*

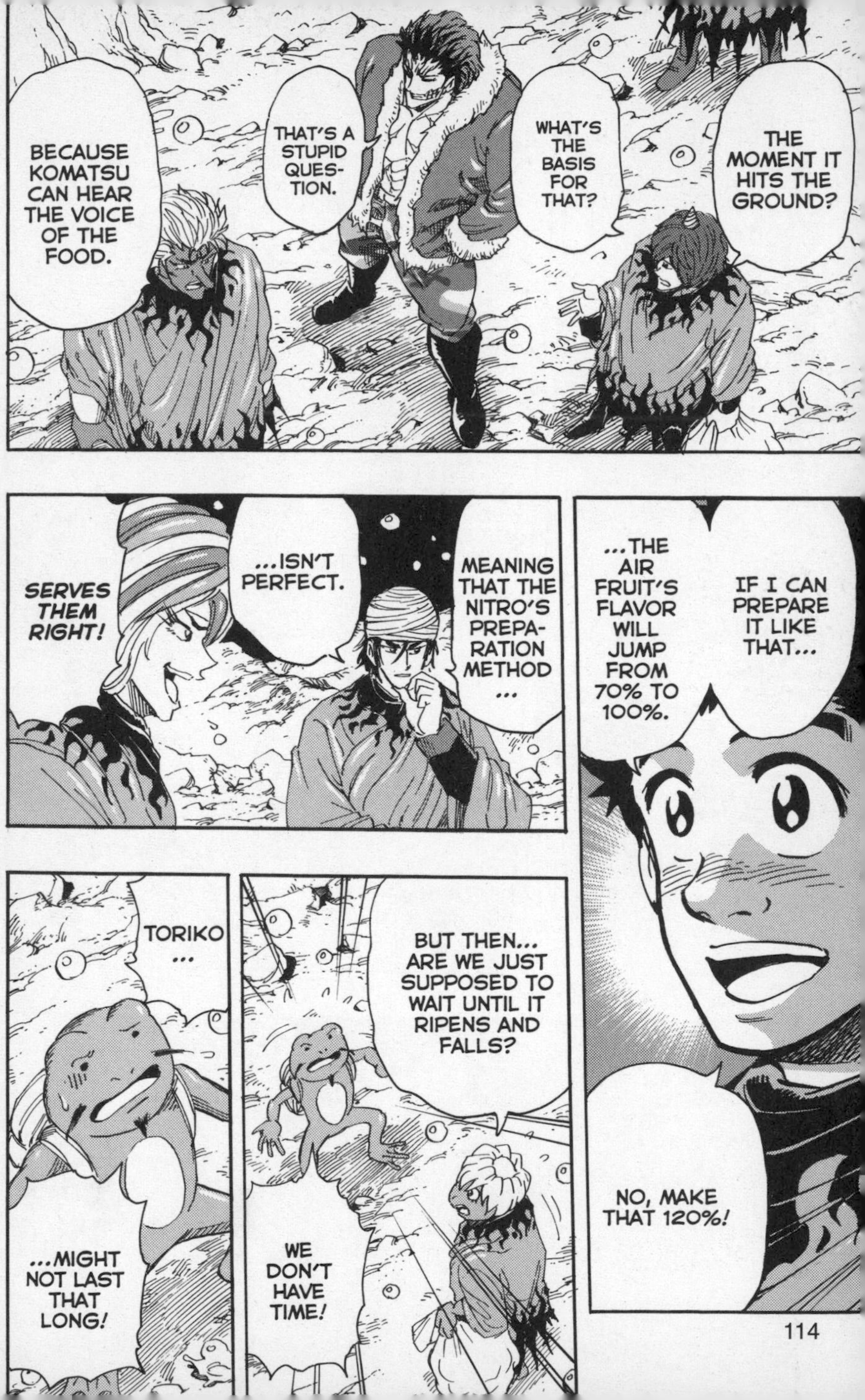
THE MOMENT IT HITS THE GROUND?
WHAT'S THE BASIS FOR THAT?
THAT'S A STUPID QUESTION.
BECAUSE KOMATSU CAN HEAR THE VOICE OF THE FOOD.
IF I CAN PREPARE IT LIKE THAT...
...THE AIR FRUIT'S FLAVOR WILL JUMP FROM 70% TO 100%.
NO, MAKE THAT 120%!
MEANING THAT THE NITRO'S PREPARATION METHOD...
...ISN'T PERFECT.
SERVES THEM RIGHT!
BUT THEN... ARE WE JUST SUPPOSED TO WAIT UNTIL IT RIPENS AND FALLS?
WE DON'T HAVE TIME!
TORIKO...
...MIGHT NOT LAST THAT LONG!

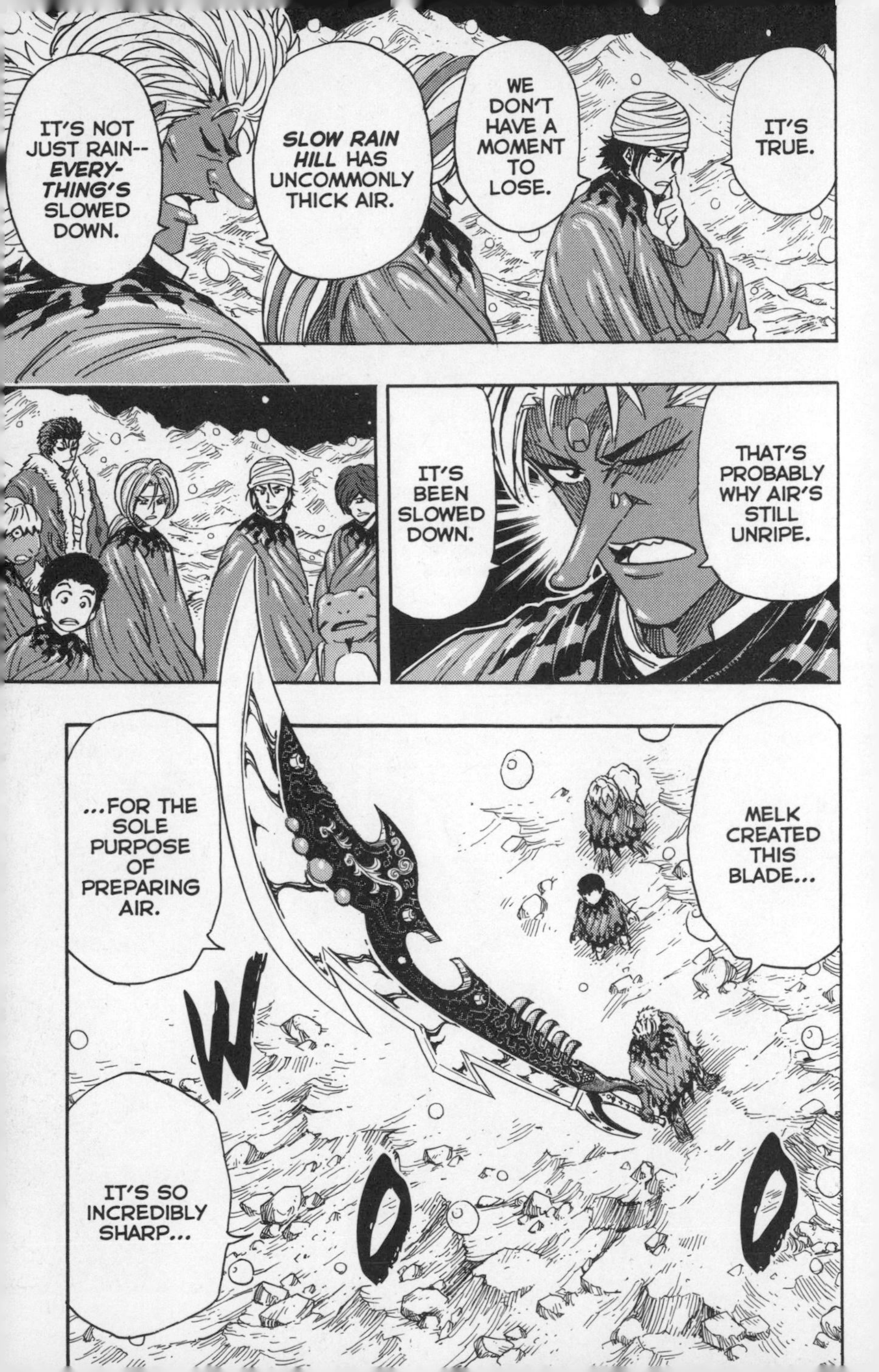
IT'S TRUE.
WE DON'T HAVE A MOMENT TO LOSE.
SLOW RAIN HILL HAS UNCOMMONLY THICK AIR.
IT'S NOT JUST RAIN-- *EVERYTHING'S* SLOWED DOWN.
THAT'S PROBABLY WHY AIR'S STILL UNRIPE.
IT'S BEEN SLOWED DOWN.
MELK CREATED THIS BLADE...
...FOR THE SOLE PURPOSE OF PREPARING AIR.
IT'S SO INCREDIBLY SHARP...

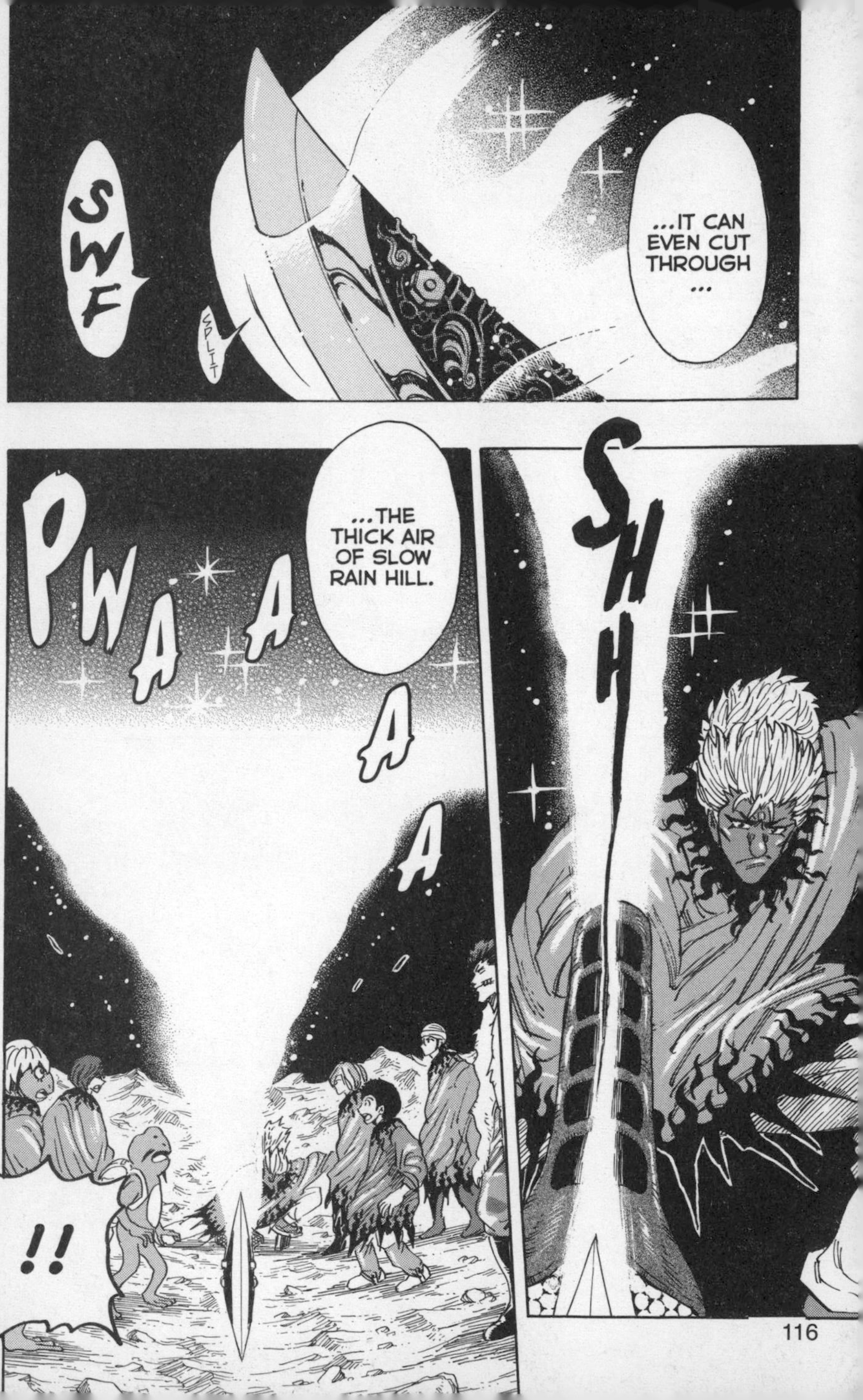
...IT CAN EVEN CUT THROUGH ...
SPLIT
SWF
SHHH
...THE THICK AIR OF SLOW RAIN HILL.
PWAAAA
!!

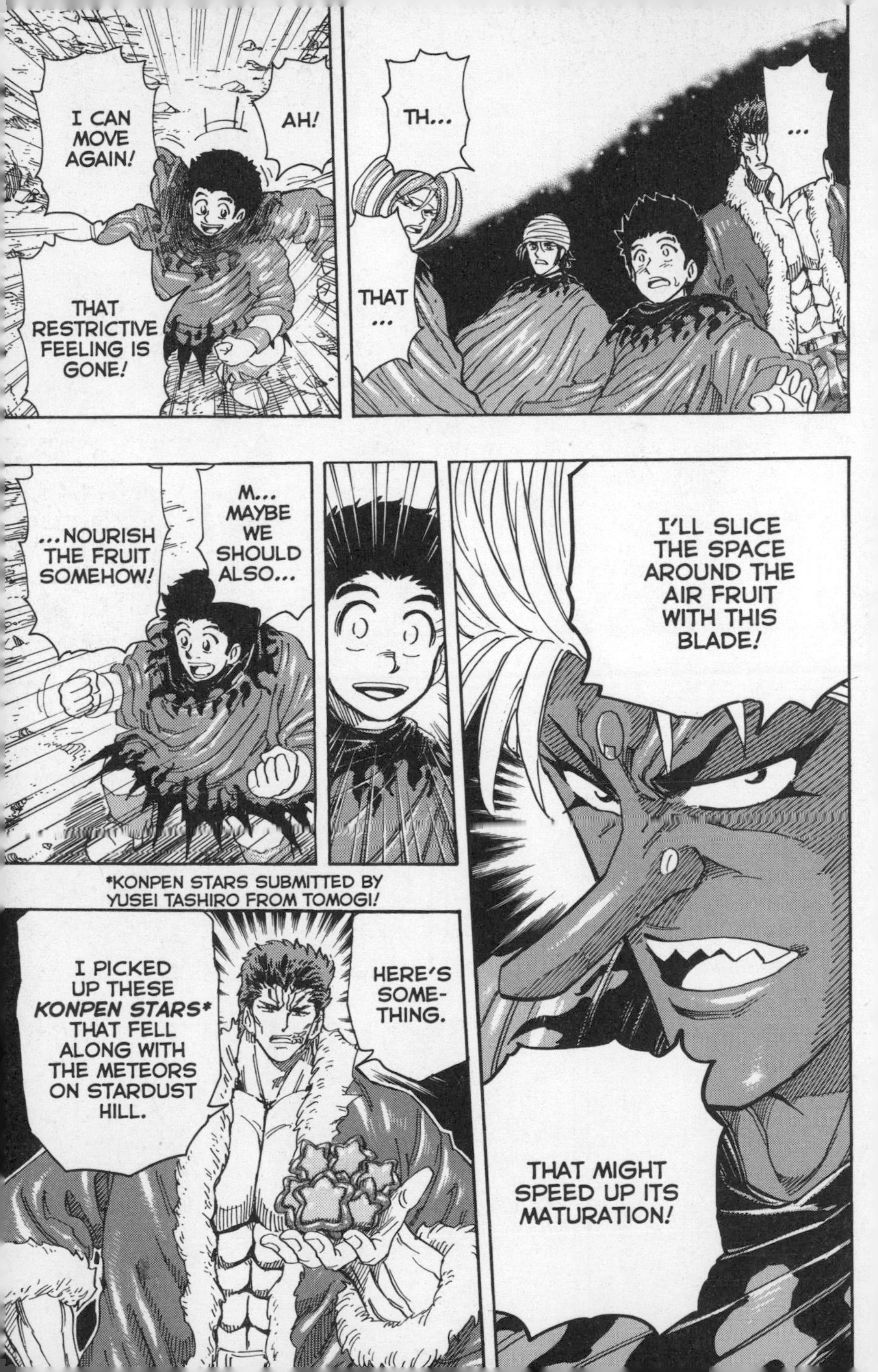
...
TH...
THAT...
AH!
I CAN MOVE AGAIN!
THAT RESTRICTIVE FEELING IS GONE!
I'LL SLICE THE SPACE AROUND THE AIR FRUIT WITH THIS BLADE!
THAT MIGHT SPEED UP ITS MATURATION!
M... MAYBE WE SHOULD ALSO...
...NOURISH THE FRUIT SOMEHOW!
HERE'S SOME-THING.
I PICKED UP THESE *KONPEN STARS** THAT FELL ALONG WITH THE METEORS ON STARDUST HILL.
*KONPEN STARS SUBMITTED BY YUSEI TASHIRO FROM TOMOGI!

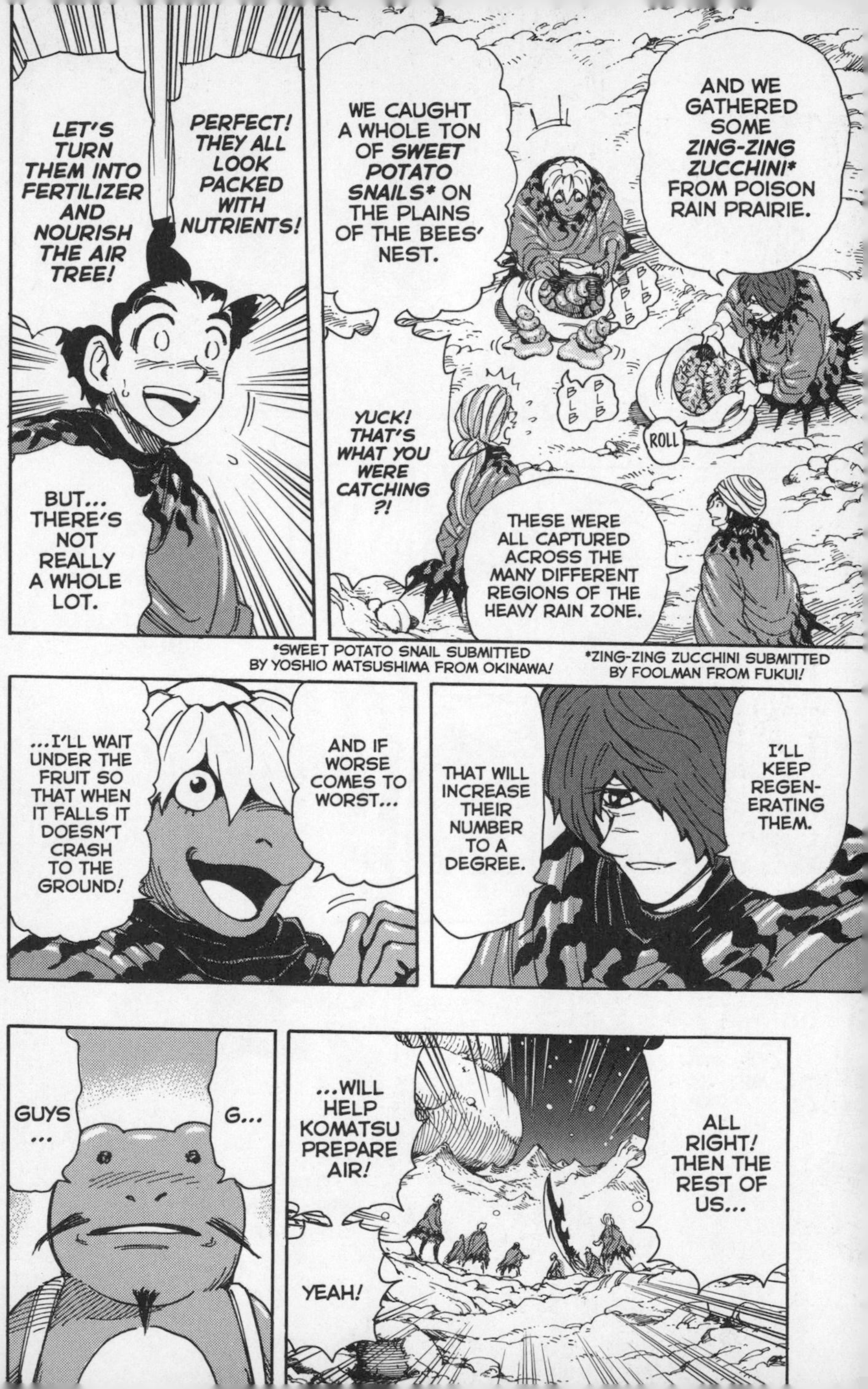
AND WE GATHERED SOME ZING-ZING ZUCCHINI* FROM POISON RAIN PRAIRIE.
WE CAUGHT A WHOLE TON OF SWEET POTATO SNAILS* ON THE PLAINS OF THE BEES' NEST.
BLB BLB BLB
BLB BLB
ROLL
YUCK! THAT'S WHAT YOU WERE CATCHING?!
THESE WERE ALL CAPTURED ACROSS THE MANY DIFFERENT REGIONS OF THE HEAVY RAIN ZONE.
PERFECT! THEY ALL LOOK PACKED WITH NUTRIENTS!
LET'S TURN THEM INTO FERTILIZER AND NOURISH THE AIR TREE!
BUT... THERE'S NOT REALLY A WHOLE LOT.
*ZING-ZING ZUCCHINI SUBMITTED BY FOOLMAN FROM FUKUI!
*SWEET POTATO SNAIL SUBMITTED BY YOSHIO MATSUSHIMA FROM OKINAWA!
I'LL KEEP REGEN-ERATING THEM.
THAT WILL INCREASE THEIR NUMBER TO A DEGREE.
AND IF WORSE COMES TO WORST...
...I'LL WAIT UNDER THE FRUIT SO THAT WHEN IT FALLS IT DOESN'T CRASH TO THE GROUND!
ALL RIGHT! THEN THE REST OF US...
...WILL HELP KOMATSU PREPARE AIR!
YEAH!
G...
GUYS...

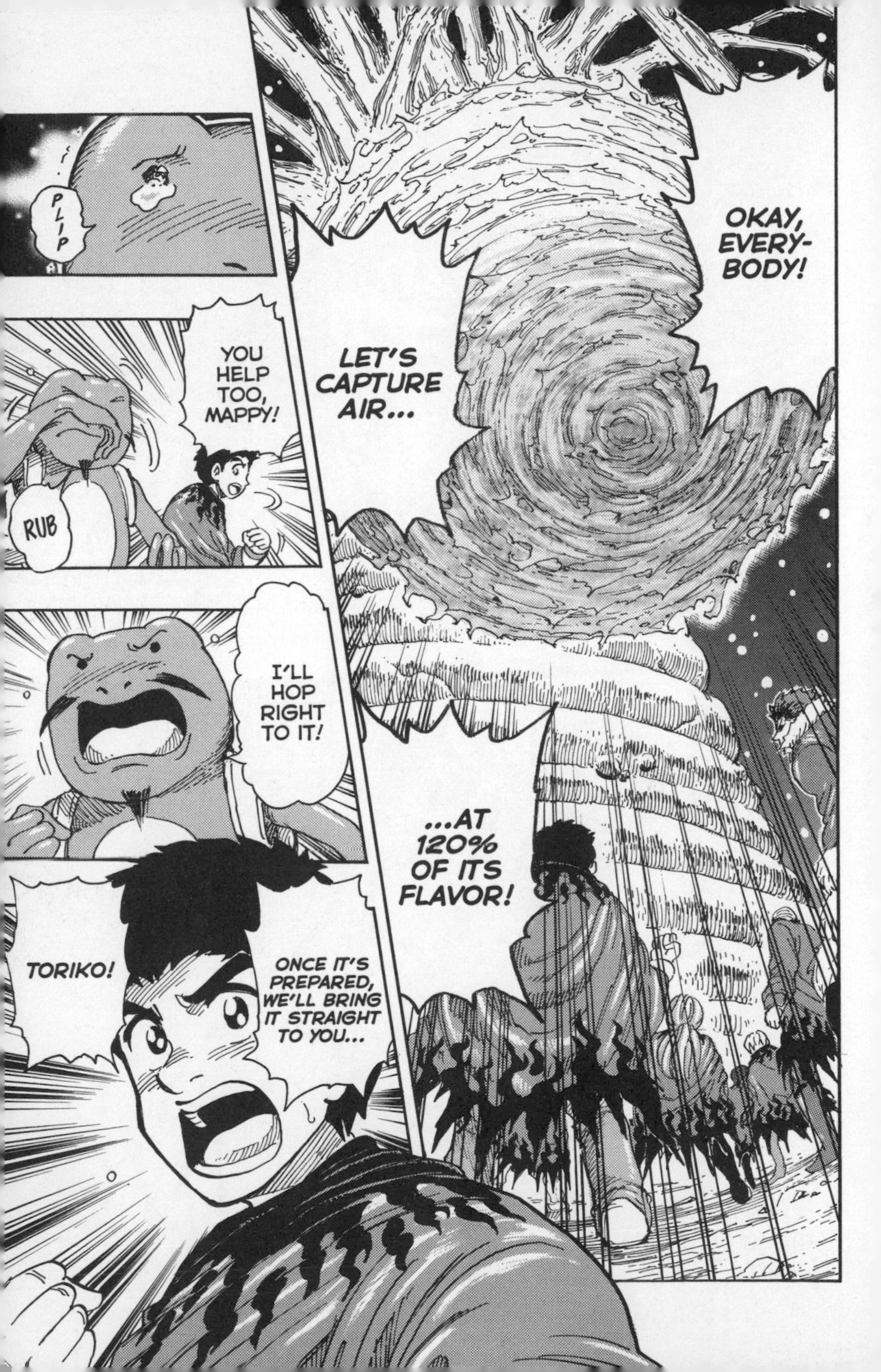
OKAY, EVERYBODY!
LET'S CAPTURE AIR...
...AT 120% OF ITS FLAVOR!
PLIP
YOU HELP TOO, MAPPY!
RUB
I'LL HOP RIGHT TO IT!
ONCE IT'S PREPARED, WE'LL BRING IT STRAIGHT TO YOU...
TORIKO!

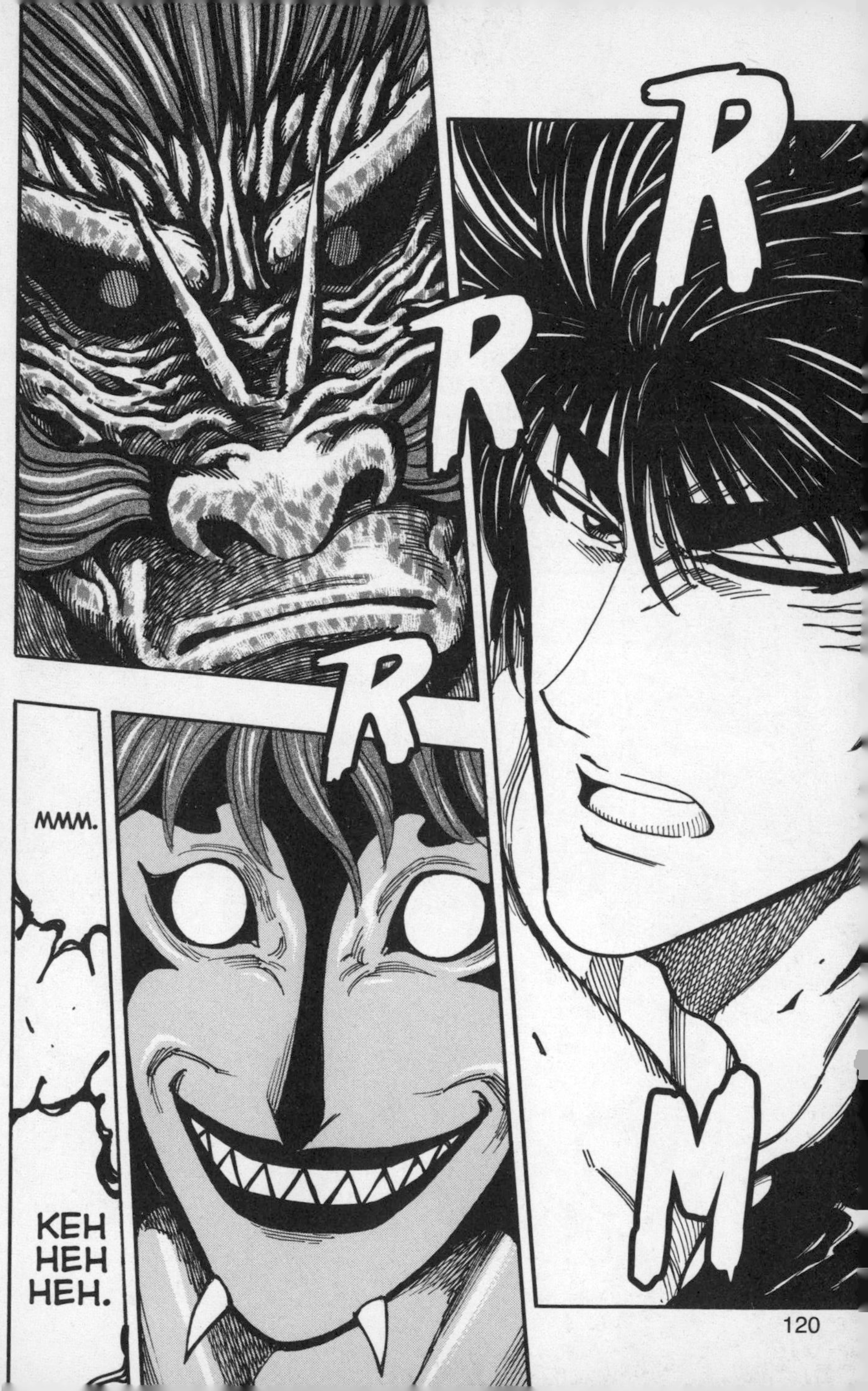
RRRM
MMM.
KEH HEH HEH.

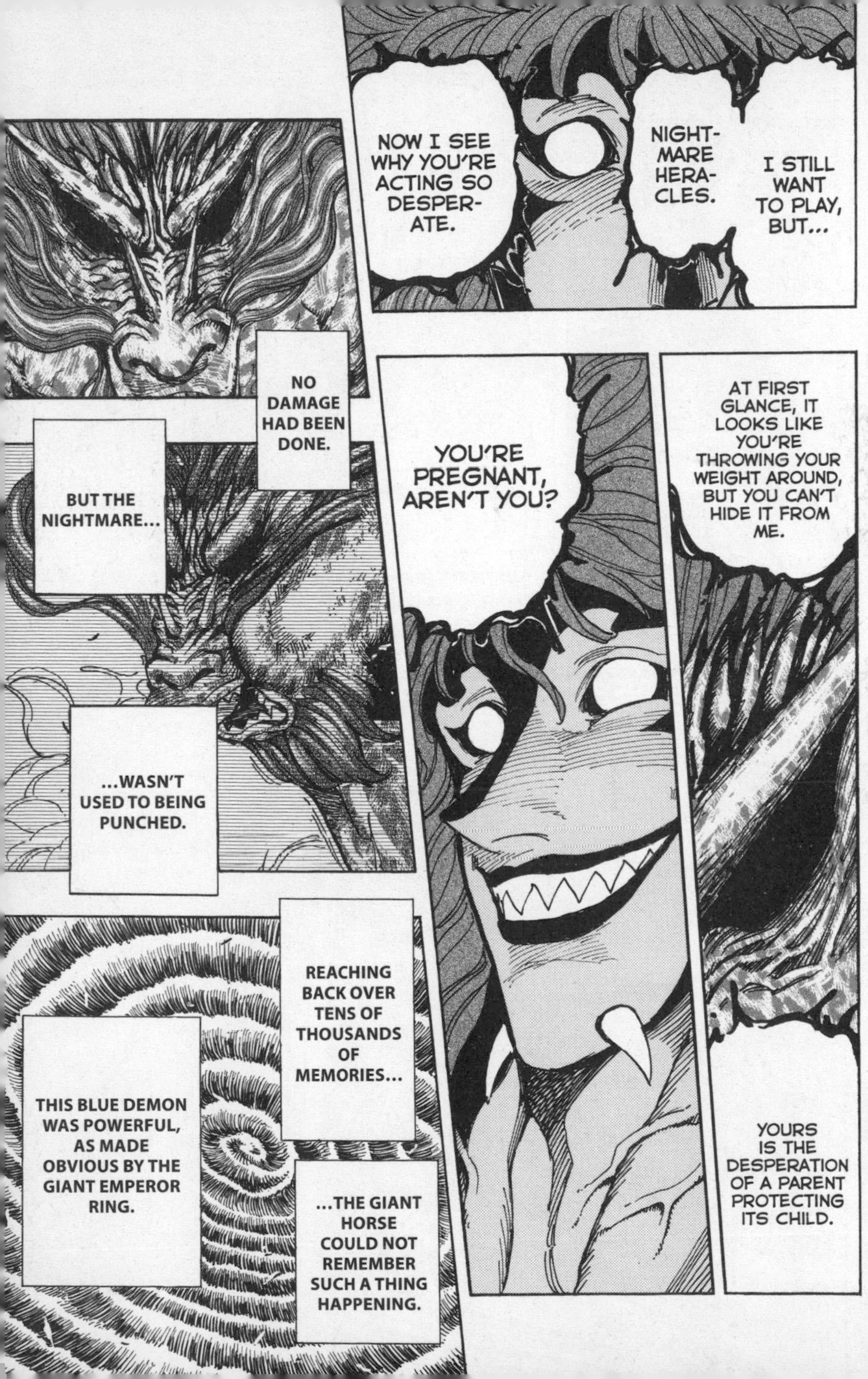
I STILL WANT TO PLAY, BUT...
NIGHT-MARE HERA-CLES.
NOW I SEE WHY YOU'RE ACTING SO DESPER-ATE.
AT FIRST GLANCE, IT LOOKS LIKE YOU'RE THROWING YOUR WEIGHT AROUND, BUT YOU CAN'T HIDE IT FROM ME.
YOURS IS THE DESPERATION OF A PARENT PROTECTING ITS CHILD.
YOU'RE PREGNANT, AREN'T YOU?
NO DAMAGE HAD BEEN DONE.
BUT THE NIGHTMARE...
...WASN'T USED TO BEING PUNCHED.
REACHING BACK OVER TENS OF THOUSANDS OF MEMORIES...
...THE GIANT HORSE COULD NOT REMEMBER SUCH A THING HAPPENING.
THIS BLUE DEMON WAS POWERFUL, AS MADE OBVIOUS BY THE GIANT EMPEROR RING.

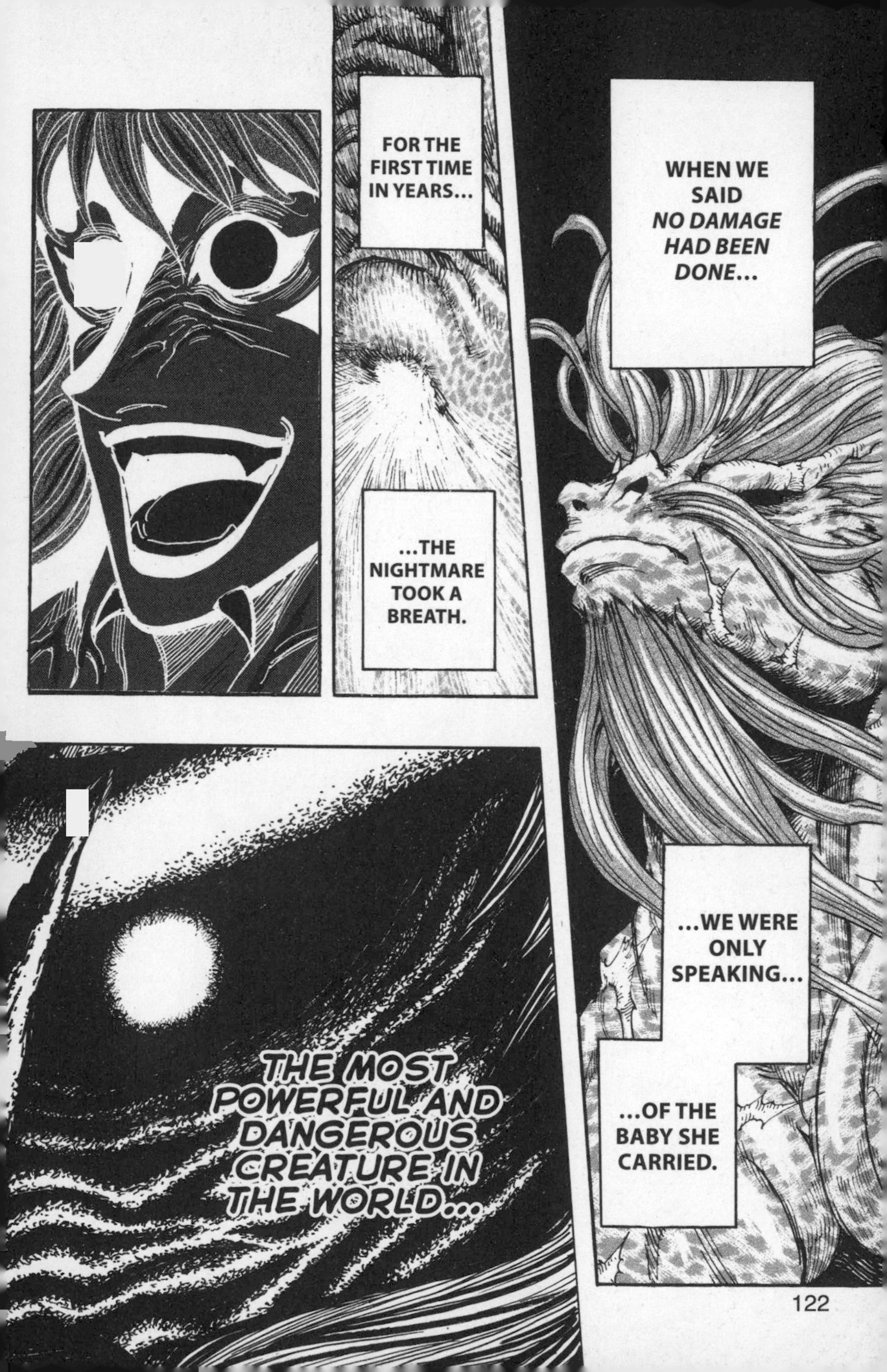
WHEN WE SAID *NO DAMAGE HAD BEEN DONE*...
...WE WERE ONLY SPEAKING...
...OF THE BABY SHE CARRIED.
FOR THE FIRST TIME IN YEARS...
...THE NIGHTMARE TOOK A BREATH.
THE MOST POWERFUL AND DANGEROUS CREATURE IN THE WORLD...

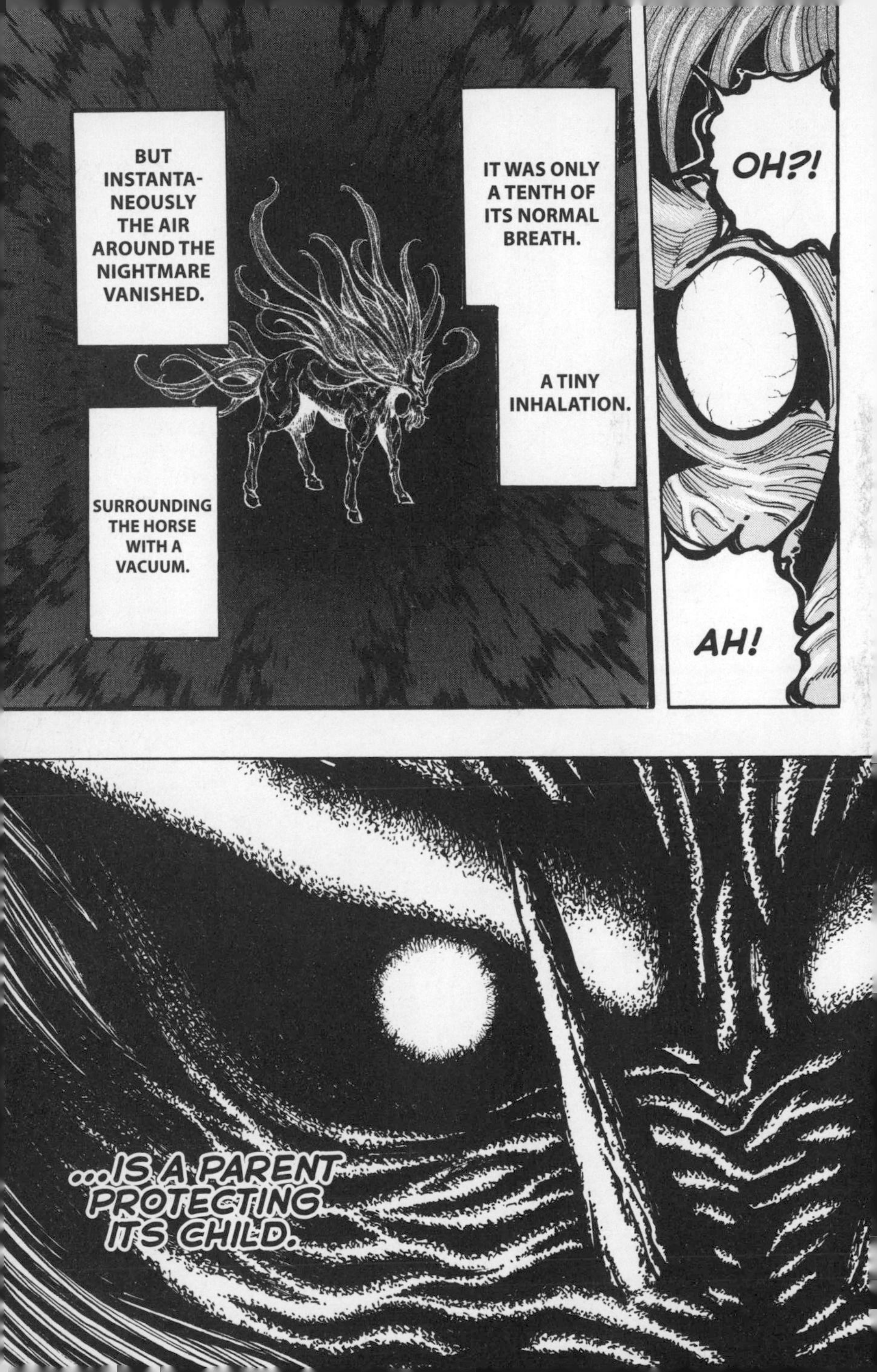
OH?!
AH!
IT WAS ONLY A TENTH OF ITS NORMAL BREATH.
A TINY INHALATION.
BUT INSTANTANEOUSLY THE AIR AROUND THE NIGHTMARE VANISHED.
SURROUNDING THE HORSE WITH A VACUUM.
...IS A PARENT PROTECTING ITS CHILD.

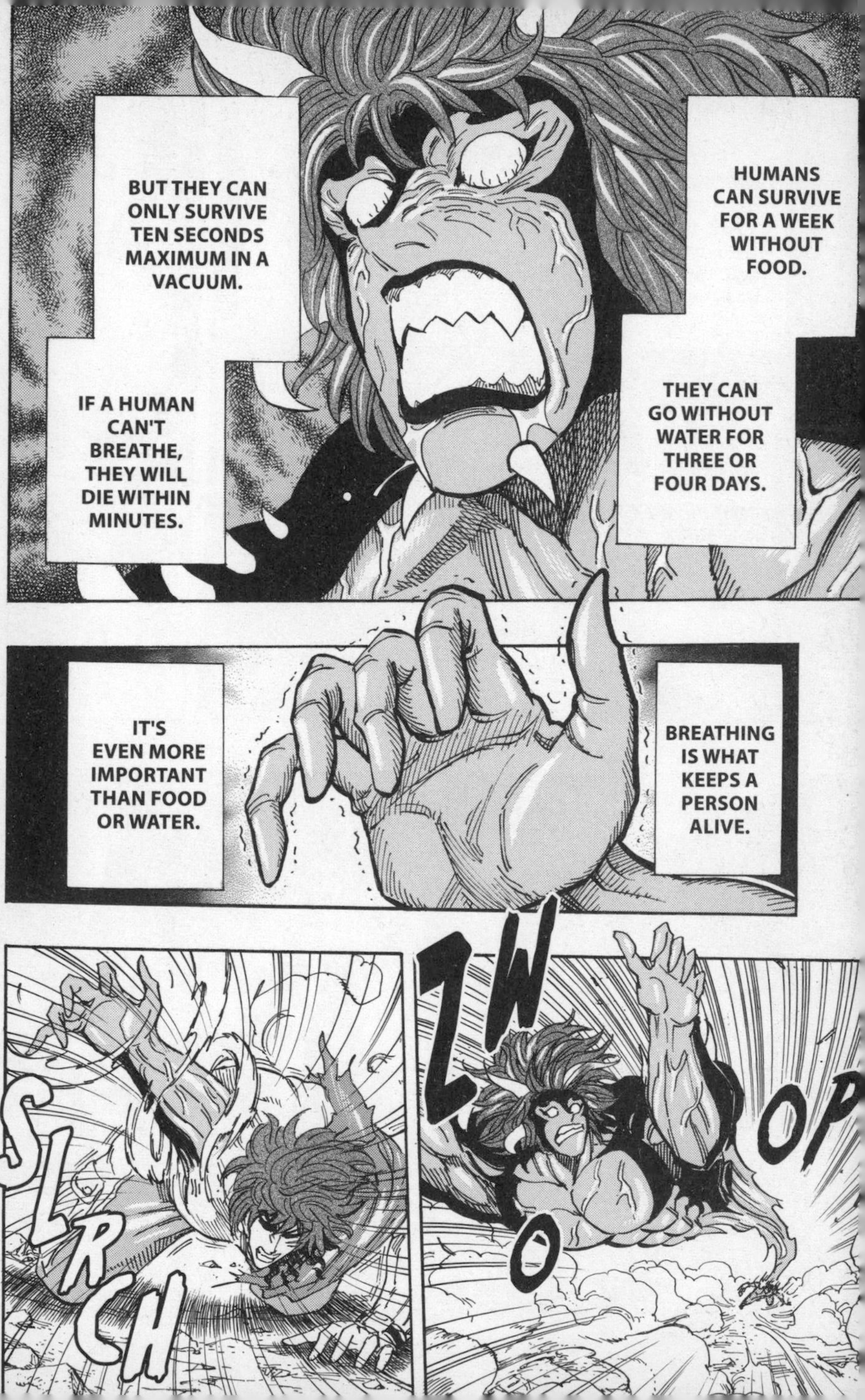
HUMANS CAN SURVIVE FOR A WEEK WITHOUT FOOD.
THEY CAN GO WITHOUT WATER FOR THREE OR FOUR DAYS.
IF A HUMAN CAN'T BREATHE, THEY WILL DIE WITHIN MINUTES.
BUT THEY CAN ONLY SURVIVE TEN SECONDS MAXIMUM IN A VACUUM.
BREATHING IS WHAT KEEPS A PERSON ALIVE.
IT'S EVEN MORE IMPORTANT THAN FOOD OR WATER.
ZWOOP
SLRCH

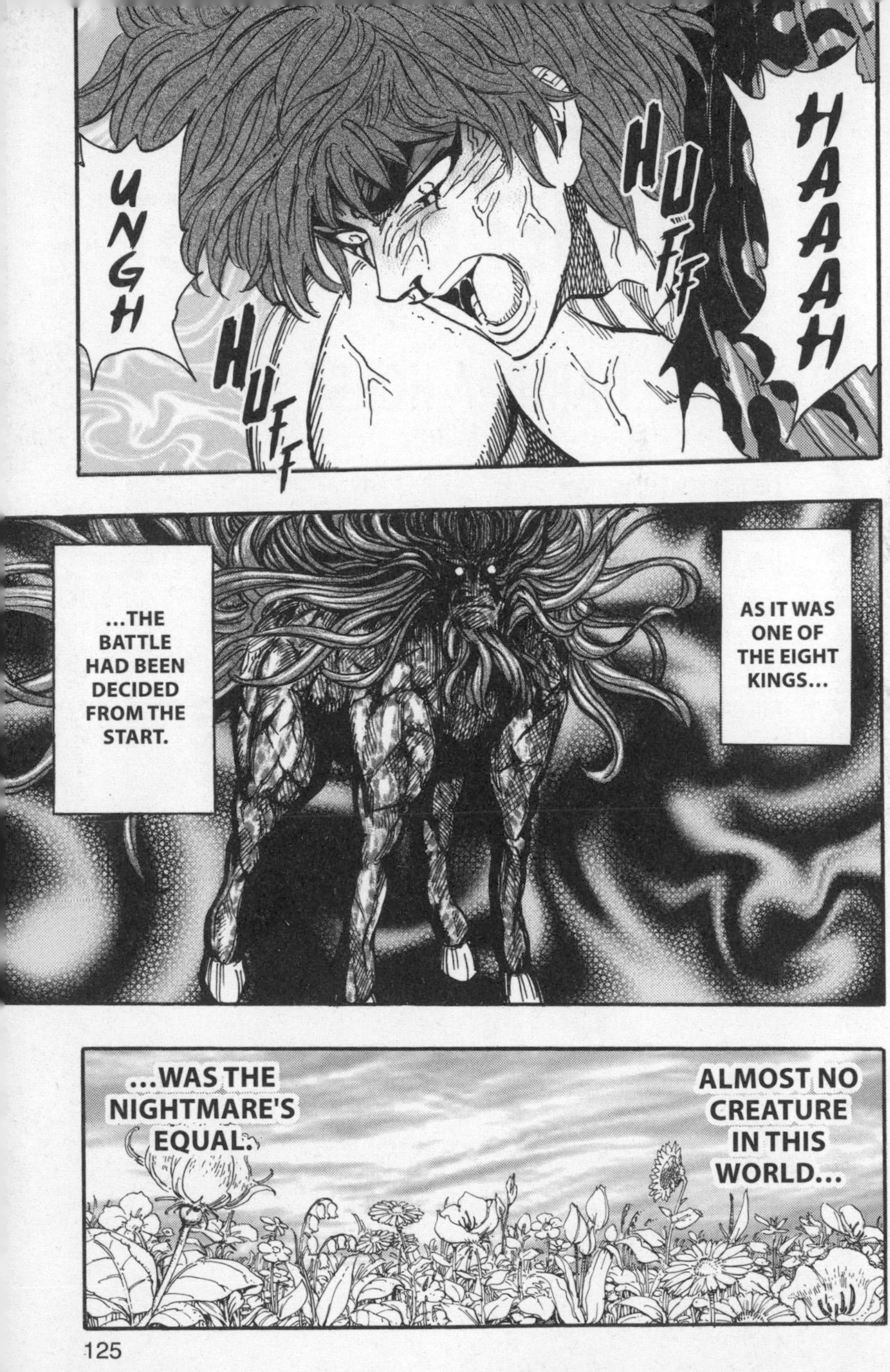
HAAAAH
HUFF
UNGH
HUFF
AS IT WAS ONE OF THE EIGHT KINGS...
...THE BATTLE HAD BEEN DECIDED FROM THE START.
ALMOST NO CREATURE IN THIS WORLD...
...WAS THE NIGHTMARE'S EQUAL.

TORIKO

GOURMET CHECKLIST

Vol. 314

DARUMA HORSE
(DEMON)

CAPTURE LEVEL: UNKNOWN
HABITAT: GOURMET WORLD (AREA 8)
SIZE: 1,300 M
HEIGHT: 1,000 M
WEIGHT: 4 MILLION TONS
PRICE: UNKNOWN

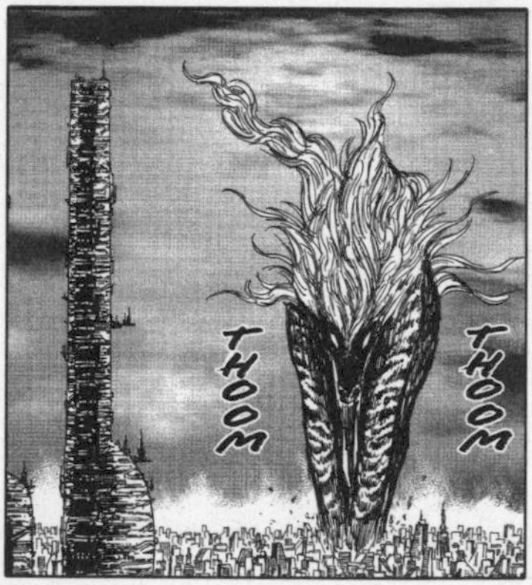
THOOM
THOOM

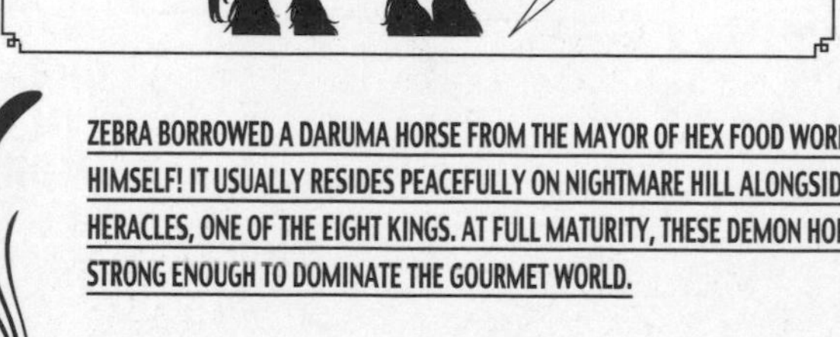

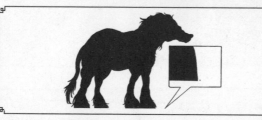

SCALE

ZEBRA BORROWED A DARUMA HORSE FROM THE MAYOR OF HEX FOOD WORLD HIMSELF! IT USUALLY RESIDES PEACEFULLY ON NIGHTMARE HILL ALONGSIDE HERACLES, ONE OF THE EIGHT KINGS. AT FULL MATURITY, THESE DEMON HORSES ARE STRONG ENOUGH TO DOMINATE THE GOURMET WORLD.

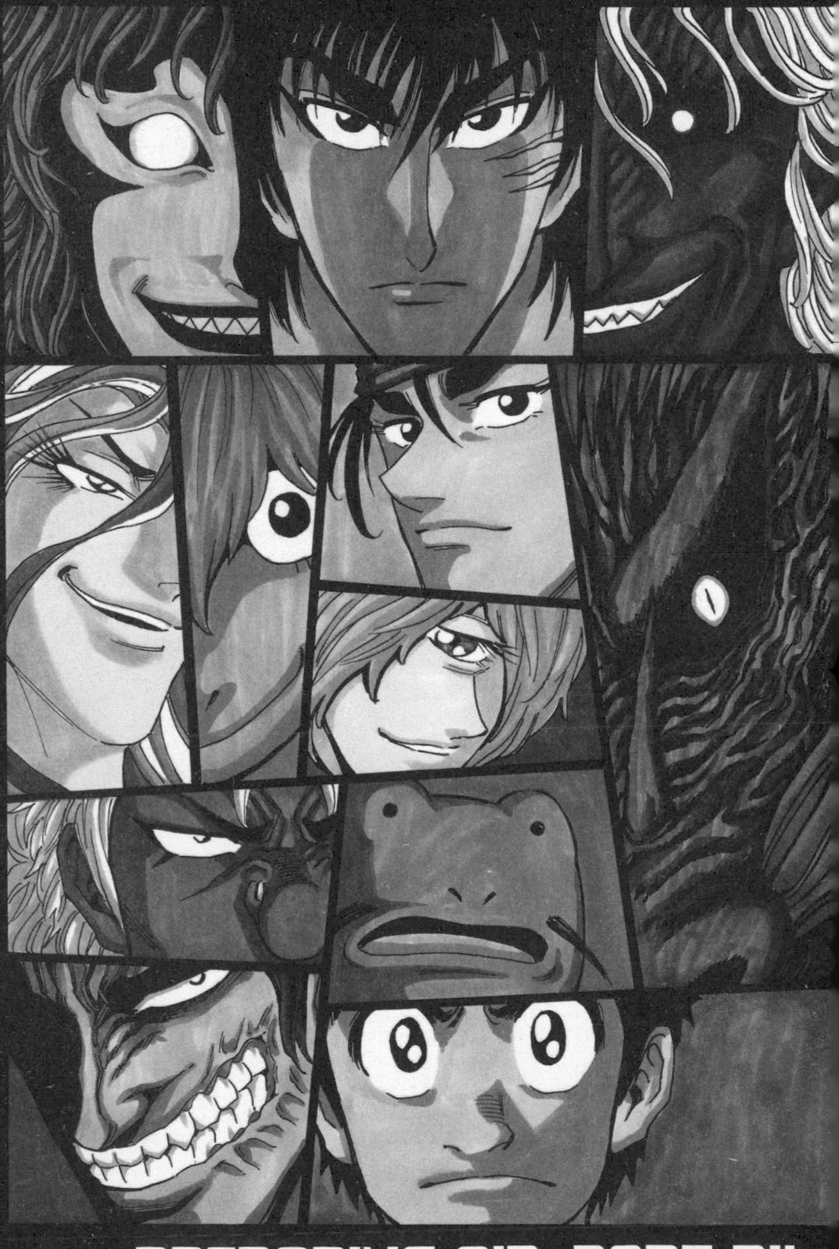

GOURMET 289: PREPARING AIR: PART 2!!

TORIKO

GOURMET CHECKLIST

Vol. 315

❖ FOUR-BEASTS: MAIN BODY ❖
(SPECIAL BLEND)

CAPTURE LEVEL: 350

HABITAT: GOURMET WORLD

SIZE: —

HEIGHT: —

WEIGHT: —

PRICE: UNKNOWN

SCALE

THE MAIN BODY OF THE FOUR-BEASTS WHO EMERGES FROM THE GOURMET WORLD EVERY SEVERAL YEARS. IT CHOOSES THE TIME WHEN HUMANITY IS AT ITS PEAK AND THEN FEASTS ON THE WORLD. THE MAIN BODY ACTS AS A CONTROL TOWER, FOSTERING SEEDS OF LIFE TO ITS EXTREMITIES, GIVING RISE TO THE FOLLOWING MONSTERS: KING FANG, INVITE DEATH, KING OCTOPUS KONG, AND MOUNT TURTLE. SINCE AS LONG AS HUMANS CAN REMEMBER, ITS OFFSPRING HUNT FOR FOOD, WHICH GETS REABSORBED INTO THE MAIN BODY AS NUTRIENTS. YEARS AGO, ICHIRYU HAD STOPPED THE EXTREMITIES FROM WREAKING HAVOC, SO THE MAIN BODY ITSELF DECIDED TO ATTACK THE HUMAN WORLD ITSELF. WITH A CAPTURE LEVEL OF OVER 350, THE FOUR KINGS COULD ONLY DEFEAT IT USING THE ULTIMATE COMBO ATTACK, "APPETITE FIT FOR A KING," AND SAVED HUMANITY FROM EXTINCTION.

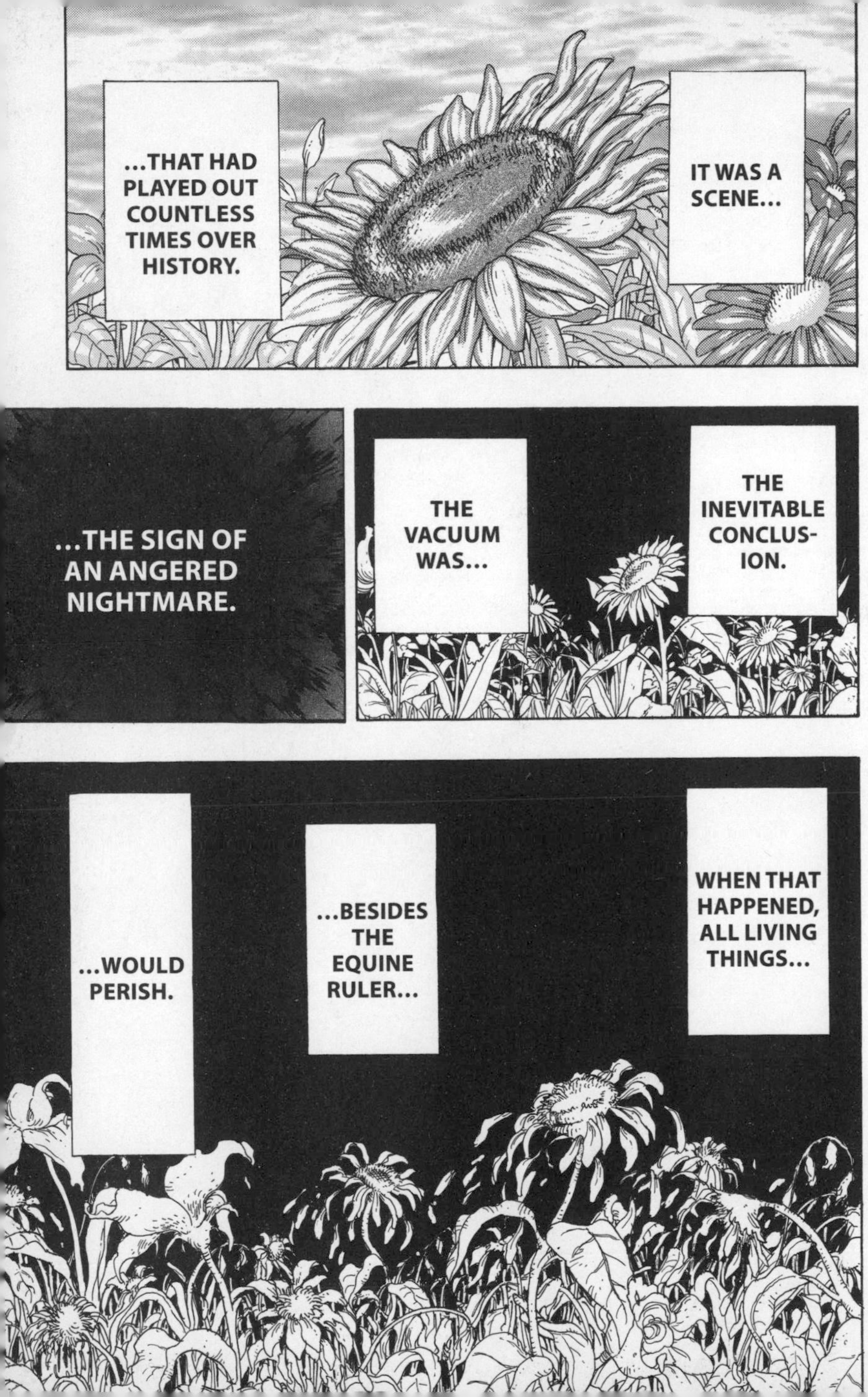
IT WAS A SCENE...
...THAT HAD PLAYED OUT COUNTLESS TIMES OVER HISTORY.
THE INEVITABLE CONCLUS-ION.
THE VACUUM WAS...
...THE SIGN OF AN ANGERED NIGHTMARE.
WHEN THAT HAPPENED, ALL LIVING THINGS...
...BESIDES THE EQUINE RULER...
...WOULD PERISH.

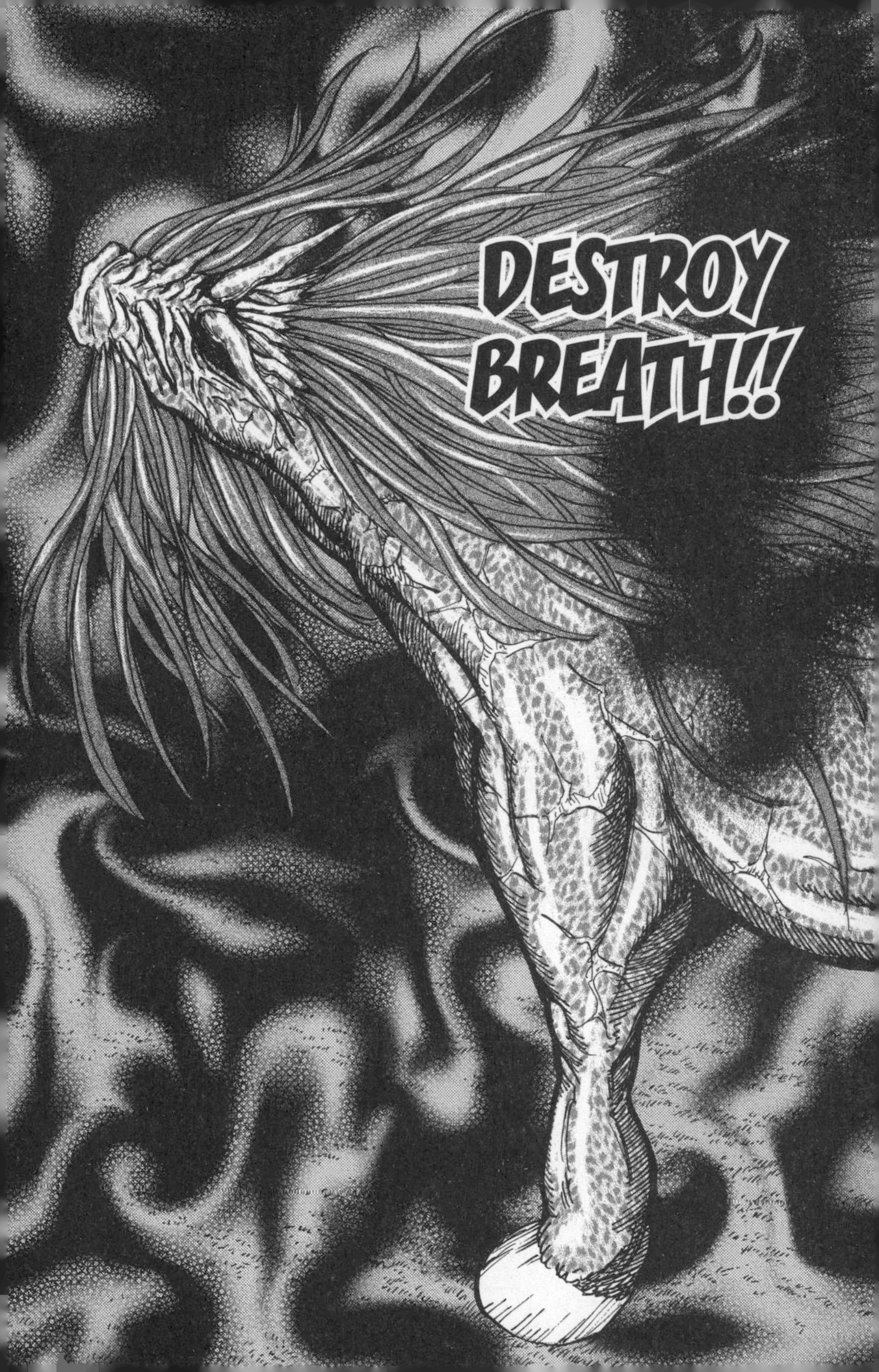
DESTROY BREATH!!

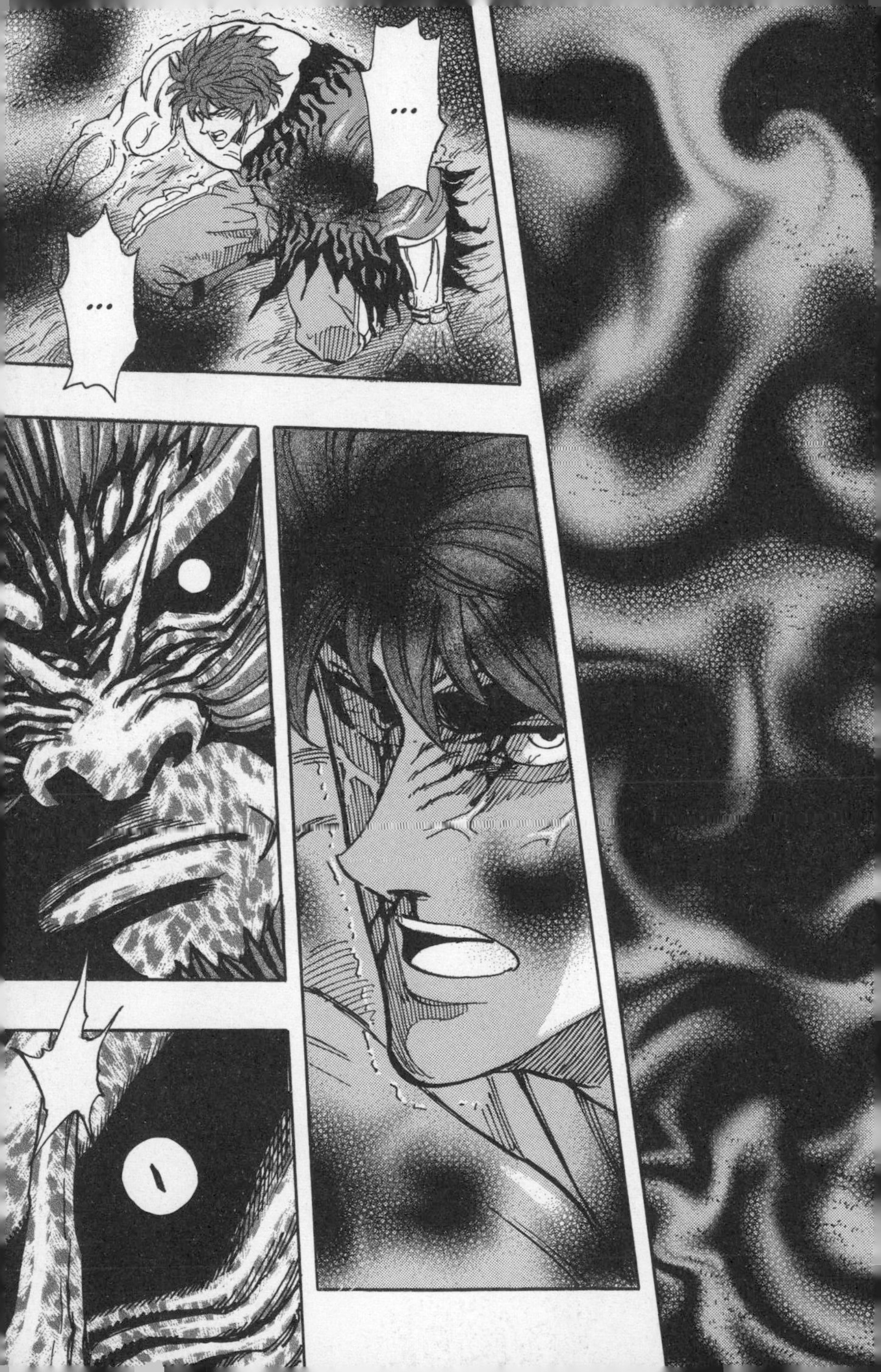
...
...

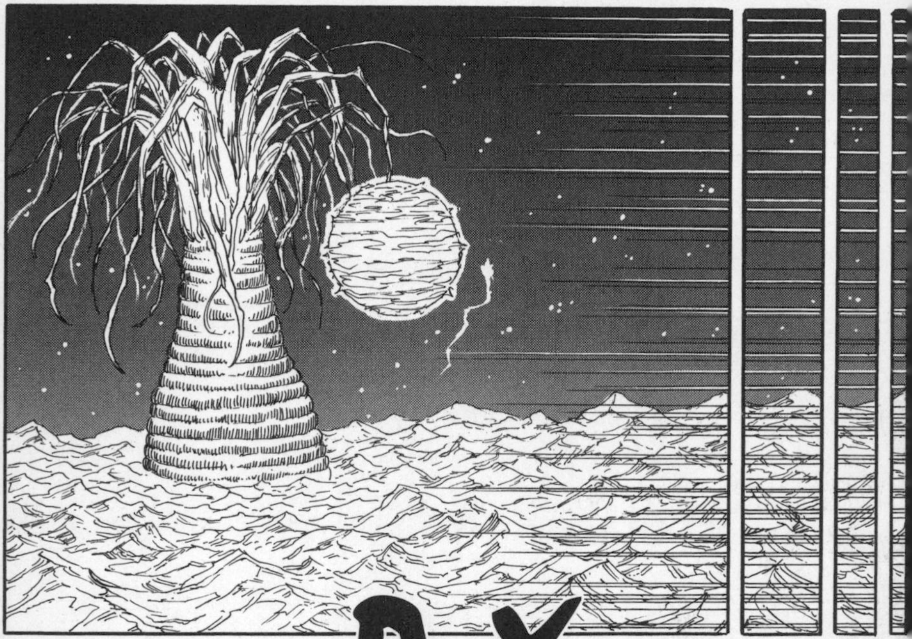

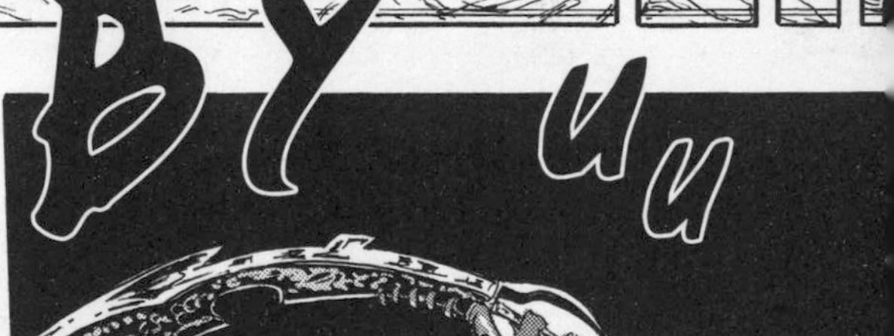
BYUU

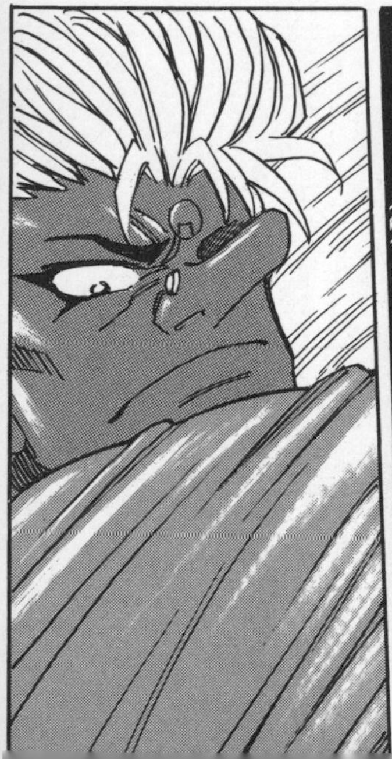

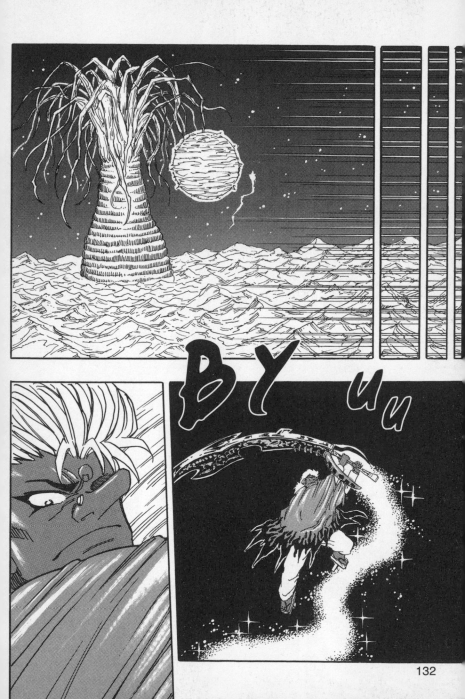

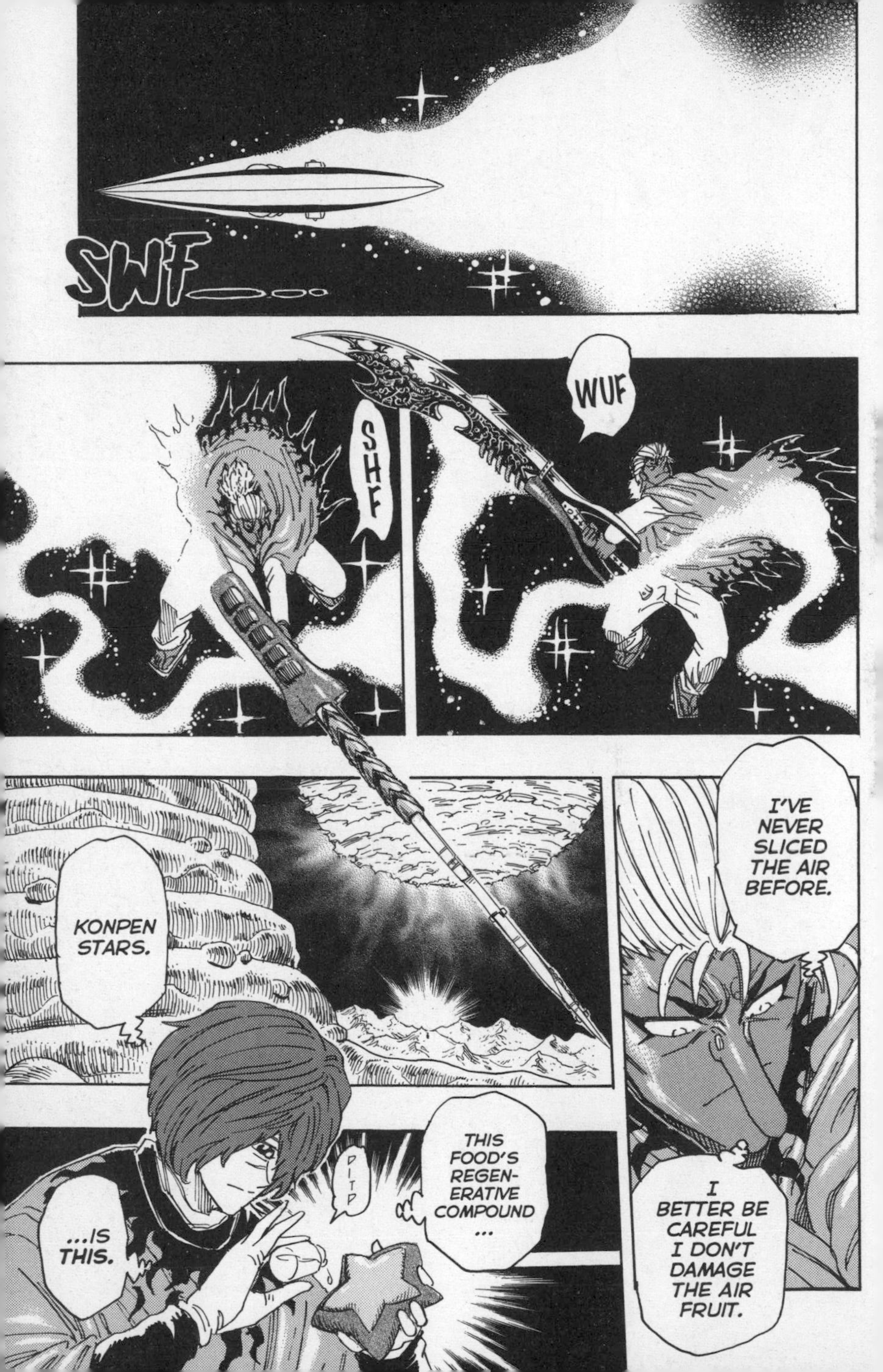
SWF
WUF
SHF
I'VE NEVER SLICED THE AIR BEFORE.
I BETTER BE CAREFUL I DON'T DAMAGE THE AIR FRUIT.
KONPEN STARS.
THIS FOOD'S REGENERATIVE COMPOUND...
...IS THIS.

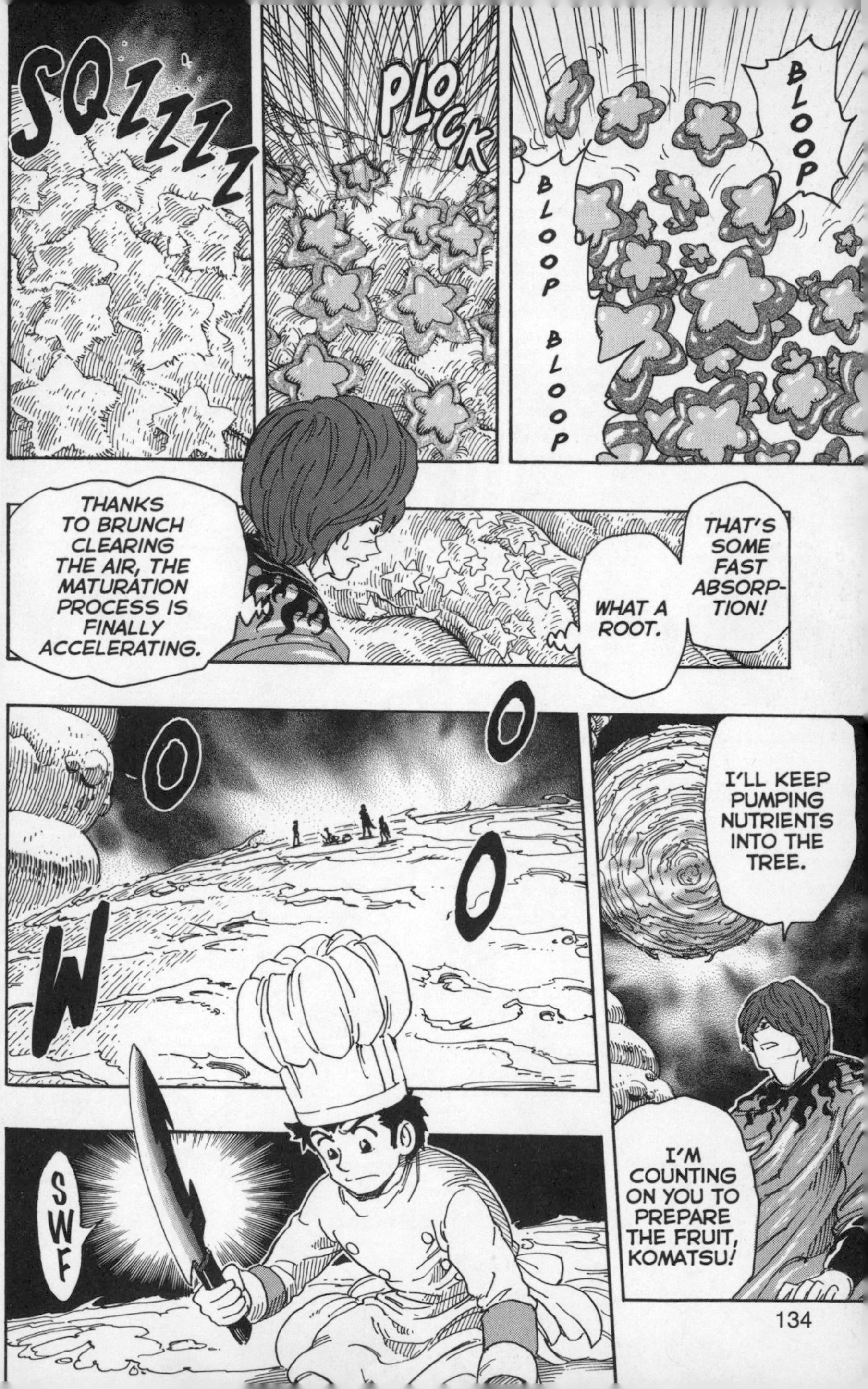
BLOOP
BLOOP BLOOP
PLOCK
SQZZZZZ
THAT'S SOME FAST ABSORPTION!
WHAT A ROOT.
THANKS TO BRUNCH CLEARING THE AIR, THE MATURATION PROCESS IS FINALLY ACCELERATING.
I'LL KEEP PUMPING NUTRIENTS INTO THE TREE.
I'M COUNTING ON YOU TO PREPARE THE FRUIT, KOMATSU!
WOOO
SWF

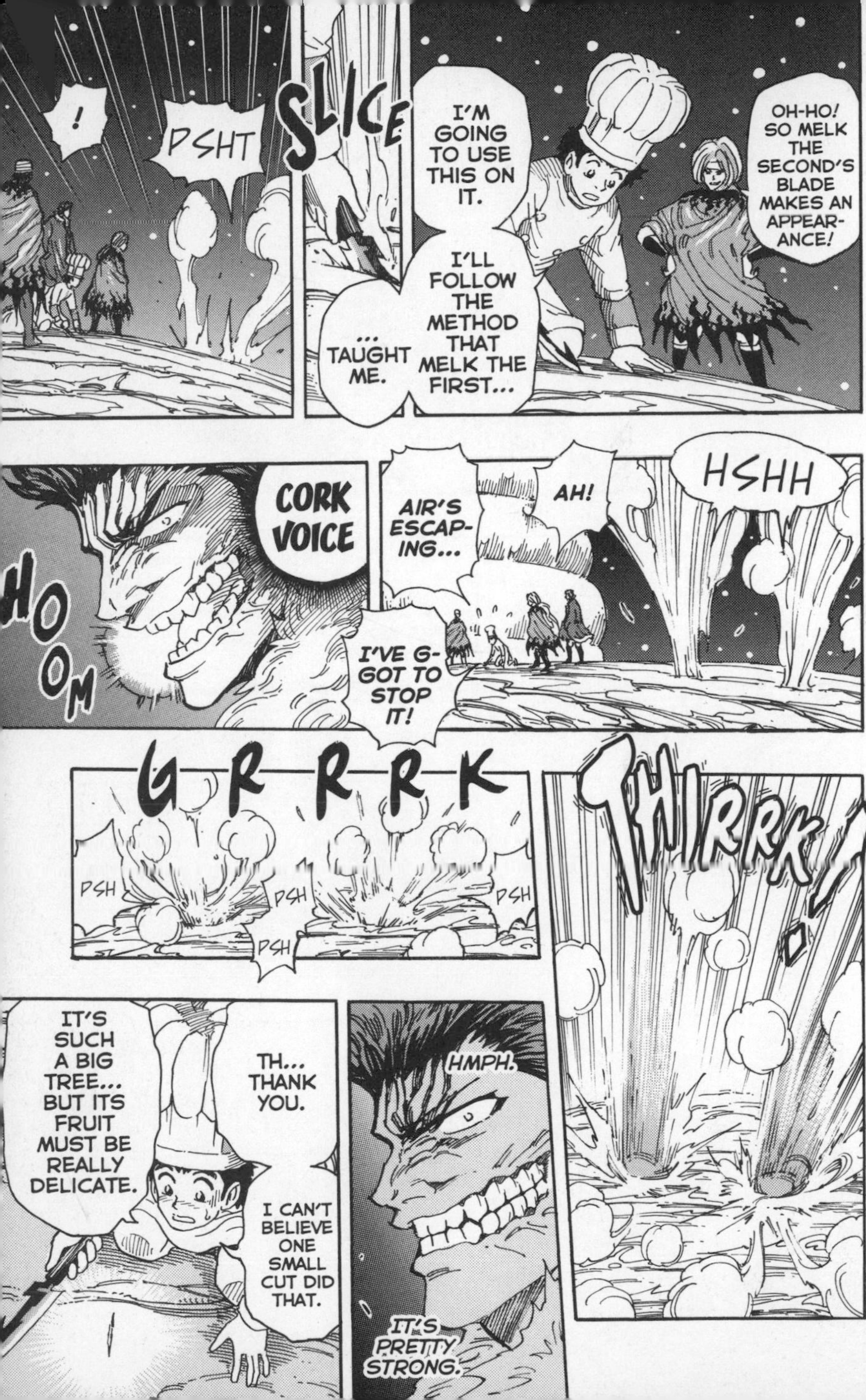
OH-HO! SO MELK THE SECOND'S BLADE MAKES AN APPEARANCE!
I'M GOING TO USE THIS ON IT.
I'LL FOLLOW THE METHOD THAT MELK THE FIRST...
...TAUGHT ME.
SLICE
PSHT
!
HSHH
AH!
AIR'S ESCAPING...
I'VE G-GOT TO STOP IT!
CORK VOICE
HOOM
THIRRK!
GRRRK
PSH
PSH
PSH
PSH
HMPH.
IT'S PRETTY STRONG.
TH... THANK YOU.
I CAN'T BELIEVE ONE SMALL CUT DID THAT.
IT'S SUCH A BIG TREE... BUT ITS FRUIT MUST BE REALLY DELICATE.

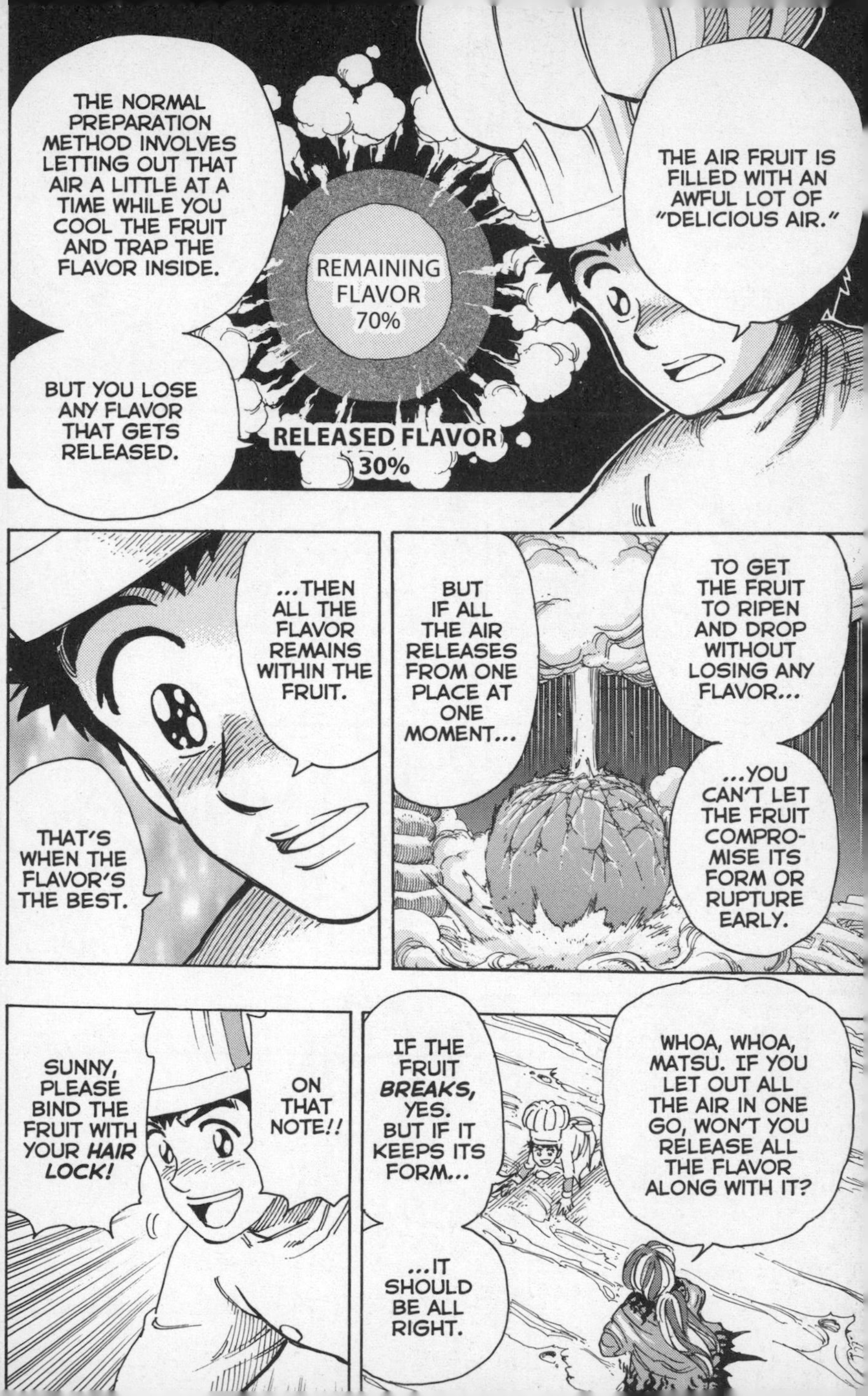
THE AIR FRUIT IS FILLED WITH AN AWFUL LOT OF "DELICIOUS AIR."
THE NORMAL PREPARATION METHOD INVOLVES LETTING OUT THAT AIR A LITTLE AT A TIME WHILE YOU COOL THE FRUIT AND TRAP THE FLAVOR INSIDE.
REMAINING FLAVOR 70%
RELEASED FLAVOR 30%
BUT YOU LOSE ANY FLAVOR THAT GETS RELEASED.
TO GET THE FRUIT TO RIPEN AND DROP WITHOUT LOSING ANY FLAVOR...
...YOU CAN'T LET THE FRUIT COMPRO-MISE ITS FORM OR RUPTURE EARLY.
BUT IF ALL THE AIR RELEASES FROM ONE PLACE AT ONE MOMENT...
...THEN ALL THE FLAVOR REMAINS WITHIN THE FRUIT.
THAT'S WHEN THE FLAVOR'S THE BEST.
WHOA, WHOA, MATSU. IF YOU LET OUT ALL THE AIR IN ONE GO, WON'T YOU RELEASE ALL THE FLAVOR ALONG WITH IT?
IF THE FRUIT *BREAKS,* YES. BUT IF IT KEEPS ITS FORM...
...IT SHOULD BE ALL RIGHT.
ON THAT NOTE!!
SUNNY, PLEASE BIND THE FRUIT WITH YOUR *HAIR LOCK!*

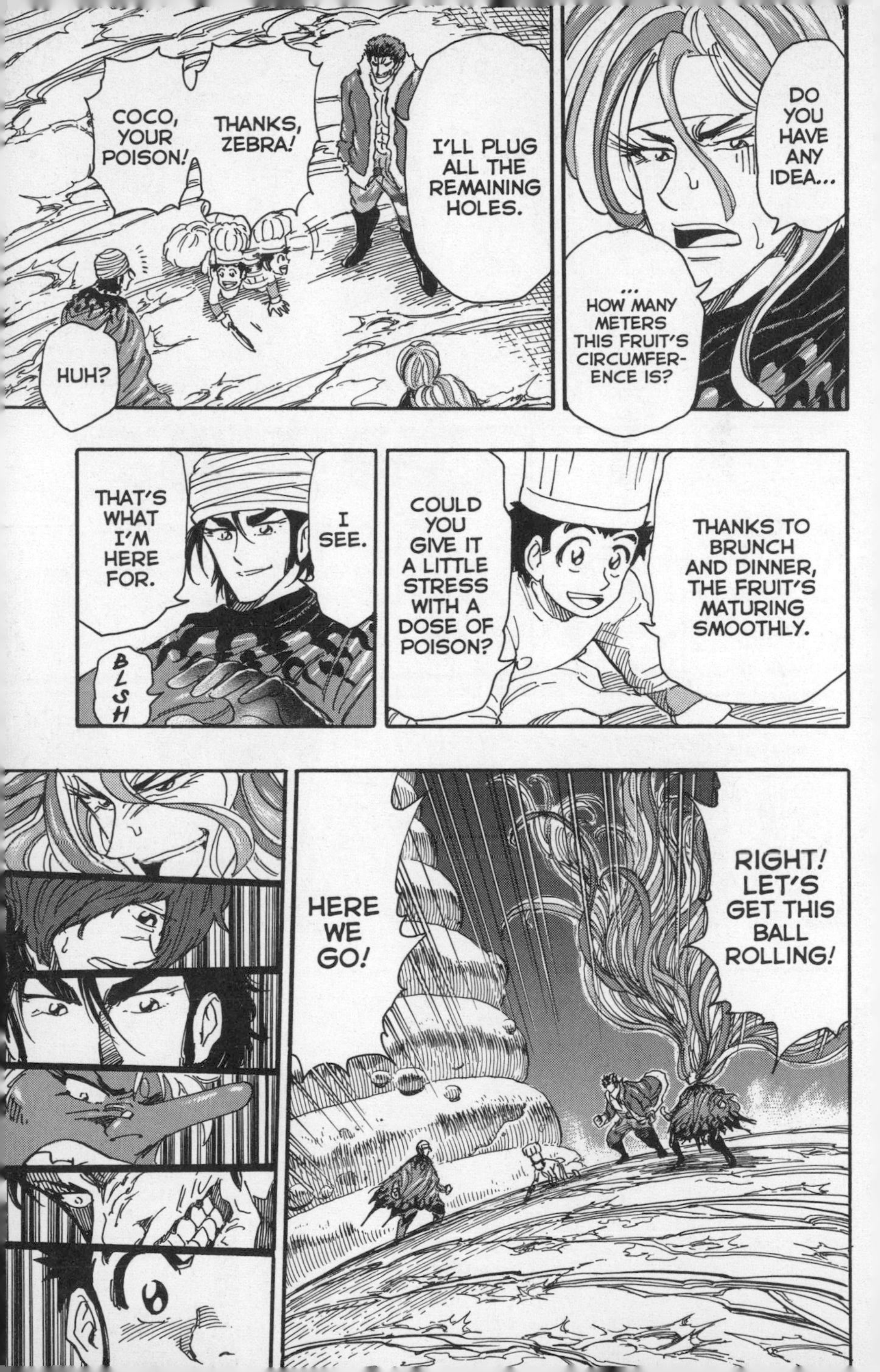
DO YOU HAVE ANY IDEA...
... HOW MANY METERS THIS FRUIT'S CIRCUMFERENCE IS?
I'LL PLUG ALL THE REMAINING HOLES.
THANKS, ZEBRA!
COCO, YOUR POISON!
HUH?
THANKS TO BRUNCH AND DINNER, THE FRUIT'S MATURING SMOOTHLY.
COULD YOU GIVE IT A LITTLE STRESS WITH A DOSE OF POISON?
I SEE.
THAT'S WHAT I'M HERE FOR.
BLSH
RIGHT! LET'S GET THIS BALL ROLLING!
HERE WE GO!

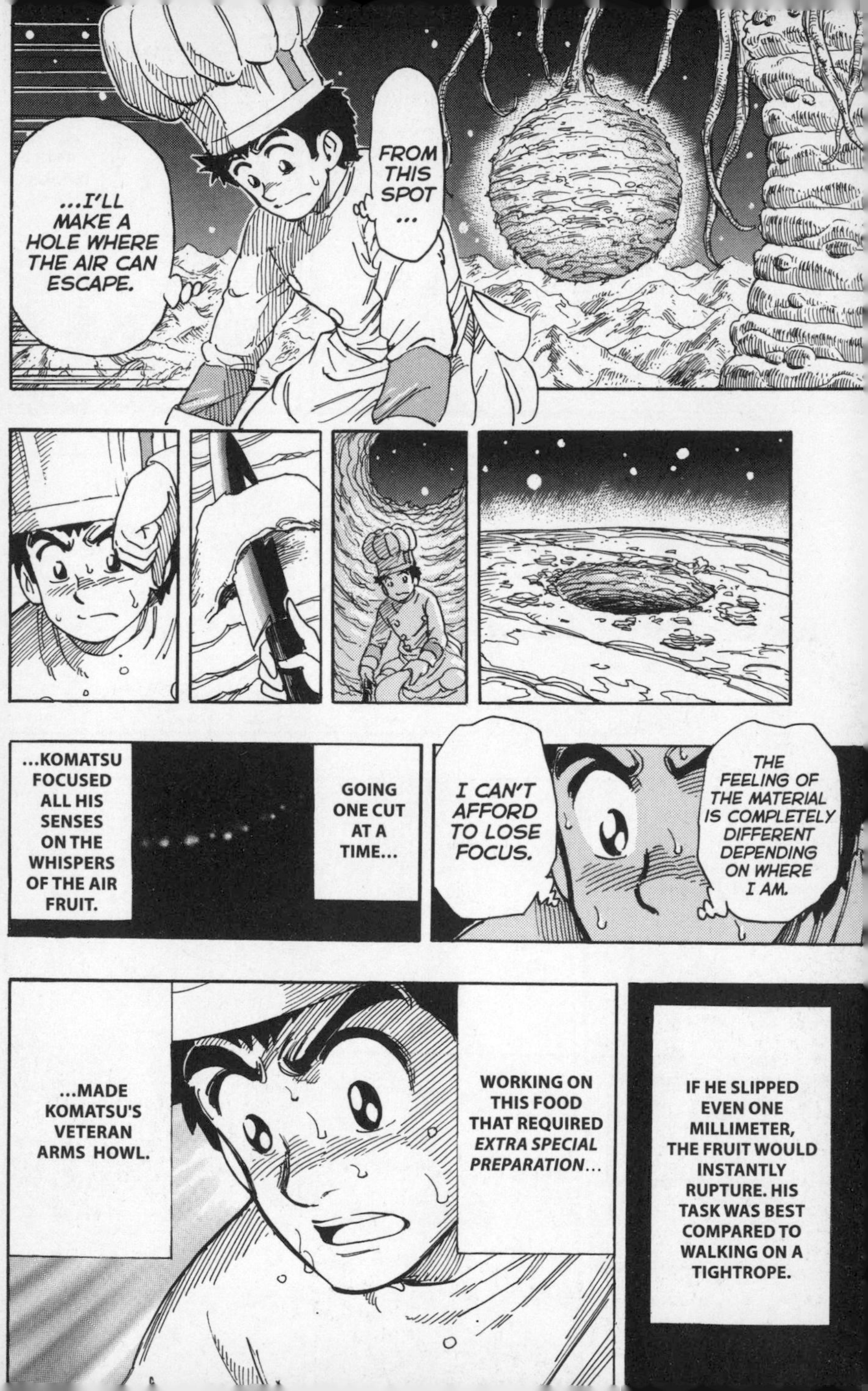
FROM THIS SPOT...
...I'LL MAKE A HOLE WHERE THE AIR CAN ESCAPE.
THE FEELING OF THE MATERIAL IS COMPLETELY DIFFERENT DEPENDING ON WHERE I AM.
I CAN'T AFFORD TO LOSE FOCUS.
GOING ONE CUT AT A TIME...
...KOMATSU FOCUSED ALL HIS SENSES ON THE WHISPERS OF THE AIR FRUIT.
IF HE SLIPPED EVEN ONE MILLIMETER, THE FRUIT WOULD INSTANTLY RUPTURE. HIS TASK WAS BEST COMPARED TO WALKING ON A TIGHTROPE.
WORKING ON THIS FOOD THAT REQUIRED *EXTRA SPECIAL PREPARATION*...
...MADE KOMATSU'S VETERAN ARMS HOWL.

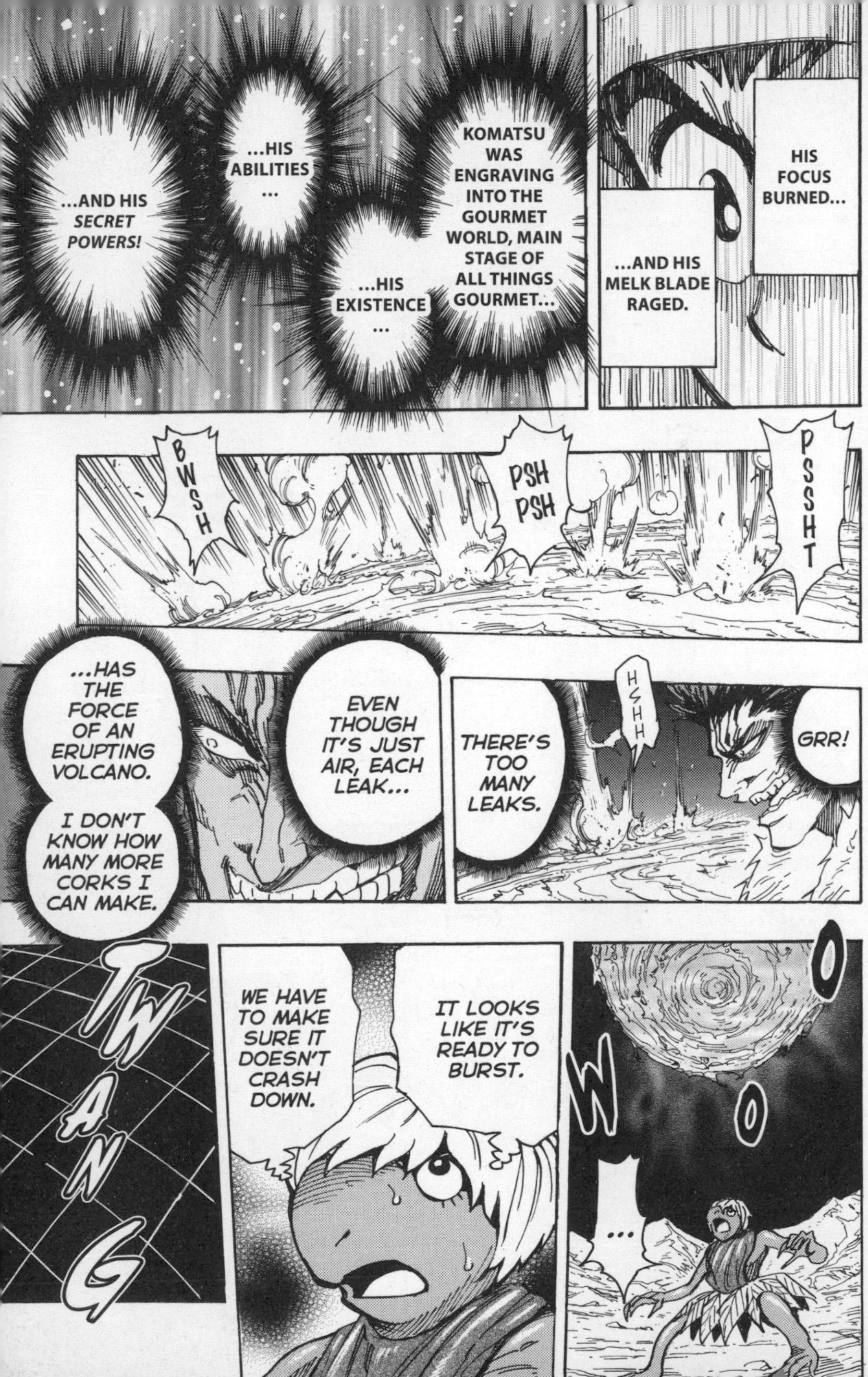
HIS FOCUS BURNED...
...AND HIS MELK BLADE RAGED.
KOMATSU WAS ENGRAVING INTO THE GOURMET WORLD, MAIN STAGE OF ALL THINGS GOURMET...
...HIS EXISTENCE...
...HIS ABILITIES...
...AND HIS *SECRET POWERS!*
PSSSHT
PSH PSH
BWSH
GRR!
HSHH
THERE'S TOO MANY LEAKS.
EVEN THOUGH IT'S JUST AIR, EACH LEAK...
...HAS THE FORCE OF AN ERUPTING VOLCANO.
I DON'T KNOW HOW MANY MORE CORKS I CAN MAKE.
WOOO
...
IT LOOKS LIKE IT'S READY TO BURST.
WE HAVE TO MAKE SURE IT DOESN'T CRASH DOWN.
TWANG

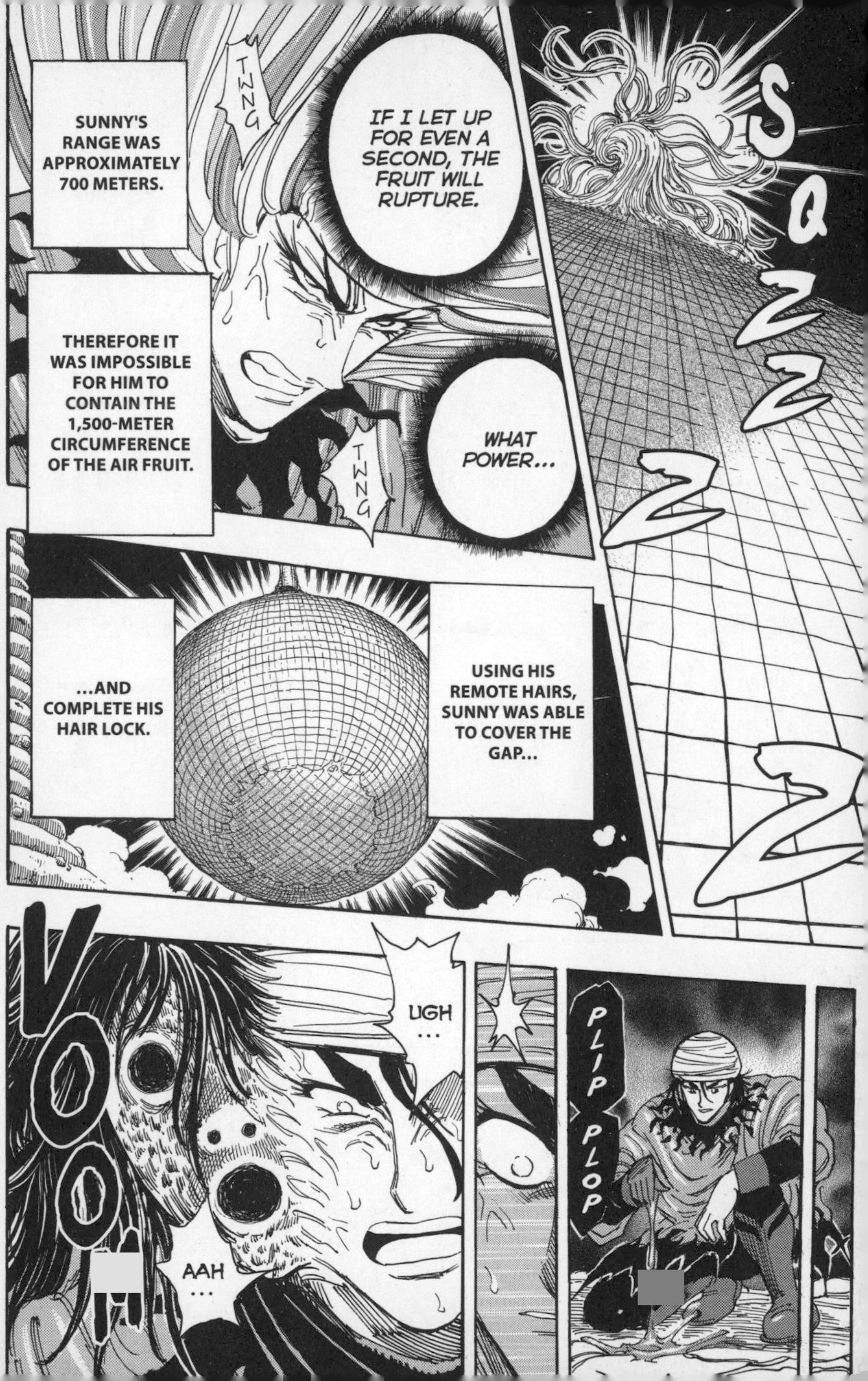
SQZZZZ
IF I LET UP FOR EVEN A SECOND, THE FRUIT WILL RUPTURE.
TWNG
SUNNY'S RANGE WAS APPROXIMATELY 700 METERS.
WHAT POWER...
THEREFORE IT WAS IMPOSSIBLE FOR HIM TO CONTAIN THE 1,500-METER CIRCUMFERENCE OF THE AIR FRUIT.
TWNG
USING HIS REMOTE HAIRS, SUNNY WAS ABLE TO COVER THE GAP...
...AND COMPLETE HIS HAIR LOCK.
PLIP PLOP
UGH...
VOOO
AAH...

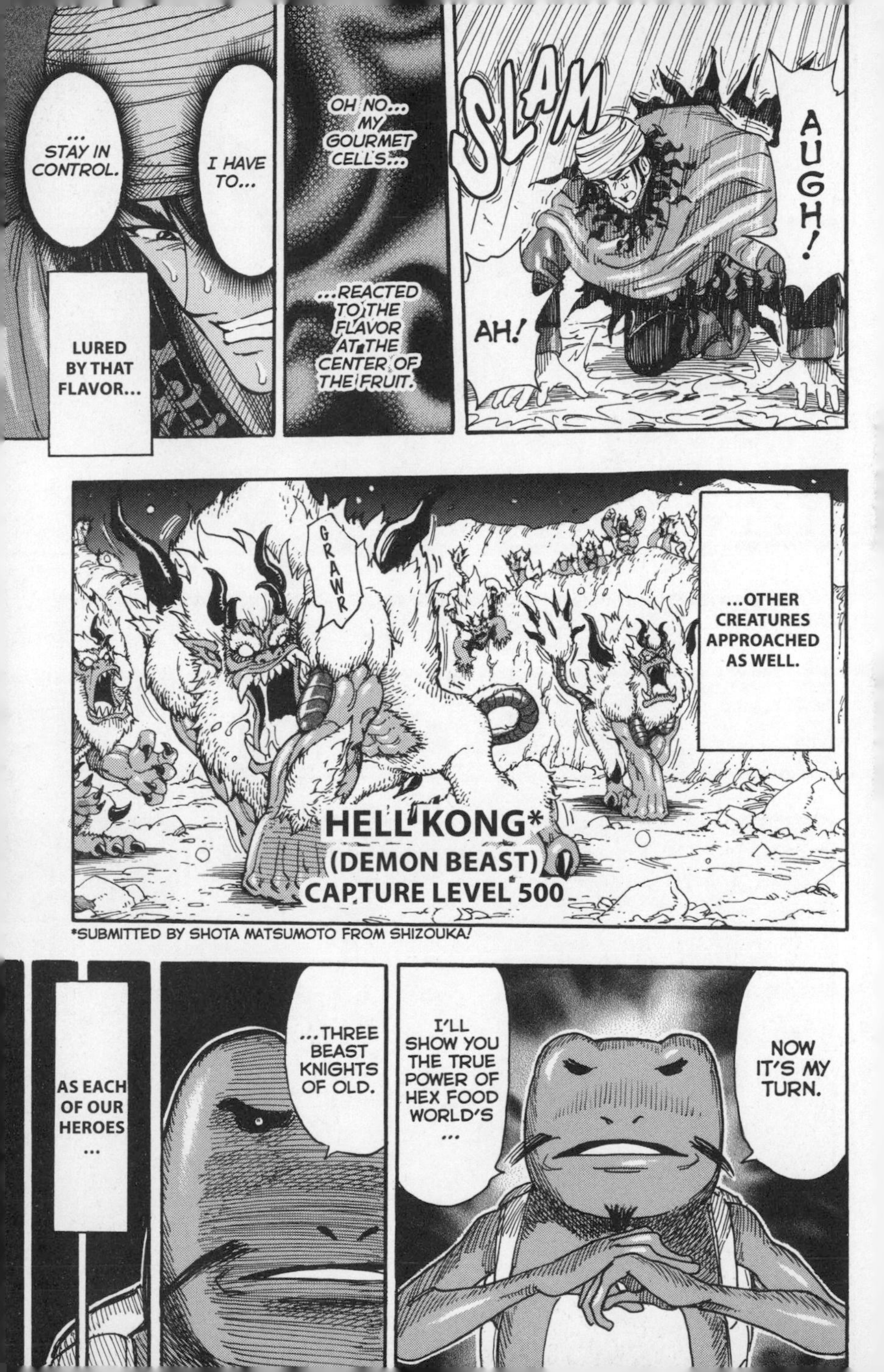
SLAM
AUGH!
AH!
OH NO... MY GOURMET CELLS...
...REACTED TO THE FLAVOR AT THE CENTER OF THE FRUIT.
I HAVE TO...
...STAY IN CONTROL.
LURED BY THAT FLAVOR...
...OTHER CREATURES APPROACHED AS WELL.
GRAWR
HELL KONG* (DEMON BEAST) CAPTURE LEVEL 500
*SUBMITTED BY SHOTA MATSUMOTO FROM SHIZOUKA!
NOW IT'S MY TURN.
I'LL SHOW YOU THE TRUE POWER OF HEX FOOD WORLD'S ...
...THREE BEAST KNIGHTS OF OLD.
AS EACH OF OUR HEROES ...

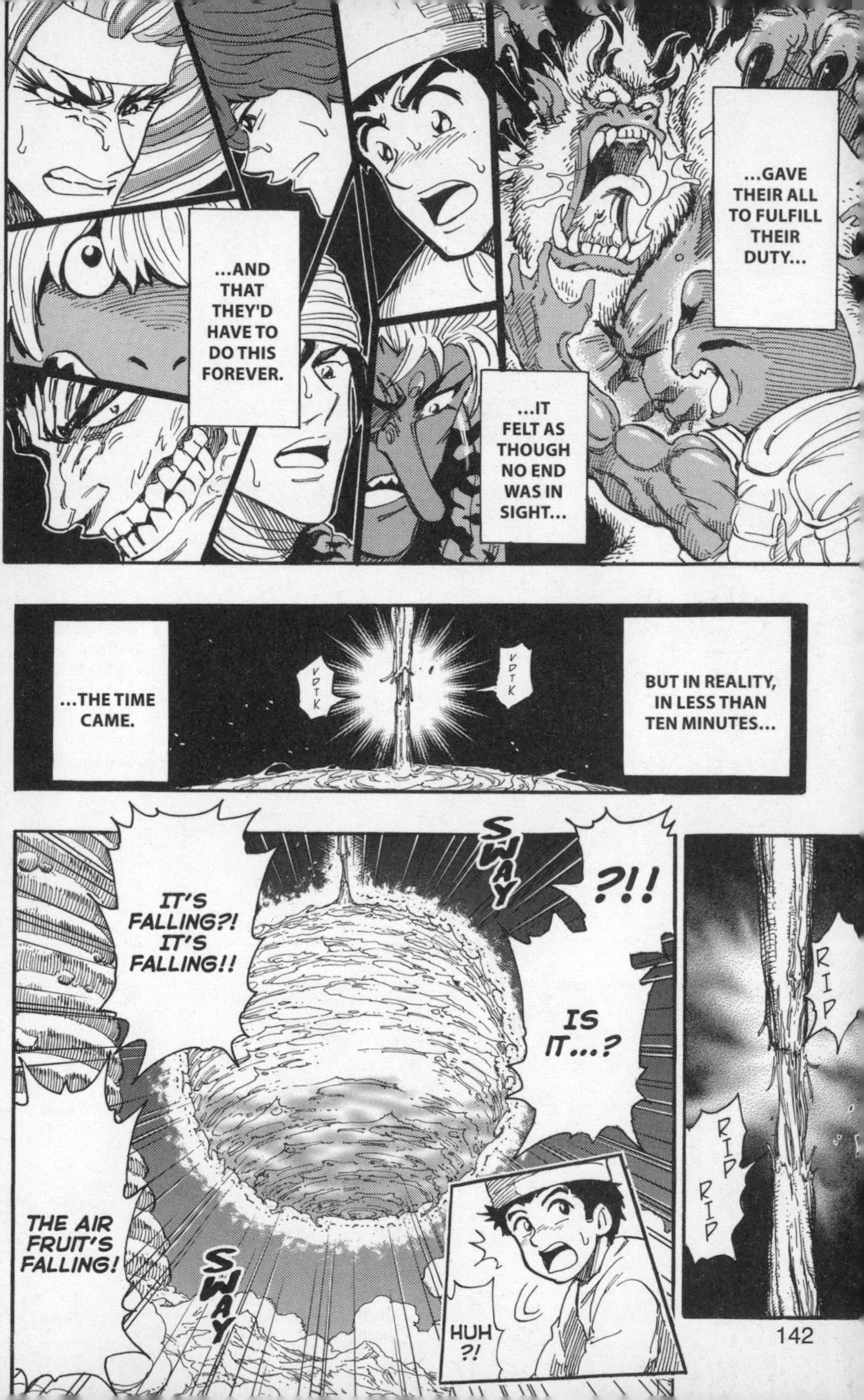
...GAVE THEIR ALL TO FULFILL THEIR DUTY...
...IT FELT AS THOUGH NO END WAS IN SIGHT...
...AND THAT THEY'D HAVE TO DO THIS FOREVER.
BUT IN REALITY, IN LESS THAN TEN MINUTES...
VDTK
VDTK
...THE TIME CAME.
RIP
RIP
RIP
RIP
?!!
SWAY
IS IT...?
IT'S FALLING?! IT'S FALLING!!
HUH?!
THE AIR FRUIT'S FALLING!
SWAY

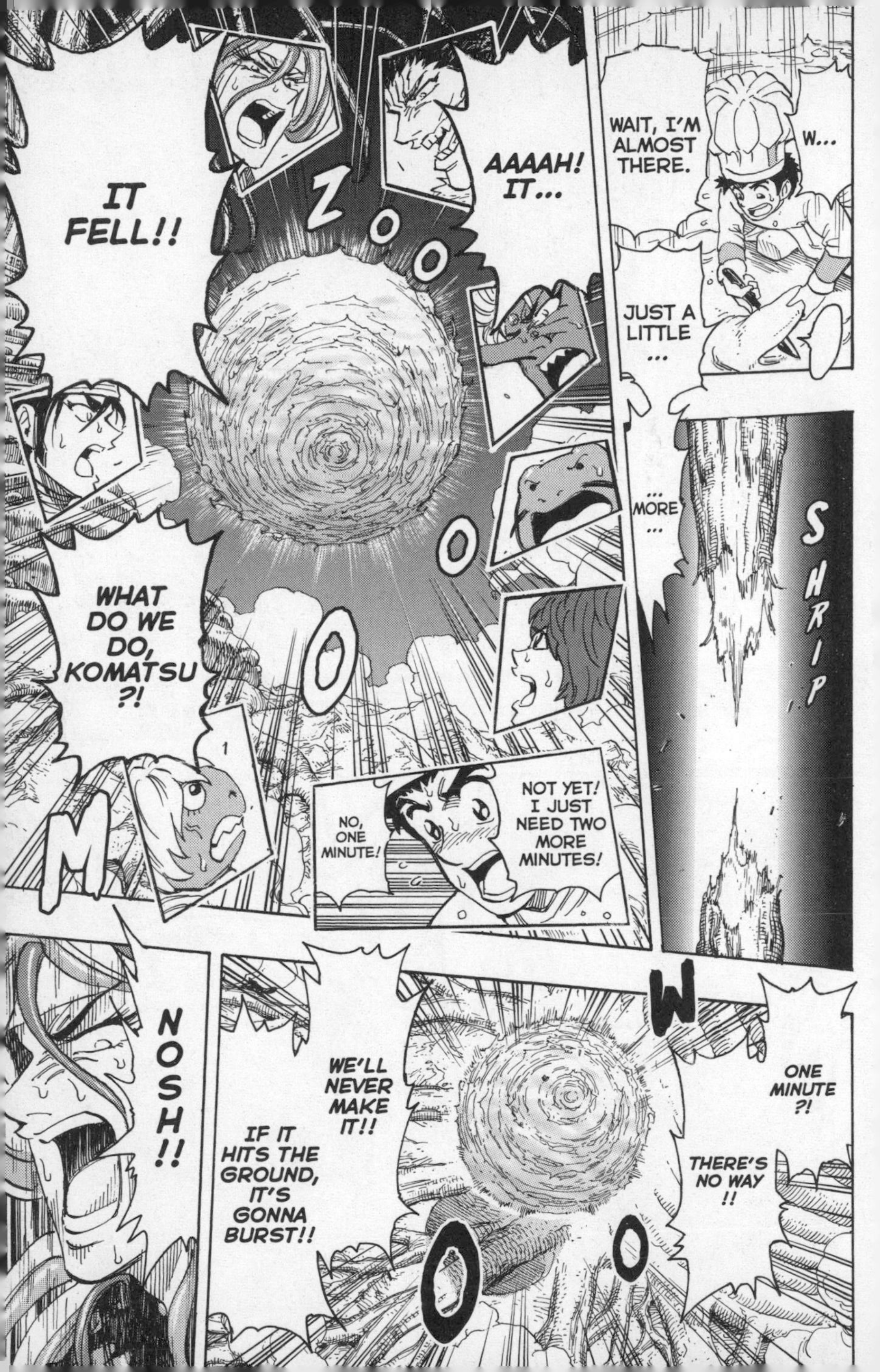
W...
WAIT, I'M ALMOST THERE.
JUST A LITTLE ...
... MORE ...
SHRIP
AAAAH! IT...
ZOOOOOM
IT FELL!!
WHAT DO WE DO, KOMATSU ?!
NOT YET! I JUST NEED TWO MORE MINUTES!
NO, ONE MINUTE!
ONE MINUTE ?!
THERE'S NO WAY !!
WOO
WE'LL NEVER MAKE IT!!
IF IT HITS THE GROUND, IT'S GONNA BURST!!
NOSH!!

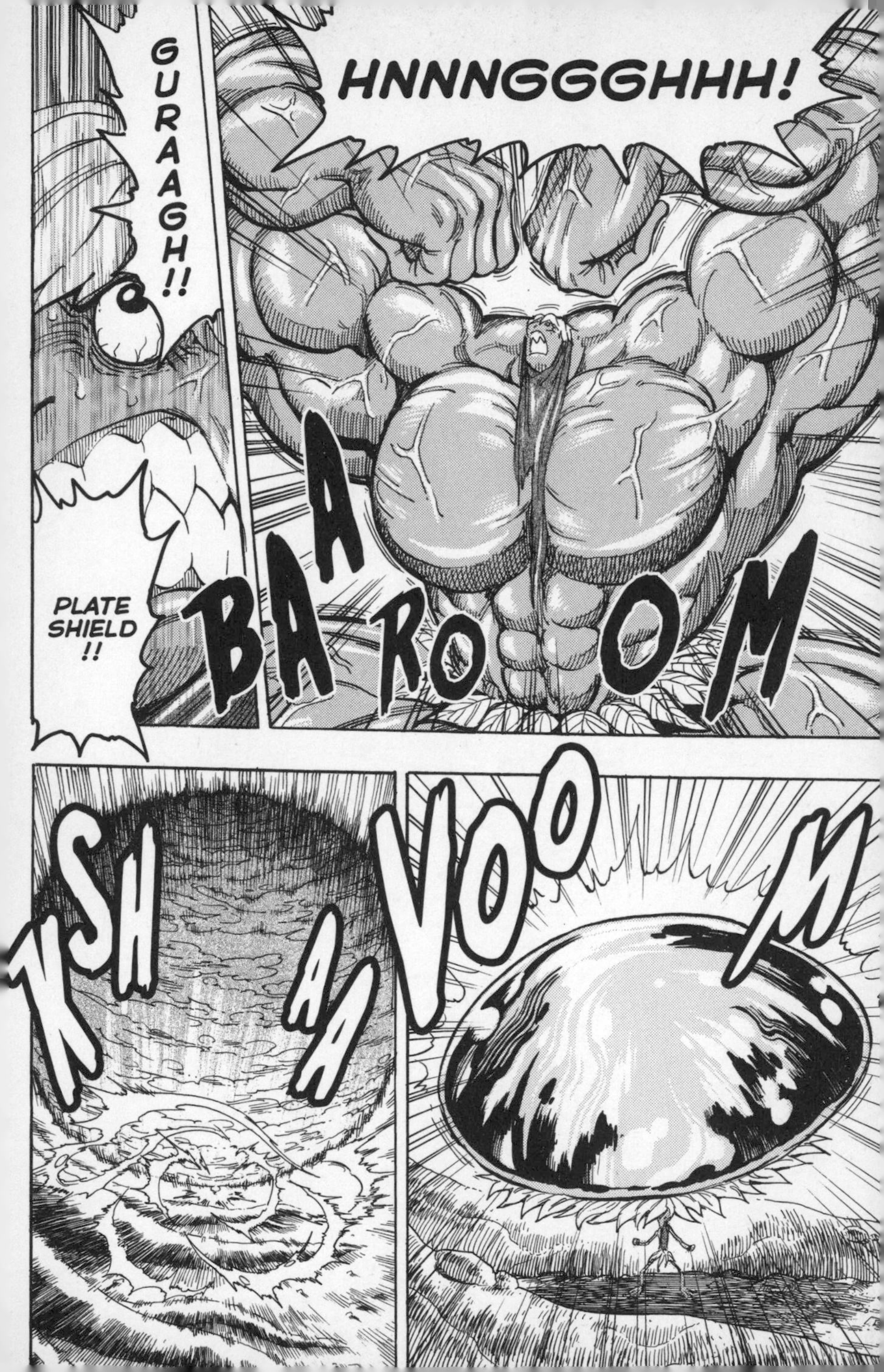
HNNNGGGHHH!
BAAROOOM
GURAAAGH!!
PLATE SHIELD !!
TSHAAVOOOM

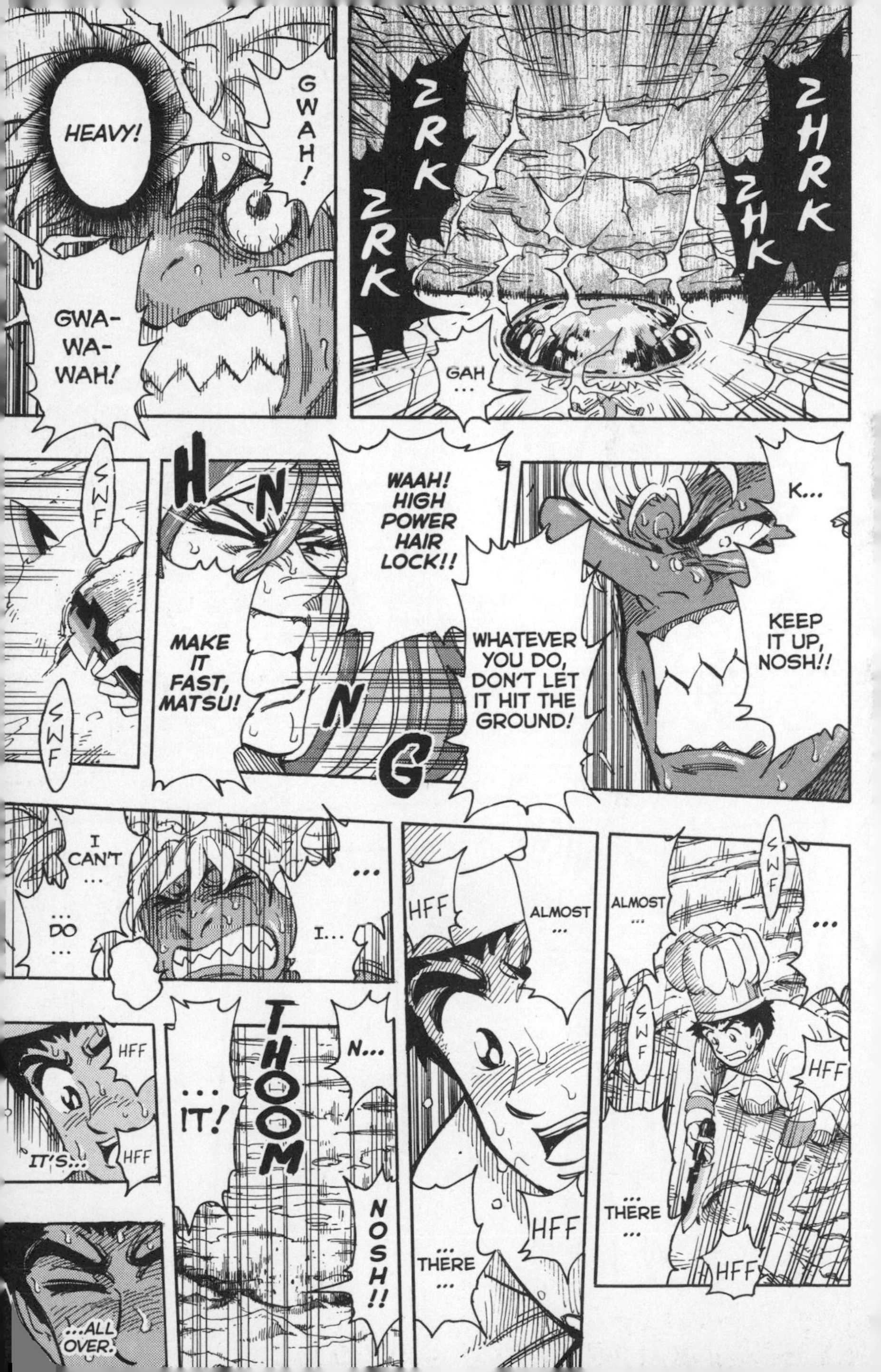

ZHRK ZHRK
ZRK ZRK
GAH ...
GWAH!
HEAVY!
GWA-WA-WAH!
K...
KEEP IT UP, NOSH!!
WAAH! HIGH POWER HAIR LOCK!!
WHATEVER YOU DO, DON'T LET IT HIT THE GROUND!
HNNG
MAKE IT FAST, MATSU!
SWF
SWF
SWF
...
ALMOST ...
SWF
HFF
... THERE ...
HFF
HFF
ALMOST ...
HFF
... THERE ...
...
I...
I CAN'T ...
... DO ...
N...
... IT!
THOOM
NOSH!!
HFF
IT'S...
HFF
...ALL OVER.

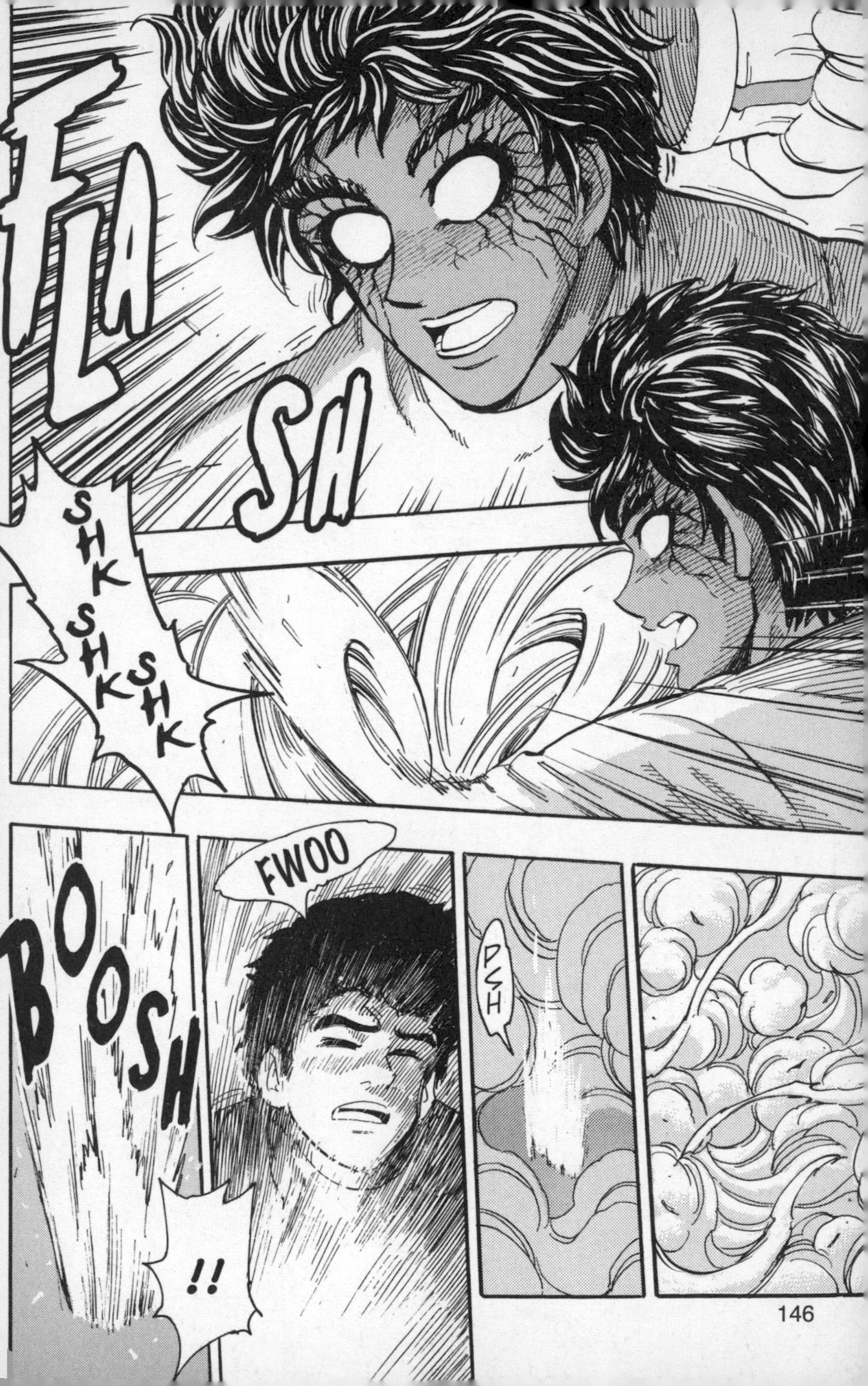
FLASH
SHK SHK SHK
PSH
FWOO
BOOSH
!!

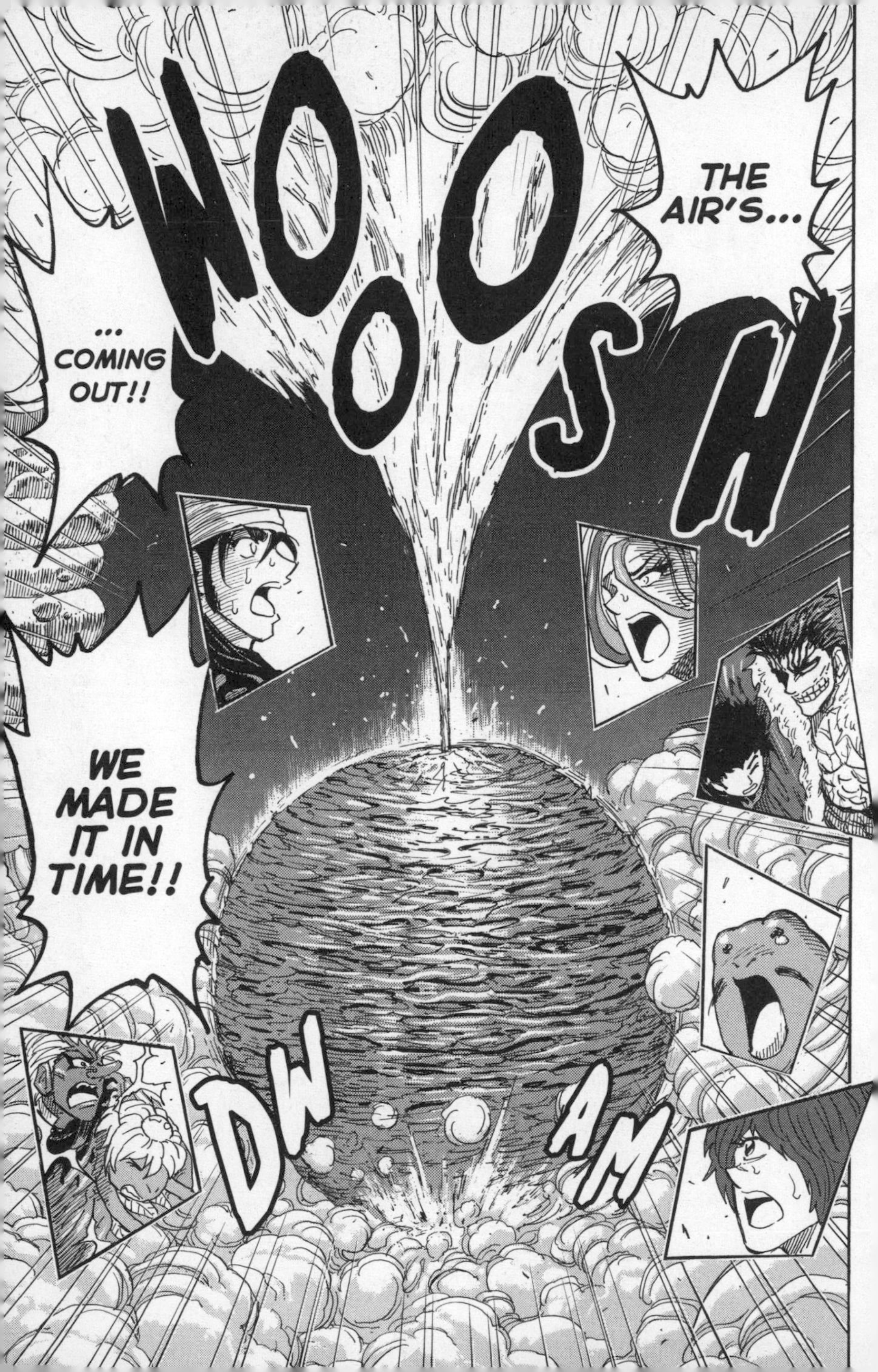
THE AIR'S...
WHOOOSH
... COMING OUT!!
WE MADE IT IN TIME!!
DWAM

TORIKO

GOURMET CHECKLIST

Vol. 316

MEDICINAL MOCHI
(DETOXIFYING INGREDIENT)

CAPTURE LEVEL: —
HABITAT: —
SIZE: 10 CM
HEIGHT: —
WEIGHT: 120 GRAMS
PRICE: NO PRICE SET

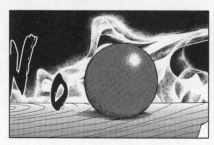

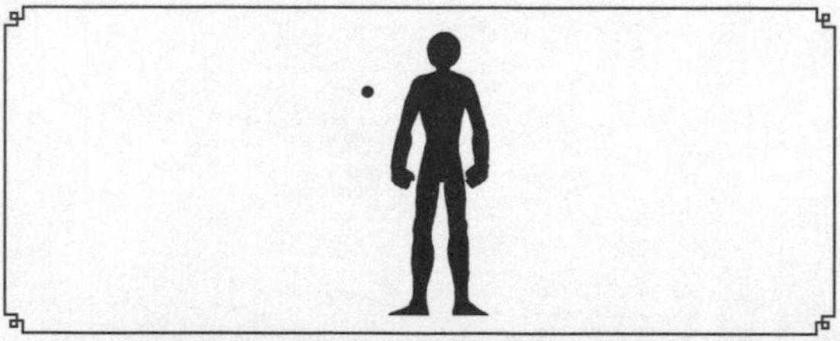

SCALE

THE MEAL KING YUDA PREPARED THIS DETOXIFYING INGREDIENT IN ORDER TO SAVE THE SEVERAL MILLION HUMANS WHO ALMOST DIED FROM THE GREEN RAIN THAT POURED OVER THE WORLD FROM THE FOUR-BEASTS MAIN BODY. WITH ONLY AN HOUR FOR THEM TO LIVE, THIS INGREDIENT NEEDED TO BE PREPARED AND DISTRIBUTED FAST. BUT EVEN WITH THE WORLD'S LEADING CHEFS ON THE JOB, THE ORIGINAL METHOD OF PREPARATION WAS JUST TOO SLOW. KOMATSU'S GENIUS CHEF SKILLS ALLOWED HIM TO SIMPLIFY THE PREPARATION SO THAT EVEN ORDINARY CHEFS COULD MAKE IT! HE EVEN MANAGED TO MAKE THEM TASTIER THAN THE ORIGINAL. WITH THE COMBINED HELP OF THE GOURMET HUNTS, CHEFS, SHOPS AND THOSE WILLING TO HELP, HUMANITY WAS SAVED FROM EXTINCTION.

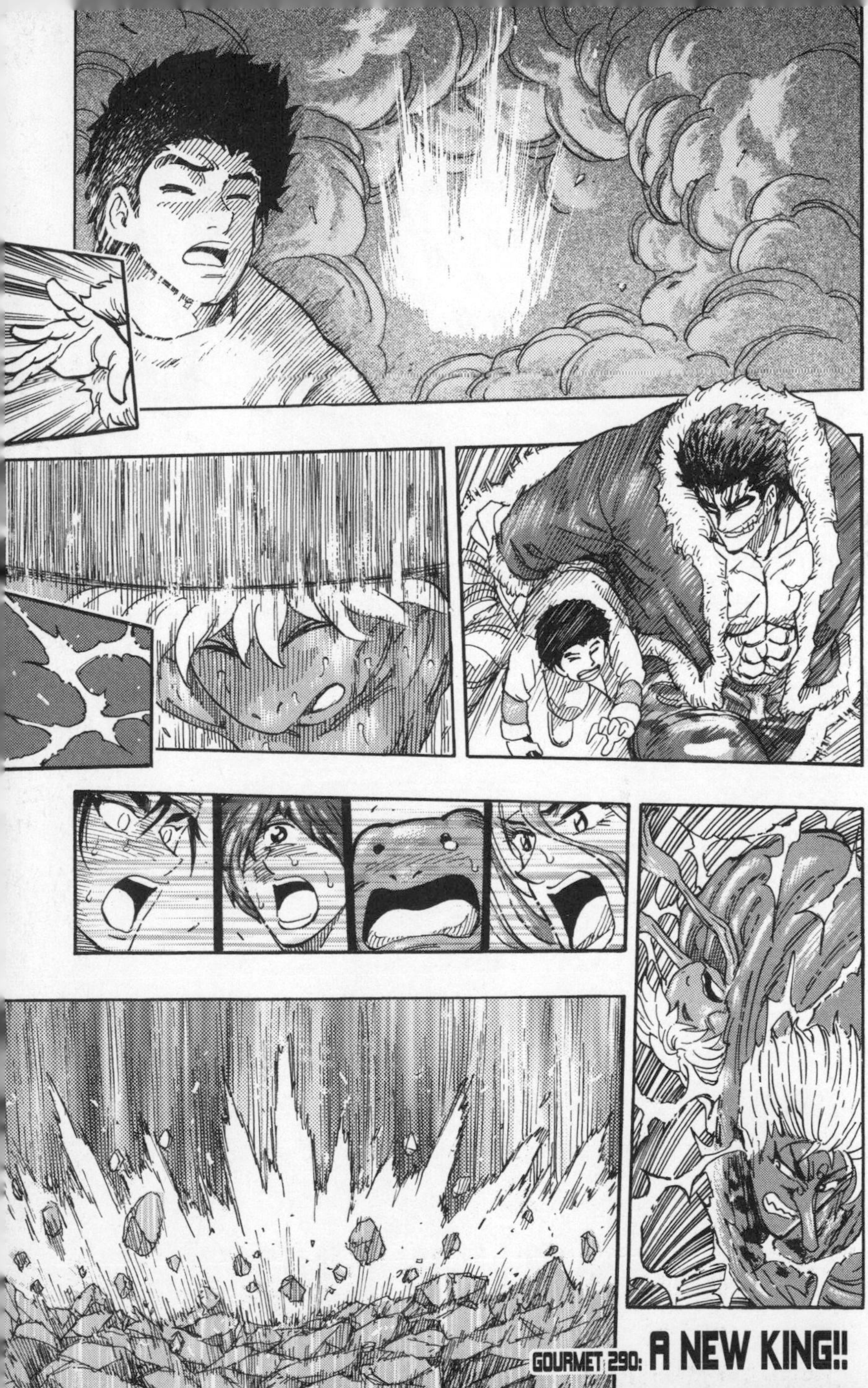

GOURMET 290: A NEW KING!!

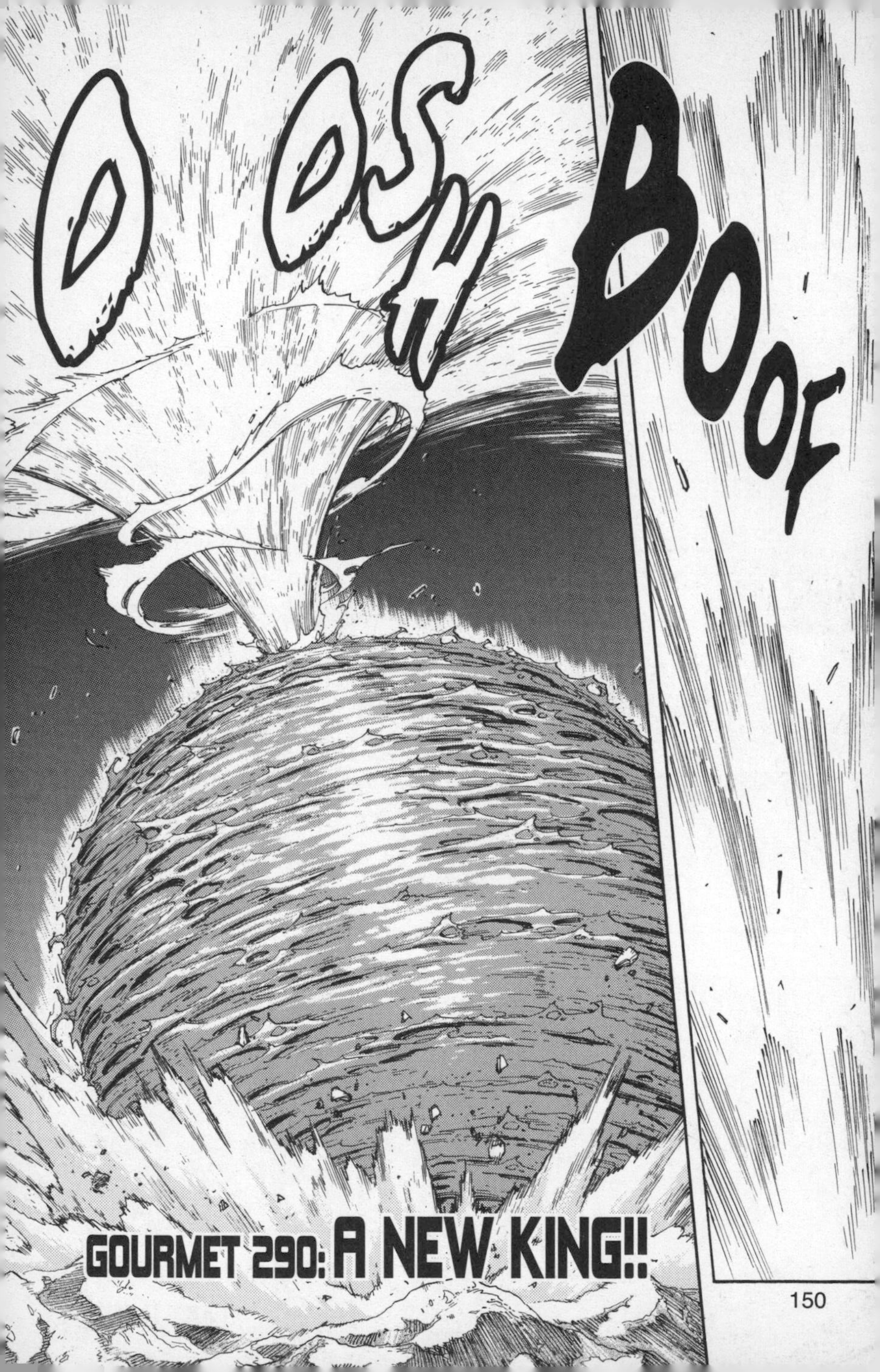
BOOF
DOSH

GOURMET 290: A NEW KING!!

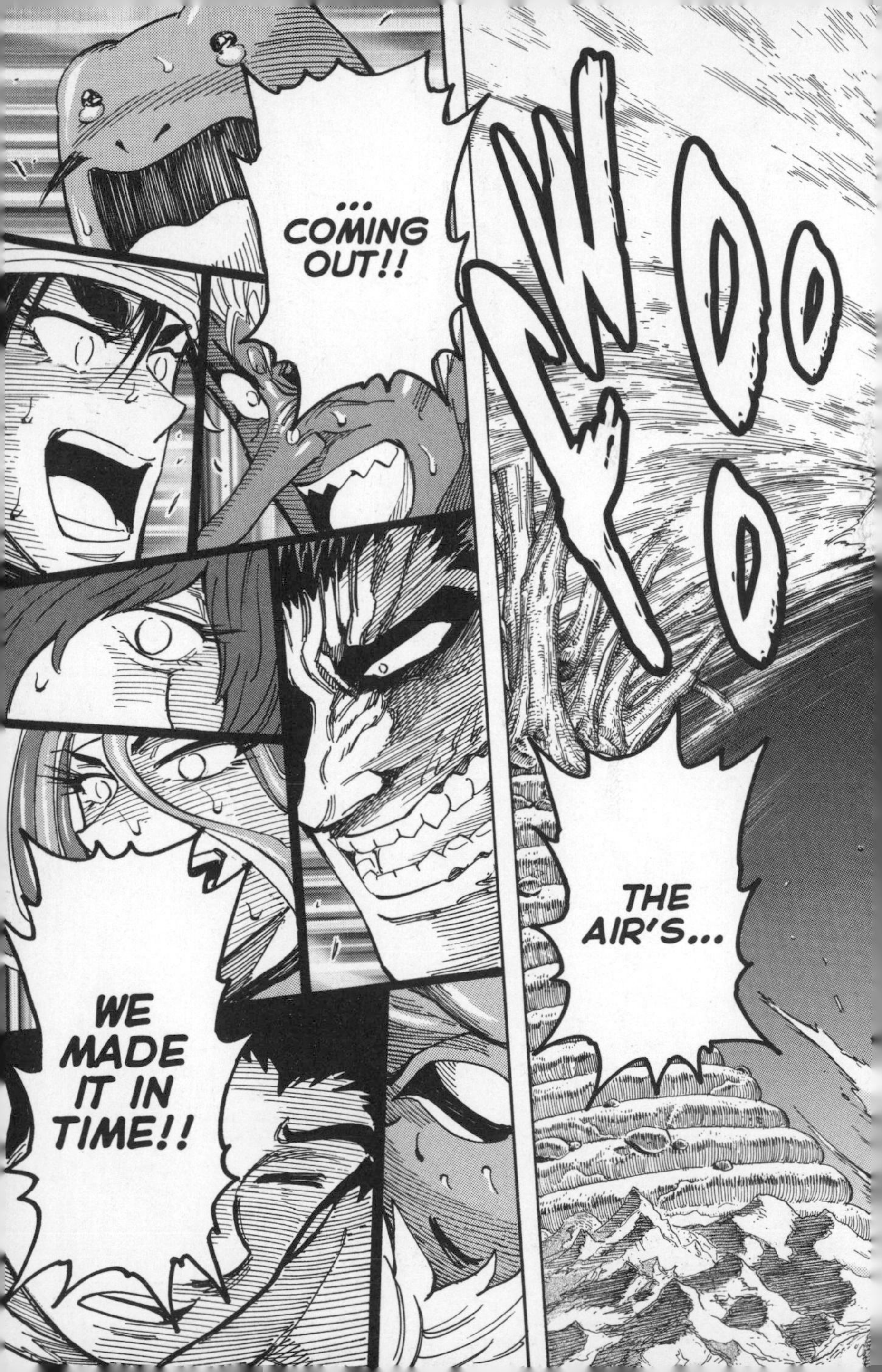
THE AIR'S...
...COMING OUT!!
WE MADE IT IN TIME!!

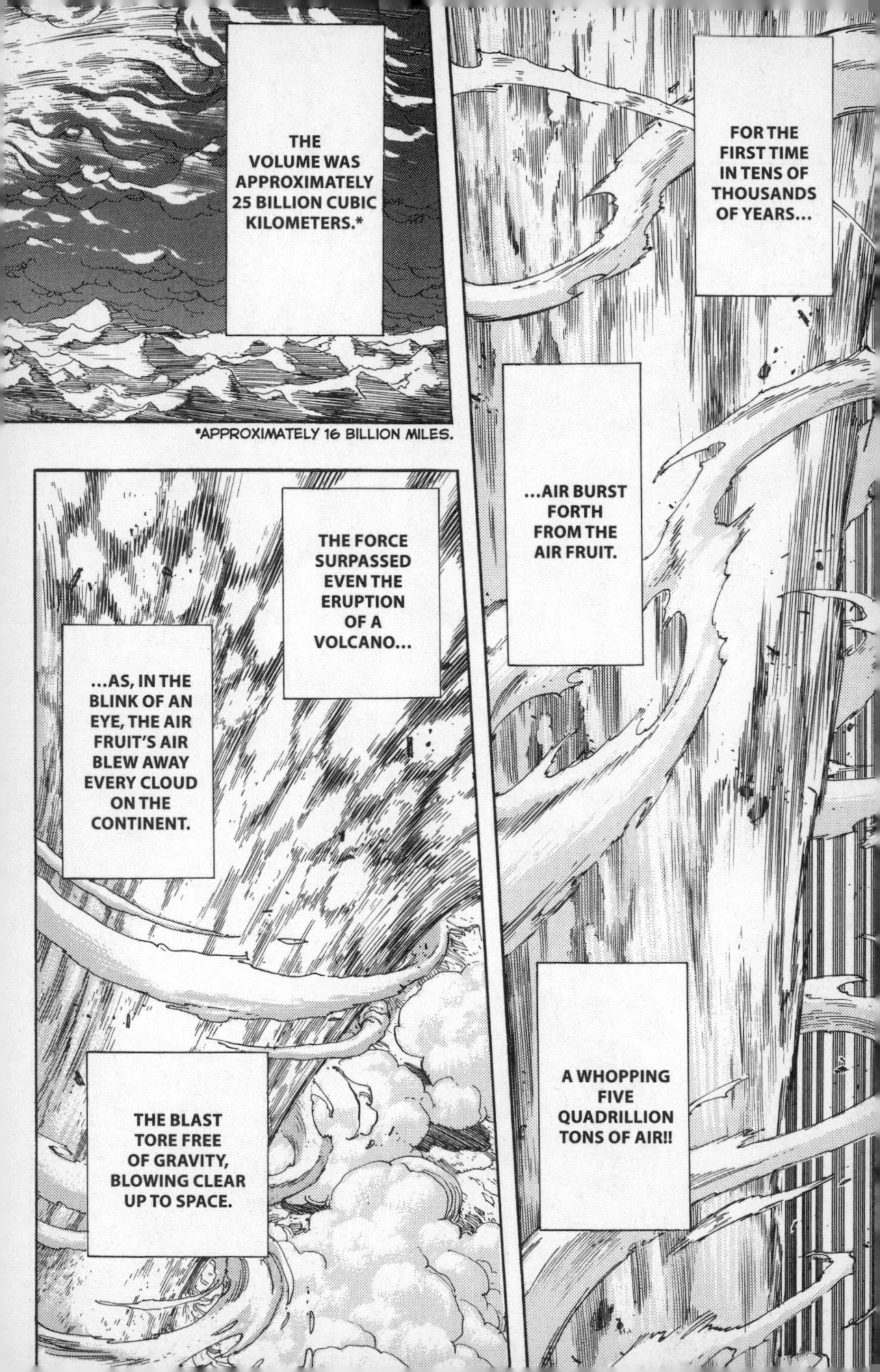
FOR THE FIRST TIME IN TENS OF THOUSANDS OF YEARS...
...AIR BURST FORTH FROM THE AIR FRUIT.
A WHOPPING FIVE QUADRILLION TONS OF AIR!!
THE VOLUME WAS APPROXIMATELY 25 BILLION CUBIC KILOMETERS.*
*APPROXIMATELY 16 BILLION MILES.
THE FORCE SURPASSED EVEN THE ERUPTION OF A VOLCANO...
...AS, IN THE BLINK OF AN EYE, THE AIR FRUIT'S AIR BLEW AWAY EVERY CLOUD ON THE CONTINENT.
THE BLAST TORE FREE OF GRAVITY, BLOWING CLEAR UP TO SPACE.

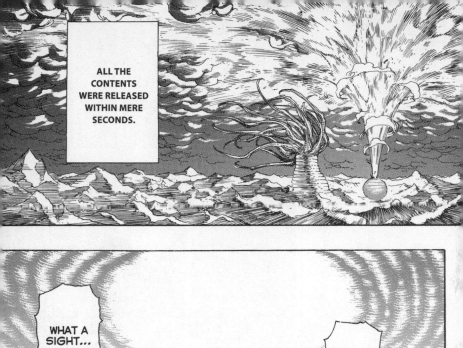

ALL THE
CONTENTS
WERE RELEASED
WITHIN MERE
SECONDS.

WHAT A
SIGHT...

W...
WOW...

TORI
...

...

KO...

T...

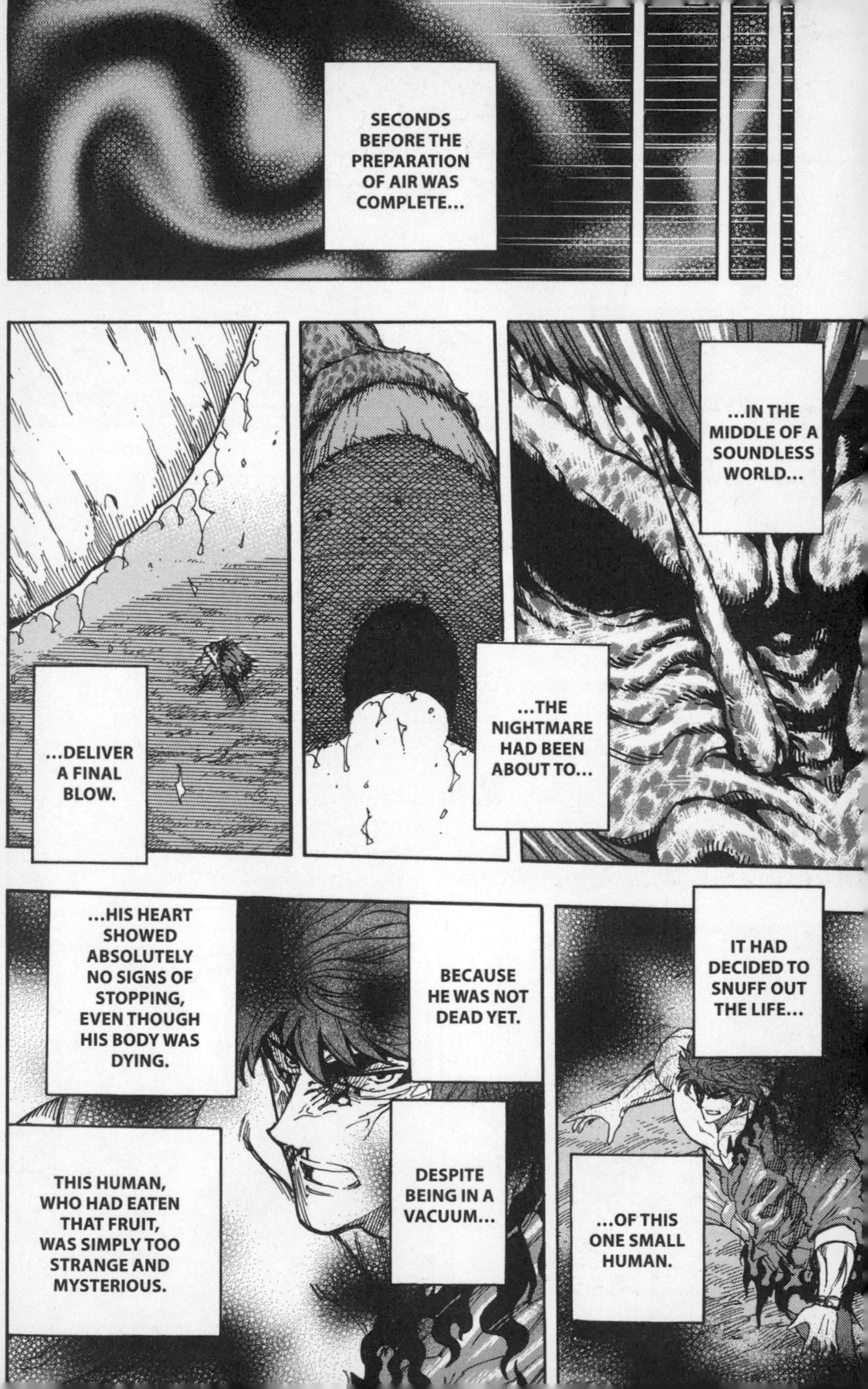
SECONDS BEFORE THE PREPARATION OF AIR WAS COMPLETE...
...IN THE MIDDLE OF A SOUNDLESS WORLD...
...THE NIGHTMARE HAD BEEN ABOUT TO...
...DELIVER A FINAL BLOW.
IT HAD DECIDED TO SNUFF OUT THE LIFE...
...OF THIS ONE SMALL HUMAN.
BECAUSE HE WAS NOT DEAD YET.
...HIS HEART SHOWED ABSOLUTELY NO SIGNS OF STOPPING, EVEN THOUGH HIS BODY WAS DYING.
DESPITE BEING IN A VACUUM...
THIS HUMAN, WHO HAD EATEN THAT FRUIT, WAS SIMPLY TOO STRANGE AND MYSTERIOUS.

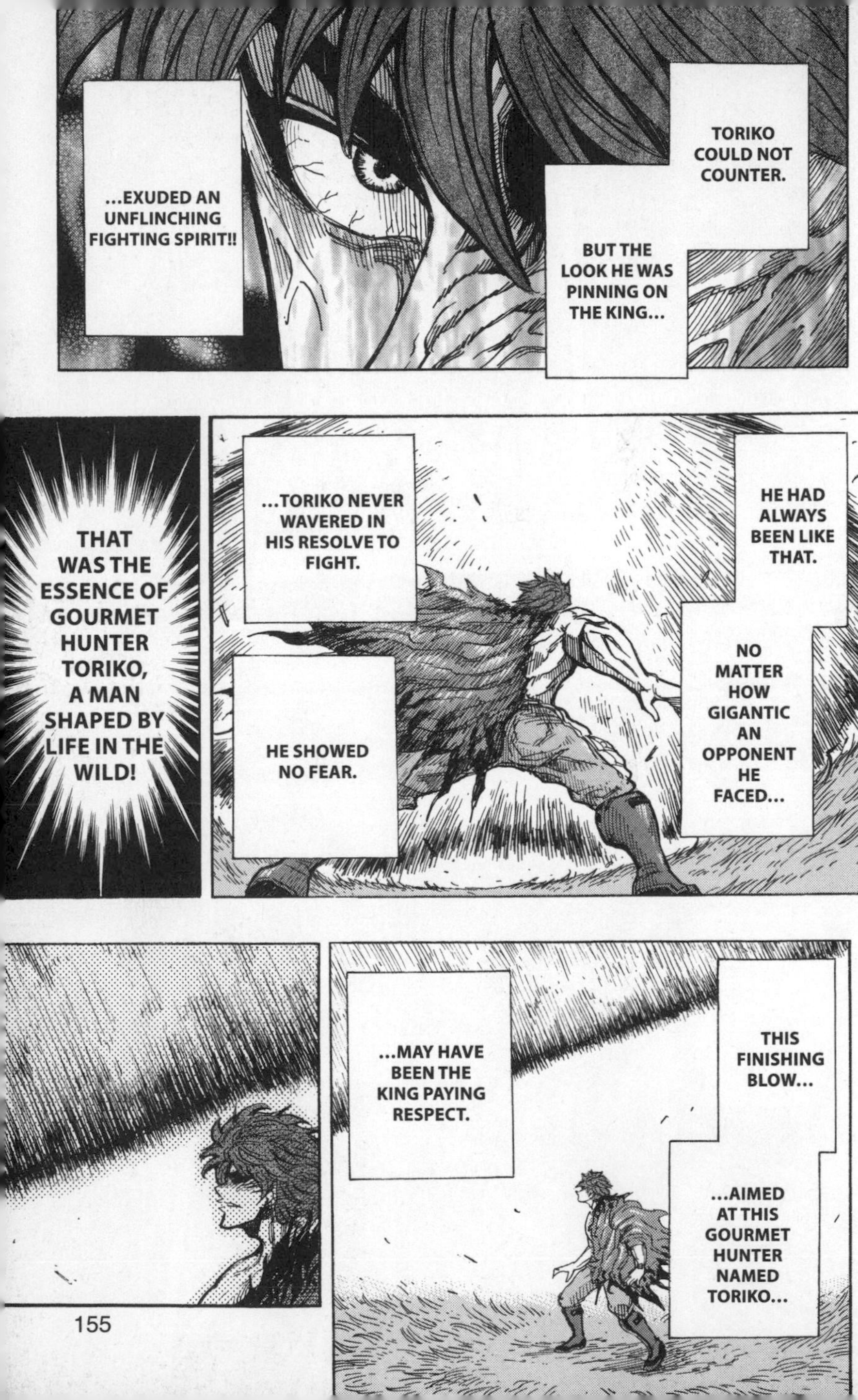
TORIKO COULD NOT COUNTER.
BUT THE LOOK HE WAS PINNING ON THE KING...
...EXUDED AN UNFLINCHING FIGHTING SPIRIT!!
HE HAD ALWAYS BEEN LIKE THAT.
NO MATTER HOW GIGANTIC AN OPPONENT HE FACED...
...TORIKO NEVER WAVERED IN HIS RESOLVE TO FIGHT.
HE SHOWED NO FEAR.
THAT WAS THE ESSENCE OF GOURMET HUNTER TORIKO, A MAN SHAPED BY LIFE IN THE WILD!
THIS FINISHING BLOW...
...AIMED AT THIS GOURMET HUNTER NAMED TORIKO...
...MAY HAVE BEEN THE KING PAYING RESPECT.

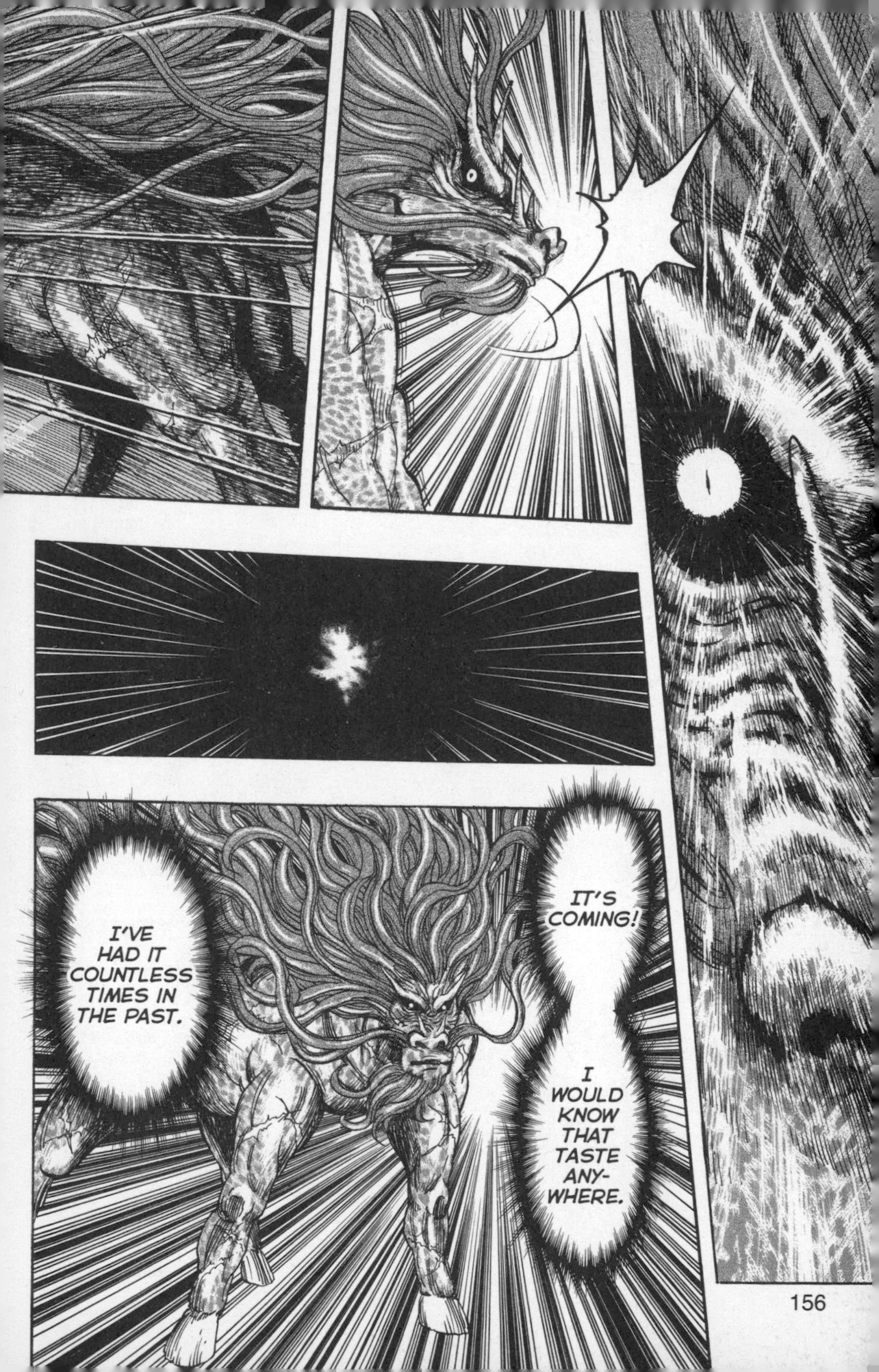
IT'S COMING!
I WOULD KNOW THAT TASTE ANY-WHERE.
I'VE HAD IT COUNTLESS TIMES IN THE PAST.

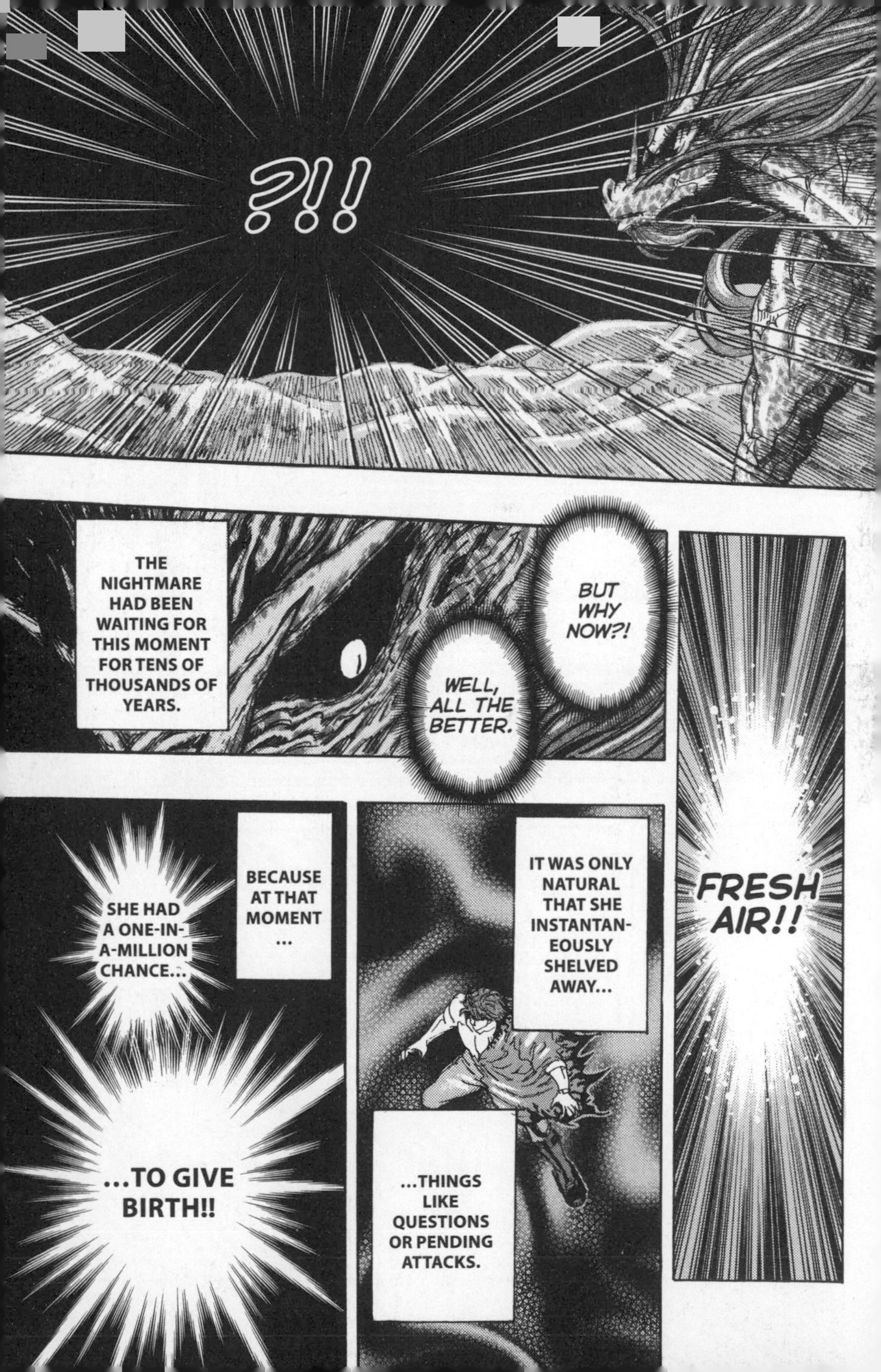
?!!
FRESH AIR!!
BUT WHY NOW?!
WELL, ALL THE BETTER.
THE NIGHTMARE HAD BEEN WAITING FOR THIS MOMENT FOR TENS OF THOUSANDS OF YEARS.
IT WAS ONLY NATURAL THAT SHE INSTANTANEOUSLY SHELVED AWAY...
...THINGS LIKE QUESTIONS OR PENDING ATTACKS.
BECAUSE AT THAT MOMENT...
SHE HAD A ONE-IN-A-MILLION CHANCE...
...TO GIVE BIRTH!!

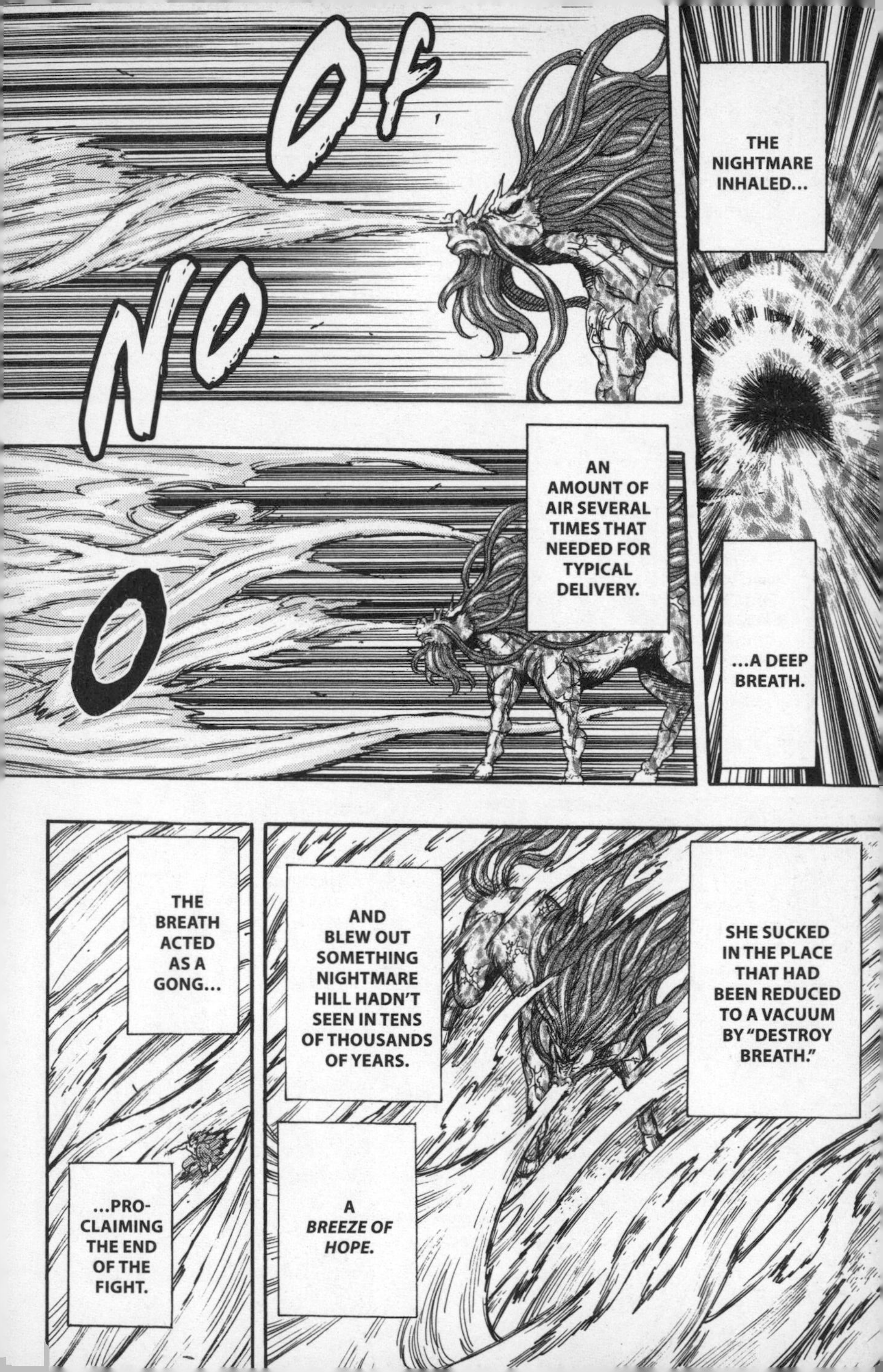
THE NIGHTMARE INHALED...
...A DEEP BREATH.
OF
NO
AN AMOUNT OF AIR SEVERAL TIMES THAT NEEDED FOR TYPICAL DELIVERY.
O
SHE SUCKED IN THE PLACE THAT HAD BEEN REDUCED TO A VACUUM BY "DESTROY BREATH."
AND BLEW OUT SOMETHING NIGHTMARE HILL HADN'T SEEN IN TENS OF THOUSANDS OF YEARS.
A *BREEZE OF HOPE.*
THE BREATH ACTED AS A GONG...
...PRO-CLAIMING THE END OF THE FIGHT.

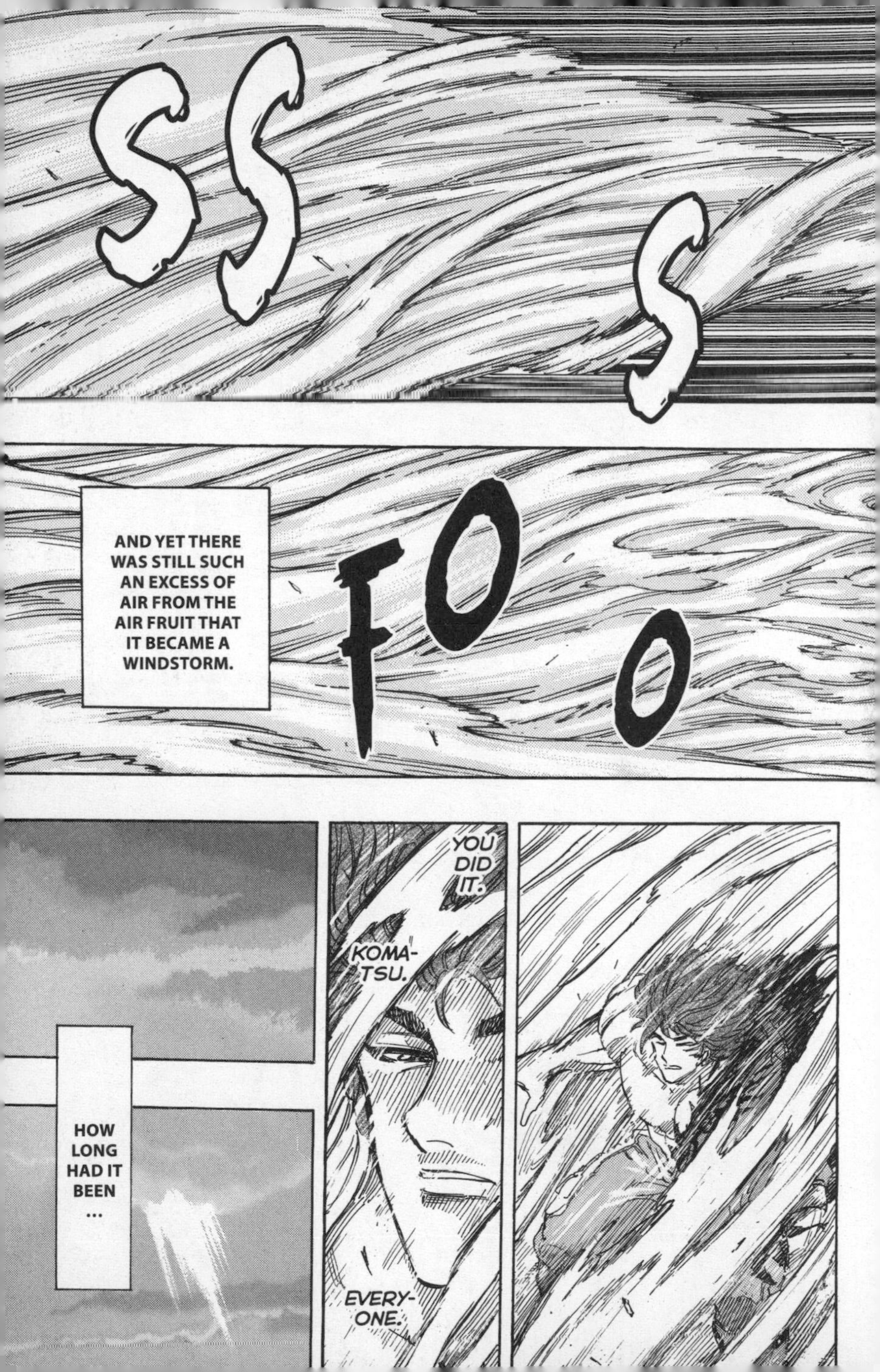
SSS
AND YET THERE WAS STILL SUCH AN EXCESS OF AIR FROM THE AIR FRUIT THAT IT BECAME A WINDSTORM.
FOO
YOU DID IT.
KOMATSU.
EVERYONE.
HOW LONG HAD IT BEEN ...

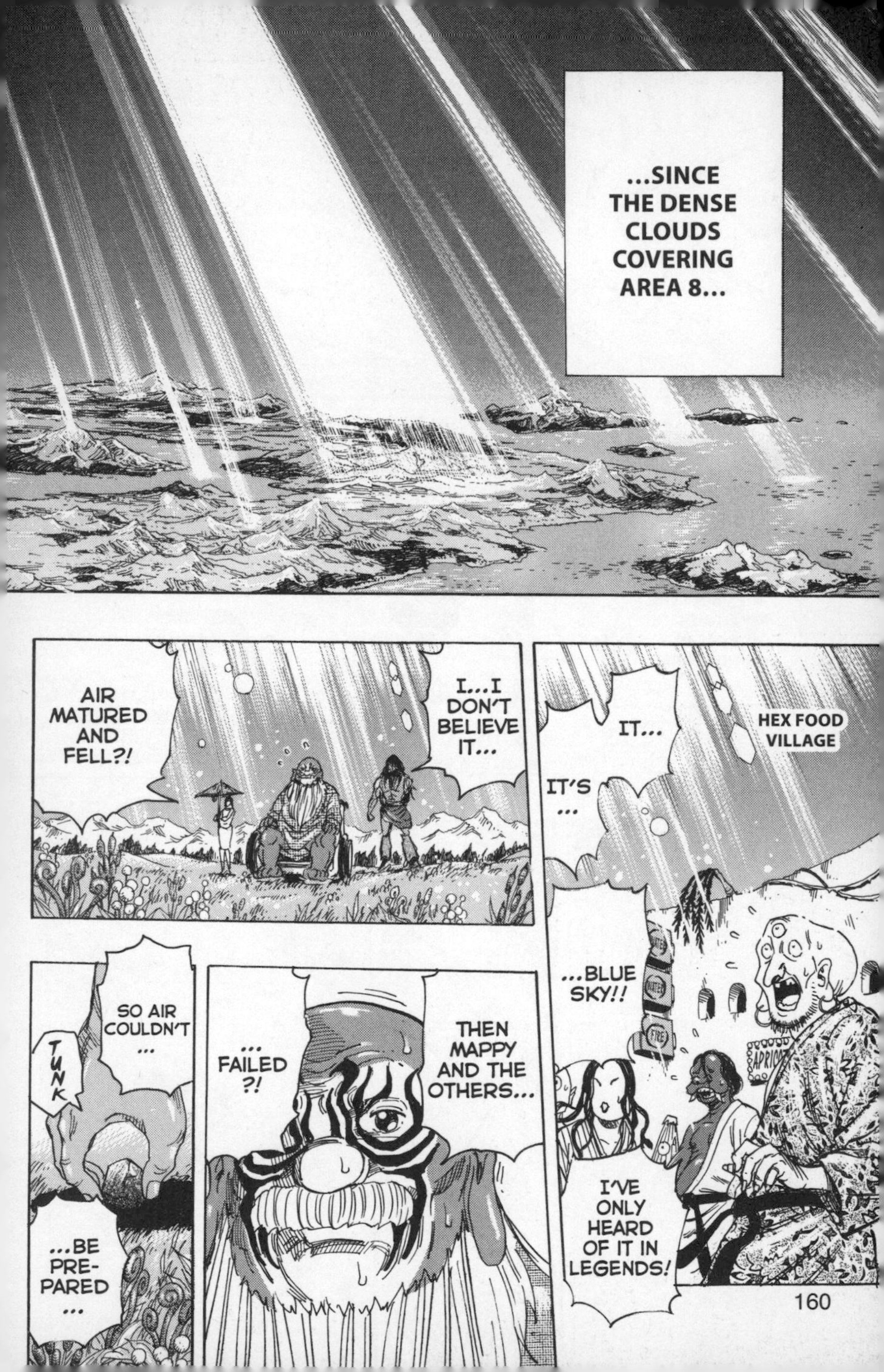
...SINCE THE DENSE CLOUDS COVERING AREA 8...
HEX FOOD VILLAGE
IT...
IT'S...
...BLUE SKY!!
I'VE ONLY HEARD OF IT IN LEGENDS!
I...I DON'T BELIEVE IT...
AIR MATURED AND FELL?!
THEN MAPPY AND THE OTHERS...
...FAILED?!
SO AIR COULDN'T...
TUNK
...BE PRE-PARED...

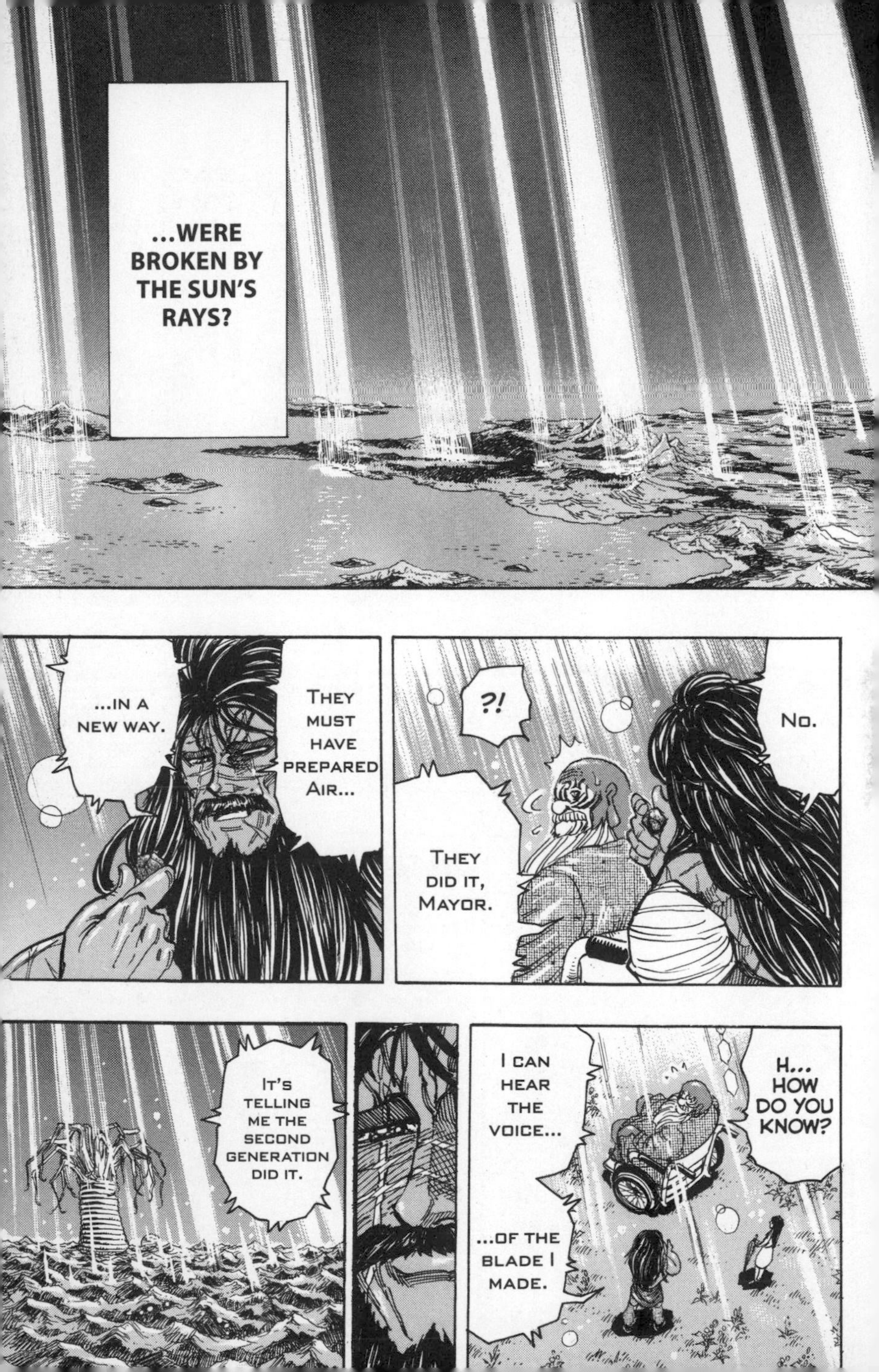
...WERE BROKEN BY THE SUN'S RAYS?
No.
?!
They did it, Mayor.
They must have prepared Air...
...in a new way.
H... how do you know?
I can hear the voice...
...of the blade I made.
It's telling me the second generation did it.

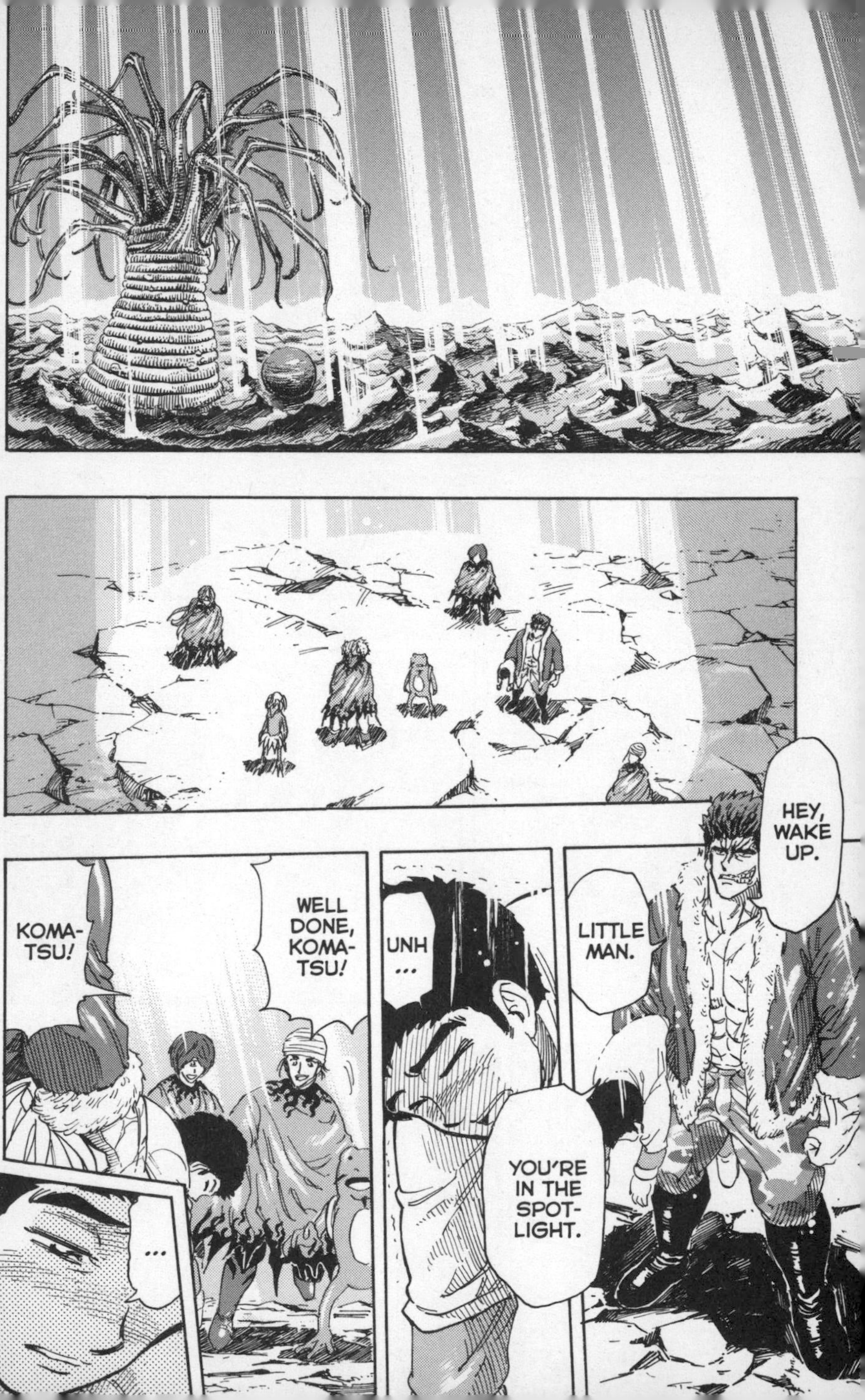
HEY, WAKE UP.
LITTLE MAN.
UNH ...
YOU'RE IN THE SPOTLIGHT.
WELL DONE, KOMATSU!
KOMATSU!
...

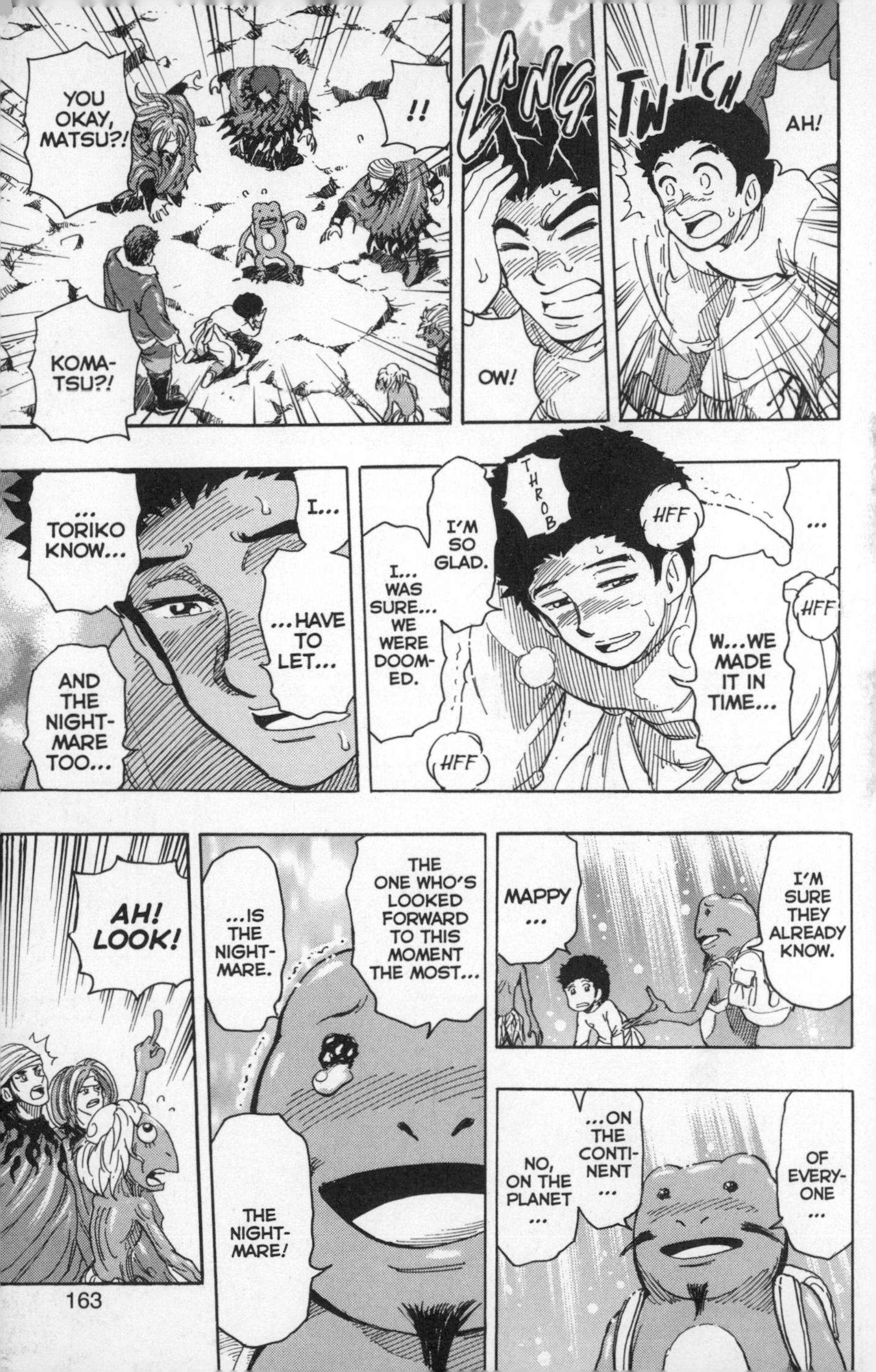
TWITCH
AH!
ZANG
OW!
!!
YOU OKAY, MATSU?!
KOMA-TSU?!
...
HFF
THROB
I'M SO GLAD.
I... WAS SURE... WE WERE DOOM-ED.
HFF
W...WE MADE IT IN TIME...
HFF
I...
...TORIKO KNOW...
...HAVE TO LET...
AND THE NIGHT-MARE TOO...
I'M SURE THEY ALREADY KNOW.
MAPPY...
OF EVERY-ONE...
...ON THE CONTI-NENT...
NO, ON THE PLANET...
THE ONE WHO'S LOOKED FORWARD TO THIS MOMENT THE MOST...
...IS THE NIGHT-MARE.
THE NIGHT-MARE!
AH! LOOK!

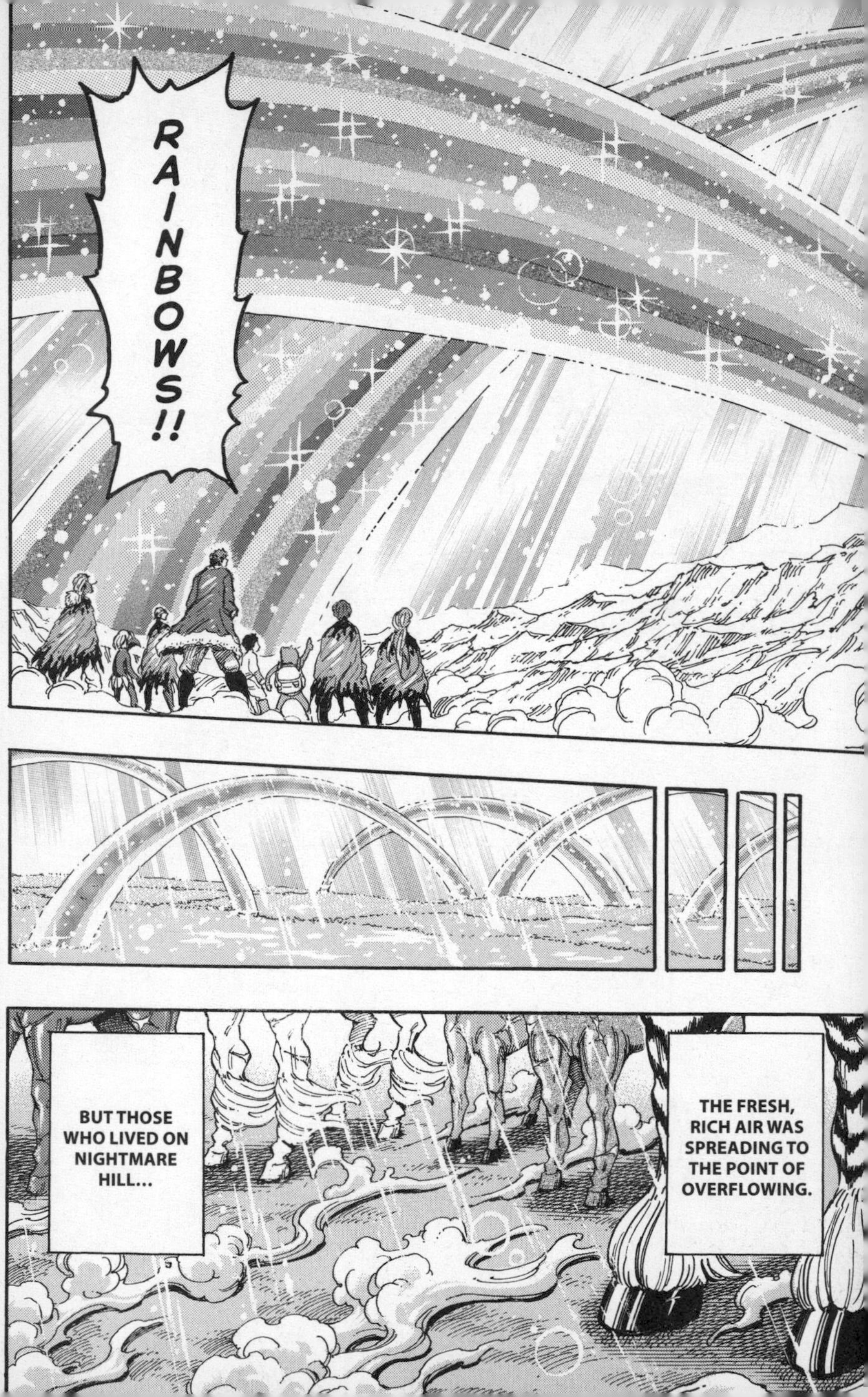
RAINBOWS!!
THE FRESH, RICH AIR WAS SPREADING TO THE POINT OF OVERFLOWING.
BUT THOSE WHO LIVED ON NIGHTMARE HILL...

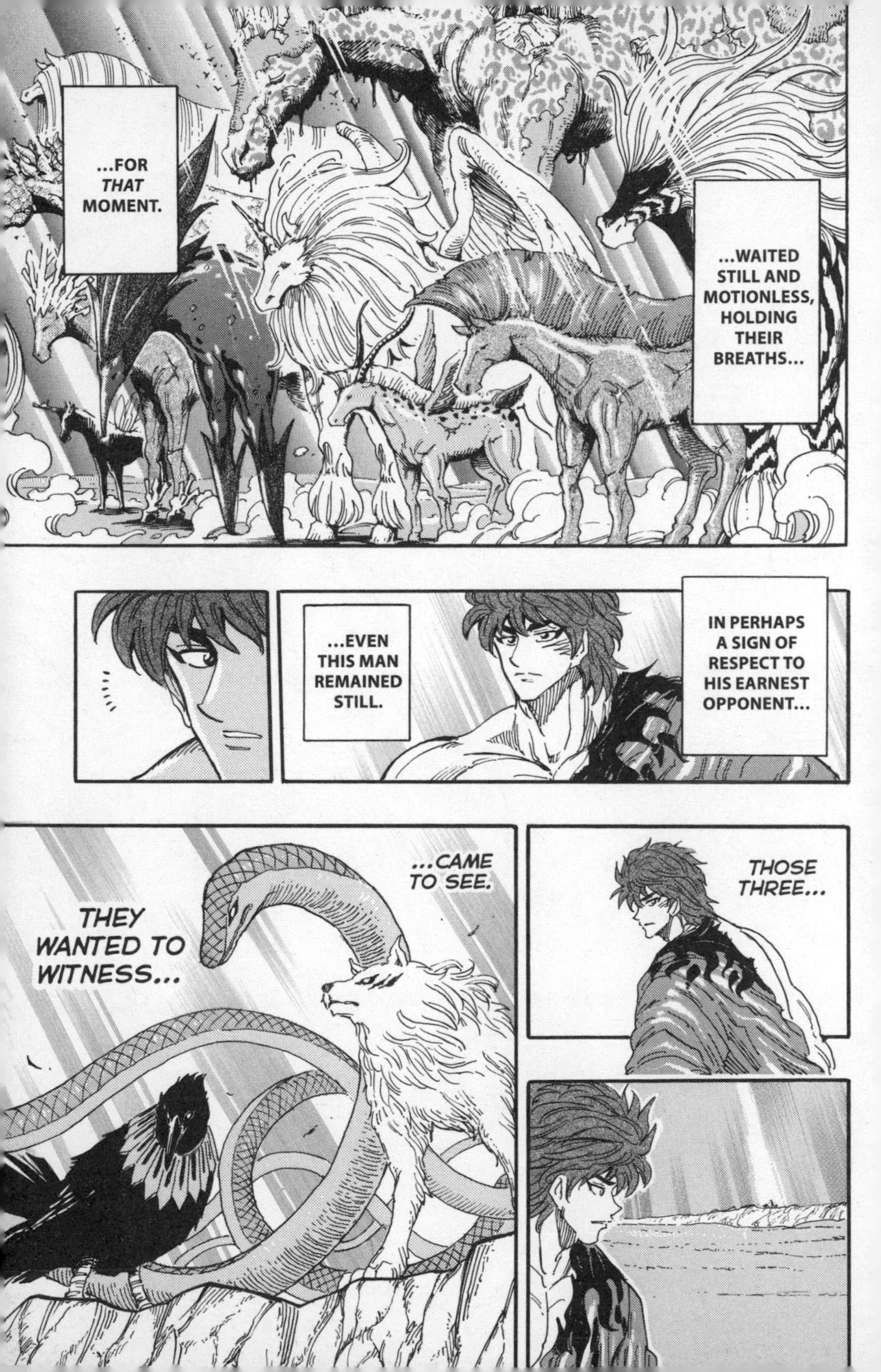

...WAITED STILL AND MOTIONLESS, HOLDING THEIR BREATHS...
...FOR *THAT* MOMENT.
IN PERHAPS A SIGN OF RESPECT TO HIS EARNEST OPPONENT...
...EVEN THIS MAN REMAINED STILL.
THOSE THREE...
...CAME TO SEE.
THEY WANTED TO WITNESS...

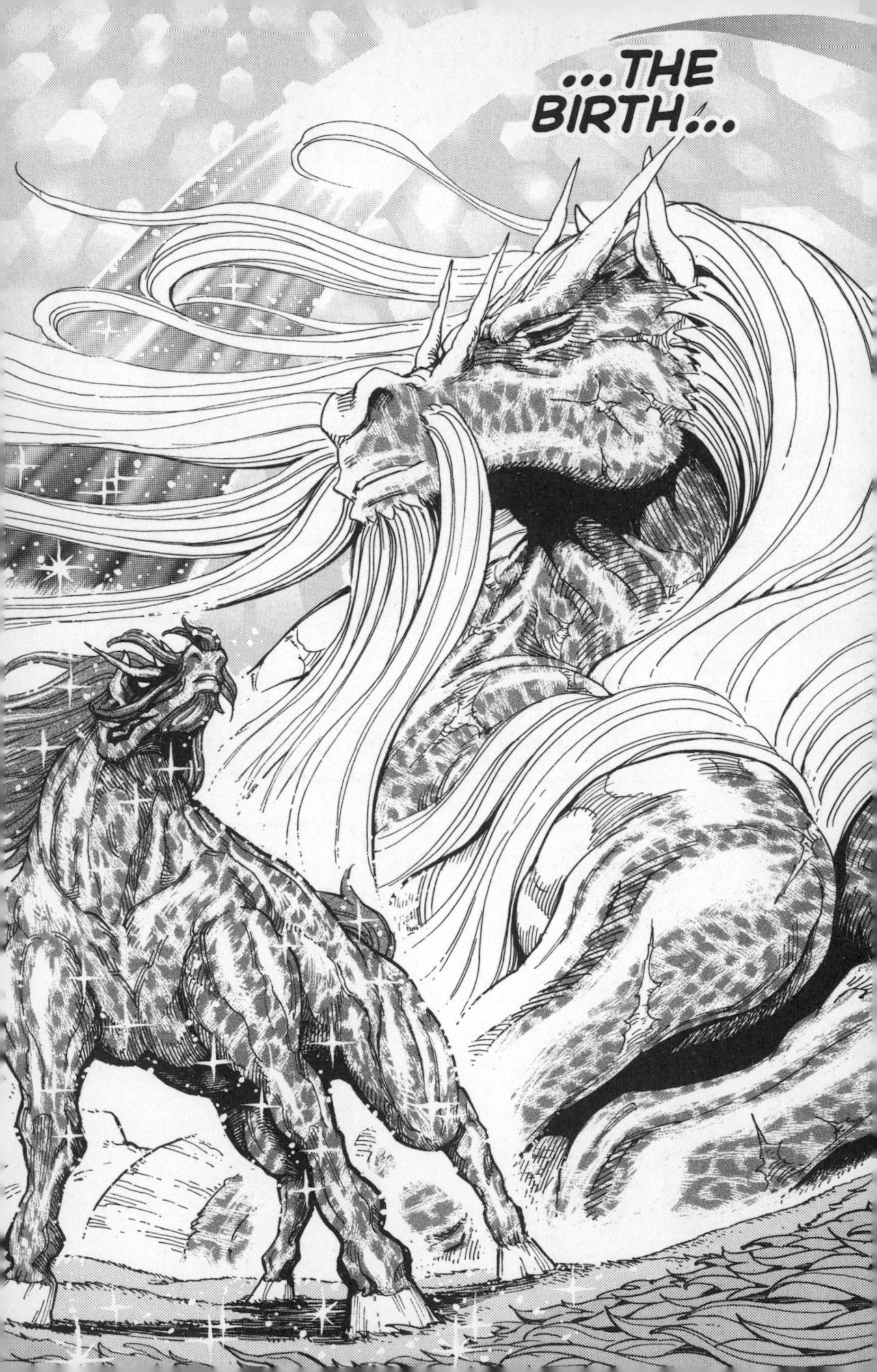
...THE BIRTH...

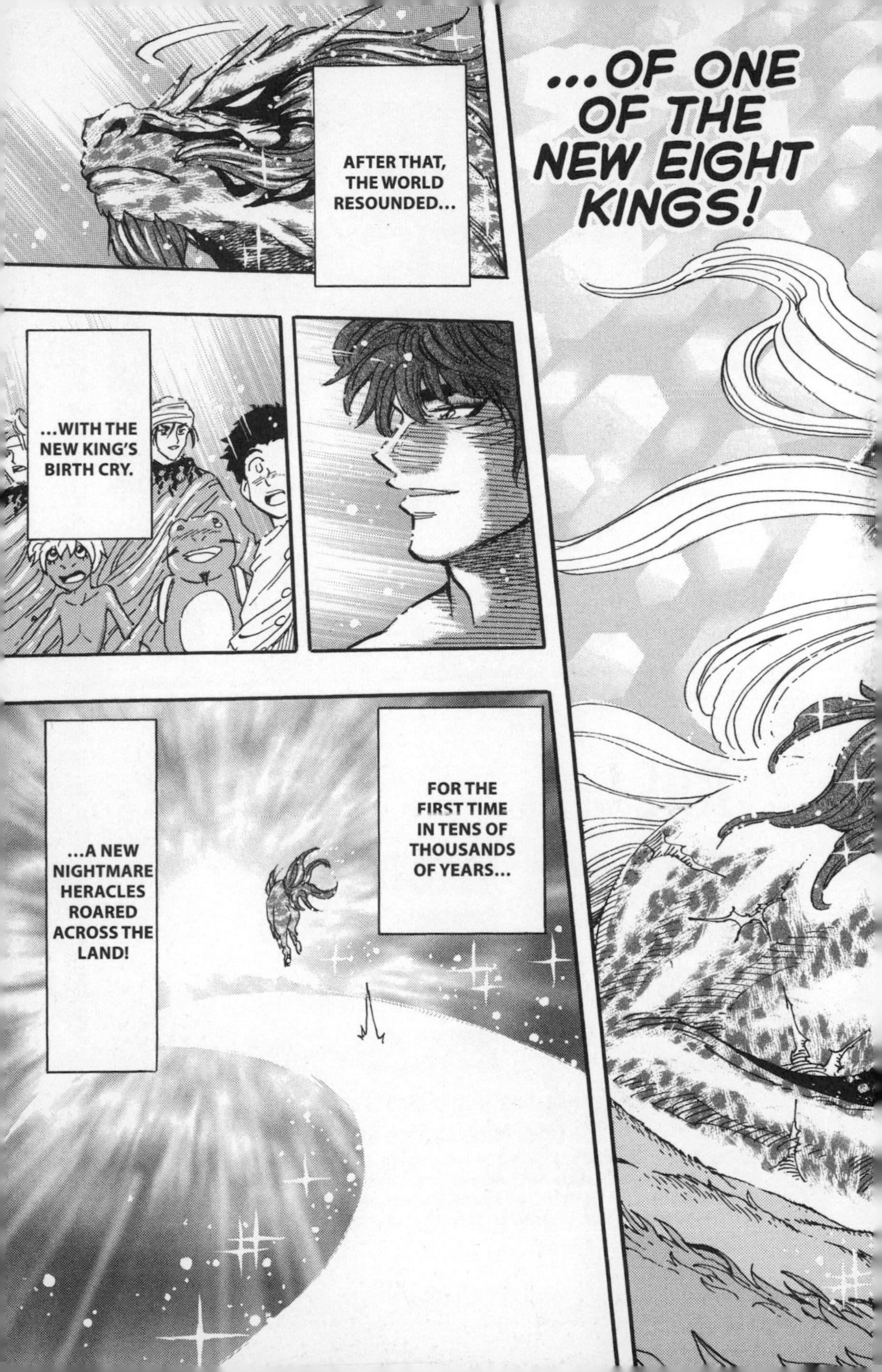
...OF ONE OF THE NEW EIGHT KINGS!
AFTER THAT, THE WORLD RESOUNDED...
...WITH THE NEW KING'S BIRTH CRY.
FOR THE FIRST TIME IN TENS OF THOUSANDS OF YEARS...
...A NEW NIGHTMARE HERACLES ROARED ACROSS THE LAND!

CHARACTER PROFILE

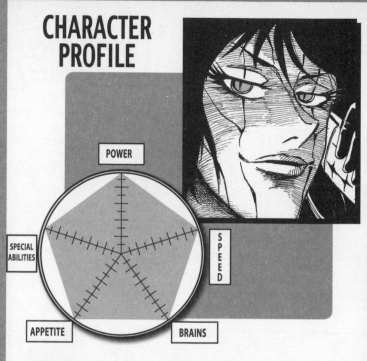

POWER

SPECIAL
ABILITIES

SPEED

APPETITE

BRAINS

JOIE

AGE: UNKNOWN		**BIRTHDAY:** UNKNOWN	

AGE: UNKNOWN

BIRTHDAY: UNKNOWN

BLOOD TYPE: UNKNOWN

SIGN: UNKNOWN

HEIGHT: UNKNOWN

WEIGHT: UNKNOWN

EYESIGHT: UNKNOWN

SHOE SIZE: UNKNOWN

SPECIAL MOVES/ABILITIES:
- Tasting Scope, Taste Change, Hundred Million Layer Fillet, Air Slice, Satanic Mince

Standing at the top of the third world power, NEO, this mysterious chef is somehow connected to both Acacia and Froese. He possesses the unique ability to change (prepare) people's thoughts (flavor) and is slowly but surely turning people from both the IGO and Gourmet Corp. over to NEO and growing his influence. His powers and ambitions are still shrouded in mystery, but it seems the day where he will have to finally face Toriko and the gang is fast approaching.

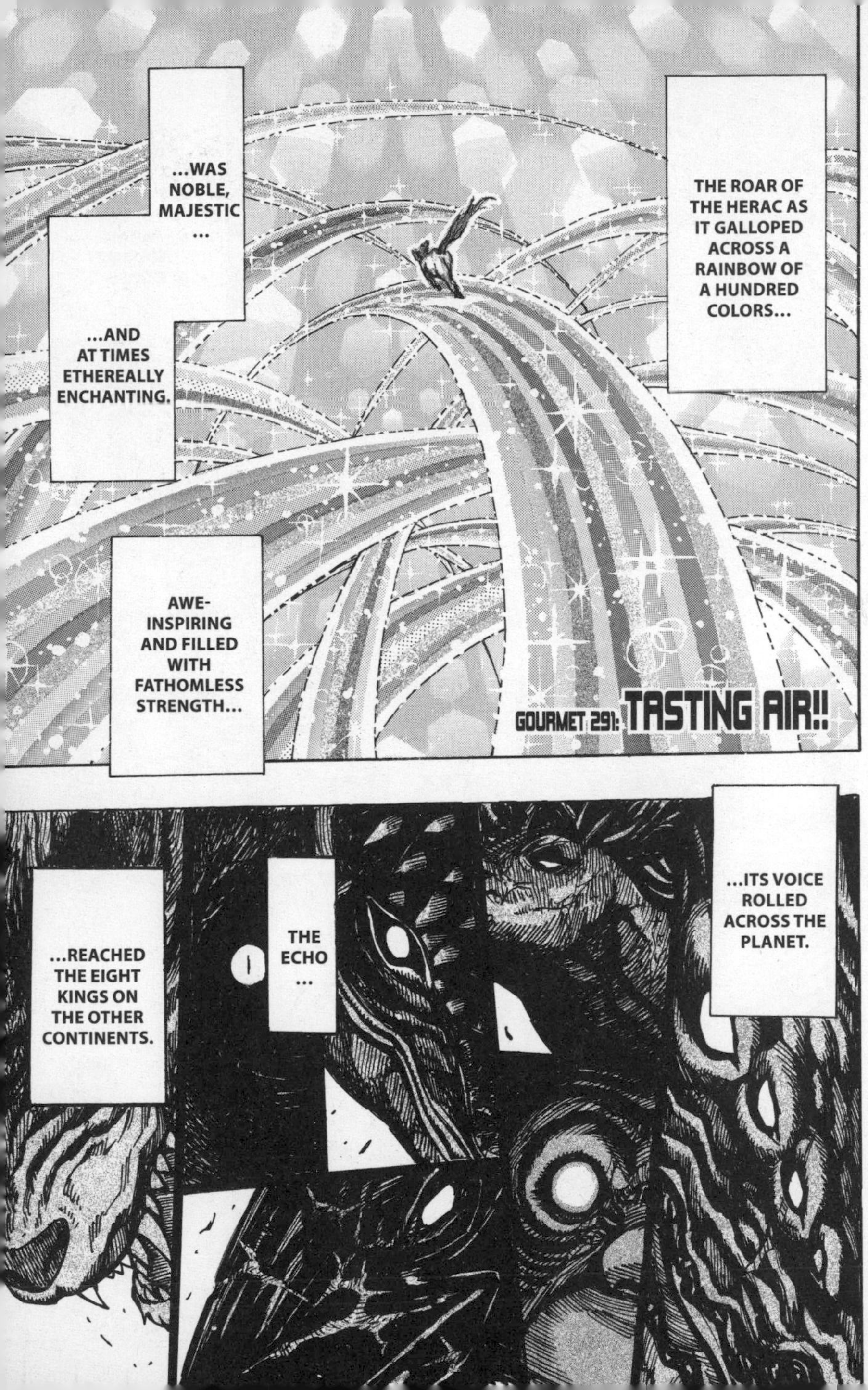
THE ROAR OF THE HERAC AS IT GALLOPED ACROSS A RAINBOW OF A HUNDRED COLORS...
...WAS NOBLE, MAJESTIC ...
...AND AT TIMES ETHEREALLY ENCHANTING.
AWE-INSPIRING AND FILLED WITH FATHOMLESS STRENGTH...
GOURMET 291: TASTING AIR!!
...ITS VOICE ROLLED ACROSS THE PLANET.
THE ECHO ...
...REACHED THE EIGHT KINGS ON THE OTHER CONTINENTS.

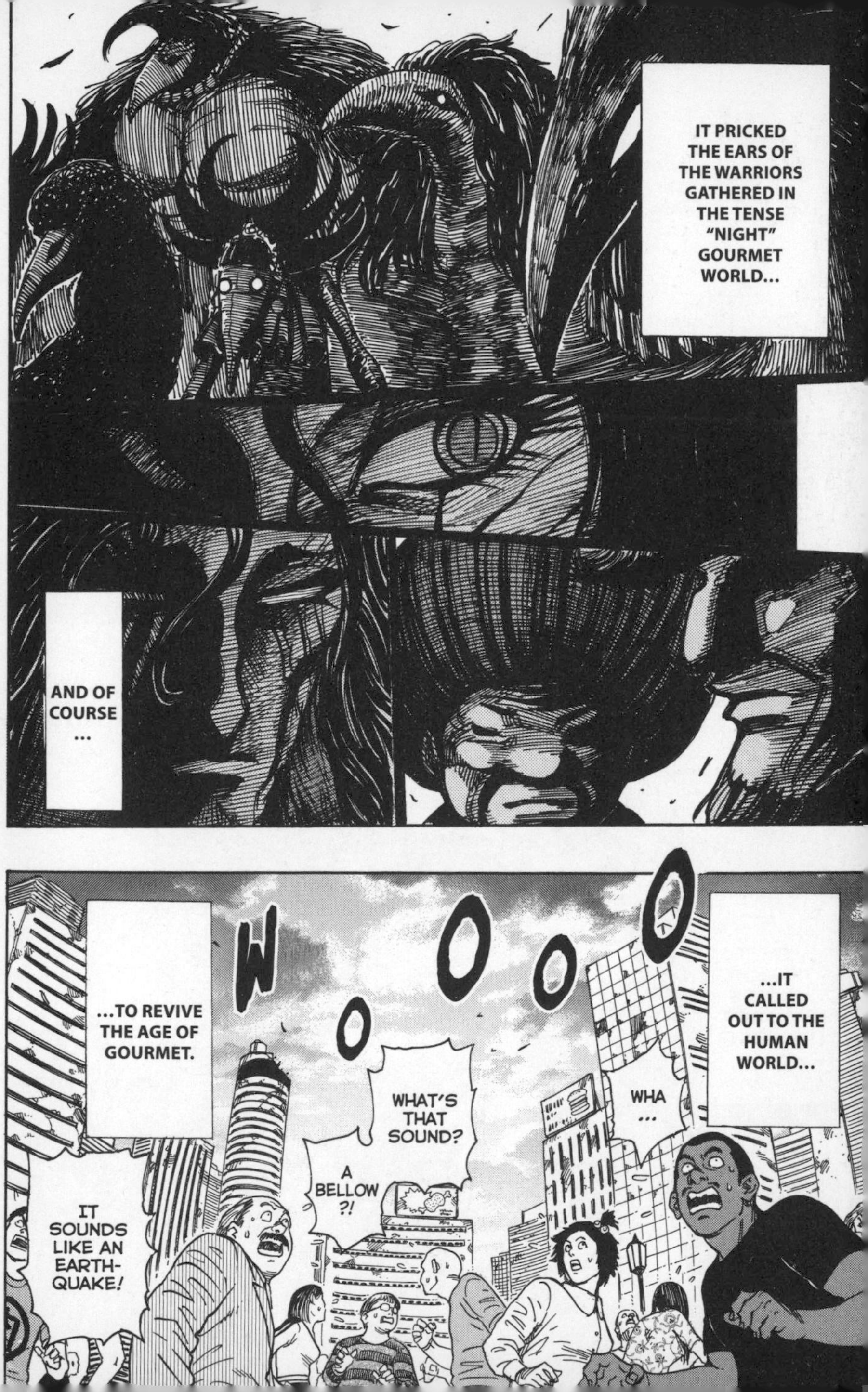
IT PRICKED THE EARS OF THE WARRIORS GATHERED IN THE TENSE "NIGHT" GOURMET WORLD...
AND OF COURSE ...
...IT CALLED OUT TO THE HUMAN WORLD...
...TO REVIVE THE AGE OF GOURMET.
WOOOOO
WHA ...
WHAT'S THAT SOUND?
A BELLOW ?!
IT SOUNDS LIKE AN EARTH-QUAKE!

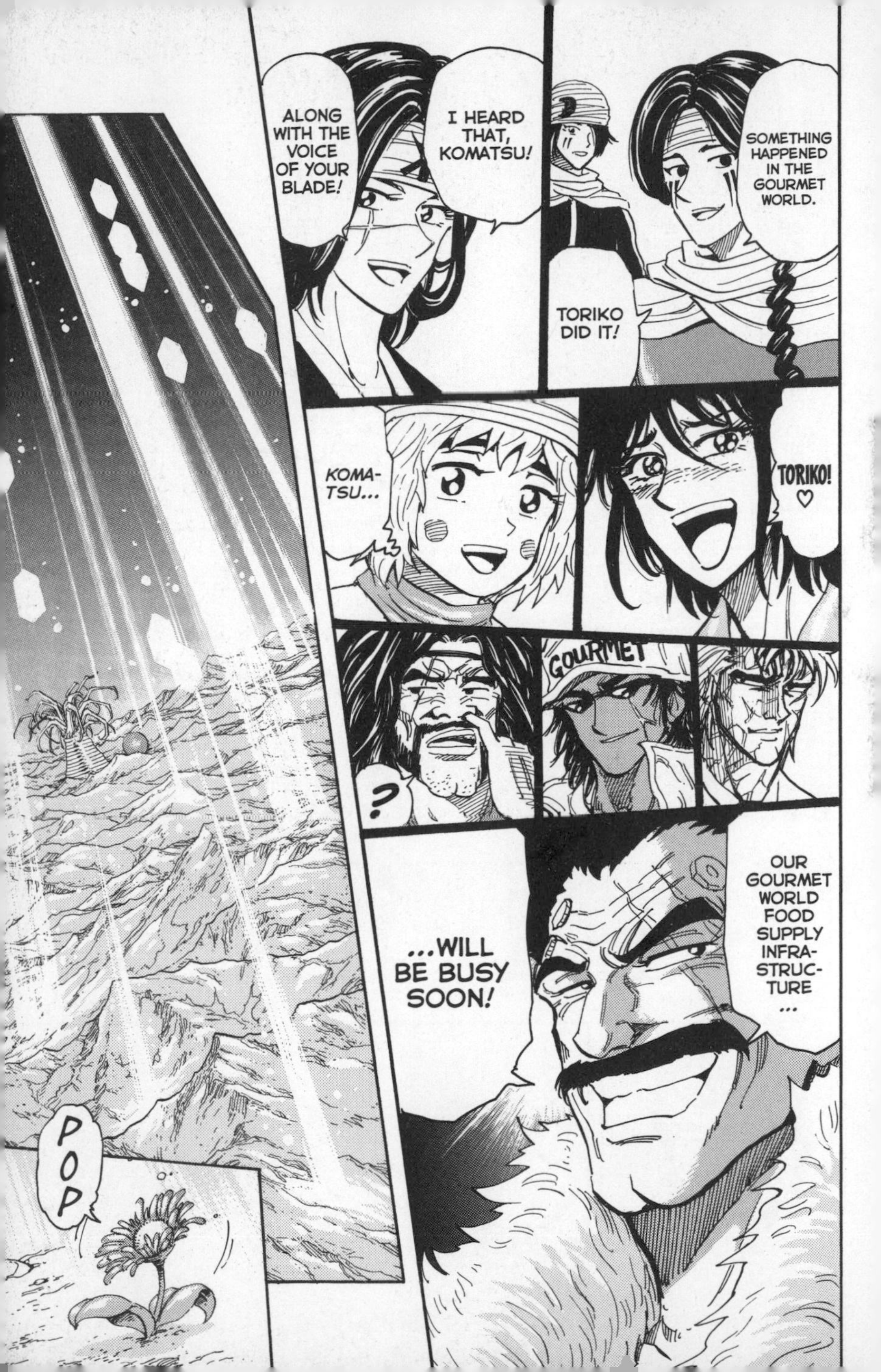
SOMETHING HAPPENED IN THE GOURMET WORLD.
TORIKO DID IT!
I HEARD THAT, KOMATSU!
ALONG WITH THE VOICE OF YOUR BLADE!
TORIKO! ♥
KOMA-TSU...
GOURMET
?
OUR GOURMET WORLD FOOD SUPPLY INFRA-STRUC-TURE...
...WILL BE BUSY SOON!
POP

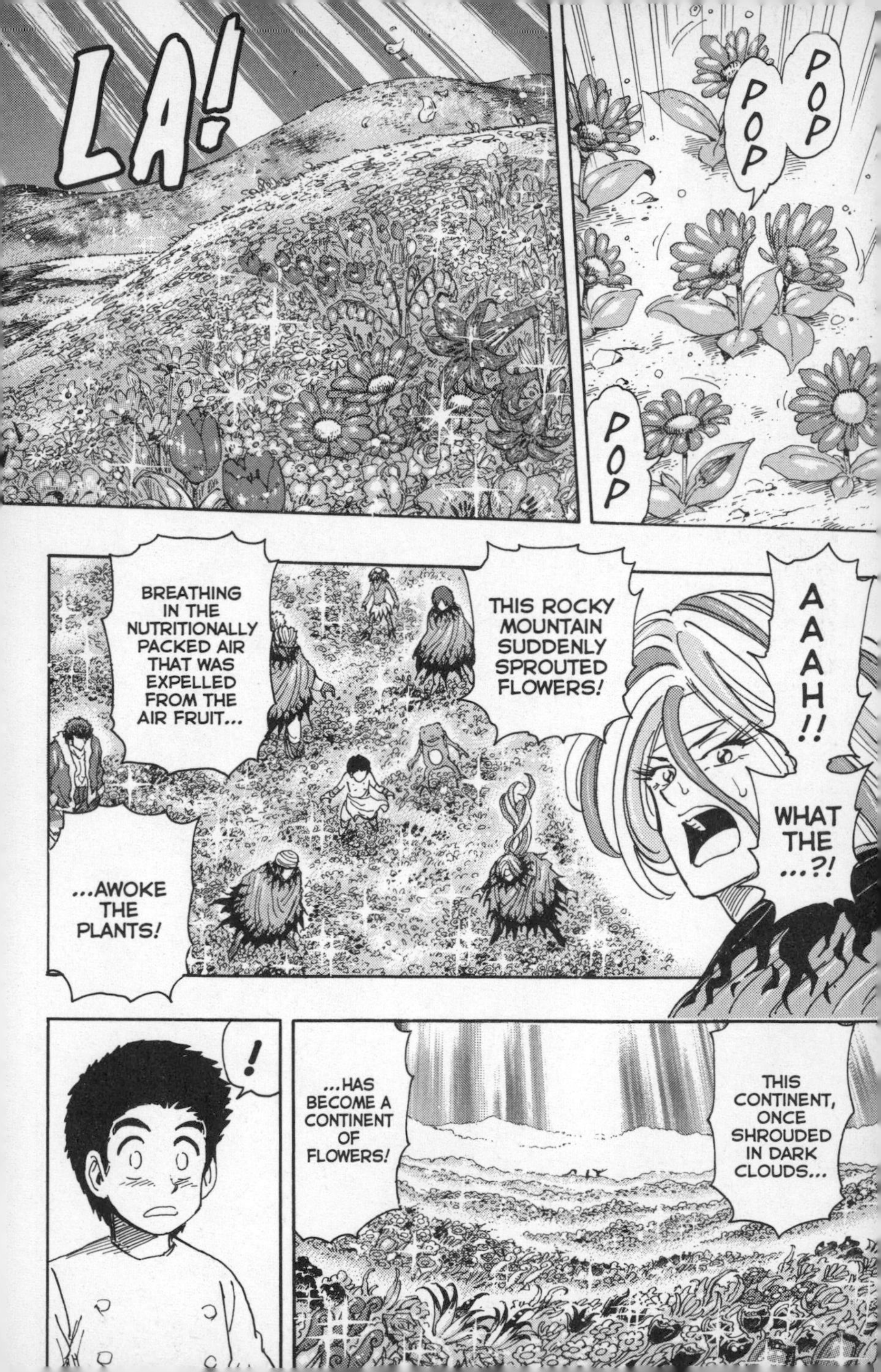
POP POP POP POP
POP POP
LA!
AAAAH!!
WHAT THE ...?!
THIS ROCKY MOUNTAIN SUDDENLY SPROUTED FLOWERS!
BREATHING IN THE NUTRITIONALLY PACKED AIR THAT WAS EXPELLED FROM THE AIR FRUIT...
...AWOKE THE PLANTS!
THIS CONTINENT, ONCE SHROUDED IN DARK CLOUDS...
...HAS BECOME A CONTINENT OF FLOWERS!
!

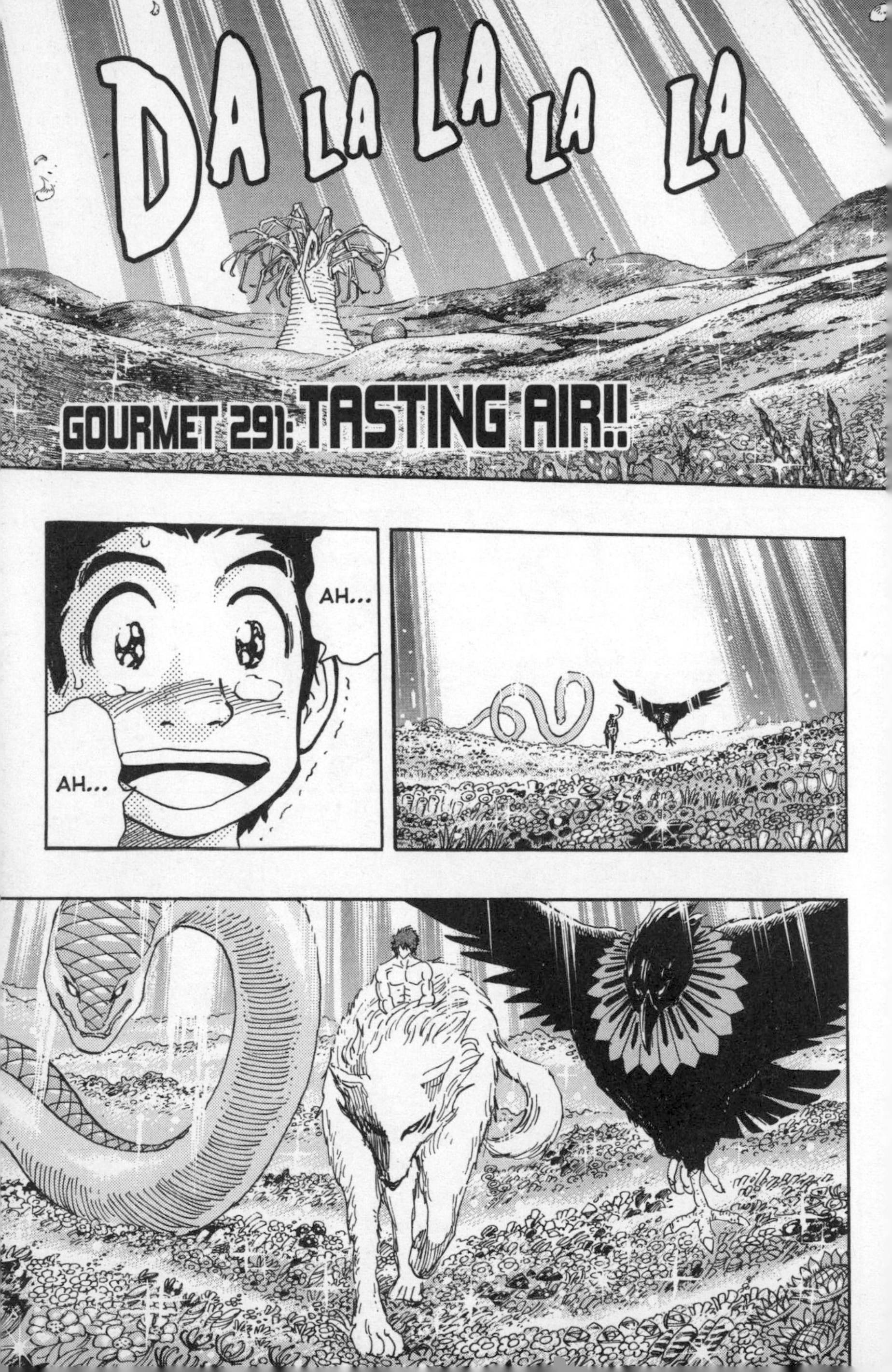
DA LA LA LA LA
GOURMET 291: TASTING AIR!!
AH...
AH...

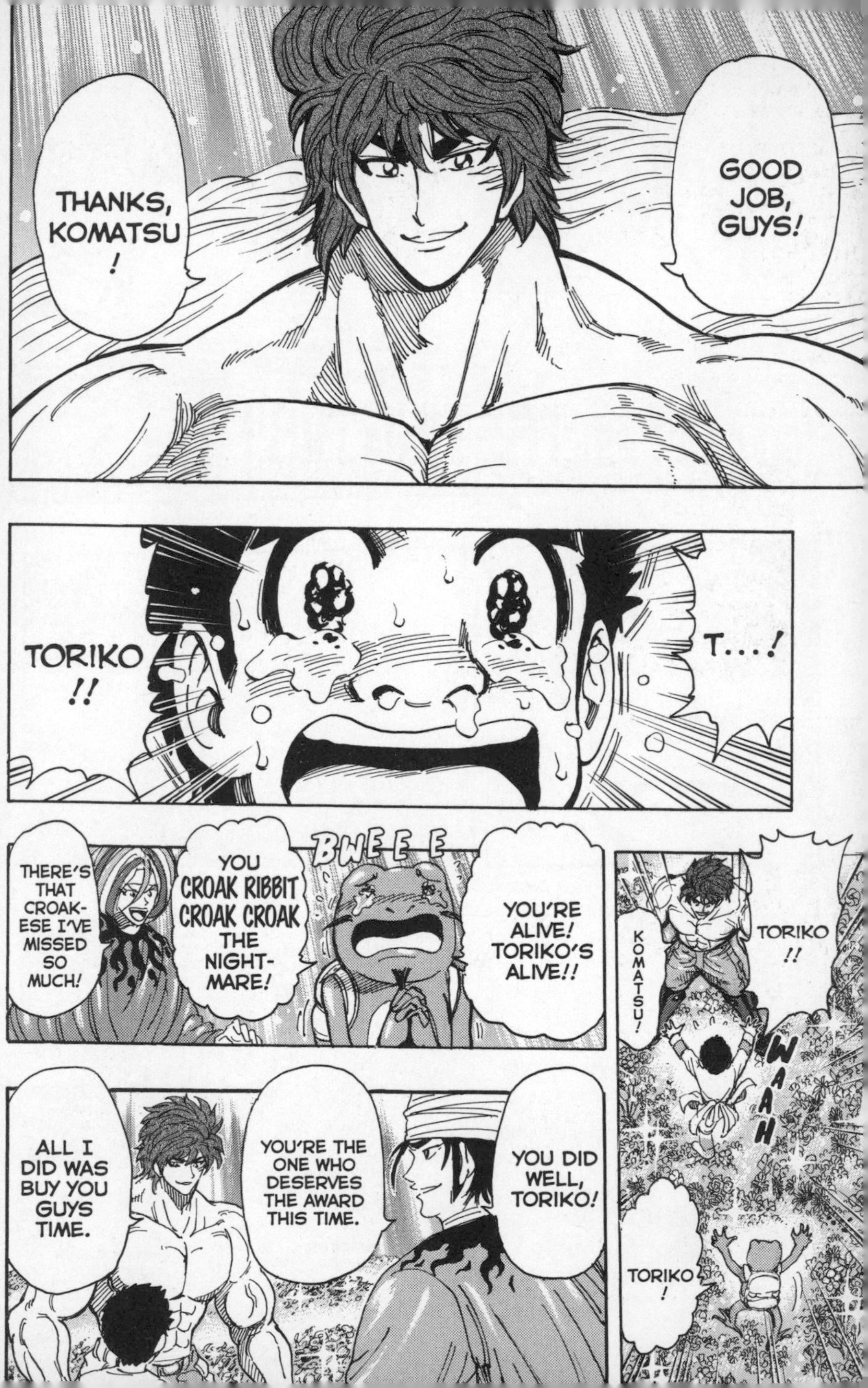
GOOD JOB, GUYS!
THANKS, KOMATSU!
T...!
TORIKO!!
TORIKO!!
KOMATSU!
WAAH
TORIKO!
YOU'RE ALIVE! TORIKO'S ALIVE!!
BWEEE
YOU CROAK RIBBIT CROAK CROAK THE NIGHTMARE!
THERE'S THAT CROAKESE I'VE MISSED SO MUCH!
YOU DID WELL, TORIKO!
YOU'RE THE ONE WHO DESERVES THE AWARD THIS TIME.
ALL I DID WAS BUY YOU GUYS TIME.

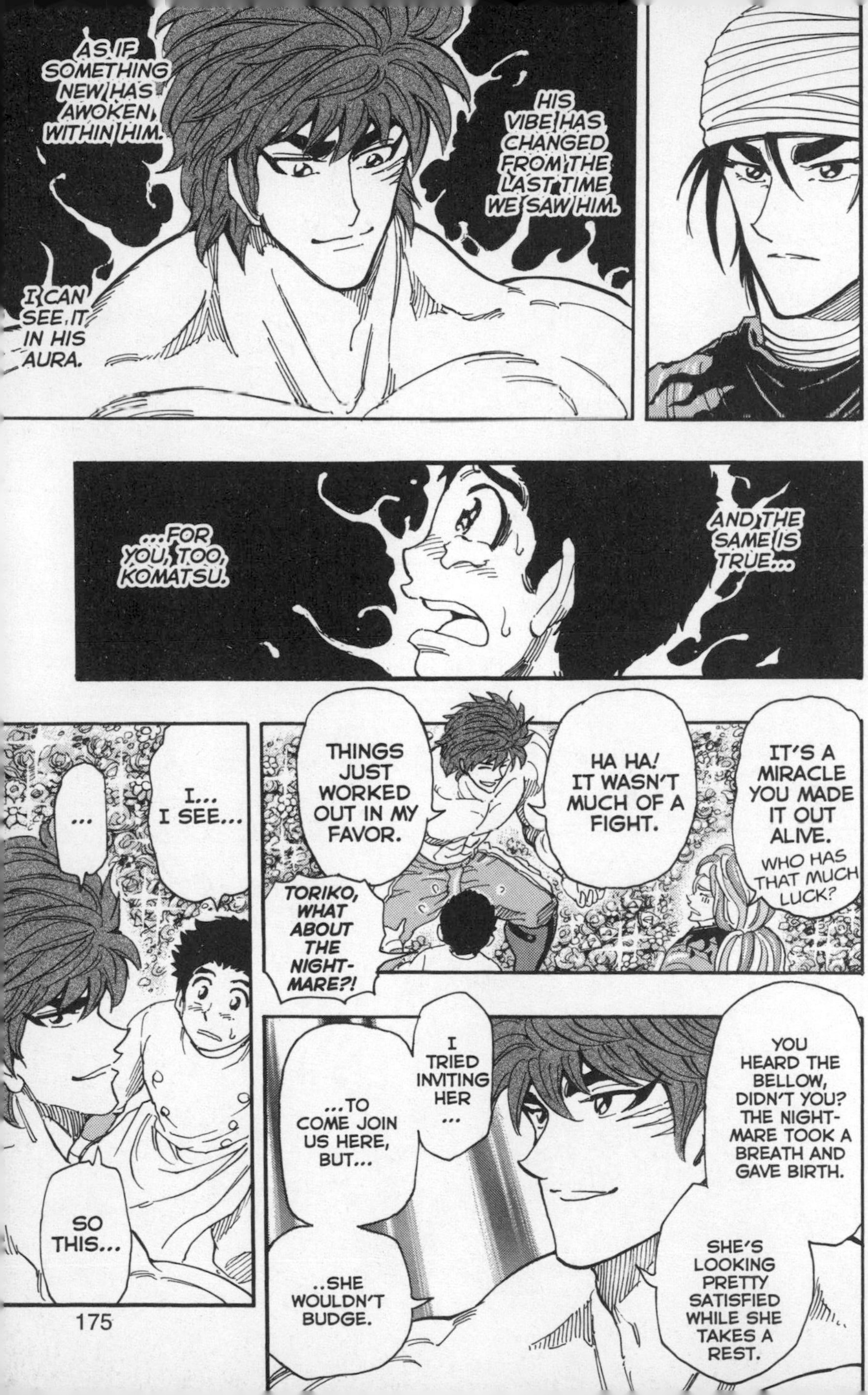
HIS VIBE HAS CHANGED FROM THE LAST TIME WE SAW HIM.
AS IF SOMETHING NEW HAS AWOKEN WITHIN HIM.
I CAN SEE IT IN HIS AURA.
AND THE SAME IS TRUE...
...FOR YOU, TOO, KOMATSU.
IT'S A MIRACLE YOU MADE IT OUT ALIVE.
WHO HAS THAT MUCH LUCK?
HA HA! IT WASN'T MUCH OF A FIGHT.
THINGS JUST WORKED OUT IN MY FAVOR.
TORIKO, WHAT ABOUT THE NIGHT-MARE?!
YOU HEARD THE BELLOW, DIDN'T YOU? THE NIGHT-MARE TOOK A BREATH AND GAVE BIRTH.
SHE'S LOOKING PRETTY SATISFIED WHILE SHE TAKES A REST.
I TRIED INVITING HER...
...TO COME JOIN US HERE, BUT...
..SHE WOULDN'T BUDGE.
I... I SEE...
...
SO THIS...

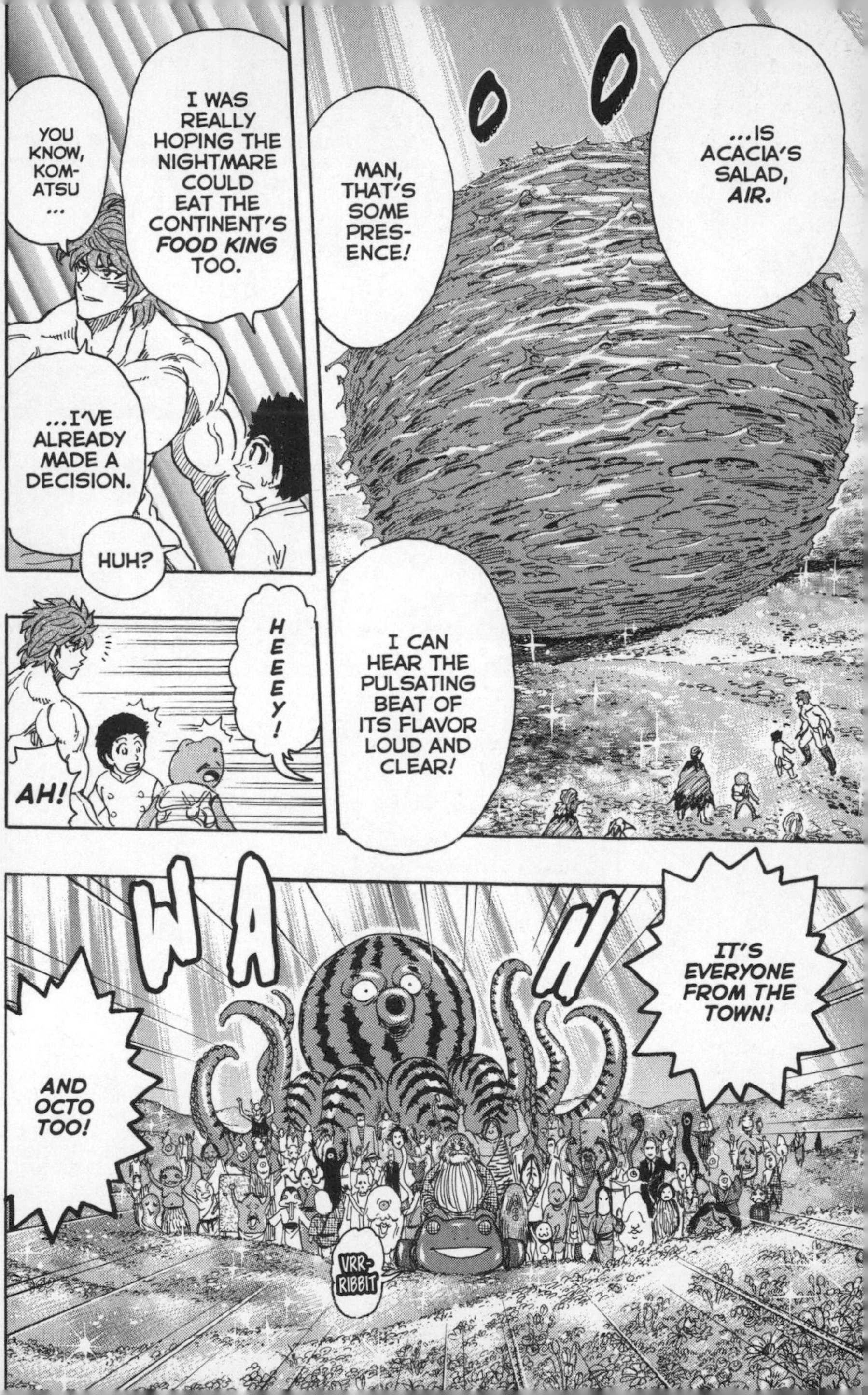
OO
...IS ACACIA'S SALAD, AIR.
MAN, THAT'S SOME PRES-ENCE!
I CAN HEAR THE PULSATING BEAT OF ITS FLAVOR LOUD AND CLEAR!
I WAS REALLY HOPING THE NIGHTMARE COULD EAT THE CONTINENT'S FOOD KING TOO.
YOU KNOW, KOM-ATSU ...
...I'VE ALREADY MADE A DECISION.
HUH?
HEEEEY!
AH!
WAH
IT'S EVERYONE FROM THE TOWN!
AND OCTO TOO!
VRR-RIBBIT

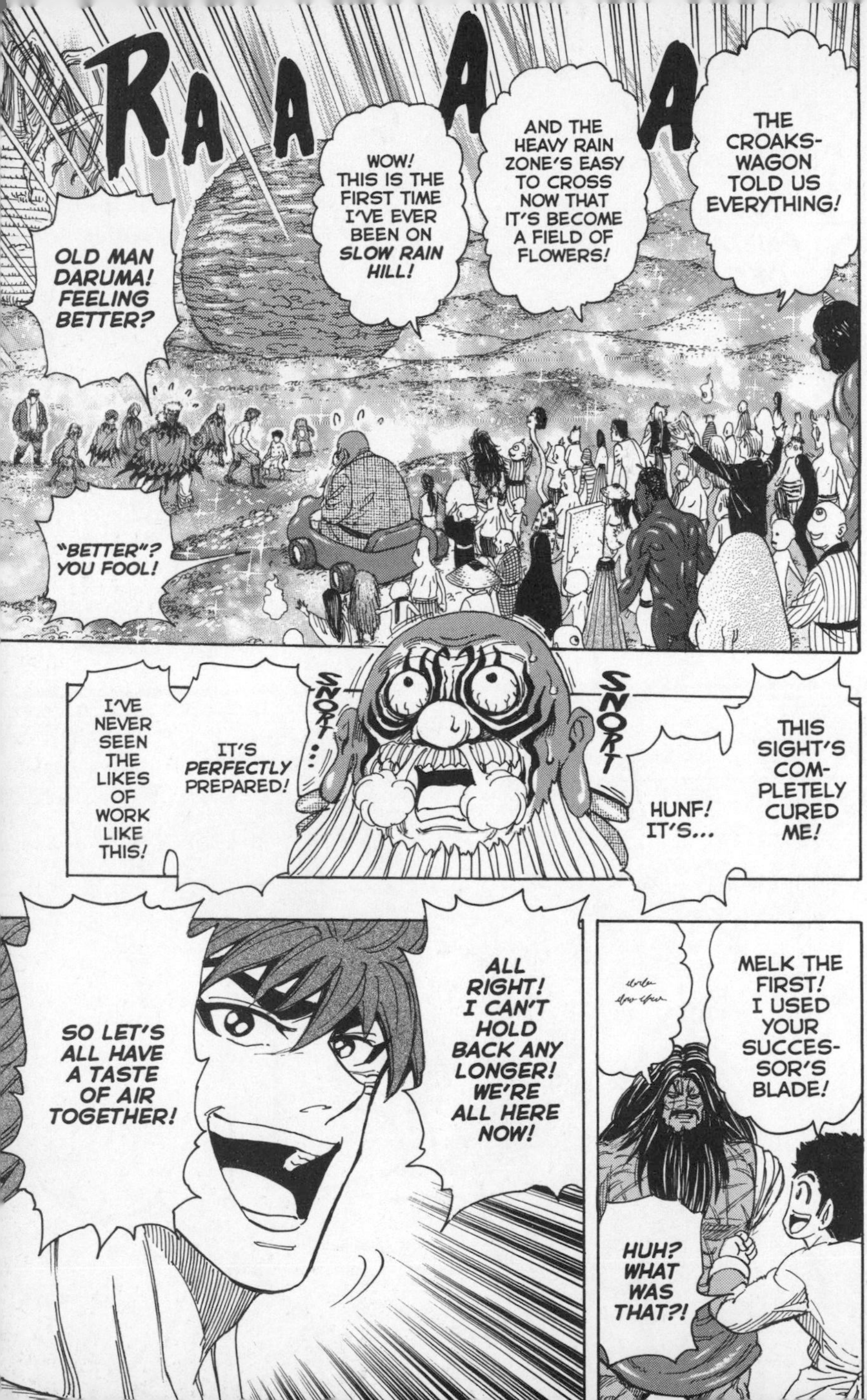
RAAAA
THE CROAKS-WAGON TOLD US EVERYTHING!
AND THE HEAVY RAIN ZONE'S EASY TO CROSS NOW THAT IT'S BECOME A FIELD OF FLOWERS!
WOW! THIS IS THE FIRST TIME I'VE EVER BEEN ON SLOW RAIN HILL!
OLD MAN DARUMA! FEELING BETTER?
"BETTER"? YOU FOOL!
THIS SIGHT'S COMPLETELY CURED ME!
SNORT
HUNF! IT'S...
SNORT...
IT'S PERFECTLY PREPARED!
I'VE NEVER SEEN THE LIKES OF WORK LIKE THIS!
MELK THE FIRST! I USED YOUR SUCCESSOR'S BLADE!
HUH? WHAT WAS THAT?!
ALL RIGHT! I CAN'T HOLD BACK ANY LONGER! WE'RE ALL HERE NOW!
SO LET'S ALL HAVE A TASTE OF AIR TOGETHER!

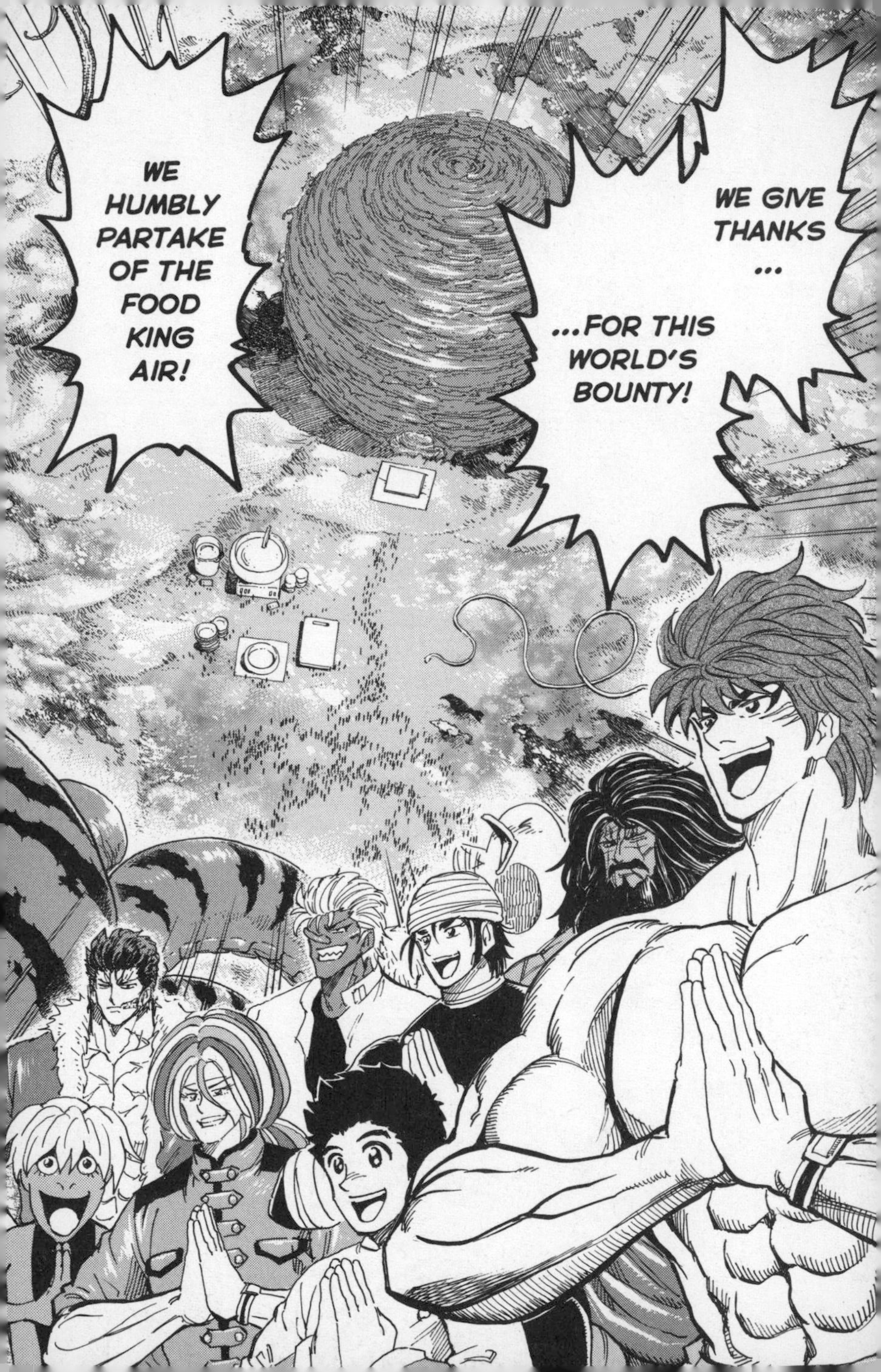
WE GIVE THANKS ...
...FOR THIS WORLD'S BOUNTY!
WE HUMBLY PARTAKE OF THE FOOD KING AIR!

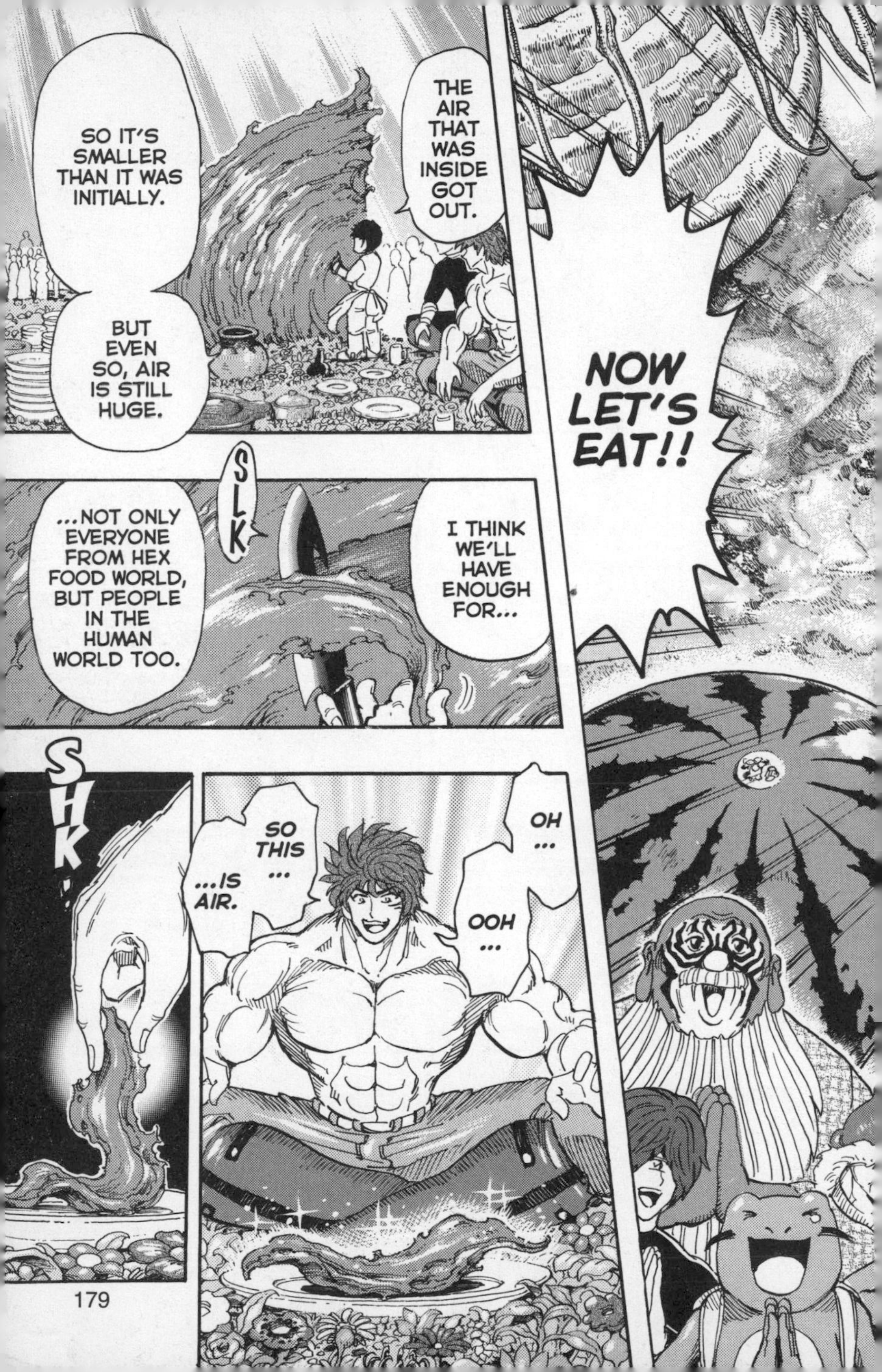
NOW LET'S EAT!!
THE AIR THAT WAS INSIDE GOT OUT.
SO IT'S SMALLER THAN IT WAS INITIALLY.
BUT EVEN SO, AIR IS STILL HUGE.
I THINK WE'LL HAVE ENOUGH FOR...
SLK
...NOT ONLY EVERYONE FROM HEX FOOD WORLD, BUT PEOPLE IN THE HUMAN WORLD TOO.
OH ...
OOH ...
SO THIS ...
...IS AIR.
SHK

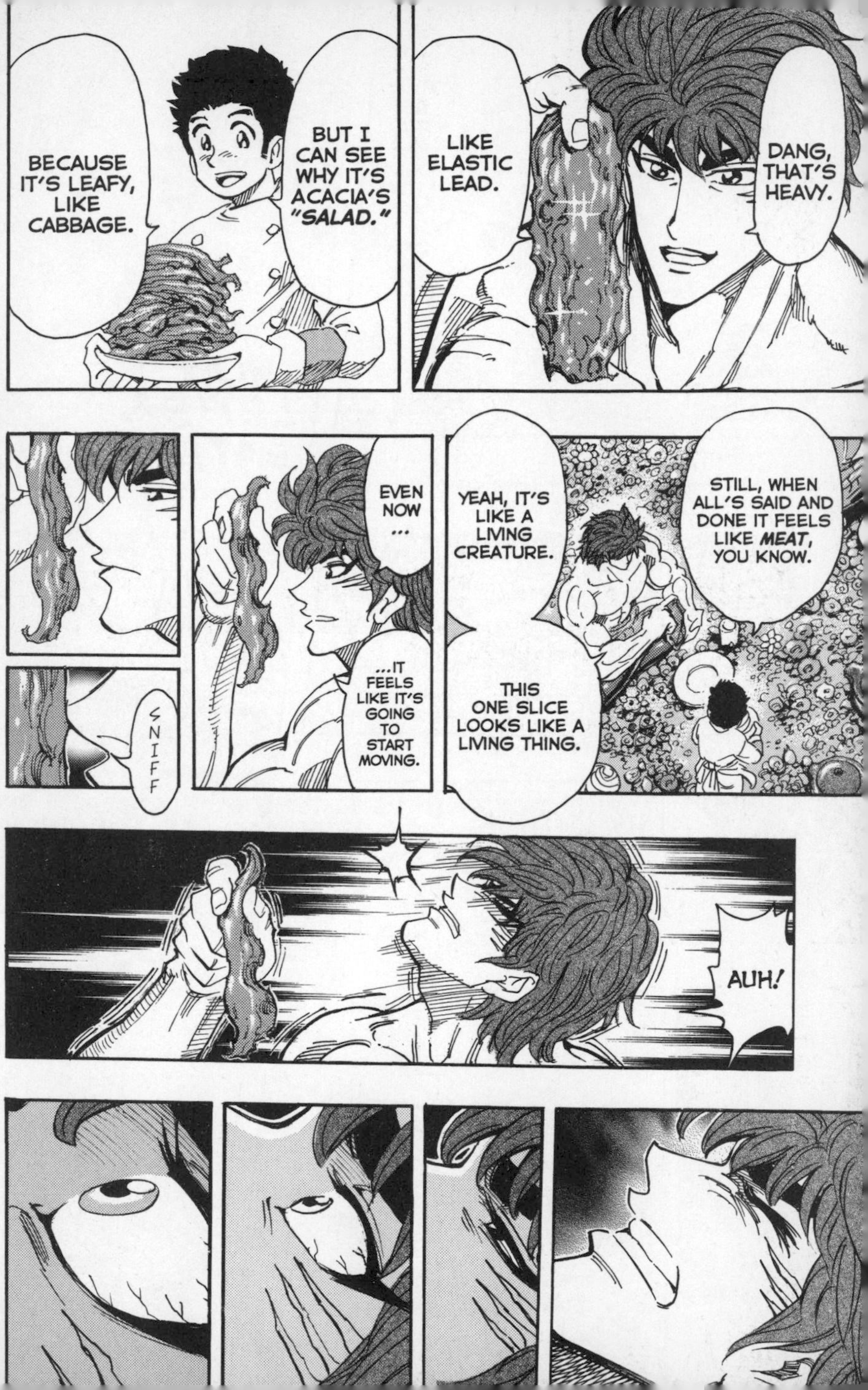
DANG, THAT'S HEAVY.
LIKE ELASTIC LEAD.
BUT I CAN SEE WHY IT'S ACACIA'S *"SALAD."*
BECAUSE IT'S LEAFY, LIKE CABBAGE.
STILL, WHEN ALL'S SAID AND DONE IT FEELS LIKE *MEAT*, YOU KNOW.
YEAH, IT'S LIKE A LIVING CREATURE.
THIS ONE SLICE LOOKS LIKE A LIVING THING.
EVEN NOW...
...IT FEELS LIKE IT'S GOING TO START MOVING.
SNIFF
AUH!

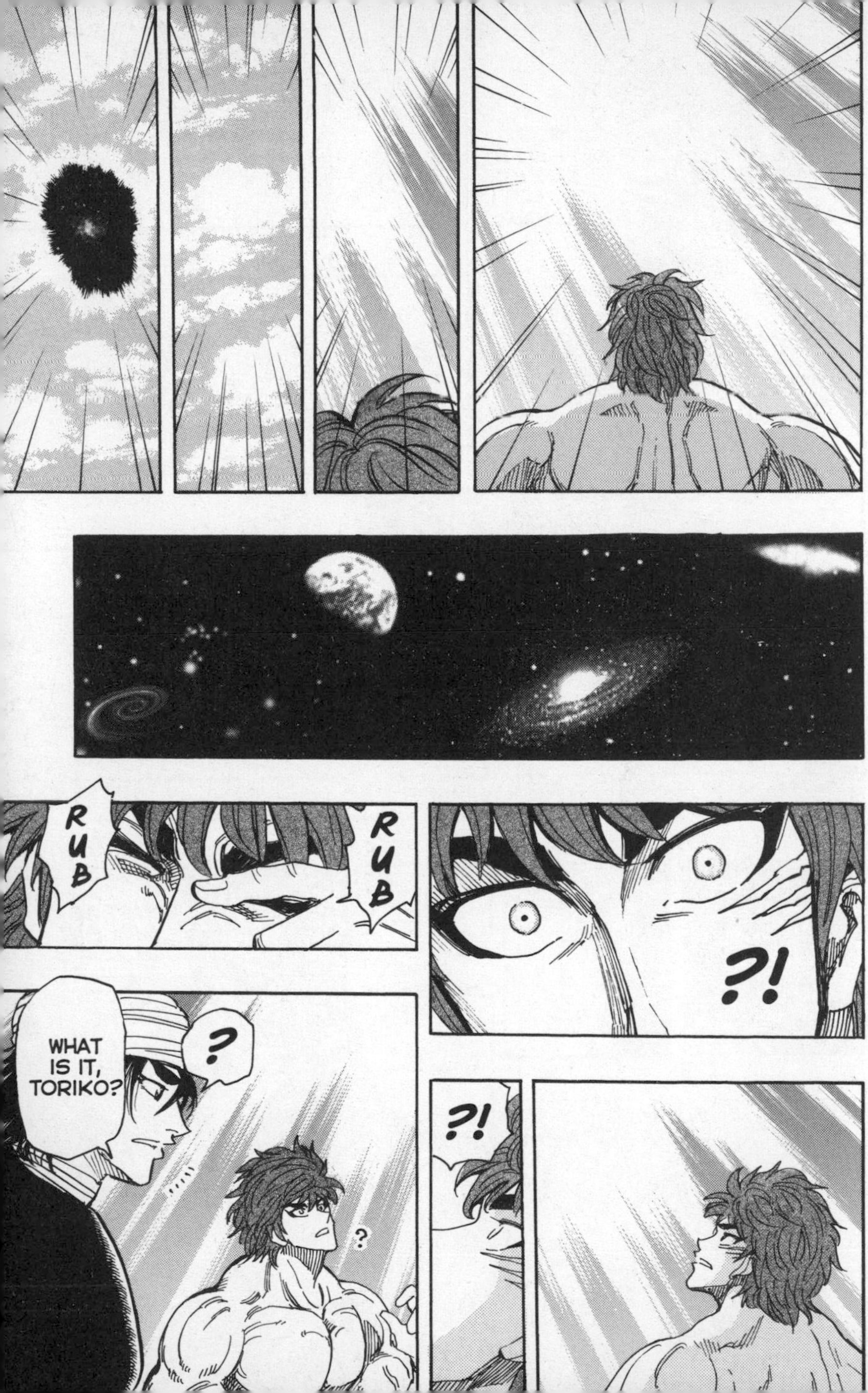
?!
RUB RUB
WHAT IS IT, TORIKO?
?
.....
?
?!

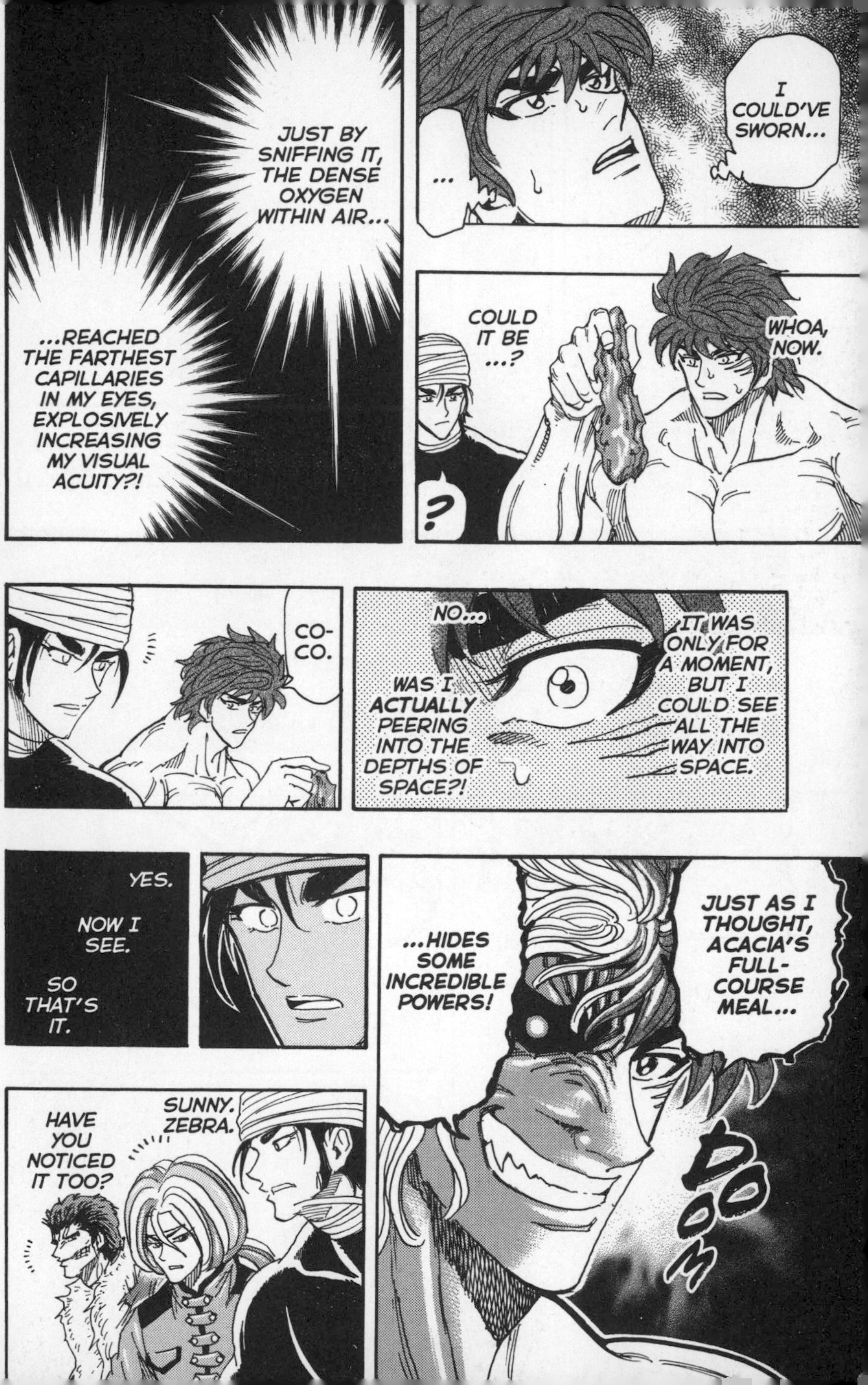
I COULD'VE SWORN...
...
WHOA, NOW.
COULD IT BE ...?
?
JUST BY SNIFFING IT, THE DENSE OXYGEN WITHIN AIR...
...REACHED THE FARTHEST CAPILLARIES IN MY EYES, EXPLOSIVELY INCREASING MY VISUAL ACUITY?!
IT WAS ONLY FOR A MOMENT, BUT I COULD SEE ALL THE WAY INTO SPACE.
NO...
WAS I ACTUALLY PEERING INTO THE DEPTHS OF SPACE?!
CO-CO.
JUST AS I THOUGHT, ACACIA'S FULL-COURSE MEAL...
...HIDES SOME INCREDIBLE POWERS!
DOOOM
YES.
NOW I SEE.
SO THAT'S IT.
SUNNY. ZEBRA.
HAVE YOU NOTICED IT TOO?

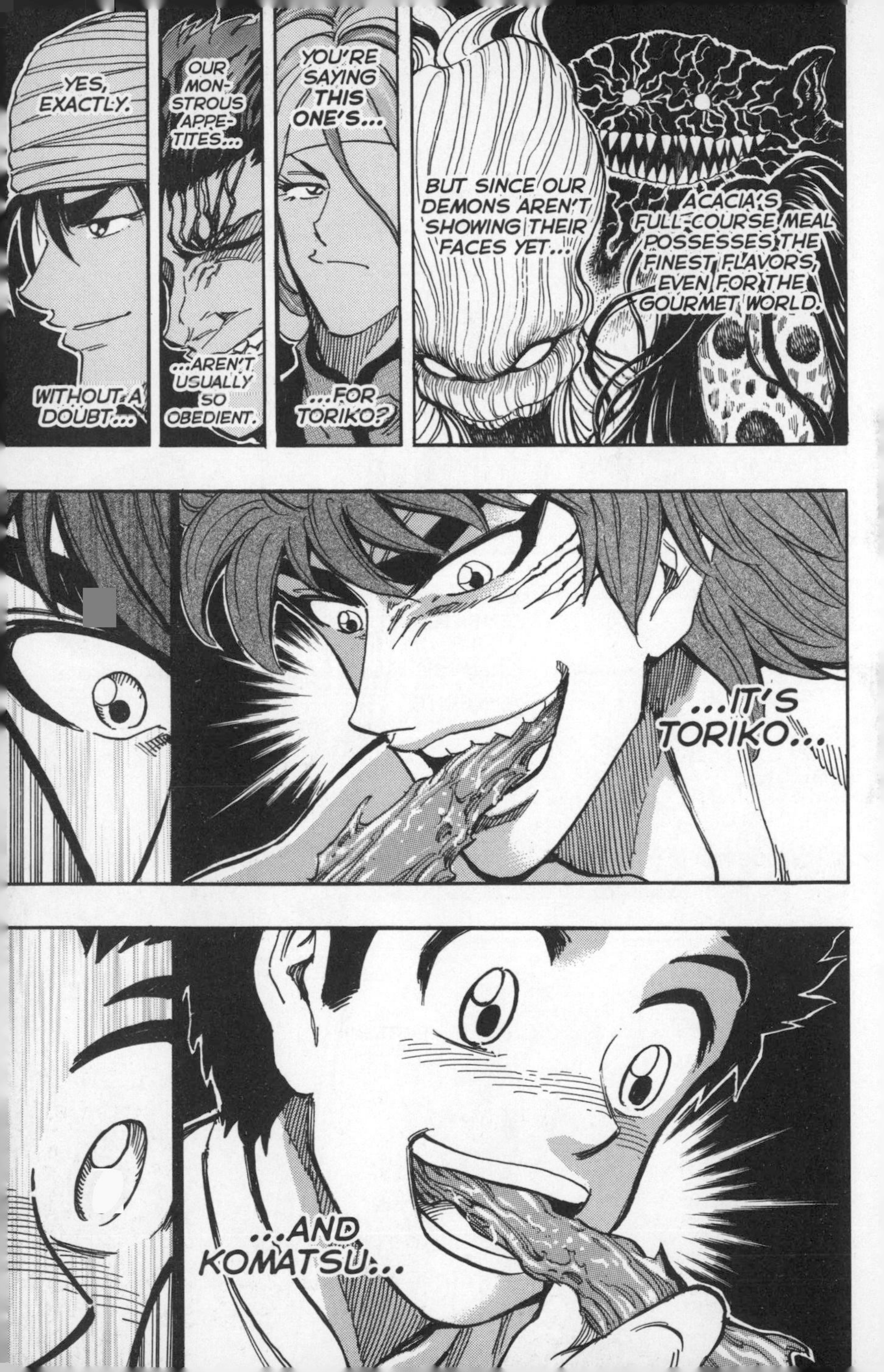
ACACIA'S FULL-COURSE MEAL POSSESSES THE FINEST FLAVORS, EVEN FOR THE GOURMET WORLD.
BUT SINCE OUR DEMONS AREN'T SHOWING THEIR FACES YET...
YOU'RE SAYING THIS ONE'S...
...FOR TORIKO?
OUR MONSTROUS APPETITES...
...AREN'T USUALLY SO OBEDIENT.
YES, EXACTLY.
WITHOUT A DOUBT...
...IT'S TORIKO...
...AND KOMATSU...

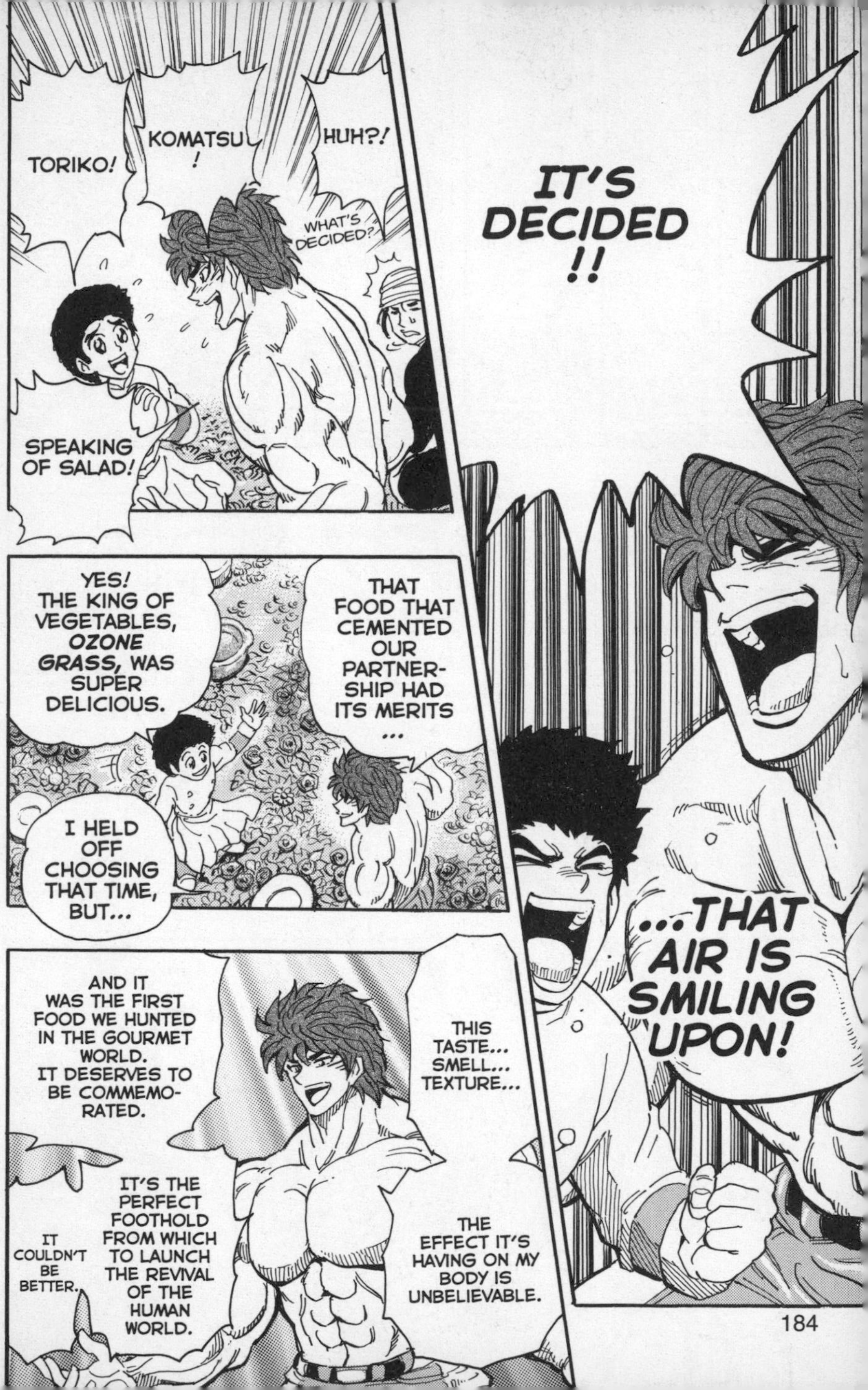
IT'S DECIDED!!
...THAT AIR IS SMILING UPON!
HUH?!
KOMATSU!
TORIKO!
WHAT'S DECIDED?
SPEAKING OF SALAD!
THAT FOOD THAT CEMENTED OUR PARTNERSHIP HAD ITS MERITS...
YES! THE KING OF VEGETABLES, OZONE GRASS, WAS SUPER DELICIOUS.
I HELD OFF CHOOSING THAT TIME, BUT...
THIS TASTE... SMELL... TEXTURE...
AND IT WAS THE FIRST FOOD WE HUNTED IN THE GOURMET WORLD. IT DESERVES TO BE COMMEMORATED.
THE EFFECT IT'S HAVING ON MY BODY IS UNBELIEVABLE.
IT'S THE PERFECT FOOTHOLD FROM WHICH TO LAUNCH THE REVIVAL OF THE HUMAN WORLD.
IT COULDN'T BE BETTER.

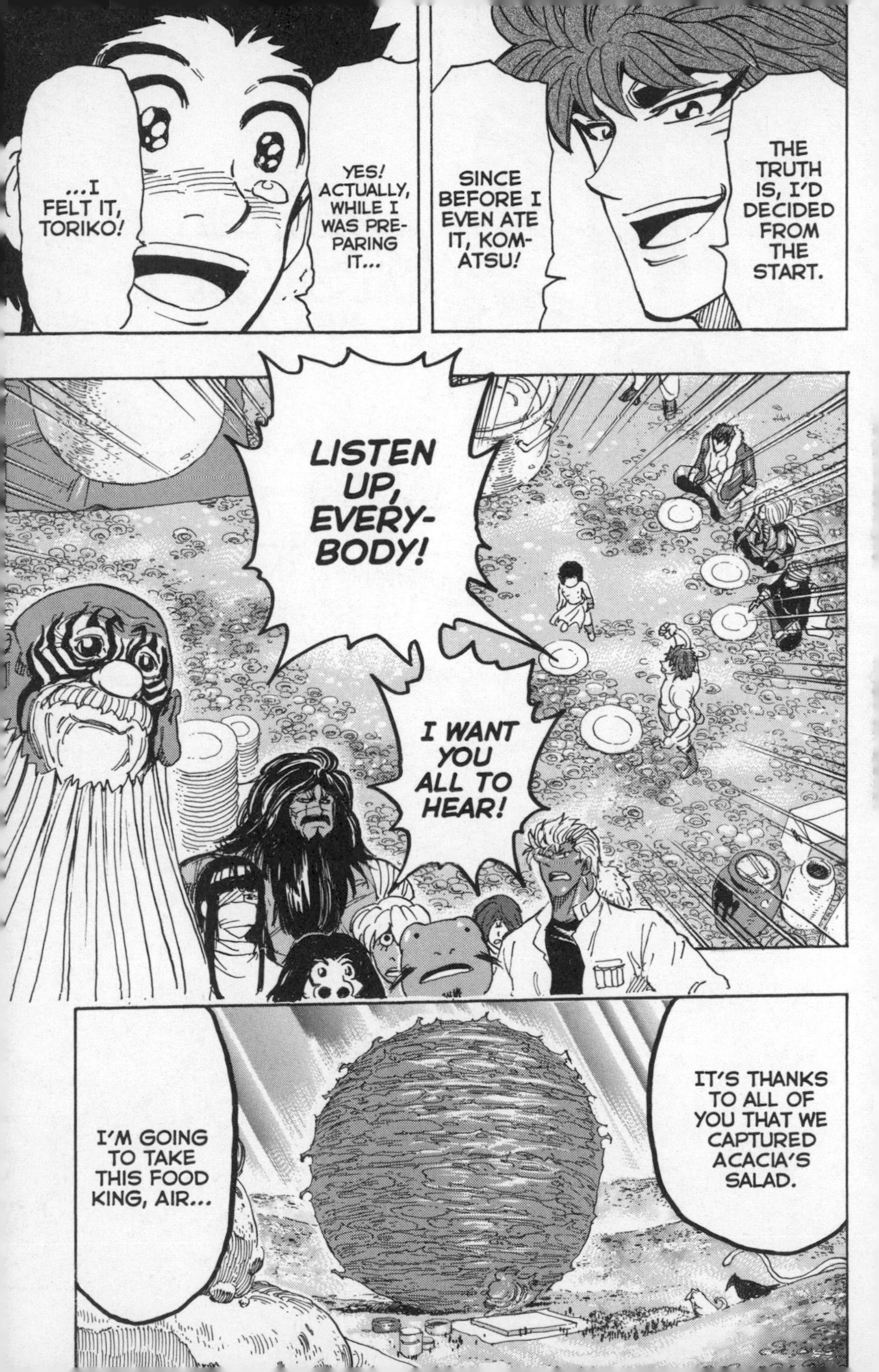
THE TRUTH IS, I'D DECIDED FROM THE START.
SINCE BEFORE I EVEN ATE IT, KOM-ATSU!
YES! ACTUALLY, WHILE I WAS PRE-PARING IT...
...I FELT IT, TORIKO!
LISTEN UP, EVERY-BODY!
I WANT YOU ALL TO HEAR!
IT'S THANKS TO ALL OF YOU THAT WE CAPTURED ACACIA'S SALAD.
I'M GOING TO TAKE THIS FOOD KING, AIR...

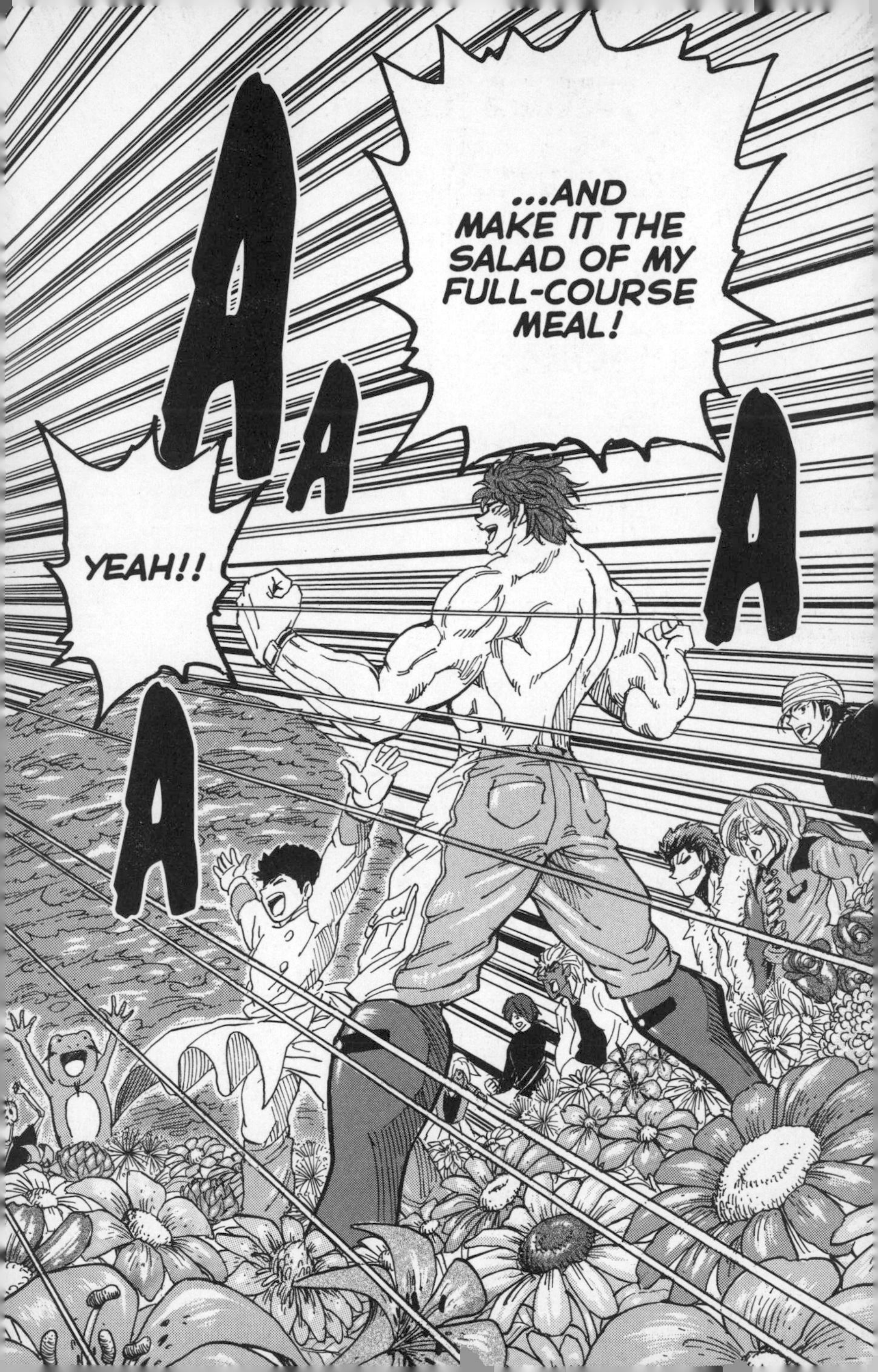
...AND MAKE IT THE SALAD OF MY FULL-COURSE MEAL!
YEAH!!
AAAA

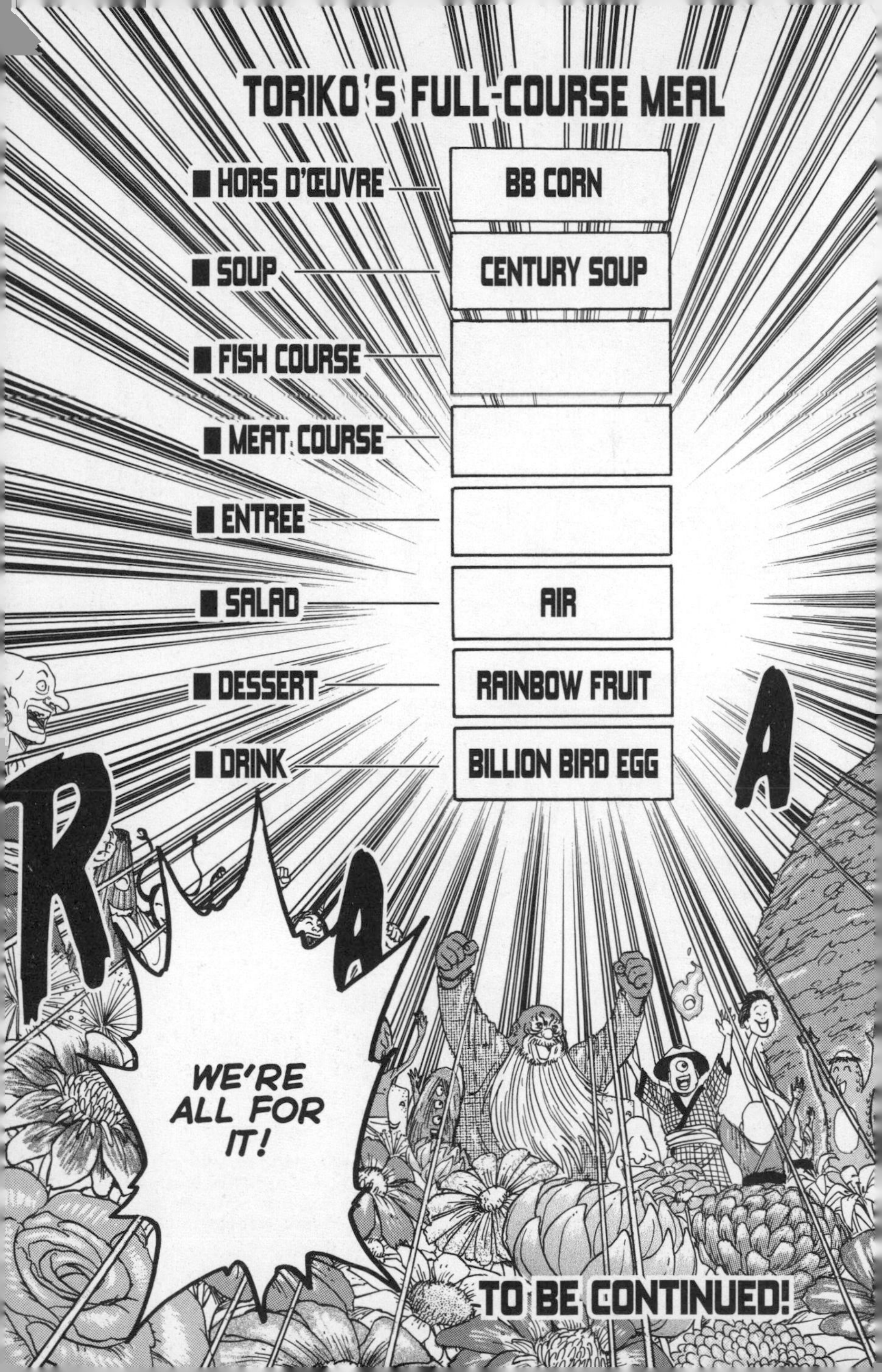
TORIKO'S FULL-COURSE MEAL
■ HORS D'ŒUVRE BB CORN
■ SOUP CENTURY SOUP
■ FISH COURSE
■ MEAT COURSE
■ ENTREE
■ SALAD AIR
■ DESSERT RAINBOW FRUIT
■ DRINK BILLION BIRD EGG
RAA
WE'RE ALL FOR IT!
TO BE CONTINUED!

CHARACTER PROFILE

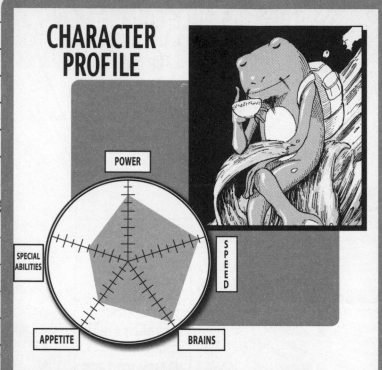

POWER

SPECIAL ABILITIES

SPEED

APPETITE

BRAINS

MAPPY (TRAVEL FROG)

AGE:	UNKNOWN	**BIRTHDAY:**	OCT 12
BLOOD TYPE:	A	**SIGN:**	LIBRA
HEIGHT:	140 CM	**WEIGHT:**	100 KG
EYESIGHT:	20/2	**SHOE SIZE:**	35 CM

SPECIAL MOVES/ABILITIES:
- Croakese

An inhabitant of Hex Food World who can be found in Area 8 of the Gourmet World. He's a guide who leads Toriko and the gang to Hex Food World. Mappy, along with Takeshi and Nopekichi, is actually one of the former members who made up the trio of Hex Food World warriors. When he gets upset, he slips into Croakese, but that's really his only shortcoming. He's a frog among frogs, overflowing with courage and bravery and willing to risk his life to capture Air.

COMING NEXT VOLUME

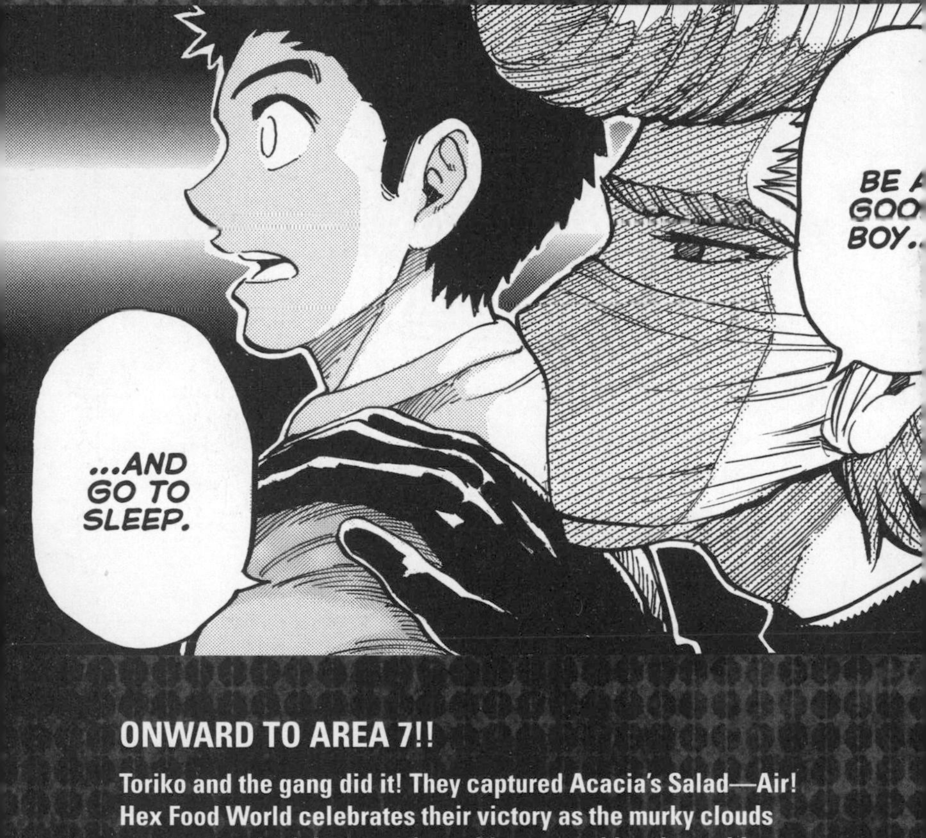
BE A GOO BOY..
...AND GO TO SLEEP.

ONWARD TO AREA 7!!

Toriko and the gang did it! They captured Acacia's Salad—Air! Hex Food World celebrates their victory as the murky clouds part to reveal rainbows and sunshine, something the residents haven't seen in years. However, the celebration is cut short when a familiar friend-now-foe, Teppei, does the unthinkable! Now Toriko and the other Four Kings must travel to Area 7 to capture Acacia's Soup, Pair, to save Komatsu! Ferocious Area 7 won't be much of a party, but they'll still have a ball…or two!

AVAILABLE APRIL 2016!

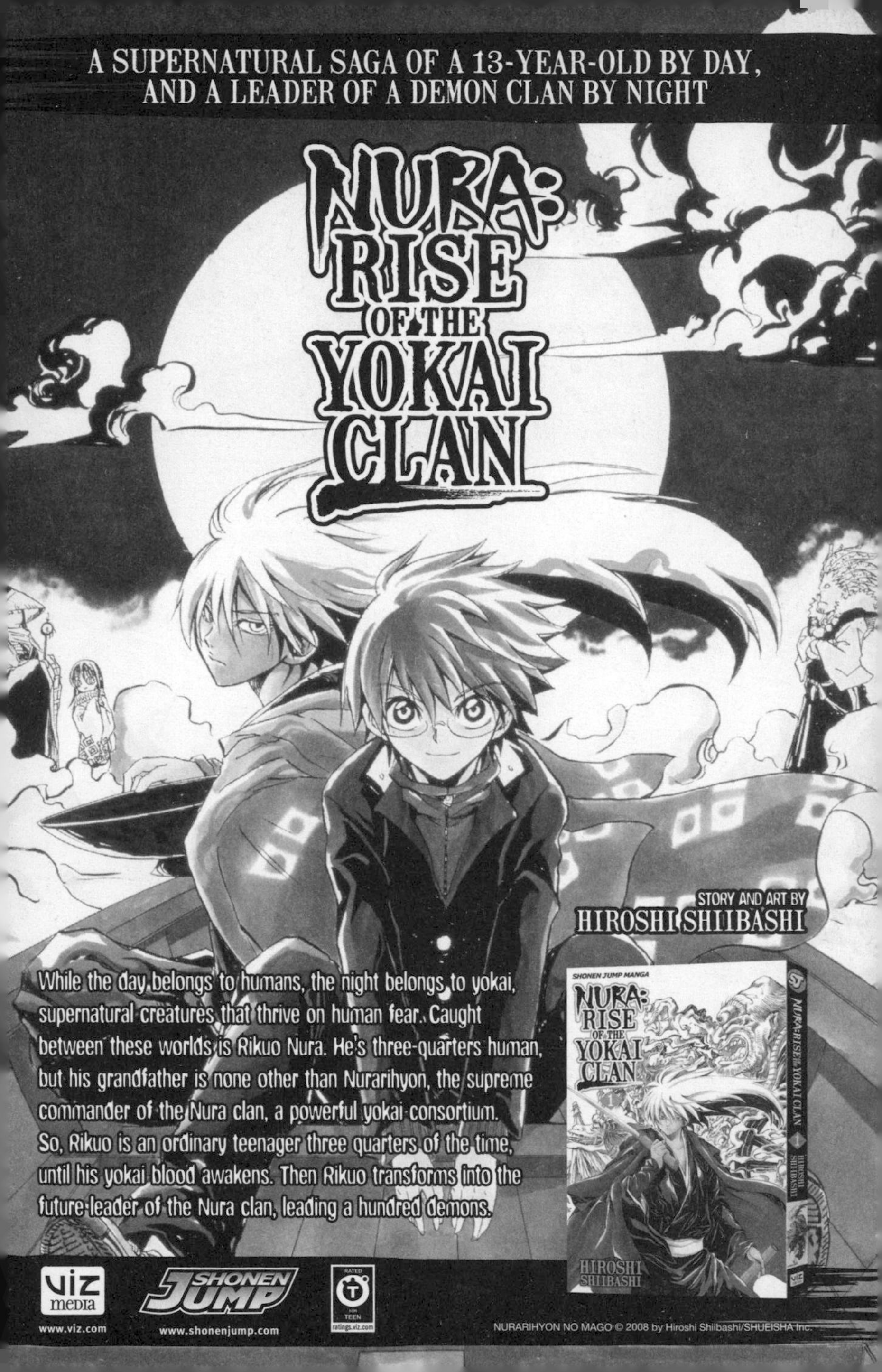
A SUPERNATURAL SAGA OF A 13-YEAR-OLD BY DAY, AND A LEADER OF A DEMON CLAN BY NIGHT
NURA: RISE OF THE YOKAI CLAN
STORY AND ART BY
HIROSHI SHIIBASHI
While the day belongs to humans, the night belongs to yokai, supernatural creatures that thrive on human fear. Caught between these worlds is Rikuo Nura. He's three-quarters human, but his grandfather is none other than Nurarihyon, the supreme commander of the Nura clan, a powerful yokai consortium. So, Rikuo is an ordinary teenager three quarters of the time, until his yokai blood awakens. Then Rikuo transforms into the future leader of the Nura clan, leading a hundred demons.
SHONEN JUMP MANGA
NURA: RISE OF THE YOKAI CLAN
1
HIROSHI SHIIBASHI
viz media
SHONEN JUMP
RATED T FOR TEEN
ratings.viz.com
www.viz.com
www.shonenjump.com
NURARIHYON NO MAGO © 2008 by Hiroshi Shiibashi/SHUEISHA Inc.

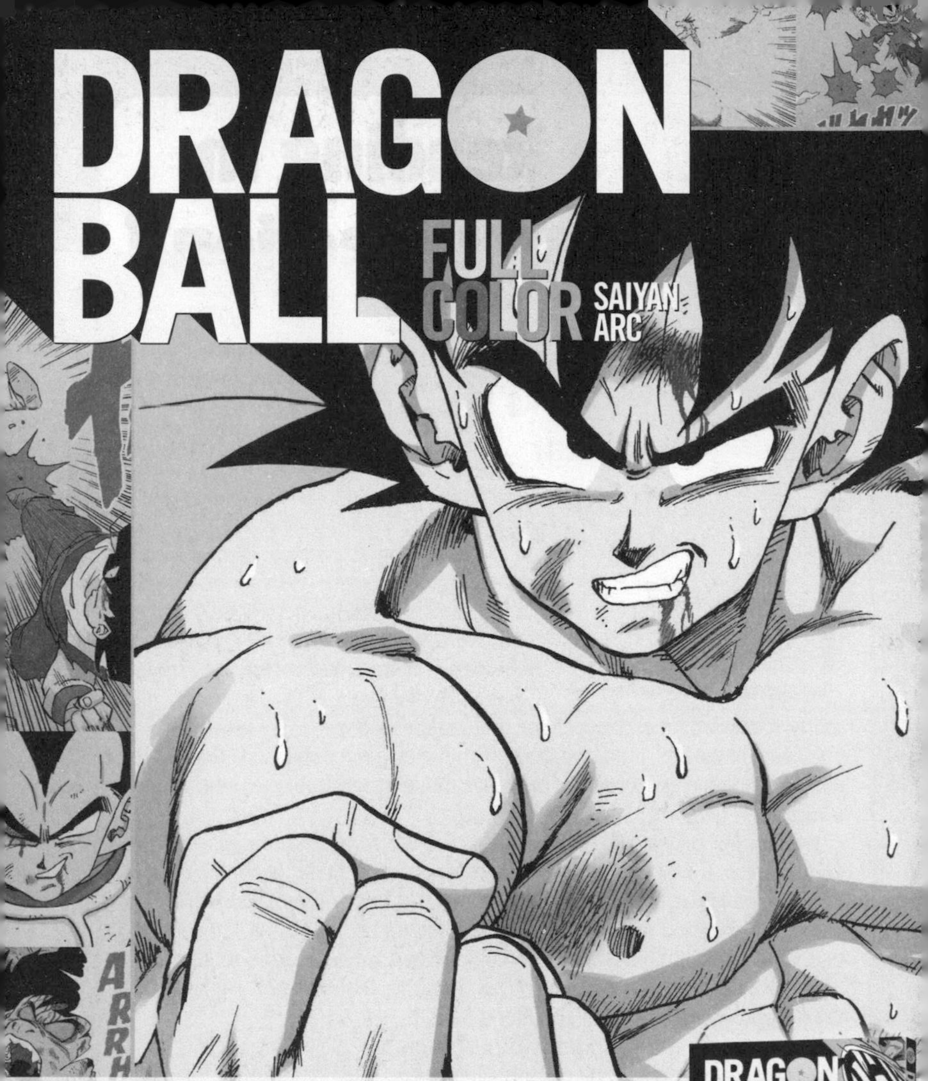

DRAGON BALL

FULL COLOR
SAIYAN ARC

After years of training and adventure, Goku has become Earth's ultimate warrior. And his son, Gohan, shows even greater promise. But the stakes are increasing as even deadlier enemies threaten the planet.

With bigger full color pages, *Dragon Ball Full Color* presents one of the world's most popular manga epics like never before. Relive the ultimate science fiction-martial arts manga in FULL COLOR.

Akira Toriyama's iconic series now in FULL COLOR!

DRAGON BALL
FULL COLOR

STORY AND ART BY
AKIRA TORIYAMA

VIZ MEDIA
www.viz.com

SHONEN JUMP
www.shonenjump.com

WEEKLY SHONEN JUMP

You're Reading the Wrong Direction!!

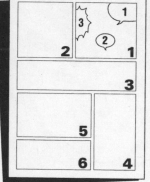

Whoops! Guess what? You're starting at the wrong end of the comic!

...It's true! In keeping with the original Japanese format, **Toriko** is meant to be read from right to left, starting in the upper-right corner.

Unlike English, which is read from left to right, Japanese is read from right to left, meaning that action, sound effects and word-balloon order are completely reversed... something which can make readers unfamiliar with Japanese feel pretty backwards themselves. For this reason, manga or Japanese comics published in the U.S. in English have sometimes been published "flopped"— that is, printed in exact reverse order, as though seen from the other side of a mirror.

By flopping pages, U.S. publishers can avoid confusing readers, but the compromise is not without its downside. For one thing, a character in a flopped manga series who once wore in the original Japanese version a T-shirt emblazoned with "M A Y" (as in "the merry month of") now wears one which reads "Y A M"! Additionally, many manga creators in Japan are themselves unhappy with the process, as some feel the mirror-imaging of their art skews their original intentions.

We are proud to bring you Mitsutoshi Shimabukuro's **Toriko** in the original unflopped format. For now, though, turn to the other side of the book and let the adventure begin...!

—Editor

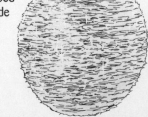

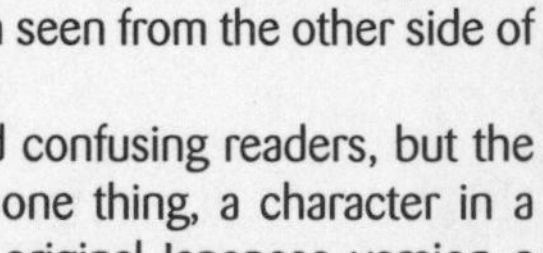

◀ • • • • • • • • • • • • • • • •